Your
Financial Plan

Your
Financial Plan
A Consumer's Guide

CAROLE ELIZABETH SCOTT
West Georgia College

HARPER & ROW, PUBLISHERS
New York Hagerstown Philadelphia San Francisco London

Sponsoring Editor: John Greenman
Project Editor: Pamela Landau
Designer: Helen Iranyi
Production Manager: Stefania J. Taflinska
Compositor: Maryland Linotype Composition Co., Inc.
Printer and Binder: The Maple Press Company
Art Studio: Danmark & Michaels, Inc.
Cartoons by Steven Duquette

Your Financial Plan: A Consumer's Guide

Library of Congress Cataloging in Publication Data
Scott, Carole Elizabeth.
    Your financial plan.

    Bibliography: p.
    Includes index.
    1. Finance, Personal. I. Title.
HG179.S34   332'.024   78-23396
ISBN 0-06-045844-5

TO ALBERT C. AND ELISABETH McGOUGH SCOTT

Contents

12

13

14

15

Preface

The objectives of *Your Financial Plan* were summarized by two of the people who helped type the manuscript. One liked it because it read like a friend telling you some things you need to know. The other liked it because "it tells the reader things that everyone needs to know."

Personal finance is a useful subject to every consumer. Therefore, the most important feature a personal finance text can exhibit is *readability*—letting the reader immediately perceive its usefulness. The reason why many personal finance and consumer economics books fail to help students is because they are intimidating encyclopedias of detail written in a lifeless style. Usefulness in a text for a course of this kind is not achieved because its material appeals primarily to the interests of the professor. Rather it is achieved by the author's constantly keeping in mind the needs and interests of the typical student, which is what I have tried to do throughout this book.

All the usual topics—savings accounts, buying real estate, investing in stocks and bonds, planning for retirement—are included, but I have tried to approach them in terms of the *average* individual's needs. By the same token, practical considerations such as buying or renting a home, buying a car, making personal consumption expenditures, taking out insurance, and using credit receive more than the usual emphasis in this text. The reader is shown the proper way to go about making an economic decision without getting into the complexities encountered in principles of economics and business finance courses.

Special features of *Your Financial Plan* are coverage of topics such as investing in coins, prints, and antiques, and end-of-chapter sections called "Your Financial Plan," which enable readers, as they progress through the text, to set up a financial plan for themselves.

Although I must bear full responsibility for the material in this text, others share the credit for getting the manuscript completed promptly. I would like to thank the following instructors, who reviewed parts or all of the manuscript and made many useful suggestions: Alfred C. Bedell, Ulster County Community College; Kenneth Manko, DeKalb Community College; Thomas E. Stitzel, Boise State University; Robert E. Tansky, St. Clair County Community College; and Clinton Warne, Cleveland State University. I am especially grateful for the help of my colleague at West Georgia College, James Overton, who pitched in when it seemed the deadline could not be met. My thanks go, too, to M. C. Hollingsworth, a secretary at my alma mater, Georgia State University, who, despite many obstacles, always came through with her share of the typing responsibilities. I also appreciate the help I received with the first draft from three secretaries at West Georgia College: Mary Ivey, Eloise Merrell, and Betty Adams.

CAROLE E. SCOTT

Your
Financial Plan

What Is Personal Finance About?

OBJECTIVES

When you have completed this chapter, you will have accomplished the following:

1. Learned why financial planning requires the setting of short-, intermediate-, and long-term goals.
2. Appreciate the importance of career selection.
3. Learned how to choose a career.
4. Recognize the problem of trade-offs.
5. Learned the proper way to make a financial decision.
6. Learned the differences between consumption, saving, investment, and hoarding.

This book is not simply an encyclopedia of facts for you to memorize. It is, instead, a plan of action for you to use in wisely making, saving, and spending money. Your first personal financial problem is obtaining an income. Subsequent financial problems involve allocating this income among various competing uses. Our free market system provides you with an unparalleled choice of products and services to select from, and the more choice you have, the more likely you are to get exactly what you want. Yet, today's ever-widening choice of products and services—often promoted by persuasive and sometimes misleading advertising—makes the job of deciding how to spend your income a difficult, complex task. Aggravating this problem is the constant reduction of the purchasing power of your dollars via inflation (rising prices), which means that, over time, a given level of income will buy less. Thus, you must constantly increase your income just to maintain your standard of living.

Because your income is limited, you cannot buy everything you would like to have. You must choose between the various products and services available to you. To choose, you must determine what expenditures will provide you with the greatest benefit per dollar, that is, you must decide just what you get out of each expenditure and how important this is to you.

THE NEED FOR GOALS

In order to rationally make any decision you must have goals. Without goals, a person is like a rudderless ship adrift in the middle of an ocean. If you do not care what happens to you, you can simply flip a coin in order to determine a course of action. But most people do care what happens to them, and, whether they realize it or not, their financial decisions have a great deal to do with what happens to them and, therefore, what they get out of life.

What do you want out of life, financially and otherwise? Once you have decided this, you can greatly enhance your chance of achieving both financial and nonfinancial goals by making appropriate financial plans and decisions. Only if you know what your goals are can you plan the most efficient—the lowest cost, in terms of time, effort, and money—method of achieving them. Of course, as you grow older your values will probably change, and, therefore, your goals will change. This means old plans will have to be scrapped and new ones made. Unforeseen events may also arise later in life which will force you to alter your goals. An athlete, for example, may suffer an injury which will force him or her into a new career and lifestyle. A confirmed loner may fall in love, marry, and have children. A college student's parents may suffer financially, forcing the student to drop out of college and seek work. A law student may be unable to pass the bar; an accountant, the C.P.A. exam.

You will have short-, intermediate-, and long-term goals. Your long-term goal might be to become a lawyer, whereas a short-term goal might be to be in the top 10 percent of your class, a goal whose achievement will give both you and your family satisfaction and help you get into a good law school. Other short-term goals, such as getting a date next weekend, may have no relationship to your long-term goals. Usually, however, goals will or should be related. For example, one of your long-term goals may be to get married, and you may end up marrying one of your weekend dates.

Many people make the mistake of seeking short-term goals that either conflict with their long-term goals or do nothing to promote their attainment. You may, for example, desire good health in your later years, but in seeking to be "cool," you may currently seek thrills by drinking and smoking heavily and taking drugs and, in this way, seriously impair your health (i.e., cirrhosis of the liver, lung cancer, and mental problems). A set of priorities which reflect what is most important to you, coupled with a long-run view, can prevent such results. People have long known that hasty, shortsighted actions usually lead to repenting them at leisure in the future.

EARNING A LIVING

People with inherited wealth often think money is nice, but that it is beneath them to go after it. Since Harvard has more wealthy students than do most colleges, perhaps this is why at its graduation ceremonies Master of Business Administration graduates have been booed by other graduates. On the other hand, people without money often believe that happiness in life depends on having money; yet, many who have inherited or earned fortunes are neither happy nor satisfied to simply go through life spending it. Even though they inherited fortunes as youths, Franklin D. Roosevelt and John F. Kennedy sought and obtained various political offices. Other people find, perhaps too late, that for them happiness lies in the striving involved in earning money. Money is, to them, merely the scorecard in the game of life. Many who claim to have no interest in money, including some college professors, constantly complain about their low salaries, particularly in comparison with those earned by less "worthy" persons in jobs oriented more toward making money rather than seeking intellectual achievement.

Whether or not earning money is crass, most people must work for a living. One must have money in order to obtain food, clothing, and shelter. Most able-bodied persons who are not heirs to fortunes prefer to earn their own living rather than depending on the charity of those who do work.

Career Selection Affects Income

How you choose to earn a living has a lot to do with how much you will earn (see Figures 1–1 and 1–2). A survey of almost 1600 men who graduated from Swarthmore College from 1929 to 1965 found that those with the highest incomes had majored in biology (a median income of $48,214 a year), economics ($43,929), chemistry ($38,900), or engineering ($37,793). Some of the lowest median salaries were found among those who had majored in philosophy ($29,000), German ($25,000), English literature ($24,857), French ($23,500), or art history ($20,625).[1] What field one prepares for also affects how quickly one can find the first job and the likelihood of getting a first job within that field. In 1976 engineering and business students got 89 percent of the job offers.[2] Less than 40 percent of college students majored in the applied fields of engineering, business, and agriculture.[3] Business and engineering students are more likely to get jobs in their field than are liberal arts graduates.

Anyone who works for someone else has a limit placed on how much he or she can earn. Only by working for yourself are your possible earnings unlimited. Working for oneself is usually more risky, however, and it may require a substantial investment of money.

How to Choose a Career

Some people will advise that you go into whatever field is currently unpopular! (Most students do the reverse!) Their logic is that when a field is crowded few people study it, thus, the number of persons in this field declines. In subsequent bidding to attract an adequate number of people to the field, employers raise the average salary paid for this kind of work. This, in turn, causes more people to study the field, and this leads to another oversupply, and so on. Engineering, over the last few decades, illustrates this process.

[1] Warren Boroson, "The New Careerism on Campus," *Money* April 1976, pp. 46–50.

[2] *Ibid.*

[3] *Ibid.*

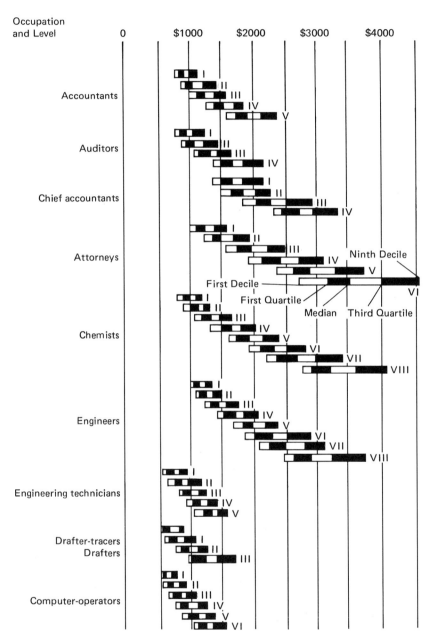

FIGURE 1–1. Salaries in Professional and Technical Occupations, March 1976 (U.S. Dept. of Labor, *National Survey of Professional, Administrative, Technical, and Clerical Pay*, Washington, D.C., March 1976)

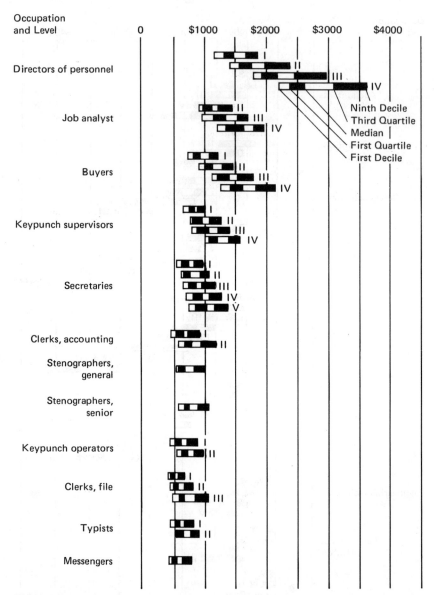

FIGURE 1–2. Salaries in Administrative and Clerical Occupations, March 1976 (U.S. Dept. of Labor, *National Survey of Professional, Administrative, Technical and Clerical Pay*, Washington, D.C., March 1976)

Others will argue that you should ignore this cycle and simply go into whatever field interests you the most, assuming you have the necessary ability. The philosophy behind this advice is that you are much more likely to do well at something you like, so even though the average salary in your field may be low, you will earn more. (Often top salaries differ less than average salaries.) There are, however, some occupations that offer virtually no opportunity to earn a high income. In fact, in some cases even earning a living is unusual. This is the plight of the poet, particularly if he or she does not wish to write greeting card verse.

If you are extremely gifted, it is probably financially safe to simply go into whatever field appeals to you the most. If you are not particularly gifted, and most people are not, selecting a career is going to involve some calculation.

Many colleges have career counselors and your college library will certainly have books that describe a variety of occupations. You may also want to read autobiographies of persons which emphasize their jobs, and talk to older friends and relatives about their jobs. The U.S. government provides a variety of publications that both describe various types of jobs and project the future demand for such work. You can also find out a lot about the options available to you by arranging job interviews with interviewers who may visit your campus. In addition to learning something about a variety of jobs and firms from interviewers, you may learn a lot about how to interview for a job by such practice and overcome the nervousness experienced by many people on their first interview. (Don't let your first interview be for a job you want very badly!) If your class has an opportunity to visit a business or government office, go! Part-time jobs can also help you to learn about possible careers. Even if the job is something you are not interested in, it can bring you into contact with persons employed in jobs you may find interesting. In addition, working at anything helps you to learn what you do and don't like and what you are and are not good at.

Consider Long-Term Outlook

In picking a career you should, as always, be careful not to take a short-sighted view. The job with the best starting pay may be a dead-end job or one which offers only a few chances to advance. Another possibility to consider is that a job in street maintenance may pay better than one of the "professions" such as teaching school. A white-collar job selling life insurance may pay you less than you would make as a long-haul truck driver. A job supported by a government contract may disappear overnight.

You would probably be surprised at the number of middle-aged people who are vastly dissatisfied with their jobs, but, due to age, responsibilities, job benefits, lack of skills, and fear, are unhappily resigned to enduring them. How did they get into such a situation? They took a short-sighted view; they took the path of least resistance. Their cousins told them about jobs where they worked. They applied and got them without considering whether they would be happy to spend the rest of their lives in such work and whether or not it offered them any opportunities. Taking such a job was a lot easier than figuring out what would be the best thing to do and maybe spending years in school, acquiring appropriate experience, leaving home, and searching for "the job" for months.

Ask around and see how the people you know got the jobs they have. How many got where they are by careful planning, and how many just fell into them? You will probably find that many were just driving by a place and thought, hey, that wouldn't be a bad place to work; heard about a job being available from a friend; well, their father was in that business; someone offered it to them out of the blue, and so on. If such jobs work out in the long-run, it is just pure luck. Do you want to depend on luck?

How Much Education?

Many people make the mistake of thinking that because, on the average, college graduates make more money than high school graduates (who make more than grade school graduates), that education alone determines how much money one makes. This is not true. Supply and demand are what determine how much money you make. People with needed skills and abilities that are in relatively short supply make the highest salaries. Because anyone can perform unskilled labor, it is in short supply only when a lot of people refuse to take such jobs, so it is usually low-salaried. A number of people will not or do not have the ability to learn difficult skills; thus, such skills are often in relatively short supply, causing education to pay off. Historically, education has paid off very well.

No matter how skilled you are, if no one wants that skill, you can't earn anything doing it. If a great number of people are as good as you are at doing something (even though a lot of people are willing to pay to have it done), you will not earn a lot. Many young people make the mistake of thinking that people will pay them simply because they can do something or because they have a degree. To keep and advance in a job, one must perform. (Would you pay someone for doing nothing or next to it?)

The difference one's credentials can make when starting a career is illustrated by the fact that in 1976 the average recipient of a Master of Business Administration degree received a starting salary of $15,132, whereas the average Bachelor of Arts graduate in humanities earned only $8,580. The M.B.A.'s higher starting salary was, of course, a product of several factors. He or she has more education. Because the academic training is applied, the M.B.A. should be productive on the job sooner. The average M.B.A. also has more on-the-job experience than does the average B.A., a fact that also makes the M.B.A. more productive and a safer bet to hire.

You Face Trade-Offs

In some professions, such as medicine, nearly everyone makes a high income. In others, there is a tremendous variance in what people earn. Lawyers, for example, may become quite wealthy or just barely scrape along. Perhaps the greatest variance is found in sales, where income is often directly based on performance, that is, what you earn is a percent of what you sell. One is often faced with a choice between something like a job with a utility, which doesn't pay well but almost guarantees you steady employment until you retire, and a job selling printing, which means a sporadic income, a greater likelihood that you may lose your job, and a possibly higher income. Financial decisions of all kinds involve trade-offs between risk and return.

Because you probably can't work when you get old, you must earn, directly or indirectly, enough in your younger years to support yourself in old age. Your standard of living in old age would clearly be maximized by currently spending as little as possible. Few are willing to make such a huge trade-off between current and future consumption; yet, most people are willing to trade off at least some current consumption in order to increase future consumption. This is particularly likely to be the case if the future consumption made possible by current saving will be greater, as it will be if you put money in an interest-bearing savings account. (Greater future consumption will be possible, however, only if the interest rate, adjusted for taxes, exceeds the rate of inflation.) Many financial decisions hinge on your willingness to exchange present for future consumption.

GETTING THE MOST FOR YOUR DOLLAR

Getting the most for your dollar involves many things. For example, if you are to maximize the benefit you get out of each dollar spent, you can't walk into the first auto showroom you see, and borrow, through the dealer, the sticker price of the first car you see so that you can buy it. You can always get a car for less than the sticker price.

All auto dealers will not, however, lower the price by the same amount; thus, you must shop around. All lenders do not charge the same interest rate or demand the same repayment schedule, maturity, and so on; thus, you should shop around for a loan as well. In addition, you may be able to sell your car for more than you will get on a trade-in (what they really give you, not what they say!). Decide what you need in a car. In other words, be both informed and rational in making purchase decisions so you get the most for your income.

Don't Look Back

*Insurance
Plans
Investments*

What you have already spent should have no effect on the decision to spend money in the future. What you've already spent is water over the dam. The only thing that counts is what new benefits will be enjoyed as a result of each future expenditure, and where is there the best ratio between new benefits and associated cost? Don't throw good money (additional expenditures) after bad. Never put more money into something just because you have already put a lot of money in it!

Consider All Costs in a Decision

False economy is one of the most common traps consumers fall into. A motorcycle costs much less to operate than does a car, but motorcyclists have far more accidents than do auto drivers and personal injury is more common and serious. How much gas must you save to compensate for being crippled for life? If you are injured, you incur the cost of medical care, the cost of the loss of income you would otherwise have earned, and the nonmonetary cost of pain and suffering. Clearly, all ramifications of a financial decision must be considered, and some of these are not financial in nature.

A purchase decision cost that is frequently ignored by consumers is the loss of the benefits provided by whatever else their money could have obtained for them. For example, if you buy a car, you won't be able to go to Europe, which might be the expenditure you place the next highest priority on. Will the car provide you with greater benefits? If it doesn't, you are giving up more than you are getting. If you make a down payment on a house, you will have to withdraw funds from a savings and loan association and lose the interest you would otherwise have earned. Is having the house worth giving the money up? Economists call the costs resulting from giving up the benefits provided by alternative expenditures *opportunity costs*.

The Tax Bite

A good part of what you earn goes to the government—either federal, state, or local—as taxes. The federal government levies a progressive personal income tax on your income, which means that the more you earn, the relatively and absolutely larger is the government's cut. Many states have personal income taxes, some states and localities charge a sales tax on the things you buy, all levy taxes on your home if you own it. If you rent, your landlord passes his property tax cost on to you through your rent. Other personal property may also be taxed. Businesses pass on to you various taxes they pay via the prices they charge their customers. Good financial management includes, as will be shown later, legally minimizing these taxes.

CONSUMPTION, SAVING, AND INVESTMENT

There are three ways in which you can use your income. You can use it for *consumption*—food, clothing, shelter, transportation, entertainment; *savings*—savings deposits in financial institutions, U.S. savings bonds, money hidden in your home; and, *investment*—a house, land, shares of stock in a corporation, government or corporate bonds. Everybody consumes, most save, and many invest, mainly in a house and land. The main concern of personal finance is how to allocate your income among these three uses and within each type of use.

Consumption

Everyone needs food, clothing, and shelter, so everyone allocates at least some of their income for consumption. Some people find that providing themselves with only these most essential goods will take all of their relatively low incomes. People with higher incomes will have enough money to purchase less essential items such as a car or washing machine, or even a trip to Europe or stereo equipment.

Some businesses pay their employees on Wednesday rather than Friday because they believe that some of the employees, if paid on Friday, would spend all their money on liquor. Since they would lose their jobs if they are drunk on Thursday and Friday, they will go home Wednesday night rather than to a bar; giving their families a chance to get their pay. Thus, the employer doesn't have hung over workers on Monday or employees' wives demanding that the employer give them their husbands' pay.

The employee who would spend all of his or her pay on a binge does not have the same set of priorities that his or her family and most of society have. But the employee is doing what we all do: we spend for this rather than that because this is more important to us than that at the time.

In order to determine the value of the net benefits of consuming a given item—whether it be a haircut or a banana—we have to know what our goals are, and how important each is. Is looking neat and being cool (the opposite of hot) more or less important than enjoying the taste of one of our favorite foods, bananas? Very few people can afford everything they want. Thus, we must have priorities to decide what we will or will not buy. Most people rank a minimum amount (at least) of food, clothing, and shelter high on their list of priorities. They will go without liquor rather than give up these things.

Saving

Most people rank having some savings above consuming more. Instead of using all of their income for consumption, they save it—for a variety of reasons. For example, any morning you might get in your car and find you have a flat tire. You open the trunk only to find you have forgotten to keep the spare full of air, so you have to pay someone to come fix the tire. You may also find yourself in a grocery store with a bill higher than you had estimated. Luckily you thought that this might happen some day and stashed some money away under your driver's license rather than spending it on that new pair of shoes! In each case you were wise to have saved your income rather than consuming it.

You also save because it is the only way you will be able to buy an expensive item. You will probably not be able to pay for a television set out of one pay check. Of course, if your credit rating is good, you may be able to buy the set now and pay for it later, usually by a series of periodic payments. Using credit will add to the cost of the TV set, as the seller will charge you interest; thus, you may decide to save up for the set to avoid this extra cost. If you put this money in a savings deposit account, you will earn interest on your money, reducing the amount you will have to put aside in order to be able to pay for the TV set. If you use credit, you will still end up "saving" some of your income, as you will have to devote a portion of your pay check for awhile to paying the seller of the TV what you owe him. Even though credit will add to your cost, you will be able to enjoy or "consume" the TV while you are doing without the money it costs.

Many people save money to pay for their children's education. Others save for their retirement. Table 1–1 illustrates how difficult saving enough money can be! Some save for trips to Europe, a boat, or a vacation home in the mountains. Many families save money for Christmas presents. Couples often save money for a honeymoon and setting up housekeeping.

forced SAVING

TABLE 1–1   Purchasing Power of the Dollar 1940 to 1976*

Year	Monthly Average As Measured By Consumer Prices	Year	Monthly Average As Measured By Consumer Prices	Year	Monthly Average As Measured By Consumer Prices
1940	$2.381	1955	$1.247	1966	$1.029
1945	1.855	1956	1.229	1967	1.000
1946	1.709	1957	1.186	1968	0.960
1947	1.495	1958	1.155	1969	0.911
1948	1.387	1959	1.145	1970	0.860
1949	1.401	1960	1.127	1971	0.824
1950	1.387	1961	1.116	1972	0.799
1951	1.285	1962	1.104	1973	0.752
1952	1.258	1963	1.091	1974	0.678
1953	1.248	1964	1.076	1975	0.621
1954	1.242	1965	1.058	1976 (May)	0.591

Source: U.S. Bureau of Labor Statistics. Monthly data in U.S. Bureau of Economic Analysis, Survey of Current Business, U.S. Statistical Abstract, 1976.

* 1967 = $1.00. Consumer prices prior to 1964 exclude Alaska and Hawaii. Obtained by dividing the average price index for the 1967 base period (100.0) by the price index for a given period and expressing the result in dollars and cents.

Investment

Some people choose to use part of their income for investment. The higher one's income, the more likely it is that he or she will invest. Investment usually has a lower priority than consumption and saving and, so, many people cannot afford to invest—nothing is left over after minimum consumption and saving is taken care of. One invests when one acquires something which will provide benefits or a return over a long period of time. Food will not do this. It is completely consumed shortly after purchase. Shares of stock, which grant their owner part ownership of a corporation, are an investment; so are bonds, which signify that you have loaned money to a corporation or a government. Holders of stock may receive dividends if the corporation has the earnings. Holders of bonds will earn interest on the money lent and eventually will receive their money (principal) back. The benefit provided by these investments is monetary. In other cases the benefit of an investment may not be received in the form of money. One also invests when one purchases a home, but the return will be monetary only if it is rented or if sold for more than was paid for it. The same is true of the land purchased on which to build the house.

Commercial banks, savings and loan associations, and other deposit-type institutions are able to pay you interest on your savings deposits because they invest some of your money and earn a return on it. They purchase bonds, which means they have loaned a corporation or government money. They also lend builders, or those who hire builders, the money they use to construct homes and businesses. Therefore, you can see that savings and investment are just two sides of the same coin. Investment requires that money be saved. One saves by not allocating all income for consumption expenditures. The government encourages you to invest some of your income by not taxing the return on direct investment as heavily as they tax your other income. It does this because without investment we would not have the equipment and buildings necessary to produce consumer goods and services (food, clothing, haircuts, movies, television sets, cars, etc.) or investment goods (houses, factories, machinery, and other goods needed to produce goods and services).

If you save money by taking it out of circulation—putting it in a cookie jar—you are said to be hoarding. If you deposit with them, financial institutions can keep money you save in circulation by lending it to business, government, and consumers, but money you hoard cannot be used to build a factory or buy someone a home.

THE SECRET TO GOOD PERSONAL FINANCING

Use your head for something other than a hat rack. Learn about money and using it. Learn how to make financial decisions. Think before you spend.

CASES FOR DISCUSSION

Case 1 Phil Baldassarri was a lackluster, but popular student in high school. He was only able to get into an open admissions college. He went to college to please his parents, get away from home, and enjoy campus life. Several of his friends were majoring in history and he figured he could handle this program without working too hard, so he majored in it too. He joined a big social fraternity and eventually became its president. Most of his time was spent on fraternity affairs and with his girlfriend. Each summer his father got him a job folding boxes with his employer. Phil is now about to graduate and get married. He won't graduate unless he can manage a B average in his last semester of work. Teaching history seems like a living death to him. One friend of his who majored in history is selling life insurance; another is in graduate school studying political science; another is looking for work; and a fourth is an assistant manager of a drive-in grocery store. Phil's family is a blue-collar family anxious for him to get a "professional" job. Phil doesn't know what to do and wonders if he could have handled things better. If he came to you for advice, what would you tell him?

Case 2 Kathy Hoehl's parents always compared her unfavorably with her older sister. Kathy didn't think she could handle college either academically or financially. In high school she played in the band until she got tired of all the practicing. She was good in typing and shorthand and her I.Q. test showed she had a bit above-average intelligence. After high school she took a course that prepared her to be a beautician, a career her mother had taken up after her children began school. Kathy thought that she would marry right after high school, but she and Jim had broken up just before graduation. After a couple of years Kathy was very dissatisfied with being cooped up all day inhaling hair spray and cigarette smoke and listening to petty gossip and idle chitchat. On her salary she can hardly make ends meet. She envies her brothers—one is a policeman and the other is a building inspector for the city. Men don't have dull, confining jobs like women do, she grumbles. She can't decide what to do and blames her parents and teachers for her unhappiness. What do you think she should do? How did she get herself into a situation she dislikes so?

Case 3 Right after the oil embargo Dwight and Betty Suzumegano replaced their 2-year old electric furnace with a gas furnace and replaced their large, almost new, American cars with very small foreign cars not handled by a local dealer. Because of rising food prices, Dwight bought a little tractor and all the implements he needs to plant a large garden on their one-acre lot. Betty bought a large freezer and canning equipment so she can put up some of what they grow, which otherwise would go to waste or have to be given away. Since they didn't know anything about gardening or canning, they took extension courses from the state university. Dwight is a young lawyer making between $25,000 and $35,000 a year, depending on what clients he has. Betty is an interior decorator making $14,000 a year. Even though their income is well above average, Dwight often has to get a small personal loan from his bank. He justifies this on the basis that no matter how much people have, they always spend more. Dwight and Betty pride themselves on how carefully they spend their money. What, if any, advice would you give Dwight and Betty?

Case 4 Mike Payne's father is a dentist and an avid football fan. All Mike's life his father has wanted Mike to play college football and enter a profession, preferably medicine. Mike enrolled as a pre-med student and played football without a scholarship. He was a substitute tackle. Mike completed a degree in biology, but his grades were not good enough to get into medical school. His father sent him to a med school in Mexico, but Mike was very unhappy in Mexico and came home after six months. He then took a job his mother lined up for him with the state highway department. His college training had little application to his job, which largely involved scheduling men and equipment to jobs. When Mike was a teenager a neighbor introduced him to woodworking, and he has a basement shop where he makes furniture for himself and friends. A building contractor hired Mike to do some carpentry on weekends. When Mike told his father he might become a carpenter full time he exploded. "How can you do this to your wife and child? You know carpenters don't make much money and are always between jobs. How will your son feel telling people his daddy is a carpenter?" What advice would you give Mike?

Case 5 Roger Klingelhofer graduated with honors in physics. After completing an employer-sponsored course, Roger became a computer programmer for a large manufacturing company, which was the first firm to offer Roger a job. A friend had tipped him off that this company had a job opening for a college graduate with a good math background. When Roger was 23 he married Ann. By the time he was 28 they had two children. Due to his family expenses, Roger has only $2000 in savings. Roger has always enjoyed mathematics, and he now believes he will be happy only if he becomes a mathematician. This requires that he go back to college and get a master's degree and a Ph.D. He's willing to teach, but would rather work in research. His current boss is clearly grooming Roger to replace him. This job would start at $30,000 and his wife is thrilled at the prospect. She has never worked and has only a high school diploma. How would you advise Roger? What, if any, mistakes has he made?

Case 6 Helen Gordon is 30 and has had five jobs. A better than average student in business administration, Helen majored in accounting, one of the best-paying fields for many years. After graduation she got a job with a national public accounting firm anxious to employ more women. She quit because of the travel involved. Helen hasn't thought seriously of marriage, but doesn't rule it out. She next got a job as assistant advertising manager of a medium-sized newspaper. She had done this kind of work for her college newspaper. A death in the circulation department led to her being transferred to circulation, but she didn't like circulation so she quit to look for a job. She had to borrow money from her parents before she found another job. Her next job was an assistant manager of a small dress shop. She quit this job because of the long hours and the fact that much of her time was spent doing work "beneath her level." Her next job was as an accounting clerk for an electric utility, which she quit after deciding that utilities were male chauvinist strongholds—the highest-ranking woman was a first-level supervisor of telephone operators. She is currently working as a buyer for a department store chain, which she believes is a job with a future for a woman. She doesn't like the chief buyer, however, and is thinking of taking her $5000 of savings and starting her own dress shop. How would you advise her? What, if any, mistakes has she made?

Case 7 Ralph Matamares is a sophomore in college. He is majoring in sociology and making better-than-average grades, but he is so bored he's thinking of dropping out of college. His father was a steel worker and the only thing Ralph has decided about his future is that he will not work in a steel mill. He says that he isn't going to spend his days in a noisy, dirty mill and his evenings drinking beer in front of a TV set. As a boy he idolized pilots, and in college he joined the Air Force R.O.T.C. Ralph would like to travel, particularly to France, since he had studied French in high school and college. He would also like to buy a car. Ralph's father has just died and a life insurance policy has paid Ralph $10,000. Ralph's uncle has just reminded him of his standing offer to take him into his auto parts business, letting Ralph buy a share of the business as he is able. Ralph can't decide what to do with the money. How would you advise Ralph?

Case 8 Mary Ezzell's favorite activity in high school was working on the school newspaper. She majored in English literature in college and worked on the student newspaper. Her lifetime ambition was realized after college when she got a job as a reporter on a large newspaper. Although the pay wasn't very good, she enjoyed her work and she saved a little. A publisher offered her a job reading manuscripts which would pay more, but she turned it down, feeling it wasn't exciting enough. One summer while on vacation she got an idea for a short story, wrote it, and sold it to the second publisher she sent it to. Soon she was regularly publishing short stories. Pleased with her work, the newspaper promoted her to assistant news editor, and gave her a large raise. Then she got an idea she was convinced would make a great novel. A friend who is a novelist says she should sell her car, get an apartment, and, using her savings of $3000 plus the $1500 she can get for her car, closet herself in the apartment until she finishes the novel. "You can't," says the novelist, "work and write a novel part time." Mary can't decide how to decide what to do. Very few novels make any money, but a really good one can make an author rich, particularly if a movie is made from it. How would you advise Mary?

REVIEW QUESTIONS

1. Why do you need goals in order to make decisions?
2. Why don't all jobs pay the same amount of money?
3. Why should short-, intermediate-, and long-term goals be related?
4. Why do you need to place priorities on your needs?
5. If you have invested a lot in something, can you afford to simply walk away from it?
6. Does education always pay off? Why or why not?
7. Name some types of decisions that you have no financial ramifications.
8. What is meant by trading present for future consumption? Why would one do this?
9. What is opportunity cost and what use is made of it?

YOUR PLAN: CHAPTER 1

**Questions to ask yourself
when deciding on a career:**

1. Is my main objective to make as much money as possible or to do something I really like to do? Would I, for example, prefer a job I enjoyed that pays $15,000 a year over one I simply find tolerable that pays $20,000?
2. How much education am I financially able to afford, and how much of the cost am I willing to absorb?
3. Am I willing to move frequently, such as every three to five years for many years?

4. Am I willing to move anywhere in the United States? In the world?
5. Am I willing to travel frequently, like every week?
6. Am I willing to take responsibility for the actions of others who I cannot personally oversee?
7. Am I willing to take responsibility for deciding questions greatly affecting others' lives, large amounts of money, and/or valuable property?
8. Am I good at making decisions, or do I dread making them and put off doing so?
9. Am I self-disciplined or does someone have to drive me to get me to do something?
10. Am I willing to exert myself even if there is no immediate, tangible reward awaiting me?
11. Do other people respect my judgment and ask me for advice?
12. Am I willing to stand up for what I think is right even when all my associates think otherwise?
13. Do I quickly get over making mistakes?
14. Do I persist in seeking a goal even when I run into a serious obstacle?
15. Am I much better than most other people at doing some things?
16. Do I always strive to do my best?
17. Do I get along with other people better than most people?
18. Do I find taking risks exciting, or at least don't mind taking them?
19. Do I usually achieve whatever I seek?
20. Is being the best at anything I do very important to me?
21. Do I get a thrill out of influencing other people, and am I able to do this?
22. Do I bore easily?
23. Does conflict fail to faze me?
24. Do I enjoy competition?
25. When I have a problem do I persist until I solve it?
26. Do I like to be outdoors? Am I miserable if I spend much time indoors?
27. Do I enjoy mental or physical activities the most?
28. Do I hate working under close supervision?
29. Do I hate operating within tight time limits?
30. How highly do I value security? Would I prefer a job I was unlikely to lose that pays $10,000 annually to one which I might easily lose but pays $20,000 annually?

How to Use Your Answers

To decide on a career you must answer these questions and apply them to each career under consideration.

The first question determines what types of careers you consider, that is, those you like or those which pay the best. Question 30 has to be considered in selecting careers within the appropriate group, that is, a more secure income or a higher one. Then, because you probably want to be successful, you will need to answer Question 15 to further narrow your list.

If one has a poor academic record, he or she isn't going to be accepted by a professional school, such as medicine. A medical education will cost a lot of money, and you will have to work very hard for many years before obtaining a reward. You will likely be making life and death decisions. Sometimes you will make mistakes that cost other people their lives. You will constantly be dealing with people. Other doctors may disagree with what you think is the correct treatment. It is up to you to keep yourself current in your field. You will be responsible for managing your office or hiring the one who runs it. To be successful, your patients must have confidence in you. Your hours will be irregular and long, but if you are reasonably good, you will have a good income.

Any position of authority requires making decisions and being responsible for them. Making decisions involves taking risks. Getting a decision carried out to a successful conclusion often requires persistence in the face of obstacles and solving problems. Mistakes will be made. One cannot constantly worry about making them and regretting those already made if one is to be an effective decision maker.

Office workers spend all their time in offices. Truck drivers and many salespeople are constantly on the move. Many companies move their executives around the nation, and some move them around the world. Jobs in advertising are centered in New York; jobs in entertainment are centered in New York and California. Lawyers are constantly involved in controversy. Some people find assemblyline work dull; others don't. Even the few successful writers often get many rejection slips for a manuscript. Coal miners risk getting hurt more than do any other workers. The small business owner has no one to fall back on. An electrical engineer's job is mostly mental, but a civil engineer spends a good deal of time outdoors engaged in physical activity. A market researcher deals with concepts; a warehouse manager deals with tangible items. A politician must sway other people; an artist must spend much time alone.

Unfortunately, it is rare for any career to fit you perfectly. Thus, you must establish priorities. For example, being a stock car racer may suit you perfectly except that you have a tremendous fear of being hurt; thus, another career may be better, as this one negative factor may outweigh all the positive factors. In other words, you must establish what things you must have and things you can do without.

Once you have decided which careers are suitable for you, you must estimate your chances of getting into and getting ahead in each of these. To do this you need to know how many openings there are likely to be the year you will be entering the field and what upper-level jobs will open later. How much competition will you face, and how do you stack up against it?

By engaging in this careful analysis you should avoid becoming a newspaper reporter because it is glamorous and you can write, only to find that you can't work under pressure and, thus, miss your deadlines, and that you can't live like you want on the relatively low pay. This analysis should also enable you to avoid going into a highly competitive field where success goes only to the exceptionally talented and hard-driving person if you hate competition and aren't talented or hard-driving.

It is essential that you answer these questions honestly. Perhaps it will help to remind yourself that some hard-driving people are driven people, and some very talented people are miserable because their achievements fall short of their wishes.

Budgeting: Your Basic Tool

Many people have difficulty living within their income. Others live within their income, but are unable to save. Many people, even if they live within their income and save, do not spend their money effectively. That is, their expenditures could be made in a way that would contribute more to the attainment of their goals. The best way to solve all these problems is by budgeting.

A *budget is a financial plan that shows anticipated receipts and expenditures.* A budget is used both to guide and control expenditures. The mere process of listing your expenditures for making out a budget may both reveal and suggest a solution to your problem.

WHY BUDGET?

Many people do not know how they spend their money. They may think they do, but if they recorded every expenditure for several weeks, they would be shocked at the results. They would find that they are spending a disproportionate amount of money for very low-priority items, thus, reducing what is available to spend on high-priority items. Gross waste may also be revealed. For example, a quarter of their food dollar may be going into the garbage can.

Often people spend a lot of time and effort trying to raise their incomes, but spend none on planning or controlling the expenditure of this money. Apparently they think that, if they get enough money, there will be no need to manage its use. This is a false philosophy. No matter how high your income is, you will enjoy it more if expenditures are carefully planned. Planning alone, however, is not enough. A plan has value only if it is followed—control of expenditures is also necessary.

Another reason for budgeting is that you can never increase your income enough to avoid financial problems. Human beings' desires are insatiable. The more you have, the more you want. There is also a tendency to spend less carefully as your income rises. When your income is low, you tend to watch your expenditures because you are afraid of running out of money. If your income rises substantially, you will probably feel there is no reason to worry about running out of money; so you may be inclined to spend with wild abandon. This type of reaction has caused people who never ran the risk of going bankrupt when they were poor to go bankrupt when they became wealthy.

The purpose of controlling personal expenditures is to obtain an optimum pattern of expenditures. This means that the most satisfactory mix of consumption and saving will be achieved, and the relative amount of your income spent on each item consumed will be appropriate in terms of its importance to you. Table 2–1 shows how people in the United States allocate their funds. (*Tangible assets* are things

TABLE 2–1   Allocation of Household Funds
(dollar amounts in billions)

Item	1973	1974	1975	1976*
Disposable Personal Income	$903.1	$ 982.9	$1,080.9	$1,181.7
Plus: Increase in Credit	94.1	60.0	62.7	102.0
Equals: Total Funds				
Available	$997.2	$1,042.9	$1,143.6	$1,283.7
Less: Spending on Non-durable Goods and				
Services	685.7	765.8	841.5	923.2
Less: Increase in Currency				
and Demand Deposits	12.7	5.1	6.9	· 6.4
Leaves: Amount Available for Investment in Tangi-				
ble and Financial Assets	$298.8	$ 272.0	$ 295.2	$ 354.1
Invested in:				
Tangle Assets	$173.4	$ 143.6	$ 141.2	$ 184.3
Financial Assets	125.4	128.4	154.0	169.8
Financial Assets Placed in:				
Savings Accounts	$ 67.9	$ 57.9	$ 84.9	$ 104.7
Insurance and Pension				
Funds	32.9	36.0	43.7	53.1
Credit and Equity				
Instruments	24.6	34.5	25.4	12.0
Percentage Distribution of Household Investments				
Total Investments	100.0%	100.0%	100.0%	100.0%
Tangible Assets	58.0	52.8	47.8	52.0
Financial Assets	42.0	47.2	52.2	48.0
Savings Accounts as a				
Percentage of:				
Total Investments	22.7	21.3	28.8	29.6
Financial Investments	54.1	45.1	55.1	61.7

Sources: Department of Commerce; Federal Reserve Board.
* Preliminary.

like houses; *financial assets* are things like savings accounts. Credit and equity instruments are stocks and bonds.)

Many people reject budgeting out-of-hand because it will inhibit them too much. They derive a lot of pleasure from buying things on whim. Being free to make a spontaneous purchase has as high a priority as having enough money available to purchase essential goods and services. One can, of course, question the wisdom of giving impulse buying a very high priority, but some people probably do. Some people certainly place a higher priority on gambling or getting drunk than on having food on the table, since this is the way they behave year after year. Budgeting, they think, will force them to change. They are confusing budgeting with spending money according to other people's priorities. The budgeting process, however, implies no particular priorities. The purpose of budgeting is simply to enable you to spend money on what you most want to spend it on; not what others think you should spend it on. If you want to spend money on gambling, you can budget for that. Budgeting simply means that you plan what percent of your income will be devoted to each possible use on the basis of your priorities. There should also be a method of assuring that this plan is followed, and if it is not, a rational decision to vary from the plan must be made.

A budget does not have to be a formal, written document, which allows for no variances. To budget, all you need to do is *plan* and *control* your expenditures. You do not have to set up an elaborate bookkeeping system. Budgeting may be as simple as dividing up the money you get when you cash your pay check and putting each batch in an envelope labeled to show what the money will be spent for. There will be an envelope for every essential expenditure and one for whatever is left over.

Just as a few people can immediately stop smoking by simply deciding they are going to do so, while others may have to be weaned off them, some people can get by with a sketchy budget in their head, while others need a detailed written budget.

Budgeting can save you money in a variety of ways. By budgeting you can reduce the frequency of borrowing and the amount borrowed. You can reduce the cost of some of your purchases, and you can earn a higher effective rate of interest on your savings. Budgeting, of course, involves spending limitations, but limitations are not something you can avoid by not budgeting. How much you can spend (and how much you can borrow) is limited by your income. Borrowing, of course, simply means that for a cost (interest), you are spending some of tomorrow's income today; thus, reducing your spending power in the future. Controlling borrowing is one of the most important functions of budgeting, because borrowing more than you can repay will force you into *bankruptcy.* By having the court declare you bankrupt, you escape having to pay your bills, but you are stripped of most of your assets, and your reputation is stained. You also lose the right to go bankrupt for several years. Many people who do not budget, of course, never go bankrupt, but many who don't budget are often too close for comfort to bankruptcy.

THE FIRST STEP

The first thing you need to do is sit down and take a hard look at yourself and, if you have one, your family. What comes first? Presumably food, clothing, shelter, and medical care will come first for everybody. After that, who can say? In the case of teenage boys, a car is likely to rank next. For a young married couple, a house. For an older couple, an education for the children may rank next. For an even older couple, retirement. Depending on who is involved, a trip to Europe, a second car, a graduate degree, a boat, or any of thousands of other things may rank next.

Once you have decided what you want and determined each item's priority, you need to estimate your income—not only currently, but into the foreseeable future. Then, do the same thing for expenses. Human memory being what it is, it is probably a good idea for several weeks to take note of what you spend. If you have a checking account or keep your past bills, you can get some idea of how you have been spending your money from these. How complete these records are depends on how much credit buying you do and how often you use a check rather than cash.

A list of major expenditure categories you might use is shown in Table 2–2, which reports on the results of research done by the U.S. Department of Labor. This table also gives you a standard by which to compare your expenditure pattern, because it lists the average annual expenditures for each item in 1972–1973 by family income and size. Many studies have shown that the level of income and family size are the two most important determinants of how much a family spends on given items. Ages of family members, educational level, place of residence, and family background also affect spending patterns. Other characteristics too numerous to mention also play a role, but their role is relatively small.

The first column in Table 2–2 (All Families) was obtained by adding up all expenditures for a given item and dividing by the total number of families in the study group. The figure underneath in parenthesis is the percent of families surveyed who spent money for this item. For example, all families spent money for food, but only 3 percent of them spent money on vacation homes. All other columns vary from this one in that the averages are obtained by dividing the total figures by the number of families who actually spent some money for the item under consideration.

There are a number of interesting things one can learn from Table 2–2. For example, as family size increases, expenditures for a given purpose normally increase, but there are exceptions. Expenditures for alcoholic beverage consumption goes down until the family size reaches six, but even then it is significantly less than for a single person. Vacation homes go up, then down. Boats, planes, and other recreational vehicles go steadily down as family size increases. Now look at what happens to these expenditures when they are classified

TABLE 2–2 Major Income Expenditures, 1972–1973

		*By Family Income Before Taxes**					
Spending for:	All Fami- lies	$8,000– 9,999	$10,000– 11,999	$12,000– 14,999	$15,000– 19,999	$20,000– 24,999	$25,000 and up**
Food	$1568 (100)	$1392 (100)	$1563 (100)	$1750 (100)	$2010 (100)	$2293 (100)	$2651 (100)
Housing (total)	2468 (100)	2128 (100)	2342 (100)	2591 (100)	3027 (100)	3495 (100)	4682 (100)
To rent	590 (39)	1545 (49)	1666 (42)	1732 (30)	2009 (24)	2020 (20)	2961 (14)
To own†	697 (63)	780 (55)	949 (62)	1060 (76)	1284 (82)	1528 (84)	2043 (89)
Fuel & utilities	429 (90)	411 (90)	463 (93)	498 (95)	558 (97)	594 (98)	711 (98)
Household operations (phones, domestic help, etc.)	317 (94)	257 (95)	277 (97)	331 (99)	363 (99)	437 (99)	688 (100)
Home furnishings & equipment	413 (88)	354 (91)	376 (93)	477 (95)	587 (97)	754 (98)	988 (97)
Clothing (buy & maintain)	671 (99)	517 (100)	617 (100)	692 (100)	867 (100)	1082 (100)	1564 (100)
Transportation (cars —buy, finance, oper- ate—& public trans. excl. trips)	1639 (93)	1466 (97)	1714 (99)	1956 (100)	2257 (100)	2712 (100)	3234 (99)
Health Care (insur- ance plus non- reimbursed costs)	491 (97)	466 (98)	487 (99)	513 (99)	584 (99)	706 (99)	896 (99)
Personal Care (selected items)	103 (84)	98 (83)	111 (87)	115 (91)	139 (94)	166 (96)	233 (97)
Education	105 (25)	194 (18)	221 (24)	232 (32)	347 (38)	551 (46)	833 (51)
Reading Materials	49 (84)	43 (84)	53 (89)	59 (92)	69 (95)	86 (96)	112 (97)
Recreation (total)	669 (93)	485 (97)	597 (98)	690 (99)	896 (100)	1297 (100)	1842 (99)

Source: Consumer Expenditure Survey Series: Interview Survey, 1972 and 1973 (Report 455-3), 1976, U.S. Dept. of Labor.

Note: All averages rounded to the nearest dollar. All figures in parentheses are the percentage of families who were actual spenders during 1973.

* Family "head" average ages in first five income brackets, 43–46 years; family sizes average 2.8–3.7 people, generally go up with income.

** Average income about $38,500 before taxes; "heads" average 48 years old; family sizes average 3.8 people.

	By Family Size			By Age of Oldest Child (husband-wife families)			One-Parent Families (at least 1 child under 18)
Singles	2 People	4 People	6 or more	Under 6	6–17	18 or over	
$693 (99)	$1330 (100)	$2061 (100)	$2894 (100)	$1282 (100)	$2248 (100)	$2461 (100)	$1451 (100)
1664 (99)	2268 (100)	3062 (100)	2922 (100)	3273 (100)	3112 (100)	2920 (100)	2303 (100)
1321 (61)	1704 (36)	1653 (29)	1380 (23)	1702 (58)	1625 (24)	1627 (15)	1493 (67)
652 (36)	876 (66)	1372 (76)	1293 (79)	1538 (54)	1446 (80)	1197 (86)	1107 (34)
291 (75)	432 (93)	551 (96)	671 (97)	460 (90)	603 (97)	615 (98)	403 (81)
255 (84)	308 (96)	405 (98)	362 (96)	464 (95)	381 (98)	358 (99)	392 (89)
242 (72)	419 (89)	597 (96)	556 (96)	622 (96)	628 (96)	587 (96)	284 (87)
341 (98)	559 (99)	888 (100)	1103 (100)	707 (100)	906 (100)	1055 (100)	675 (99)
980 (79)	1520 (95)	2214 (98)	2463 (97)	1804 (99)	1938 (99)	3015 (99)	1145 (87)
280 (95)	522 (98)	581 (99)	621 (98)	512 (98)	594 (99)	713 (99)	269 (90)
80 (69)	128 (87)	133 (91)	141 (89)	76 (82)	134 (92)	167 (93)	106 (70)
236 (5)	280 (10)	396 (45)	569 (51)	202 (25)	195 (45)	806 (57)	209 (26)
42 (71)	57 (86)	71 (91)	65 (85)	59 (88)	71 (91)	69 (93)	46 (66)
427 (82)	709 (93)	897 (99)	929 (97)	670 (99)	916 (99)	997 (98)	381 (91)

TABLE 2–2   (*Continued*)

				*By Family Income Before Taxes**			
Spending for:	All Fami- lies	$8,000– 9,999	$10,000– 11,999	$12,000– 14,999	$15,000– 19,999	$20,000– 24,999	$25,000 and up**
Vacation and pleasure trips	247 (62)	257 (64)	303 (68)	314 (73)	408 (79)	544 (87)	861 (87)
Other recreation (TV, sports, per- formances, etc.)	309 (91)	248 (95)	312 (97)	352 (98)	414 (99)	547 (99)	742 (99)
Vacation homes†	21 (3)	††	573 (2)	493 (3)	613 (4)	775 (6)	1013 (8)
Boats, planes, other recreational vehicles	92 (16)	431 (15)	384 (17)	472 (20)	607 (23)	811 (29)	836 (31)
Alcoholic Beverages	79 (63)	95 (66)	124 (68)	110 (72)	134 (79)	144 (81)	202 (88)
Tobacco Products	130 (56)	226 (60)	232 (61)	243 (64)	264 (65)	272 (63)	256 (58)
Personal Insurance (life, endowment, annuities, income)	258 (71)	237 (74)	298 (79)	326 (85)	415 (89)	510 (90)	857 (90)
Retirement & Pensions	584 (73)	537 (73)	715 (78)	773 (81)	988 (83)	1245 (86)	1721 (86)
Gifts & Contributions	430 (86)	354 (88)	356 (88)	424 (95)	518 (95)	689 (97)	1637 (98)

† Includes interest, taxes, maintenance and repairs; excludes mortgage payments toward
     equity.
†† Inadequate data.

by income size rather than family size. How can you explain these variances?

Note that income is before taxes. Since we have a progressive federal tax system—higher-income families have to allocate more of their income for taxes than do lower-income families—after-tax income will vary less. Since this data was gathered prices have gone up substantially. By 1977 you needed to add one-third to these figures because of this price increase. In other words, you need to multiply the figure in Table 2–2 by 1.33 to see how much this amount of consumption would have cost in 1977. Since this data was gathered patterns of spending have changed because all prices have not gone up at the same rate. The price of heating and cooling a home, for example, has gone up more than the price of most things. And while people have turned their thermostats down in the winter and up in the summer, their bills have still risen, forcing them to consume less of other

	By Family Size				By Age of Oldest Child (husband-wife families)			One-Parent Families (at least 1 child under 18)
Singles	2 People	4 People	6 or more	Under 6	6–17	18 or over	
306 (48)	484 (63)	389 (73)	386 (66)	272 (70)	386 (73)	454 (73)	240 (38)
196 (78)	272 (90)	446 (98)	508 (96)	368 (99)	475 (98)	488 (97)	257 (91)
689 (1)	703 (4)	592 (4)	643 (3)	826 (1)	563 (3)	824 (5)	††
859 (5)	626 (13)	620 (23)	580 (24)	502 (20)	550 (26)	531 (25)	298 (6)
147 (51)	120 (61)	117 (74)	121 (69)	102 (81)	123 (74)	132 (73)	94 (49)
179 (40)	226 (54)	246 (65)	272 (69)	202 (63)	250 (67)	272 (68)	193 (58)
164 (47)	315 (72)	448 (85)	471 (82)	376 (81)	442 (86)	524 (86)	213 (55)
536 (63)	771 (68)	942 (82)	896 (83)	764 (81)	979 (81)	992 (83)	563 (77)
448 (77)	615 (89)	399 (90)	564 (86)	295 (87)	414 (91)	645 (92)	215 (67)

items. Tastes, too, have changed since this data was gathered, causing less consumption of some things and more of others.

All the columns labeled by family size include all levels of income from zero up. The same is true of subsequent columns. Keep in mind that major purchases—home, car, or major appliances—are not made every year, thus people are not always paying for these items. As a result, you cannot simply multiply an expenditure by ten, say, and conclude that is how much would be spent in ten years on this item.

KINDS OF EXPENSES

Expenses can be classed as *avoidable* and *unavoidable*. A trip to the beach or prime cuts of beef are avoidable expenses. Traveling to work and eating are unavoidable expenses. It is important to distinguish between the two because, if your expenditures are too high, you can reduce them only by reducing or eliminating avoidable expenditures. If you fail to identify all avoidable expenses, you may fail to cut expenditures enough or may do so in an unsatisfactory manner, that is, you may cut an avoidable expense that is more important to you than another you failed to identify. A budget must cover all unavoidable expenses.

Over the period of time your budget covers, some costs will be *fixed* in size. For example, whether or not you use your house or car, you will have to make given-sized payments to those who loaned you the money to buy them. On the other hand, how much gasoline you buy for your car will vary with how much you drive it; thus, gasoline is a *variable* cost. Some portion of that gasoline cost is *avoidable*, such as that you use to take a Sunday drive. Assuming that there is no cheaper way to get to work, the cost of the gasoline you use to drive to work is an *unavoidable* cost. For the time being, your mortgage payment is unavoidable, as it is a legal obligation. Over a longer period of time it is avoidable, because you can sell the house. However, you cannot avoid having some housing cost; in other words, either you will have to pay the mortgage on a cheaper house or rent on an apartment for less than you would pay on a mortgage.

A cost is fixed only in the short-run. In the long-run, you can sell a piece of property and, thus, change the size of your mortgage payment and your property tax. You must consider fixed costs, because you must budget for the short- as well as the long-run.

Some variable costs are unavoidable, such as the cost to a salesperson of buying the gasoline necessary to visit customers. Some fixed costs, such as the monthly fee for parking your car at work, are unavoidable. Other variable and fixed costs are avoidable, such as movie tickets and a country club membership fee.

Variable costs are usually the hardest to predict, and, therefore, if many of your costs are variable, it is risky to have a rigid budget. Fixed costs, if they are a large part of your total costs, give you headaches if your income falls, forcing you to reduce your expenditures. The more of your costs that are unavoidable, whether fixed or variable, the tougher is your problem if you have to trim expenditures. To cut total expenses by reducing your country club expense requires dropping your membership; whereas, to cut them by reducing your grocery bill means buying cheaper food and/or less food; not doing without any.

You have some control over whether a cost is fixed or variable or whether it is avoidable or unavoidable. You can have a fixed medical expense in large part via taking out insurance to cover medical costs. If you take out such insurance, this means that you can't cut cost by sticking it out a few days to see if you get well without seeing a doctor. On the other hand, the need for a lot of medical attention will not ruin your budget via an unavoidable, huge increase in your medical bill. By taking out medical insurance, you make medical costs unavoidable, in other words, you will pay a premium whether or not you get sick. This decision will also affect the total size of your outlay for medical purposes over your lifetime. You may spend either more or less by taking out insurance. Most people pay more, otherwise, insurance companies would find it difficult to stay in business. It might be worthwhile to pay more, if it prevents you from periodically going into the "hole," which could, at worst, send you into bankruptcy, ruining your credit rating and stripping you of your assets, or at least make it necessary for you to get a high-cost, emergency loan to bail yourself out.

Your budget must cover all unavoidable expenses. Since you cannot predict their size with 100 percent accuracy—your budget will have to include margin for error. If you find that your unavoidable expenses are too large, you should determine if some of them could ultimately be converted into avoidable expenses. You don't, for example, have to keep up with the Joneses, who have a $75,000 home. You can sell yours and buy a cheaper one, thus, reducing your monthly mortgage loan payment.

By looking at the figures in Table 2–2, you can see what other people, on the average, spend for various items depending on their level of income and family size—the two most important influences on the level of expenditures. Remember, however, that these are only averages. Are you average? If you think you are, you should look into any significant differences between your spending and that in the Table. If you don't think you are average, are variances in line wtih the differences in your tastes or objectives and those of the average person or family?

THE BUDGETING PROCESS

Budgets range from the very informal to the very formal. They may be extremely rigid or extremely flexible. The flexible budget allows for unforeseen expenditures or it simply allows you to spend some money on impulse or whim. If the future turns out different than you anticipated, a rigid budget will cause you difficulty, because your plan will not be appropriate. If, however, your financial position is desperate, a rigid budget may be your only salvation. You simply cannot spend more than a relatively small amount no matter what happens. Very low-income individuals always face such a situation, but others' financial positions are equally bad because they have allowed avoidable expenses to rise so high that total expenses exceed income.

Before going anywhere, you must have a starting point. Otherwise, you don't know what direction you need to go in to reach your objective. Thus, no matter what type of budgeting process you choose, you must first determine where your starting point is, and what are your financial objectives.

Your starting point is your current financial position. Table 2–3 illustrates a hypothetical consumer's current financial position. Using this format, you can determine if your *assets* (things you own) exceed or fall short of your *liabilities* (money you owe). The difference between your assets and your liabilities is your *net worth*. If you have a *negative net worth* (you owe more than you own)—you may have a problem! A negative net worth means you have no estate to leave to your heirs and may have trouble paying your debts. Via budgeting, you can bring your net worth into a positive position.

Assets

Assets are things owned and things you are entitled to. Cash is an asset; so is a checking account in a bank. A savings account in a bank, savings and loan association, mutual savings bank, or credit union is also an asset. Unlike cash and a checking account, savings accounts earn interest. Savings certificates, savings bonds, corporate and municipal bonds, and corporate stocks are other types of assets you might have. All of these pay you a return. An insurance policy is also an asset. It entitles you or your beneficiaries to receive payment if certain disasters strike. Some life insurance policies have a cash value, that is, if they are terminated, you will receive a cash payment. These are known as *liquid assets* because they can readily be converted to cash.

TABLE 2–3 A Personal Balance Sheet

Assets (+)		Liabilities (−)	
Cash	$ 800	Credit cards	$ 450
Savings account	4,000	Auto loan balance	1,600
10 shares of stock	3,500	Mortgage loan balance	30,000
Jewelry	400	Total Liabilities	$32,050
Furnishings	3,350		
Cars	4,500	Net Worth	$14,500
Equity in home	30,000		
		Total Liabilities	
Total Assets	$46,550	plus Net Worth	$46,550

Other assets you may hold are said to be less liquid than these because it is more difficult to convert them into cash quickly without loss. These are called fixed assets. Such assets include your home, automobile, boat, camper, mobile home, motorcycle, jewelry, furs, furniture, power tools, hunting rifle, antiques, and so on. Determining a value for these assets is usually much more difficult than in the case of more liquid assets. Often such assets can be sold only for a price well below what you paid for them. Table 2–4 tells a good bit about what assets Americans hold.

The value of an asset is not determined by what you paid to obtain it, but what you can sell it for. What are houses like yours selling for now? How much is that stock you own trading for now on the stock exchange? At what price does a reputable jeweler appraise your diamond ring? What price does a used-car value guide list for your car?

Liabilities

A *liability* is something you owe—a debt. Did you borrow money in order to buy your home? Have you used a credit card to make some purchases this month? Did you fail to pay off all your charge account balances last month? Have you taken out a loan based on your life insurance policy's cash surrender value? Have you bought stock on margin, that is, the broker you dealt with has loaned you part of the price of the stock you purchased through him or her? Are you buying something on lay-away? Are you withholding less from your paycheck than you are going to have to pay in taxes this year? Do you owe property taxes?

Unfortunately, while you may have to sell an asset for less than you paid for it, creditors are not going to be willing to accept less than they loaned you, plus interest. Thus, you can find yourself being unable to sell something for the amount you still owe on it—cars are a good example.

The fact that the value of your assets exceeds the amount of your liabilities does not mean that you will have no problem paying off these liabilities. To take an extreme example, suppose the only asset you possess is a house; your only liability is a mortgage loan taken out to buy the house. A monthly payment on this loan is now due. Let's say you've lost your job, and thus, you don't have the cash you need coming in. The value of the house may far exceed the sum of all the payments, but to sell the house in time to meet this one payment would mean taking a big loss because to sell it quickly you would have to set a price below its true value. In addition, selling a house involves a lot of costs. *Therefore, you should include in your budget an adequate*

TABLE 2–4   Percent of Households Owning Motor Vehicles and Television
Sets and Having Available Selected Other Appliances, 1974

Annual income of household	1 or more motor vehicles	1 car	2 or more cars	TV set	Air Conditioning Central	Air Conditioning Room	Refrig- erator	Freezer	Washing machine
Under $3,000	46.2	37.0	6.2	89.7	7.9	21.7	96.6	19.7	50.7
$3,000 to $4,999	64.2	51.9	8.8	94.4	10.7	27.0	98.7	23.6	55.4
$5,000 to $7,499	79.4	60.4	15.6	96.1	13.0	30.5	98.7	26.6	62.6
$7,500 to $9,999	88.3	61.9	23.1	97.0	13.6	35.2	99.1	30.4	68.5
$10,000 to $14,999	93.9	54.9	36.8	97.9	18.2	35.5	99.4	37.0	77.2
$15,000 to $19,999	96.7	45.4	50.1	99.0	24.4	36.1	99.5	40.6	85.3
$20,000 to $24,999	97.4	36.8	60.1	99.0	28.7	34.3	99.7	44.2	86.0
$25,000 and over	97.2	29.4	67.2	98.7	38.6	30.4	99.7	48.4	89.2

Source: Statistical Abstract of the United States 1976, U.S. Department of Commerce, Bureau of the Census, table 689, p. 424.

amount of cash and/or demand deposits (checking accounts) to pay all currently maturing obligations.

A budget can be used in minimizing your tax bill. This subject will be gone into in detail in Chapter 3; therefore, all that will be said here is that by moving your income and non-tax expenditures around in time, you can reduce the amount of taxes you have to pay. This is one liability whose size you can alter!

After you determine your starting point—your financial position—your next step is to itemize your anticipated cash receipts and expenditures so that you can manage them and thus, achieve your goals, which may include improving your financial position. You usually roughly list receipts and expenditures in the distant future because you cannot accurately estimate them and need a detailed plan only for the immediate future. Table 2–5 illustrates a hypothetical consumer's budget.

Clearly, if projected cash income in a future time period falls short of projected cash expenditures during that time, you have a problem. If this problem can be seen far enough ahead, and you will

TABLE 2–5   A Weekly Personal Budget

Cash Income:		
Salary (received every other week)		$500.00
Cash Expenses:		
Groceries	$ 45.00	
Meals out	15.75	
Transportation	25.00	
Monthly mortgage payment	300.00	
Monthly electric bill	90.00	
Monthly telephone bill	15.00	
Total cash expenses:	$490.75	
Deposit in savings account:	25.00	
Total outlays of cash:		$515.75
Difference: surplus or (deficit)		($ 15.75)
Cash on hand at beginning of week:		100.00
Cash on hand at end of week:		84.25
Cash balance needed for next week:*		75.00
Cash surplus or (deficit)		$ 9.25

* Since no salary will be received the following week, this cash is needed for the following week's expenses. Note that it was necessary for a cash balance to be carried over from the previous week in order for there to be enough cash available to cover this and the following week's expenses. This ending balance is $9.25 more than is needed. This amount is available to be allocated to other uses. If the week had ended with a projected deficit, plans for earlier weeks or this week would have to be changed or money would have to be borrowed.

experience cash surpluses in the meantime, this problem can easily be solved by holding these anticipated cash surpluses until they are needed to cover the later excess of cash outflows over inflows. Even if borrowing is the only way to acquire this cash, by anticipating the need for it far in advance, you have more time to shop around for the best loan available. You also need to hold some cash to handle expenses that you cannot predict and to handle overestimates of income or underestimates of expenses. (Losing your job would lower your income!)

Savings

The purpose of saving is to provide you funds to buy things in the future. You may be saving to buy a house or a car, or to finance your children's education or your retirement. The checking account and cash balance you hold for emergencies are also called savings in that they, too, represent income not spent. Their purpose is, however, different from that of other funds saved, because their purpose is to improve your liquidity. Cash balances to handle emergencies are a form of insurance whose purpose is to avoid a worsening of your condition.

Savings planned for the future should be subtracted from anticipated income just like an expense; otherwise, there is no sound rationale for your savings. They will simply be what is left over, and what is left over may be either more or less than you need to save. If you subtract both savings and expenses from income, anything left over should be allocated to either or both savings and consumption, based on their relative priorities.

BUDGETING CAN SOLVE PROBLEMS

There are many common consumer problems that budgeting can eliminate. One problem might be called the Christmas syndrome. Lulled by the Christmas spirit and enticed by retailers' promotions, many people buy so much before Christmas that after the holiday season, not only are they unable to take advantage of after-Christmas sales, but they have to borrow to finance basic needs. What might be called the college blues can also be wiped out. For a few days after some students receive a check from home, money is burning a hole in their pockets. Just before the next check comes, they are desperately living off snack food and staying in the dorm—that's all they can afford to do! Another problem budgeting can solve is how to handle lumpy expenditures—large expenditures that have to be made at one time rather than being spread evenly over the year.

With a budget, you will decide before Christmas—not while listening to Christmas carols in a store—how much you will spend on the holiday. You will leave yourself some funds for the after-Christmas sales and necessities. Before the Christmas buying season you will refrain from spending some of your income so that you will not have to borrow to finance Christmas. If you do decide to borrow, you will have a plan for repaying the loan without undue strain.

With a budget, the college student will deposit most of his or her check in a bank account; thus, there will be no money burning a hole in his or her pocket. There will be a plan for spending the money, and it will cover the period until the next check comes. The student will withdraw funds as the budget calls for their use. Checks will be written for major expenditures, both for safety and to provide a record of expenditures that can be used in future budgeting and shown to parents when asking for more money.

With a budget, you will not be running out at tax time to borrow money to pay your taxes. Anticipating such lumpy expenditures, you will accumulate the necessary funds during the months preceding the date when taxes are due.

Another problem budgeting will solve is not being able to borrow or having to pay an above-average interest rate due to your poor credit rating. A good *credit rating* is a history of good personal financial management: you can pay your debts on time. By budgeting, you will be able to pay off your obligations on time and you will not be writing checks for more than you have on deposit in the bank. You will not be paying off your credit accounts late, incurring a higher interest charge. In addition, when you go in for a loan, you will not already have a staggering debt burden, and you will have plenty of information at your fingertips about how you are going to be able to repay a new loan. Loan officers will be overjoyed to see you and give you a good deal—assuming you can convince them that you are really as good as you seem. They see very few good personal financial managers; thus, they make take some convincing!

THE NO-NO's OF BUDGETING

A budget should not be a straitjacket. Not only is planning and controlling expenditures down to the last penny impossible; if you try it, it is so maddening and so time-consuming that you will probably get disgusted and give it up. *Neither should a budget be immutable.* You cannot forecast even the immediate future. Your budget should be

flexible enough to allow for small errors without having to scrap the.
budget. It should probably be flexible enough to allow you to take
advantage of nonrecurring bargains, that is, an item you would normally have bought later is currently on sale. Experience wlil show
you how flexible your budget needs to be.

It will do you no good to prepare a budget and then throw it
in a drawer and forget about it. You should refer to it regularly so
that you can follow it and know when you aren't following it. If you
are not following it, why not? Is it impossible to follow because it is
all wrong? If so, learn from these mistakes and make a better budget
for the future. Identify your mistakes and analyze why they happened.
Constantly monitor the financial decisions embodied in your budget.
Are they assisting you in obtaining your objectives? If not, why not?

Don't set spending limits which are clearly impossible to meet.
To reduce expenditures, don't simply zero in on the larger expenses
and slash them. For half the price of a refrigerator, you can't buy a
refrigerator. Maybe your refrigerator is likely to break down during
the period covered by your budget and have to be replaced. You can,
however, wear your clothes longer; thus, you can avoid this expenditure. You can eat less expensive meat. You can go to the movies less
often. Big expenditures, in short, may seem the easiest way to cut costs,
but they often aren't.

Don't plan to do without something you clearly aren't going to
be able to do without. Don't forget to allow for the unexpected—
unexpected expenses are always cropping up. Check over your list
of essentials. Are they really essentials? Must you drive your car to
work and carry no riders? Couldn't you go with someone else cheaper
or earn money by carrying riders? When you have a party, do you have
to serve expensive refreshments? Must you have an expensive set of
golf clubs or the very best tennis racket?

BUDGET COMPONENTS

The first item in a budget is your income. This includes salaries, wages,
bonuses, commissions, tips, gifts, interest, dividends from corporations,
profit distributions by unincorporated businesses, and a gain from the
sale of an asset. Usually this is the easiest figure in your budget to
come up with.

The second item in your cash budget is expenses. These expenses
can be categorized as: (1) those that occur annually, but do not occur
as often as once a month; (2) those which occur at least once a month,
but do not occur weekly; (3) those which occur at least once a week;

and, (4) irregular expenses that may or may not reoccur, and, if they reoccur, it is not on a regular basis.

Typical of the first group are insurance payments. Auto and home insurance, for example, are often paid one or two times a year. Rent or home mortgage payments, however, are usually paid monthly. Food is bought weekly. Money may be spent on transportation daily. Buying a wedding ring or having an appendectomy illustrates the fourth type of expenditure, the irregular expenditure.

Food, clothing, and shelter are, of course, essential expenses. Medical care and transportation are basic expenses. Because of the high cost of doing without it, most people consider some insurance a basic expense. Many states require that automobile drivers carry insurance, and a large number of Americans have health, life, property, and casualty insurance policies.

Even people with very low incomes spend some money on recreation and entertainment. Both savings and education are significant uses of funds by the average American consumer. And, like it or not, taxes account for a larger slice of the average consumer's income than any other single item. Common, but not relatively very large, are expenditures for gifts and contributions.

Debt repayment also accounts for a sizable amount of consumer income. In 1976 consumer debt outstanding—mortgages, installment credit, and other consumer credit—rose by $96 billion, a record increase. In the first quarter of 1977 consumer debt rose by another $19 billion, lifting total consumer debt to a record $897 billion. In the first quarter of 1977 consumer installment credit outstanding amounted to 14.7 percent of after-tax consumer income. Consumers were, on an annual basis, spending nearly $61 billion (4.9 percent of after-tax income) on debt service.

In recent years there has been a significant lengthening of the average loan period. It appears that in 1977 around 82 percent of the new-car loans were for more than three years. A year earlier this figure was only 57 percent, and two years earlier it was only 42 percent. Longer-term loans were also being taken out for the purchase of used cars, mobile homes, and conventional housing. Personal loans were also lengthening. Somewhat surprisingly, perhaps, is that at the same time the loan period has been lengthening, the size of the average down payment has been declining.

Consumers' holdings of *liquid assets* (cash, savings accounts, etc.) are higher relative to income than at any time in three decades. The ratio of their total *financial assets* (intangibles) to income, including stock holdings, is well below previous peaks, but this ratio is climbing. Financial assets are securities, cash, and so on. In addition to securities, intangibles include such things as copyrights.

What portion of their income consumers save, how much they borrow, and in what form they hold their wealth is determined by the current level of their income; their expectations about the level of their future income; the current cost of borrowing, and the return on savings and investments; their anticipations about the level of interest rates and dividends in the future; current prices and expected future prices, and mob psychology. Changes in the relationship of prices to one another also plays a role in consumer decisions. Will, for example, housing costs rise more or less rapidly than rent? Will bond yields rise or fall more or less rapidly than dividends?

DAILY FINANCIAL MANAGEMENT

Obviously you cannot include every item you buy, down to the last button, in your budget. Every expenditure, however, must be carefully weighed if you are to stay within your budget. You don't want, for example, to find out that buying a much needed winter coat will cause you to exceed your clothing budget because you bought some clothes for a party, or find that your food budget doesn't have enough left in it because you bought a bunch of snack food for the party. You also don't want to buy a refrigerator one day and find out a few days later that you could have purchased it for much less next door to the store where you bought it. (Perhaps if you had bought the cheaper refrigerator, you could have afforded the party snacks and clothes!)

To control your daily expenditures it is a good idea to, either in writing or in your head (preferably the former), keep track of what you spend every day. Thus, you will quickly see when you are spending at an unsustainable rate and make plans for slowing your spending in the least painful manner.

Staying Within Your Food Budget

Never head for the grocery store without a list. Without a list, you are likely both to spend too much and fail to get some needed items. The person in the family who is least susceptible to the intentionally alluring items in the supermarket should do the shopping. Shop by yourself —a companion will likely distract you from your objective: getting what you need for the least and staying within your budget.

Clearly, you want to get a given quality food for the lowest cost per ounce, pint, or so on. You don't want to buy fancy grades unless they are worth it to you and you can afford this luxury. Although they are not so heavily advertised, the store's own brand-name products are usually cheaper than are national brands and are of similar quality.

Certainly it is worth trying the store brands once to see if they are satisfactory. Package size is not important. What counts is what is in the package. Certain types of packages are, however, more convenient to use, and some can save you money by reducing waste, that is, the food will keep longer in them.

By shopping in more than one store you can compare prices and buy where a given item is the least costly, but you must beware of spending more to run around from store to store than you can save by buying the cheapest goods. A good way to reduce this running around is to watch food advertisements. It may be well worth your while to subscribe to a newspaper just for the advertisements for food, clothes, furniture, and appliances. Because they are largely advertising mediums, many suburban newspaper subscriptions are very cheap. Sometimes money-saving coupons appear in newspaper advertisements. If you can work it out, shopping with a neighbor and, therefore, sharing transportation costs is another good way to save money. You should not, of course, run out for only a few items at a time. This is another reason for making a shopping list, because you are then less likely to forget an essential item and have to make an extra trip for it. Combining your grocery shopping trip with taking children to school or shopping for clothes is another way to save on transportation.

Don't shop in a store just because it offers trading stamps or games. These have to be paid for in the prices the store charges! The store without the contest may be the best place to shop because its prices may be lower, besides, you stand very little chance of winning the other store's game.

Convenience foods—already prepared dishes ready to put in the oven—cost more than similar unprepared foods. Before buying them you should carefully consider whether or not the convenience they provide is worth the cost and whether you can afford this cost. Much snack-type food is what is called "junk" food—it offers little in the way of nutrition. Can you afford to throw money away on such food? Check the dates on perishable items and don't buy them if you don't think you can eat them up in time. Don't buy in bulk to get a lower price per unit if you will end up throwing a lot of it away because it has spoiled before you can eat it. Can you afford to patronize a convenience store? Their prices are a good deal higher than a supermarket's.

Check the directions on the package about how to prepare food; proper preparation reduces waste. When buying meat take into account that there will be shrinkage in cooking. Familiarize yourself with the government grading systems for food so that you won't think something is cheap when it is simply properly priced because it is inferior. Do not delude yourself that only the top grade is fit to eat.

Staying Within Your Clothing Budget

When you shop for clothes you are interested in a variety of things. You are concerned with durability, appearance, fit, comfort, practicality, ease of upkeep, and cost. Because of its greater durability the more expensive piece of clothing may be the best buy, however, many high-priced pieces of clothing provide you nothing that lower-priced pieces won't provide except status or snob appeal. As in the case of groceries, you should shop around and watch advertisements. If you don't want to waste money, don't shop for clothes for fun. Only shop for clothes when you determine that you need some new clothes.

Obviously, you should familiarize yourself with the various types of fabrics and their characteristics. *Cotton,* for example, is very comfortable, but it doesn't hold a crease well unless it is combined with another fabric and is permanent press. Cotton shrinks unless treated ("shrinkage controlled" isn't the same as "guaranteed not to shrink"). *Worsted* fabric provides longer wear and serviceability. *Nylon* is hot to wear in the summer, but is a good windbreaker in the winter and is warm when lined and is lightweight. *Polyester knits* pack well and dry quickly. *Bonded* fabrics may separate.

Good quality clothing doesn't have uneven, narrow seams which are neither bound nor pinked to resist raveling. Good quality clothes have neat buttonholes that are reinforced, hems are even and the weave is vertical, patterns are matched at seams, finishings are securely fastened. Where appropriate, they are certainly lined and lined with a durable material. Collars and facings are reinforced.

Clearly, you are not extremely interested in durability if an item of clothing will very quickly go out of style. However, clothing that will quickly go out of style is seldom a good buy because its cost is excessive relative to the amount of wear you will get out of it. This is because stores know they have to sell such clothing at a loss unless it sells fast, so they sell it at a higher price than they would if they had plenty of time to get rid of it. This pricing policy makes up for the items they have to sell at a loss.

Children present some special buying problems. The fact that they quickly outgrow their clothes suggests that durability isn't a major consideration; yet, they are usually much harder on clothes than are adults. To a substantial extent the answer to this problem lies in the particular child involved. Is he or she growing rapidly? Is he or she very hard on clothes? Is there a younger child to hand the clothes down to? Because children's clothes are not much cheaper than adults', and because they outgrow their clothes, a major part of the clothing budget of a family with children is absorbed by the children. It is good training for older children to include them in the budget-making and acquisition processes.

Always read the labels that come on your new clothes. Are they colorfast? Can they be washed? How should they be washed? Are they Sanforized (will not shrink more than 1 percent)? What kind of fabric or fabrics are they made of? Do they have repellent finishes? Are they permanent press? Are they wash and wear?

A good time to buy clothes is after their main selling season which, fortunately, is well before the season they will be worn. Retailers must get rid of fall fashions to make room for winter fashions, and so forth. Of course, your selection is reduced, particularly if you are of average size, but most people can find suitable clothing from among the "leftovers" and often save one-third or more.

Staying Within Your Furniture and Appliance Budgets

Because furniture and appliances have a longer life and generally higher cost, greater consideration and more comparison shopping should precede their purchase than is the case with food and clothing. The larger of these purchases must be specifically included in your budget.

As is the case with clothing, furniture may be bought directly from a retail store or ordered through a catalog. The latter has the advantage of eliminating the necessity of leaving your home, but can produce a serious problem if you are not satisfied with the merchandise received. In some cases you may obtain a better price from a catalog seller because he probably deals on a volume basis, and many furniture retailers do not. Speciality furniture not locally available may also be obtained through catalogs. Retail stores which do a high volume of business will generally have lower prices and provide more services than will stores which do a small volume of business. By selling directly from a warehouse, some furniture retailers have been able to significantly lower prices. Delivery charges can be substantial, so if you have the capability, you may be able to save by transporting your new furniture yourself. Used furniture and appliances have low resale values. A good way to dispose of them is to advertise in the classified advertising section of your local newspaper.

Before buying a piece of furniture or a large appliance, measure it and the space you plan to put it in. Also measure the doorways and hallways in your home to be sure you can get it inside. Always have people who will use chairs and beds try them out for comfort before buying them. Check carefully for flaws and poor workmanship. In furniture, buy durable fabrics, wood, plastics, and finishes. Be sure the piece will blend in with your other furnishings, draperies, and wallpaper. If you expect to move, will the furniture you are considering be practical to move and fit into, perhaps, substantially different surroundings?

The price range of small household appliances is substantial. Your need for them, perhaps, varies even more. Manufacturers have become very creative in recent years in developing new small appliances. The tendency is to increasingly limit an appliance's use so that you will need a different one for nearly every job. For example, you can cook either a steak or a hamburger in an electric fry pan, but you can't cook a steak in a hamburger cooker. You can boil a hotdog and many other things in a pot, but you can only cook a hotdog in a hotdog cooker. Thus, before buying an appliance with very few uses, be careful to consider how often you will use it, and whether it will do a better job than would an appliance with broader uses. Then decide if it is worth the price asked for it.

It is always a good idea to talk with friends who have an appliance you are considering buying in order to find out what they like and don't like about it. You then learn both about the desirability of the brand they have as well as what to look for in other brands. Examine the appliance carefully and try to imagine yourself using it. In this way, if it has some major flaws, you are likely to become aware of them. Think twice about buying a luxury model.

A large appliance represents a substantial investment. You should receive many years of service from a large appliance. A relatively long warranty period and high-quality service facilities are of particular importance. (Because doing without the services of large appliances, such as a refrigerator, is normally a greater problem than doing without the services of a small appliance, speedy repair service is much more important.) The availability of inexpensive repair parts is also very important. If the particular brand or type of large appliance you are considering buying will soon cease to be produced, getting it repaired may become a real problem in a few years. Very new and unestablished appliances, and those a very long time in the marketplace are the prime candidates for going out of production.

You should always look at an operating model. The reliability of the manufacturer is very important, but so is that of the retailer. Dealing with the retailer is more convenient than dealing with the distant manufacturer if you encounter problems. Safety and capacity to handle the job are often major areas of concern.

CASES FOR DISCUSSION

Case 1 In 1972 Keith Christensen got a good job with an airline, earning $12,000 a year. One of the fringe benefits of the job was a drastically reduced rate on air travel for him and his family. In 1972 he and his wife Marie had one child, who was then seven years old. Marie worked then, but quit after their second child came in 1974. Keith and Marie, for less than $2,000 a trip, have been to London, Paris, Rome, and Tokyo. Encouraged by the fact that he now makes $14,000, Keith and Marie put down $5,000 on a $38,000 home a year ago. They are still paying for two luxury automobiles. To keep from cutting into his family's standard of living, Keith has been borrowing for the past few years. He currently owes $6,000 in addition to the money owed for his house. He is two months behind on his house note and a credit card company has turned his account over to a collection agency. What should Keith and Marie do? How could they have avoided getting into this situation?

Case 2 Donald Maloney grew up in a lower-middle-class home. Now he is "in the chips." He finished medical school only five years ago and he is already making between $75,000 and $85,000 a year. He and his wife Susan and their three children enjoy an elegant home in the city where Donald practices, and a home in the mountains and at the beach. Donald recently learned to fly, and he now has his own two-engine plane to fly his family to their vacation homes. Because they now can get there so quickly, they are able to use these homes far more than in the past. Susan loves shopping, and she has tastefully decorated their home with her acquisitions. Their grocery bill runs $200 a week, which Donald thinks is a bit high even for today. Donald is upset because he can't seem to save a dime. Sometimes he is late paying a bill. Assume you are a financial consultant he has approached for a solution to his problems.

Case 3 Janice Abernathy works in one of the crews that clean planes at the end of their runs. Her husband Kip is unemployed but is receiving unemployment checks, and he gets a $50-a-month disability pension from the army. Kip was laid off work due to a strike at a firm which supplied the plant he worked in. His job paid $700 a month when he was working. Janice earns $550 a month. Their rent is $180 a month, and they have four children under 12 years old. Her mother lives with them. She receives social security and pays $20 of the rent. Sometimes the children have to go to school with no lunch money. This makes Janice mad because Kip goes down to the local pool hall several times a week and her mother always plays bingo two nights a week. Since Kip was laid off, they have fallen behind in paying several of their bills. You work for a social service agency and Janice has come to you for help. Draw up a budget for her.

Case 4 Fernando Ortega opened a small automobile accessory store eight years ago. He barely made it the first few years, but now he is doing well. He takes home about $25,000 a year, yet his personal life is just one financial crisis after another. Although he has two brothers and two sisters, they all have families and leave it up to Fernando, a bachelor, to support their aged parents. Both are in a nursing home and this costs $1,500 a month. The only income his parents have is social security, and they turn this money over to Fernando. His parents are also covered by Medicare. Fernando complains that he's so concerned about money that he is afraid to even buy a paperback book without thinking it over carefully. Can you make up a budget to help Fernando?

Case 5 Celia Westbrook and Matthew Blake plan to be married in two months. Celia has just finished law school and was recently employed by a small law firm at $10,000 a year. Matthew is just started working toward a Ph.D. in geology. He has a graduate teaching assistantship which pays $4,000 a year. It is 50 miles from Celia's law office to Matthew's campus, and there is no public transportation in the area. Rental housing is scarce. All low-rent housing is reserved for low-income families, and they make too much money to qualify. It looks like they will have to pay around $300 a month for an apartment or buy a house. There are no houses available for less than $35,000 in the vicinity. Because you are their friend and have had good luck budgeting your expenditures, they have come to you for help.

Case 6 Irving Akerman will soon be going off to college. He will be attending the state university about 110 miles from home. The university is on the quarter system, and tuition is $200 a quarter. A two-man room in a dorm is $230 a quarter. A meal ticket at the college cafeteria for three meals a day for the quarter costs $175. Irving will not have a car. His father has promised him $250 a month, and, he told Irving that if he's old enough to go off to college, he's old enough to manage his own finances. Irving is worried that he can't manage. Since you are an old hand at this kind of thing, he has come to you to work out a budget for him.

Case 7 Michael Mancini is a commercial marketing engineer for an electric utility. His wife Lois is just starting her junior year in college and is majoring in chemistry. Michael makes $13,000 a year. When Lois finishes school she plans to work a year and then start a family. They plan to have two children. She plans to return to work after about eight years. Before then they want to buy a house. They now have only $500 in savings. They own a 2½-year-old car. Their apartment costs them $280 a month, including utilities. Can you set up a budget for them which will enable them to buy a house in five or six years?

Case 8 Oliver and Cora Blalock are looking forward to Oliver's retirement next year from the foundry where he has worked for the past 30 years, but they are worried about whether they can live comfortably. They would like to move from Michigan, where they have lived all their lives, to St. Petersburg, Florida. They expect to have a retirement income of $600 a month. They own their 3-year-old car and their home, which they could sell for around $28,000. Oliver's health is not too good. Last year he had medical bills of $1,000, which included one short hospital stay. Make out a budget for the Blalocks.

REVIEW QUESTIONS

1. What is a budget?
2. What is accomplished by budgeting?

3. What is the difference between a fixed and a variable expense?
4. What are the major advantages of a variable budget?
5. What is a negative net worth?
6. Is it true that as long as your net worth is positive that paying your bills off in full and on time will not be a problem?
7. Why is it, do you suppose, that few businesses or governments fail to budget, but many individuals fail to do so?

YOUR PLAN: CHAPTER 2

Questions to answer to decide whether to budget and how to budget:

1. Do you often find yourself without the money necessary to buy badly needed things?
2. Is your income below average?
3. Do you frequently have to go further into debt in order to pay off existing debts?
4. Do you often regret having made a purchase?
5. Do you often fail to pay a bill when it comes due?
6. Do you sometimes have several of the problems mentioned in the preceding questions?
7. Do you know what your total income is this year? (Your total income is all salaries, wages, tips, interest, dividends, gifts, etc.)
8. Do you have any idea how much you spend in a year?
9. Are you able to save any money?
10. Do you greatly value being able to act on impulse?
11. Do you have any dependents?
12. Do you have trouble keeping your checkbook balanced?
13. Do you ever save up to buy something?
14. Do you usually plan your purchases a good while before making them?
15. Is the size and timing of most of your expenses pretty certain?
16. Can you rather accurately project your annual income?

How to Use Your Answers

If you answered any of Questions 1–6 yes, you need to budget. If you answered either Questions 7 or 8 no, this is a major reason you answered one or more of the first six questions yes. Budgeting will certainly help you because, at a minimum, you will learn the answers to these two vital questions. Even if you answered Questions 1–6 no, you still need budgeting if you answered 16 and/or 9 no. Even if you answered one yes, you may still need to budget. You also need to budget if you are simply not saving enough.

If buying on impulse is very important to you, you had better stick to a flexible budget. If you have dependents, this increases the flexibility your budget should have, as it is difficult to plan exactly for several people. Control of expenditures becomes more difficult when several people are involved; thus, more effort must be expended in controlling expenditures.

If you have trouble balancing your checkbook and/or saving up money for a future purchase, budgeting will be difficult for you. If someone else in your family has no problems with checkbooks and saving, it would be a good idea to have them do the budgeting. If you must do the budgeting, it would probably be best if you use the "envelope" method, that is, place the proper amounts for each expenditure and savings in envelopes appropriately marked. If saving is difficult for you, savings should be immediately put in the bank, preferably in an account where you are penalized for removing the money before a given date.

If you have not been planning purchases a good while in advance of making them, budgeting will involve making a major change in your behavior—you need to face up to this fact. Initially, perhaps, your budget should not extend too far into the future. Once you have achieved some success in short-run planning, extend the period of time covered by your budget.

If you cannot forecast either or both income and expenses very well, budgeting is made much more difficult. Under these circumstances, your budget should be very flexible. You should plan expenditures based on both the worst and best possibilities, that is, the lowest possible income and the highest possible level of unavoidable expenses, and the reverse. Until you are certain the worse will not be the case, operate as though it will be the case.

**Questions you should answer
before making a purchase:**

1. Do I really need it? (Maybe you can make do with something you already have.)
2. Do I want this particular item?
3. Would another item serve my needs better?

4. Does it fit into my budget?
5. Is it worth what it costs?
6. Do I need it now? (A better product may be available later.)
7. Is it reasonably durable?
8. Can I return it?
9. If it is an item which might need servicing, how can I obtain service, and how much will it cost? Is the service prompt and of good quality?
10. Will buying it require I make other, related purchases? If so, what are they and how much will they cost?
11. How will I get it home? (Is delivery by truck necessary? Must it be mailed?)
12. What warranty or guarantee does it have? How good is it?
13. Can I rely on the seller to treat me fairly if some dispute arises about it?
14. If replacement parts may some day be needed, can they be readily obtained? What will they cost?
15. If I don't pay cash, how will I finance it? Are the terms of financing reasonable? Would it be better to finance it through, say, a bank rather than through the merchant?
16. Am I letting a salesman talk me into something I'll later regret?

Expenditures Made Less Often Than Weekly or Daily

Estimates	Jan	Feb	Mar	Apr	May	June	July	Aug	Sept	Oct	Nov	Dec	Total 12 months
Housing:													
Rent or mortgage													
Utility													
Furniture													
Appliances													
Painting, roofing, etc.													
Other													
Insurance:													
Life													
Health													
Auto													
Home													
Other													
Children:													
College, etc.													
Other													
Debts:													
Installment													
Other													
Clothing (major):													
Adults													
Children													
Vacation:													
Contributions:													
Other:													

Total of all nonweekly expenditures for the year: _____

Income earmarked weekly to cover these (divide by 52): _____

PLANNING FORM 2

Purchases Made Weekly or Daily

Income per Week   _____

Estimated Weekly Expenses

Food and beverages:
    At home   _____
    Away   _____

Transportation:
    Auto   _____
    Other   _____

Household:
    Routine upkeep of house   _____
    Routine upkeep of yard   _____
    Other   _____

Recreation and entertainment:
    Recreation (includes magazines, books,
       etc.)   _____
    Entertainment   _____

Children:
    Allowances   _____
    Incidentals   _____

Clothing:
    Routine purchases   _____
    Dry cleaning   _____
    Home laundry   _____

Medical and dental:
    Routine medical   _____
    Routine dental   _____

Impulse buying: _____

Set Aside Weekly   _____

Savings*   _____
Earmarked for nonweekly expenses**   _____
Emergencies***   _____

Total Uses of Income   (_____)

Difference Between Income and Uses of Income   _____

    (If negative, some adjustment must be made: money
    must be borrowed or some of the above must be
    reduced.)

      * To provide for needs in the future
      ** From Planning Form 1
      *** Illness or other irregular expense

The Benefits of Saving

59

9. Know how to evaluate different saving media;
10. Be familiar with the following terms:

insurance	certificate account
liquid saving media	negotiable instrument
	endorse
checking account	special checking
demand deposit	account
bank	regular checking
savings and loan association	account
	cancelled check
credit union	passbook
overdraft	certificate of deposit
float	government savings
bonus account	bond
investment account	simple interest
	compound interest

Many people spend every nickel they get their hands on, and then they borrow more. The fact that many people behave this way doesn't make it right. Even some of the people who live this way will tell you they wish they could do otherwise. They claim that it is impossible for them to save. Some claim their income is too low; others say they don't have the necessary self-discipline. In some cases the reason people don't save isn't due to either of these causes, even though they say it is. The real reason is that they underestimate how beneficial saving is and fail to make realistic savings plans. Unrealistic planning or no planning at all leads to failure.

Saving can serve many functions. Savings can provide peace of mind; reduce expenditures by enabling you to avoid paying interest; enable you to weather financial emergencies; avoid the problems caused by fluctuating income; make it possible to get more benefit from consumption; and provide the wherewithal to invest.

WHY SAVE?

Saving is not an end in itself—*you save in order to obtain certain goals.* You save to provide yourself with security and to enable you to acquire things at a minimum cost. Americans save less than 10 percent of their income (see Table 3–1).

TABLE 3–1 Savings in the United States (billions of current dollars)[a]

	1974	1975	1976
Total personal income	1154.9	1253.4	1382.7
Less: Personal tax and nontax payments	170.3	169.0	196.9
Equals: Disposable personal income	984.6	1084.4	1185.8
Less: Personal outlays	913.0	1004.2	1119.9
Equals: Personal saving	71.7	80.2	65.9

Source: Board of Governors of the Federal Reserve System, Washington, D.C., "Federal Reserve Bulletin" (January 1978), p. A53.

[a] No adjustment is made for changes in the purchasing power of the dollar due to changes in the price level.

The old saying that a lender will only lend you money if you don't need it has enough truth in it to justify having some savings in order to provide yourself with the wherewithal to handle the many emergencies everyone experiences. Knowing you can handle emergencies gives you peace of mind.

Interest

A lot of people use credit instead of savings to make purchases of items not bought regularly, such as kitchen appliances. Yet, credit card companies and retail stores usually charge an 18 percent annual interest rate! This is not an unusually high rate for consumer credit. At an 18 percent annual rate, after only four years, you have paid interest equal to the cost of what you have bought if your outstanding balance remains level. By saving, you can avoid these steep charges for using credit.

This is not to say that you should never use credit. By using credit you get things sooner, but you will get less because part of your income will go for interest. *Interest is the cost of getting things sooner.* Clearly, there is a limit to how much it is worth to get something sooner.

Typical goals of saving are acquiring enough money for a down payment on a house; a college education for your children or more education for yourself; retirement; a vacation; an automobile, camper, or boat; serious illness or other unexpected expense; or, to invest in securities.

Insurance

Insurance is an alternative to putting aside money to handle a disaster, but it is not available in every case, and it may not handle 100 percent of the cost. Instead of periodically depositing money in a savings account and, therefore, having available whatever has accumulated to handle an emergency, you can make periodic payments for an insurance policy which will pay a certain amount if disaster strikes. The amount you receive may be either more or less than you have paid the insurance company. The sooner a disaster strikes after you have taken out a policy, the more likely it is that you will have spent less on insurance than you would have had to put aside to be able to cover the cost of the disaster. In a short time you will not be able to save up as much as an insurance policy will pay off. Obviously, an insurance company cannot survive if this is usually what happens! Therefore, most people pay more than they collect.

You cannot insure every hazard in life. Insurance companies also may refuse to sell you a policy that will cover your entire loss or may charge you very dearly for doing so—so dearly it's not worth it.

You can provide for your family in case something happens to you by purchasing life insurance, health and accident insurance, and income protection insurance. *Life insurance* will pay benefits to your survivors. *Health insurance* and *accident insurance* will cover medical bills so that your family doesn't have to go without to pay them. *Income protection insurance* will replace your salary if you are disabled and unable to work. You can also take out insurance to cover expenses other members of your family incur.

Insurance should certainly be used in place of savings in some cases. Today a major illness can easily cost many thousands of dollars. Very few people can save enough to cover a major medical expense without sacrificing basic current needs. Most people simply can't save this much. But, just because you need medical insurance to protect you against huge medical bills, this doesn't mean you need medical insurance to cover much smaller bills.

Relatively small medical bills, are, by far, the most common type. Huge ones seldom occur. Thus, an insurance company will charge you relatively more for coverage of small medical bills than for huge bills. As a result, it may be more economical to set aside savings at interest to handle relatively small medical bills (which you cannot cover out of your current pay check), rather than taking out an insurance policy to cover them.

Another type of insurance it is wise to have is *fire insurance*. Just as saving for an unlikely, but huge, medical expense is usually not possible, neither is saving to protect yourself against the huge expenses you would face in the event that your house burned down. On the other hand, insurance which will cover major and minor damage to your house is rather expensive, therefore, saving may be the most economical way to pay for minor repairs. Insurance companies may require that you partially insure yourself, that is, absorb part of any loss you suffer. Savings enable you to do this. If you live where hurricanes, earthquakes, floods, and so on are likely, you will want to insure yourself against these too.

Insurance is actually a form of savings where, instead of each person saving individually, a group of people save to protect the group. Since everyone will not experience the disaster insured against, collectively these people do not need to save as much as they would if each one saved just for oneself. Thus, insurance can substitute for personal saving.

You may be insured against job loss because you are eligible for federal and/or state unemployment insurance. Through a union contract, your employer may have agreed to pay you while you are temporarily laid off. These benefits, however, may be inadequate or you may not have this type of protection. Thus, one goal of savings is to tide you over periods of little or no income. You are likely to have no income or low income after you retire. Through social security and/or some other pension plan you may be assured of some income, but this is likely to be a lower income than you are used to. (The average couple on social security receives $4800 a year.)

Investment

The reason for some saving is to acquire funds to invest in income-generating assets. The minimum amount of money you can invest in some things, such as rental housing, is comparatively large. Thus, you often have to save money for a good while before you have enough to invest. Because of the large amount of money which is usually required and the high risk involved in a direct investment like a business, a lot of people invest indirectly via such things as shares of stock. Financial institutions (such as commercial banks, insurance companies, mutual funds, etc.), using money they receive from you, also make such investments. The amount of individual direct investments, however, is significant, particularly if you include the money people put into their own homes as investment.

HOW MUCH SHOULD YOU SAVE?

Your savings *goals* and *income* determine how much you should save. If you are still in your teens or early twenties and unmarried, the income you will have will likely be determined largely by your selection of a vocation. You will need to save to finance the formal education necessary for this job and to finance the things you need to start out on your own, such as furniture, automobile, and so on. These are all short-term savings objectives, but many young people are unable to afford to save for anything other than the short run. If they are financially able, however, they should save for more distant needs such as marriage, if this is planned, children, a house, and retirement.

Whatever your circumstances, you will need to save for your expensive luxuries, as it is best not to dissipate your credit on luxuries. Save your credit for necessities. In other words, to borrow for a vacation home and get so heavily in debt you have to go without necessities because you can't borrow any more is not very smart. Some people might say, "So what, I'll just stop making payments on my loan and let them repossess." Do this, and you have thrown away what you have repaid and your good credit rating. *A good credit rating reduces how much you need to save for emergencies.*

As you acquire a family, both your short- and long-term savings objectives will have to be altered. Your savings will have to be adequate to meet the needs of a family, such as providing for the education of your children and the support of your family if something should happen to you. Usually a rising level of income as you get older enables you to save more, putting things within reach that you earlier could not even consider.

When you are young it is difficult to foresee your long-term needs. You will probably have a relatively low income, and you may feel that the future will take care of itself. As a child someone else handled long-range planning; thus, you developed no awareness of the need for it or that it even existed. For these reasons, young people's savings are typically short-term with respect to objectives. This is shortsighted, as many people recognize as they grow older. Then their savings goals will include many more long-term goals. Retirement draws nearer as you get older, encouraging you to save for it, but it is also the case that, as you get older, you realize that the future catches up with you sooner than you used to think.

As you age, more than your circumstances, needs, and perspective change. Your desires change too. Earlier a sports car may have been your heart's desire; later a cabin by the lake may be your fondest desire. Once you may have planned to retire at 65—later you may decide to retire at 55; thus, you will need to save more for retirement than you first estimated. The prospects for future inflation may look grim, and this, too, will raise your savings goal. Once, you had not planned to have any children, but eventually you may, thus, your need for savings will increase.

As you age, the circle will close. Once your savings goals were short-term because you were either shortsighted or in financial straits. Eventually your savings goals will become short-term because you do not have many years to plan for, and your income, if you didn't save and/or insure yourself adequately when you were young, may be very low.

Clearly, how much you should save depends on your needs, your ambitions, and your ability to save, which depends on the level of your

income. Your needs and ambitions determine what your essential and desired short- and long-term savings goals are. Both these and the level of your income change over time. Thus, you must either anticipate this or alter your goals when these changes occur. The former is to be preferred because it is more efficient—the sooner you start saving, the sooner you will save enough to obtain your goals.

To develop the saving habit, you should make a point of always saving. Never spend every nickel. Do not begin saving with overly ambitious goals, as you are likely to fail to achieve them and give up. Learn how to save before you try to save very large amounts.

As was noted in Chapter 2, the amount you save is not properly determined by simply saving whatever is left over from your previous pay check when you get the next one. This is no more rational than spending on food whatever is left over after spending on everything else. Also, if you follow this route, you are likely to have nothing left over!

CHOOSING THE WAY TO HOLD YOUR SAVINGS

Putting your savings in a mattress or similar place is foolish in two different ways. The first, and most obvious, is that it isn't safe. The second is that it costs too much! The people who print your money— the federal government—offer you savings bonds and guaranteed savings accounts in savings institutions that will pay you interest. Unless you need your savings instantly, there is no reason to forego the interest earnings you could obtain by placing your savings in either of these places—they are as default-free as money.

How rapidly you can get your money from various savings mediums (savings bonds, savings accounts, and so forth) and how much chance there is that you will lose some of your money or all of it, varies among mediums. Unfortunately, those mediums where you might lose some money are those that normally pay you the highest yield. *A medium from which you can get your money rapidly, without loss, is called a liquid medium.* It will, unfortunately, pay you the lowest yield. Thus, you must decide what portion of your savings will be placed for easy retrieval with little or no possibility of loss, and what portion you want to put elsewhere to earn a higher return. The higher the yield on your savings, the less you need to save to accumulate a given amount.

Savings are funds set aside for future use. They are set aside where they will earn interest so as to reduce how much has to be set aside. Funds set aside to generate income in the future are invested funds.

Commercial Banks

A *commercial bank* is a financial institution that accepts deposits of money and provides a variety of other financial services. Banks do not pay interest on some deposits. A deposit that earns interest is best for all your savings except those held for a short period of time.

A *checking account* is a deposit-type account that pays no interest. A checking account is a *demand deposit,* which means you can retrieve your money from this type of deposit on demand. A check can usually be used in place of cash, and it is safer to deal with checks than cash, as they are not so readily spendable by thieves. You obtain your money from a demand deposit by writing a check on your account made payable to *Cash* where a payee's name would otherwise appear. As is always the case when you write a check, you sign it on its face as the payer. In this case you also sign it on the back. By doing this you *endorse* the check, which means you authorize the bank to cash it. To cash any check the payee is required to endorse it. (In this case you are both the payer and the payee.)

Checks are more often used to pay people for goods and services or to repay obligations than they are used to withdraw funds from a demand deposit. If, say, you owe the electric company $60 for a month's service, you can write a check for this amount with the electric company named as the payee. By endorsing and presenting this check to a bank, the electric company will get $60, assuming that you have this much in your account. If you don't, the bank will not honor the check, and your bank will charge you for an *overdraft.*

The electric utility can also collect its money by endorsing the check and depositing it in its bank, which may or may not be the bank you have your account with. If the check is deposited at a different bank than it is drawn on, the electric company gets credit for a deposit of $60 before the money is collected from the bank on which the check was drawn and before that bank reduces your account by $60. This is called *float*—float exists while both your account and the electric company's contains the $60. This will be the case for only a short period of time. If, during this time, or before the payee deposits your check, you write another check on that $60, you are *kiting.* Kiting is rather risky, however, because you must make a $60 deposit before the second check shows up at your bank!

A check is a *negotiable instrument,* which means the payee can assign his rights to someone else. Thus, if it wishes to, and its creditor is willing, the electric company can simply endorse the check and give it to its creditors, who can cash, deposit, or pay a bill with it by endorsing it again. The holder of an endorsed check should be very careful not to lose it unless the endorser has specified in the endorsement that the check is only to be paid to a certain person or company. If the endorsement is open (the payee only signed it), anyone who steals the check can cash it without having to engage in forgery. If the payee of a check wishes to deposit it in his or her account, he or she should, unless it will be endorsed at a bank teller's window, be sure to make the endorsement restrictive by writing that the check is to be deposited to an account only ("For Deposit Only").

There are two types of checking accounts you may open. The bank will charge you for each check written if you open a *special checking account*. If you open a *regular checking account*, you will not be charged for each check you write, but you will not be able to let your balance in this account fall below some specified level. Therefore, by opening a regular checking account, you lose the interest you could have earned on the minimum amount (minimum balance) you are required to keep in this account. *You should open a regular account only if the interest lost is less than the amount you would pay for the checks you write if you had a special checking account.* You cannot consider this minimum balance part of your savings because you can't withdraw the money without losing the regular checking account. If you need money badly, of course, you may be willing to give up this account.

Using checks is a safe and convenient way to pay bills. A thief naturally prefers cash to checks. When you decide to spend the funds you have accumulated in a savings account, you may wish to transfer them to your checking account rather than withdrawing the cash because of the greater safety involved. If you pay by check, a receipt (the check) is generated because your bank will return to you your *cancelled checks* when the payee has been paid. You can prevent a thief from forging your name on a stolen check by calling your bank and ordering them to *stop payment* on your checks. (They may require this order be put in writing.) You can also do this if you write a check and later decide you shouldn't have.

Because you can stop payment on a check, and because it is always possible that you don't have enough in your account to cover a check you have written, a creditor may refuse to accept your check. A solution to this problem, other than paying cash, is to offer him a cashier's check, a certified check, or a money order. A *cashier's check* is one drawn on a bank by the bank itself, which you obtain by paying the bank the amount you wish to pay by check. You do not have to be a depositor in a bank to obtain this service. A *certified check* is one of your checks that the bank certifies will be paid because it has already reduced your account by the amount of the check, making it impossible for you to withdraw the money. A *money order* is a check-like instrument sold by most commercial banks, the U.S. Postal Service, and several private financial institutions such as American Express.

Banks offer a wide variety of accounts which pay interest, and, thus, are normally more appropriate for your savings than demand deposits. They can be opened with a very small deposit and added to at will if they are of the *passbook* type. Withdrawals can be made at any time the bank is open, but banks can legally require 30 day's notice on a withdrawal. A few banks have automatic tellers (machines) so that you can deposit and withdraw money when the bank is closed. If your account is a passbook account, all deposits, withdrawals, and interest payments are recorded in this passbook. You keep the passbook and the bank keeps a duplicate record of transactions shown in the passbook. Banks also have *no-passbook savings accounts.* If you have one of these, instead of a new balance being recorded in your passbook everytime a deposit or withdrawal is made, you receive either a validated deposit receipt or a withdrawal receipt; thus, eliminating the need for the passbook.

Banks also offer savings certificates called *certificates of deposit* (CD's). They pay the saver a higher rate of interest than is paid on other savings accounts. The catch is that a minimum amount of money (usually very large) is required to open this type of account, and your money must remain in it for a certain length of time to earn this higher interest rate. Certificates of deposit are usually denominated in multiples of $1,000, with $10,000 frequently being the lowest denomination available. The interest rate paid on them varies with their value. The larger ones carry the highest rates. Longer maturities (redemption by the bank is relatively far off) carry higher rates than shorter maturities. All CD's mature within one year. CD's may or may not be negotiable, that is, capable of being sold by the holder. (This is a way to get your money before a CD matures.) Most CD's are held by businesses.

If a bank belongs to the Federal Deposit Insurance Corporation (FDIC), an agency of the federal government, individual deposits in this bank are insured by the FDIC for up to $40,000. By placing some of your money in deposit accounts listed as belonging to members of your family, you can get more than $40,000 of your money covered. Another way to do this is to open accounts in your own name at several banks. (Legally a deposit belongs to the person whose account it is in. Thus, you would not want to put your money in just anybody's name!) You can also gain more than $40,000 of coverage through joint accounts and accounts for persons for whom you are the guardian and, thus, have control of their money.

If you need the money you have in a certificate of deposit, your solution varies with the type of CD you have, that is, negotiable or nonnegotiable. The negotiable CD can be sold if there is a buyer, but if the buyer wishes to earn a higher yield than the CD carries, she will buy it from you at a discount; thus, you will earn a lower yield than if you had held it until it reached its maturity. (Say you acquire from a bank a $10,000 CD that will yield 5 percent if held to its maturity. For simplicity's sake, say you immediately sell it to someone who wants to earn 6 percent. This person will pay you $9,905.66 for the CD because $9,905.66 times 6 percent is $594.34, and $9,905.66 plus $594.34 is $10,500—what the CD will be worth when it matures.) Yields on CD's fluctuate often. Thus, discounting is not uncommon. Of course, the reverse, selling at a *premium*, is also possible. If the CD you hold is not negotiable, you will have to ask the bank which issued it to redeem it, and they will do so at a discount.

Thus, we see that the higher yield on the CD is accompanied by a greater risk—if you need your money, getting it may reduce your yield. With a passbook account, once you have had an amount in an account for a very short period of time, you can withdraw this without a reduction in your yield. You can always withdraw from your passbook account, but you may find no buyers for a negotiable CD.

Commercial banks are chartered either by the federal or state government. All federally chartered commercial banks must belong to the FDIC; most state banks choose to do so or are required to do so. The maximum interest rates banks can pay on their various savings accounts are set by whichever government body chartered them. Very large CD's, which are bought by businesses, are not so restricted, but they are not insured by the FDIC, as the FDIC only insures individuals.

There are several reasons why the government regulates how much banks can pay on savings accounts and prohibits the paying of interest on demand deposits. The government is trying to prevent commercial banks from drawing funds from other savings institutions by offering higher rates than others can offer, and it is seeking to hold down bank costs and competition to prevent bank failures that could ruin many depositors. This policy is increasingly being questioned for a variety of reasons. Largely because of the FDIC, bank failures in recent years have not hurt depositors. Many question the government's keeping uncompetitive financial institutions afloat and making larger profits possible by holding down their interest costs and, thus, depriving the depositor of a higher return on a deposit. Opponents of change claim that without these ceilings on interest rates and the prohibition on interest being paid on demand deposits, a great many banks would fail, and that, without causing severe inflation, the government couldn't prevent harm to many depositors. If interest on deposits rose, they say, mortgage loans would become a less attractive use of deposits for savings institutions, since mortgage yields are relatively low, and this would hurt the vital home building industry.

In recent years some financial institutions which compete with banks have been allowed to offer interest-bearing deposits which serve the same purposes as demand deposits. As a result, the pressure to allow commercial banks to pay interest on demand deposits or to outlaw these near-demand-deposit accounts has grown. There are two types of savings accounts that transfer funds without a check being written. These savings accounts substitute for holding a demand deposit account for making payments. *Negotiable orders of withdrawal* (NOW's) can be used to order a savings institution to pay to a payee funds on deposit in a savings account. A NOW is a draft (an order to pay). *Share drafts* can be used to order a credit union to pay funds on deposit in a savings account to a payee. Some savings and loan associations have placed computer terminals in retail stores so shoppers can withdraw funds from their accounts and deposit funds into some other person's or business' account. Thus, shoppers can pay for purchases made in a store by transferring funds from their accounts to the retailer's. You can also make such transfers by telephone. These methods eliminate the need for the paper work associated with checks, NOW's, and share drafts, and some believe this is the way all fund transfers will take place in the future; thus, eliminating drafts, checks, and cash. You can also arrange for a savings institution to pay regularly occurring bills from your account. Commercial banks sometimes offer similar services.

Because these alternatives are now available in some parts of the country and more may be available in the future, you should investigate all such options before deciding to open a checking account.

Savings and Loan Associations

Savings and loan associations differ from commercial banks in that they are not allowed to offer demand deposits and must make loans almost exclusively to consumers wanting to purchase homes. Government regulation largely confines savings and loan associations to financing home purchases. Banks lend mostly to business, and their consumer lending is largely confined to things other than mortgages on homes. Savings and loan associations, sometimes known as building and loan associations, also differ from commercial banks in that most of them are mutuals—a financial organization owned by its customers. Any profits a mutual makes are credited to its customers. An institution very much like a savings and loan association is a *mutual savings bank*. Unlike savings and loan associations, which are scattered across the nation, mutual savings banks exist in only a few states. The main difference between the two organizations is that while control of the savings and loan association lies with its owners, who, in the case of the mutual, are its customers, control of the savings bank is in the hands of a group of trustees. A *trustee* is legally obligatel to manage the assets of a trust in a manner beneficial to the beneficiaries of the trust. The deposits in the savings bank are the assets of the trust, and the depositors are the beneficiaries of the trust.

Savings and loan associations (S & L's) offer passbook accounts like those offered by commercial banks except that they are allowed to pay a slightly higher rate of interest to the depositor. Interest may, as is also the case with commercial banks, be compounded in a variety of ways. The effective rate of interest you earn varies with how the interest rate is calculated, that is, an annual rate compounded monthly gives you a higher effective rate of interest than one compounded quarterly, as will be illustrated later in this chapter.

Savings and loan associations offer so-called *bonus accounts* which are like passbook accounts except that they earn a higher rate of interest if a specified amount is deposited each month over a set period of time. Another account offered by these institutions is the *investment account*. These accounts are available in specified minimum amounts and interest is paid periodically to the depositor by check. A similar type of account is the *certificate account*, which is like a nonnegotiable CD, but is usually smaller. A larger amount of money is required to open one of these accounts than is required for others S & L's offer, but it pays a higher return than does a passbook account. (Table 3–2 shows the variance in interest rates between different types of accounts.) A certificate account must remain intact for a specified period of time to earn the maximum interest rate. If the certificate is presented for redemption before it matures, a lower interest rate will be paid than if it had been held until its maturity. Renewal at the same rate may or may not be possible. Several different maturities are normally offered, with the longer maturities paying a higher interest rate than the shorter maturities. Interest can either be paid to the depositor or placed in the depositor's account; thus, raising the value of the certificate, which is the base upon which interest is computed. If interest is credited to your account, you earn *compound interest*—interest on interest; otherwise, you earn *simple interest* which is a lesser amount.

Say you place $1000 in an account paying 5 percent a year, and interest is compounded annually. One year after making the deposit, if interest is credited to your account, you will have $1050 on deposit. If interest had been compounded every six months, however, you would have $1050.63. This is because:

First six months:

Interest = principal × interest rate × time
Interest = $1000 × 0.05 × ½
Interest = $25, which is earned at the end of six months

Second six months:

Interest = $1025 × 0.05 × ½ as the principal is now $25 greater
Interest = $25.63

End of year:

Total interest = $25 plus $25.63, which is total earned over one year
Total interest = $50.63

Thus, the effective rate of interest if the 5 percent annual rate is compounded semiannually is 5.063 percent. A faster way of figuring how much the deposit would grow would be to use the following equation:

$$V = P(1 + i/m)^{mn}$$

where V is the value of the deposit at the end of n years, m is the number of times interest is computed annually, i is the annual stated rate of interest, and P is the amount deposited at the beginning of the period. Therefore:

$$V = \$1000(1 + .05/2)^{2 \times 1} \text{ or } \$1000(1.025)^2$$

$$V = \$1050.63.$$

Note that if interest is compounded annually, this equation becomes:

$$V = P(1 + i)^n.$$

Table 3–3 shows you how frequent compounding at a given annual rate increases the effective yield on your deposit.

All federally chartered savings and loans associations are required to insure each account with the Federal Savings and Loan Insurance Corporation (FSLIC). This insurance covers up to $40,000 for each individual depositor at a savings and loan association. Most state-chartered savings and loan associations join the FSLIC. All the insured savings and loan association's deposits are covered by this insurance.

TABLE 3–2 Interest Rate Ceilings on Savings at Federal Home Loan Bank Members Savings Associations

	Effective Month and Rate Ceiling						
Type of Account	Sept. 1966	Dec. 1969	Jan. 1970	May 1973	July 1973	Nov. 1973	Dec. 1974§
Regular Passbook	4.75%	4.75%	5.00%	5.00%	5.25%	5.25%	5.25%
90-Day Notice	†	5.00	5.25	5.25	5.75	5.75	5.75§
Certificate:							
30 to 89 days:							
No minimum	†	†	†	†	5.25	†	†,§
90 to 179 days:							
No minimum	†	†	5.25	5.25	5.25	5.75	5.75
$1,000 minimum	†	†	5.25	5.25	5.75	5.75	5.75
180 to 364 days:							
No minimum	†	†	†	†	5.25	5.75	5.75
$1,000 minimum	5.25	5.25	5.25	5.25	5.75	5.75	5.75
1 but less than 2 years:							
No minimum	†	†	†	†	5.25	5.75	†
$1,000 minimum	5.25	5.25	5.75	5.75	6.50	6.50	6.50
2 but less than 2½ years:							
No minimum	†	†	†	†	5.25	5.75	†
$1,000 minimum	5.25	5.25	5.75	5.75	5.75	6.50	6.50
$5,000 minimum	5.25	5.25	6.00	6.00	6.50	6.50	6.50
10,000 minimum	5.25	6.00‡	6.00	6.00	6.50	6.50	6.50
2½ but less than 4 years:							
No minimum	†	†	†	†	5.25	5.75	†
$1,000 minimum	5.25	5.25	5.75	5.75	5.75	6.75	6.75
$5,000 minimum	5.25	5.25	6.00	6.00	6.75	6.75	6.75
$10,000 minimum	5.25	6.00‡	6.00	6.00	6.75	6.75	6.75
4 but less than 6 years:							
No minimum	†	†	†	‡	6.75	†	†
$1,000 minimum	5.25	5.25	5.75	5.75	none	7.50	7.50
$5,000 minimum	5.25	5.25	6.00	6.00	none	7.50	7.50
$10,000 minimum	5.25	6.00‡	6.00	6.00	none	7.50	7.50
6 or more years:							
No minimum	†	†	†	†	6.75	†	†
$1,000 minimum	5.25	5.25	5.75	5.75	none	7.50	7.75
$5,000 minimum	5.25	5.25	6.00	6.00	none	7.50	7.75

Source: Federal Home Loan Bank Board.

Note: Certain details of a technical nature, and rate ceilings prevailing only for a short time or in limited geographic areas, have been omitted.

† Not authorized.

‡ Applicable only to certain certificate renewals.

§ Effective November 27, 1974, associations may pay the maximum certificate rate on all governmental unit certificate accounts with 30-day minimum terms and balances less than $100,000, and on all governmental unit notice accounts.

TABLE 3–2   (*Continued*)

Type of Account	*Effective Month and Rate Ceiling*						
	Sept. 1966	Dec. 1969	Jan. 1970	May 1973	July 1973	Nov. 1973	Dec. 1974§
$10,000 minimum	5.25	6.00‡	6.00	6.00	none	7.50	7.75
$100,000 minimum:							
30- to 59-day maturity	†	†	†	†	none	none	none
60- to 89-day maturity	†	†	6.50	none	none	none	none
90- to 179-day maturity	†	†	6.75	none	none	none	none
180- to 364-day maturity	5.25	5.25	7.00	none	none	none	none
1 or more year maturity	5.25	5.25	7.50	none	none	none	none

TABLE 3–3   Effective Annual Rate of Interest

Compounded	Stated Annual Rate (%)		
	5	6	7
Quarterly	5.0945	6.1363	7.1859
Monthly	5.1161	6.1677	7.2290
Daily	5.1267	6.1831	7.2500

Normally, you can withdraw funds from your savings and loan account on demand. However, if the savings and loan association wishes to, it can require a written, 30-day notice.

Credit Unions

Credit unions are one of the least publicized types of financial institutions in the United States; yet, they often pay a relatively high rate of return on savings and charge a relatively low rate on loans. The reason for this low profile is that the average credit union is rather small, and many people are not eligible to become a member of a credit union.

A *credit union* is a mutual organization operated exclusively for the benefit of its members. It may be either federally or state chartered. It accepts savings from its members and normally lends this money only to them. A small membership fee is required to become a member of a credit union. When you deposit money in a credit union you become a *shareholder* and the interest on your account is called a *dividend.*

A credit union can pay a higher rate of return on your deposit than other financial institutions can because the federal government sets a higher allowable ceiling rate for them than for other financial institutions, and some states sets none. Credit unions are often capable of paying higher rates than other financial institutions because their costs are lower. Credit unions pay no federal income taxes. Ordinarily, credit unions may legally serve only those people who have an occupational, residential, or associational "common bond." As a result of their limited clientele, an organization, often an employer, provides the credit union with free or low-cost facilities and/or services. Loan losses are also exceptionally low because an employer may withhold the last check of an employee who quits without paying off the credit union. Peer pressure may also force a borrower to pay on time. The average loan is usually small, so paying it off is no great burden.

Credit unions serving predominantly low-income members can accept deposits from nonmembers. This way individuals with no real common bond can utilize the services of a credit union. Accounts in either a federal or state credit union may be insured by an agency of the federal government, the National Credit Union Administration. Thus, your account may be insured in a credit union just as it is in a commercial bank or a savings and loan association. Withdrawals may normally be made whenever the credit union is open. As a rule, credit unions are open for far fewer hours than are commercial banks and savings and loan associations.

Government Savings Bonds

The *U.S. government bonds* that individuals are likely to use as a savings medium are Series E or H bonds. Neither of these bonds can be sold; nor can they be used as collateral for a loan. To obtain the money you have in them you must either hold them until their maturity, when the U.S. Treasury will retire them, or have the Treasury redeem them before or after their maturity. (You may continue to hold these bonds after their maturity if you wish, and they will continue to earn interest after maturity.)

Series E bonds carry no interest rate. A return is earned because the saver pays only three-fourths of the bond's *face value* to acquire it. The face value is what the Treasury will pay the saver when the bond matures. If you redeem a Series E bond before its maturity, you will receive more than you paid for it, but your rate of return will be lower than if you had held it to its maturity. Series H bonds, in contrast, do carry interest. They are sold at face value. Interest on this value is paid semi-annually. Both Series E and H can be purchased via a payroll withholding plan or from a commercial bank or the U.S. Postal Service.

In the recent past people did far worse by saving via government savings bonds than by using savings accounts because government paid a much lower interest rate than you could get elsewhere. Many bonds were bought during and right after World War II when other interest rates were much lower than they were a few years later. Thus, the yield on savings bonds looked attractive when they were issued, but not later. Well before they matured the rate they paid was relatively low. New bonds issued by the government did not offer much higher rates than those maturing. As a result, redemptions began running ahead of new sales. This forced the government to offer higher rates.

Life Insurance

Life insurance will be covered in detail in a later chapter, but it is necessary to mention it here because it serves as an individual savings medium as well as a group savings medium like other forms of insurance

Everyone's house won't burn down, so fire insurance companies don't have to charge policyholders enough to pay off each of them. They only have to collect enough each year to pay current claims. Everyone, however, will die sometime; thus, in the case of permanent life insurance, the life insurance company has to charge enough to pay off everybody's beneficiaries. The company usually collects money before it needs to pay it out. (Actually, the policyholders don't quite pay in full for benefits paid out, as the insurance company is able to earn a return on what they collect by investing it until they have to pay it out.) A permanent life insurance policy is both a way to insure yourself and provide yourself with a form of savings account (because the policy builds up a cash value over the years). You can cancel your insurance and receive the cash value of the policy. You can also borrow money from the insurance company using this cash value as collateral for the loan. The "interest" you will earn on this type of "savings account" is relatively low. If, however, you lack the self-discipline to get yourself down to the bank to make a deposit, this may be the only way you can save money. A major portion of individual savings in the United States are accounted for by permanent life insurance policies' cash values.

Comparing Saving Media

Every saving medium has three characteristics by which it should largely be judged: *liquidity, safety, and return.* (Table 3–4 shows how return varies depending on where you invest your money.) Cash is the most liquid form of savings, but it earns no return. U.S. savings bonds are the safest form of savings, but they are not as liquid as cash and do not pay the highest rate of return. (If a savings bond is lost or stolen, it can be replaced; money can't. If the government's bonds become worthless, so will its money.) Certificates of deposit pay the highest return, but they are not as liquid as cash or as safe as savings bonds because they aren't insured.

No one savings medium is likely to be appropriate for all your

TABLE 3–4   Average Annual Yield on Selected Uses of Your Money

Year	Savings Deposits in Savings Associations	Savings Deposits in Mutual Savings Banks	Time and Savings Deposits in Commercial Banks	United States Government Bonds	State and Local Bonds	Corporate Aaa Bonds**
1950	2.52%	1.84%	0.94%	2.32%	1.90%	2.62%
1955	2.94	2.64	1.38	2.84	2.57	3.06
1960	3.86	3.47	2.56	4.01	3.69	4.41
1965	4.23	4.11	3.69	4.21	3.34	4.49
1966	4.45	4.45	4.04	4.66	3.90	5.13
1967	4.67	4.74	4.24	4.85	3.99	5.51
1968	4.68	4.76	4.48	5.25	4.48	6.18
1969	4.80	4.89	4.87	6.10	5.73	7.03
1970	5.06	5.01	4.95	6.59	6.42	8.04
1971	5.33	5.14	4.78	5.74	5.62	7.39
1972	5.39	5.23	4.66	5.63	5.30	7.21
1973	5.55	5.45	5.71	6.30	5.22	7.44
1974	5.98	5.76	6.93	6.99	6.19	8.57
1975	6.24	5.89	5.92	6.98	7.05	8.83
1976*	6.31	5.98	7.32	6.78	6.67	8.43

Sources: Federal Deposit Insurance Corporation; Federal Home Loan Bank Board; Federal Reserve Board; Moody's Investors Service; National Association of Mutual Savings Banks; United States League of Savings Associations.

 * Preliminary.
 ** Lowest risk corporate bonds.

funds because none is superior in all three characteristics. To determine which media to use and how much money to put into each, you must examine each of your savings objectives. Money you are setting aside for handling unexpected expenses should not be placed in anything but a very liquid medium; neither should savings which you know will be needed very soon. Money that you absolutely cannot afford to lose because of the importance of your objective in saving it should be put in a very safe medium. If neither liquidity nor safety is essential, but setting aside enough money is a problem, a high-yield should be sought.

Other factors will also play a role in determining which media you will use. Series E savings bonds, for example, can be registered in the name of one person, two persons as coowners, or in the name of one person and a beneficiary. In the latter case, the beneficiary gains control of the bond if the other person dies. Until then, the beneficiary has no control over the disposition of the bond. A deposit account can be in more than one name, but you cannot have the beneficiary arrangement. A life insurance policy must have one or more beneficiaries.

The owner of a Series E bond can either pay income taxes on the increase in the bond's redemption value each year, or he can wait and pay all taxes when he redeems it. Income taxes will have to be paid every year on interest or dividends from savings accounts and shares in a credit union. Income taxes cannot be postponed on Series H bonds either. If you will be subject to a lower tax rate in the future, postponing owing income taxes will save you money.

The cash value of your life insurance policy can be borrowed against. Series E bonds cannot be used as collateral for a loan or be sold or given to another person. Certificates of deposit may be negotiable; thus, they can be sold and used as collateral for a loan. A commercial bank or other savings institution is more likely to lend to its depositors than to others. A credit union may be able to lend only to shareholders. Are you likely to need to borrow money? If you are not a very good credit risk other sources of loans may be closed to you. How much will collateral reduce the cost of borrowing or increase your chances of getting a loan? You need to answer these questions in order to determine how important it is to you to save in a way that will help you borrow money.

A MATTER OF INTEREST

As has already been illustrated, how often interest is compounded at a given annual rate determines the effective annual rate. Although financial institutions make a big to do about how often interest is compounded, the effect of this is not very large. Of course, there is no reason to pass up even a very small increase in interest if everything else is comparable.

The interest you receive is also affected by what base is used to figure interest on. Is interest figured from the day each deposit is made to the day of withdrawal? Or is it figured on the balance in your account at the beginning of the period? Is there any grace period? (Maybe money deposited by the tenth of a month is treated as if it was all deposited on the first day of the month.) Is there a penalty for early withdrawals?

The variations in the base on which interest is figured and in how often interest is computed causes a substantial variance in what you will earn on a given set of deposits and withdrawals. The easiest way to discover which is the best set of conditions is to make up a hypothetical set of deposits and withdrawals and, applying each institution's method of computation, see how much interest you would earn.

You may be surprised to see how rapidly your savings will grow at even rather modest rates of interest. Table 3–5 shows several rates of interest and how much $1 would grow after a number of years at that rate. By multiplying the value of a $1 deposit after a given number of years by a larger amount of money, you can see how much a larger deposit would grow. (Table 3–5 can be used for interest periods of less than one year by considering the interest rates to be for a period other than one year and the periods to be less than one year in length. For example, an annual rate of 16 percent compounded quarterly would be a 4 percent quarterly rate. If this deposit was held for two years, there would be eight interest periods.) Table 3–6

TABLE 3–5   How Much $1 Will Grow

	Interest Rates		
Years	6%	8%	10%
1	1.06000	1.08000	1.10000
2	1.12360	1.16640	1.21000
3	1.19102	1.25971	1.33100
4	1.26248	1.36049	1.46410
5	1.33823	1.46933	1.61051
6	1.41852	1.58687	1.77156
7	1.50363	1.71382	1.94872
8	1.59385	1.85093	2.14359
9	1.68948	1.99900	2.35795
10	1.79085	2.15892	2.59374
20	3.20713	4.66096	6.72749

shows how much money you would have if you deposited $1 a year at various rates.

Table 3–5 shows you that if you put $1 on deposit today at 8 percent, two years from now you would have $1.16. If you deposited $10,000 at 8 percent, ten years from now you would have $21,589.20. Table 3–6 shows that if you deposited $1 today at 10 percent and $1 more each year, at the end of five years you would have $6.72. If you had deposited $1,000 a year, you would have $6,715.60. (If you deposited $1 today at 10 percent, one year from now you would haxe $1.10. One year from now you would deposit another $1; thus, two years from now the first $1 would have grown to $1.21 and the second to $1.10, for a total of $2.31.) In formulating your savings plans, it is a good idea to consult tables like these. Savings institutions can provide you with them, and you can get them in a bookstore or a library.

In 15 years, an annual deposit of $1 a year at 6 percent would grow to $24.67. At 10 percent, it would grow to $34.95. (This is not shown in the table.) The former is computed thusly: $1.00(1.06)^{15}$.

SAVING FOR RETIREMENT

Saving for retirement differs from all other savings in that options are available for this type of saving that are not available in any other case. This subject will be discussed at much greater depth in Chapter 14.

Some employers deduct money from each of your pay checks for retirement purposes. This money, along with, perhaps, money contributed by your employer, goes into a fund from which a pension will be paid to you. In some cases your employer provides all the money which goes into this fund. Any money your employer puts

TABLE 3–6   How Much $1 A Year Will Grow

	Interest Rates		
Years	6%	8%	10%
1	1.0600	1.0800	1.1000
2	2.1836	2.2464	2.3100
3	3.3746	3.5061	3.6410
4	4.6371	4.8666	5.1051
5	5.9753	6.3359	6.7156

Note: This table is derived from Table 4–1. For example, in the 6 percent column and the 2 year row, the number 2.1836 is the sum of the first two figures in the 6 percent column in Table 4–1. The third figure, 3.3746, is the sum of the first three figures in Table 4–1.

into a pension fund for you is called a *fringe benefit*. (Your salary is not a fringe benefit. Meals in a company cafeteria, sold below cost, are a fringe benefit.) Self-employed persons can set up retirement funds for themselves. Often income taxes on the money placed in these funds and the interest earned on it is deferred until you withdraw the money as a retirement pension. The cash value of a life insurance policy can be used to set up a fund from which you will be paid a pension when you retire.

Just as you have no choice about paying into social security, if you work in "covered" employment, you have to pay into any group pension fund your employer has set up. If you are self-employed, you decide if and how much you will set aside in a pension fund. You also decide if you want to buy life insurance that includes a pension fund. Pension funds are a major form of individual savings.

REVIEW QUESTIONS

1. What needs does saving meet?
2. What substitutes for saving are available?
3. How much you save depends on what factors?
4. If you anticipate needing more money in the future than you will be earning, why save money between now and then to handle this problem? Why not just plan to borrow the money?
5. How are your savings goals likely to change as you grow older?
6. What savings media are available, and what are their chief differences?
7. Why shouldn't you put all your savings in one savings medium?
8. What causes stated and effective rates of interest to differ?
9. What is the difference between saving and investing?

CASES FOR DISCUSSION

Case 1 Delores Bush is a junior at a large state university. A lot of her friends plan to spend their spring holidays in Florida. This will be about four months from now. Delores is trying to talk her father into letting her use his credit card so she can go with them, but it doesn't look like he is going to let her. So, last week she looked for a job and found one typing in a lawyer's office three afternoons a week. She makes $30 a week. She will stay in Florida a week. She will fly down. It is a 1500-mile trip. Delores also wants to save up some money to buy her boy friend, Ed Cone, a $200 watch next Christmas. She has come to you for advice as to where she should put her savings. What would you tell her? Why?

Case 2 Joel Lee and his wife Mary Jane want to buy a house, but not if this will prevent them from sending their two children to college. Gene is 14 and Raymond is 8. Joel and Mary Jane together earn $18,500. Joel has a $40,000 permanent life insurance policy. Through their employment, they have health insurance on themselves and the children. They have $4,000 in Series E savings bonds, $6,000 in a savings and loan association passbook account paying 5½ percent, and $600 in a checking account. Joel is an avid golfer and hunter and has a good bit invested in sporting equipment. Mary Jane likes tennis, but has much less invested in equipment. Both would like to join a country club, but this costs $1,000 a year. This would eliminate, however, the $5 fee Joel pays for a game of golf and the $1 Mary Jane pays to play tennis. Joel would probably take fewer hunting trips if they joined. They can't buy a house in their community that they would be happy with for less than $40,000. Mary Jane and Joel are at a loss as to how or if they can finance these things. How would you advise them?

Case 3 Joe Brown was talking to his coworker Jane Hawkins, and he happened to mention that he had $3000 in a passbook savings account at a bank. She told him she was surprised at his lack of financial acumen. He would be much better off with a certificate account at a savings and loan association. At about this time, their boss, Anita Florrid, walked by and overheard Jane's remark. Neither of these are good investments, she said. Joe should look into putting his money into the stock market. Now Joe is concerned. Should he leave his money where it is? Should he move it? If he moves it, where should he move it? How should he go about deciding which is best?

Case 4   Howard Chen is 25, unmarried, and earns $14,000 a year as a ceramic engineer. He lives in a very expensive apartment and drives an expensive, foreign sports car. Seldom is he in debt, but he saves nothing. This didn't worry him until a few months ago when he had to have major surgery. Except for a couple of childhood diseases, Howard had never been sick in his life, so the surgery was a shock. More shocking, however, was the bill: $6,000. If he hadn't been able to count on his parents to help him, it would have been a disaster, since he was out of work for two months, and his employer only paid him for two weeks. As a new employee, this was all Howard was entitled to. Howard had no medical insurance. Because his parents were able to handle only $3000 of his bill, Howard had to borrow the rest. His parents also paid his $750 rent for three months. Howard thinks that, perhaps, he should change his ways. In addition to worrying about his own finances, he is worried about his parents'. His father will retire in two years, and spending this money on Howard didn't help their retirement plans. Howard is very fond of his parents, and they have spent a lot of money on him over the years. His parents hope to travel extensively after they retire. How would you advise Howard?

Case 5   Al Tranakos and Michele Shue plan to get married when they finish college next year. Al plans to go to law school. Michele, who is completing a master's degree in economics, hopes to work in economic forecasting, hopefully for a large bank. Neither has any savings. Al's parents will give him $2000 a year while he is in law school. Michele's parents will have them over for dinner and give them some modest Christmas and birthday presents, as this is all they can afford. They also think it will be good for the couple to be on their own. You appreciate what you earn, they say. Al and Michele think that they had better start saving some money. Al's parents currently pay his tuition and board. He pays everything else from his earnings working as a groundskeeper on campus. He earns $200 a month. Michele clerks in a department store. She is on call; thus, she never knows how much she will work. She works regularly, however, in December. She expects to average about $125 a month except for this month, when she will probably earn $500. Most of Michele's tuition and board is paid for by a student loan which she will have to repay once she finishes college and gets a job. Her parents pay for most of her clothes and furnish her with a car. Their parents will pay for their wedding. What kind of savings plan would you suggest for them?

Case 6 Charlie Mann was a good friend of yours in college. Charlie joined his mother in the real estate business after graduation. The two of you have kept in contact with one another over the decade since you graduated. Charlie has always respected your judgment. He is running for Congress this year, and you volunteered to work in his campaign. Charlie feels that the average taxpayer is largely being ignored by the government, and he is running as a reformer. He has asked you whether you think government regulation of financial institutions has harmed or helped the average saver. You ask for time to think about and study the issue. After you do this, what would you tell him?

Case 7 Your coworkers have selected you to sell your boss on a credit union. What would you tell him?

YOUR PLAN: CHAPTER 3

**Questions you must answer to decide
how much and where to save:**

1. What proportion of your annual after-tax income is accounted for by unavoidable expenses?

2. What kind of individual and group insurance do you have?
3. How much credit is available to you via credit cards you now have and ones you could get, plus signature loans (no collateral required)? How much credit could you obtain at one time? How much could you borrow by offering collateral?
4. Are you covered by social security? A pension plan?
5. How many dependents do you have, and how long are they likely to remain your dependents?
6. How long will it be before you retire?
7. Is anyone in your family or yourself afflicted with any chronic health problems?
8. Will you likely inherit money or property? If so, how much?
9. Can you depend on any help from relatives in a financial emergency, and how much help can you expect? (Are you willing to accept it?)
10. Do you wish to help any of your relatives if they run into a financial emergency? How much help are they likely to need?
11. Is your job secure?
12. Is your income regular?
13. By how much is your income likely to rise over the years?
14. Is your spouse employed? If so, answer Questions 11, 12 and 13 relative to his or her situation.
15. If either you or your spouse lost your job, how long would it likely take to find another?
16. How much time from work might you lose, and how often (from a strike or layoff due to lack of work, loss of a contract, etc.)?
17. Are you considering divorce?
18. Are you considering buying a house?
19. Are your children planning careers which will require extensive education beyond high school?
20. What major purchases would you like to make in the near and distant future?
21. Based on the maximum amount you can save (consider your answer to Question 1), are there any savings media that you cannot afford?
22. Are most of your savings needs such that you need to place most savings in a highly liquid medium? (Consider your answers to Questions 6, 7, 9, 10, 11, 12, 14, 15, 16, and 20.)
23. Are you willing and able to take some risk in order to obtain a higher rate of return on your savings?

How to Use Your Answers

These questions are designed to cause you to determine how much you can save, what alternatives to saving you currently possess, what needs you have for saving, and what type of savings media are appropriate. You determine how much to save by considering your savings needs and your alternatives to saving. The nature of your savings needs, your willingness to take a risk, and your need for a high return determines where you place your savings. Clearly, if your need is greater than your ability to save, you will need credit. Even if this is not the case, you may not wish to save for all possible expenditures. You would rather gamble that you will not need these savings. You may prefer to sacrifice some savings in order to make current, avoidable purchases. This choice depends on your priorities.

Making the choice between savings and insurance is examined in detail in Chapter 13.

Taking Advantage of Consumer Credit

10. Know what types of loans savings and loan associations and credit unions make.
11. Know how to go about obtaining credit.
12. Be familiar with the following terms:

rebate	passbook loans
revolving credit	single payment loans
consolidation loans	personal installment
regular charge	loans
account	credit card loans
conditional sales	promissory note
contract	acceleration clause
credit bureau	prepayment
character	privilege
capacity	line of credit
capital	overdraft account
travel and enter-	
tainment cards	

The secret to using consumer credit is to use it rather than having it use you. When it is used for convenience or to speed up the acquisition of something at a reasonable cost, you are improving the quality of your life. If, however, it is used in an attempt to consume beyond your income, the consumer credit habit destroys you financially just as a drug habit destroys you physically.

Consumer credit can refer to any purchase made by an individual for consumption, which is either not paid for at the time of purchase or is paid for with borrowed money. Generally, however, consumer credit excludes the purchase of a home on a credit basis. Even though by using it, it is "consumed," the purchase of a home is usually considered an investment. One reason for this is that your home normally has a significant value when you dispose of it, and you usually dispose of it by selling it at a profit. This is not true of a pair of shoes or your automobile. In addition, it takes many years to "consume" a home, whereas most other consumer goods are consumed within one year. Many, however, such as appliances and furniture, are used for several years.

It is obviously futile to attempt to increase your lifetime consumption by using credit. Creditors can't make money by lending more than they receive as principal repayment and interest. Most of the time, most creditors make money. Hence, you shouldn't plan to increase your consumption above the level afforded you by your earnings from your job and investments. Whenever the use of credit causes you to pay finance charges, such as interest, you reduce your consumption because you gain no material consumption from having made these expenditures. This expenditure pays for a service. It is the cost of having something before you could save the money to pay for it. The money you spend on interest will not benefit you at all to the extent that you could have obtained the loan more cheaply by shopping around more or it causes a disproportionate reduction in your future purchasing power. In other words, suppose you could obtain a 20-cent doughnut without payment today if you agree to pay the baker 40 cents tomorrow. Assume tomorrow you could buy two doughnuts for 40 cents. Unless that doughnut stood between you and starvation today, you probably would not be willing to pay this outrageous 100 percent finance charge. You also wouldn't pay it if another baker offered a better deal. As the starvation possibility illustrates, the use of credit is most justified in an emergency, and some borrowing power should always be reserved for emergencies. *Everyone* needs some combination of insurance, savings, and borrowing power to handle emergencies.

Credit turns some people into addicts. Going into a store or restaurant and paying by signing their name gives some people a sense of power. Without credit, they can go into a store without buying anything. With credit, they cannot resist buying. The fact that so many people are addicted to credit is the main reason sellers offer credit. They figure that you will buy more if you have credit, and offering credit gives them a second way to earn a return.

Assume that the fellow who sells you a doughnut for 20 cents has incurred 15 cents in costs of production and selling. His rate of return on the money he has tied up in the doughnut is 33.3 percent. That's what he makes for selling that doughnut if you pay cash for it. If he, in effect, lends you the doughnut for one day, he makes 20 cents more. Thus, if he sells his doughnuts on a cash basis, his profit on each sale is 33.3 percent, but if he sells them on a credit basis it is, in effect, 166.6 percent ($25¢/15¢$ rather than only $5¢/15¢$). Of course, it takes him two days, rather than one, to earn it. In short, credit selling is a way for retailers to add to their profits by going into the lending business. That they are, in effect, lending money can easily be seen in that the results are the same as if you borrowed 20 cents from him today and paid him back 40 cents the next day. The seller is simply giving up money today in exchange for a larger amount tomorrow, and that's what lending is all about.

An addiction to credit can easily turn into credit slavery—you have to go ever deeper in debt to pay off maturing obligations. If this spiral is not halted, you will go bankrupt.

Because it is convenient to both buyer and seller, some things are only available on a credit basis. For example, you use electricity for a month before paying for it. As long as you pay your bill in full monthly, there is no charge for this credit. Other providers of services, such as doctors and dentists, often work this way. Many purchases are made from retail stores on this basis. If you do not pay on the due date, a penalty rate will be levied, and the one on overdue *consumer sales credit* is almost always substantially higher than the one levied on similar *consumer cash credit* (a loan of money rather than a good or service). Thus, it often pays to borrow the cash necessary to pay for the items bought on credit on time rather than let your account with a retailer become overdue, causing you to pay the penalty rate charged on an overdue amount. In other words, it is cheaper to repay a loan than a late retail account. Another advantage of the cash loan is that legal proceedings are required to take some of your assets from you to pay this type of overdue debt. If you buy something on credit, you do not own it until it is fully paid for. Thus, if you do not pay, the seller can simply *repossess* it, since the seller still owns it.

If you can obtain credit, you should always consider whether to 1) buy using your own money, 2) borrow the money, or 3) obtain sales credit from the seller or a third party. If the seller offers free credit, that is, if you pay by the due date, you pay no more than if you pay cash now (e.g., use a credit card). It is often to your advantage to take credit, assuming this will not lead you to buy things just because it's easy, because you will not have to carry as much money around with you, and, if you buy several items from one seller or several sellers, you will receive only one bill and will write one rather than a number of checks. This will also enable you to build a credit record, and having a credit record helps you get additional credit. Needless to say, sales credit grantors only want those customers who will pay, but they prefer delayed payment so they can collect interest. Thus, credit card issuers won't be happy about you not paying interest! In contrast, those who lend consumers money normally want their money by the due date, since they are paid interest on amounts paid by the due date.

There are two kinds of repayment methods. There is the kind where you pay the *principal* amount—the amount borrowed—plus any interest on one given future day, and a second kind, called *installment credit*, where you pay the principal amount and interest in periodic installments over some period of time.

THE COMPUTATION OF INTEREST

There are a variety of ways in which the interest on either *consumer sales credit* (for goods and services) or *consumer cash credit* (money) is computed. The most simple rate to compute, and the one federal law dictates that a credit grantor tell you, is simple annual interest. The federal *Truth in Lending Act* calls this the annual percentage rate (APR). This rate is the real or effective cost of the loan, because it is computed by dividing what you spend a year for the loan by how much of the creditor's money you have in hand throughout the year.

If your bank lends you $1200, letting you walk out with $1200, net, of their money, on the condition that you return in a year with $1320, the simple annual interest rate is 10 percent: $120 divided by $1200. If, however, you get an *installment loan,* which requires that you repay the loan by monthly installments of $110, your simple annual interest rate is more than 10 percent, even though you repay the same amount: $1320. This is because you do not have the use of the $1200 throughout the year. You have $1200 only for the first month. The second month you have $1100. The third you have only only $1000. By adding $1200, $1100, $1000, $900, $800, $700, $600, $500, $400, $300, $200, and $100 and dividing the total, $7800, by 12 you can determine how much of the bank's money you average having throughout the year, $650. By dividing the $120 interest charge by $650 you will obtain the effective cost of the loan, 18.5 percent. (You might want to refer to the previous chapter where you were shown how to compute interest.)

A 1.54 percent monthly rate of interest applied to the unpaid balance of an installment loan of $1200 repaid in 12 monthly principal payments of $100 is a simple annual rate of 18.5 percent. This annual rate is obtained by multiplying the monthly rate by 12. (These numbers have been rounded. $120 divided by $650 is 18.46153 percent, and 1.53846 percent times 12 equals 18.4615 percent.) The interest rate on installment loans or sales credit is often computed via a *monthly rate on the unpaid balance,* but some credit card issuers will also charge you interest on the entire amount now due unless you pay all of this amount. Thus, the larger is the ratio of your payment to the amount due, the greater the effective interest rate, since the ratio of fixed interest charge to your real unpaid balance increases. *The APR, therefore, will not be the effective rate of interest if only a partial payment of the balance due is made.* The effective interest rate may far exceed the APR if partial payment is made, because there is no resulting reduction in the amount of interest due. (The APR and effective rate of interest will be considered to be the same in subsequent discussion except where noted.) Some credit grantors, however, will give you a better break when a partial payment is made. Then they charge you interest only on the average amount of credit outstanding during the month, rather than the total amount.

It is not uncommon to borrow, say, $1200 at a stated rate of 10 percent and have the lender give you $1080, which is 90 percent of $1200. This is called *discount interest*. You will get $1080 and return the lender $1200. Thus, the APR is 11.1111 percent, since this is what percent $120 (the cost of credit) is of $1080. ($120 plus $1080 equals $1200.) A like method of charging interest is called *add-on interest*. If you want to borrow $1080, you will sign a note for $1200, because $1080 is 90 percent of $1200. Thus, the effective interest rate is again $120 divided by $1080 or 11.1111 percent. If a discount or add-on loan is an installment loan, the APR is further increased by periodic repayment of the principal amount.

Lenders have increasingly favored the add-on method of figuring interest. Using this method, however, presents a problem when the borrower wishes to repay an installment loan early. Suppose you obtain an add-on installment loan of $1080, payable monthly at an annual stated rate of 10 percent. Your monthly payment would be $100. Ninety dollars of this would be for repayment of principal. The APR is $120 divided by $585, the average unpaid balance, which means the APR is 20.51 percent.

A monthly rate of 1.71 percent on the unpaid balance is equal to both a 20.51 APR and effective rate. Table 4–1 shows what the

TABLE 4–1   Comparative Monthly Payments on Two Loans of $1080

Month	1.71% on Unpaid Balance		10% Add-on (20.51% APR)	
	Principal	Interest	Principal	Interest
1	$90	$18.47	$90	$10
2	90	16.93	90	10
3	90	15.39	90	10
4	90	13.85	90	10
5	90	12.31	90	10
6	90	10.77	90	10
7	90	9.23	90	10
8	90	7.70	90	10
9	90	6.16	90	10
10	90	4.62	90	10
11	90	3.08	90	10
12	90	1.54	90	10
Totals	$1080	$120.05[1]	$1080	$120

[1] Error of five cents is due to rounding of 0.017094 to 0.0171 and rounding of the product of 0.0171 times the unpaid balances every month.

monthly payments on an installment loan of $1080 for one year at 1.71 percent per month on the unpaid balance would be, and what the payments on the add-on loan of $1080 at 20.71 percent would be. This table shows one advantage of the add-on method: because the payments are level, the $120 interest is paid more slowly. This causes the effective rate on the add-on to be a bit lower than on the other loan, which makes you pay interest more rapidly.

The variance in when interest is collected creates a problem if the borrower wishes to pay the add-on loan early. If, for example, the borrower pays off the remaining principal with the fourth monthly payment, with an add-on loan, she has paid only $40 in interest; with the other loan she has paid $64.64 in interest. (Add up the first four interest payments.) To avoid this, lenders often use what is called the *Rule of 78* to compute how much interest you owe if you repay an add-on loan early. Many states require that small loan interest computations be made this way. The figure 78 is obtained by adding the figures from 1 through 12. The lender is allowed to consider that at the end of the first month of the loan period 12/78ths of the interest due on the loan has been earned. At the end of the second month, 11/78th has been earned, and so on. The amount of interest it is assumed the lender has earned monthly is shown in Table 4–2, along with the difference between this amount and what the borrower actually pays in interest monthly (shown in Table 4–1). If the loan is repaid early, the lender collects this difference.

Table 4–2 shows that if repayment is made at the end of the fourth month, the borrower will have to pay $24.60 in additional interest, so that he will pay the same interest he would have paid if the loan had been on the basis of 1.71 percent per month on the unpaid balance. (Note that the Rule of 78 produces the same-sized monthly interest payments as does computing 1.71 percent of the unpaid balance.) Thus, using the Rule of 78, the borrower would pay off the loan with a final payment of $844.60 (8 times $90 plus $100 plus $24.60).

Observe that *the add-on method is to the borrower's advantage* because, relative to the percent per month on the unpaid balance method, it defers the payment of interest. The equal interest payments also make your budgeting easier.

CONSUMER PROTECTION

The *Truth in Lending Act* (formally known as the Consumer Credit Protection Act) was passed in 1968. One of its major purposes was to assure that the lender discloses in a meaningful way all credit terms so that the consumer can readily compare the various credit

TABLE 4–2   Use of the Rule of 78 on $1080 Loan

Month	Fraction of 78	Interest Earned Fraction × $120)	Interest Paid	Differ- ence in Interest	Cumula- tive Differ- ence
1	.153846[1]	$18.46	$10	$8.46	$ 8.46
2	.141026	16.92	10	6.92	15.38
3	.128205	15.37	10	5.37	20.75
4	.115385	13.85	10	3.85	24.60
5	.102564	12.30	10	2.30	26.90
6	.089744	10.76	10	.76	27.66
7	.076923	9.23	10	(.77)	26.89
8	.064103	7.69	10	(2.31)	24.58
9	.051282	6.15	10	(3.85)	20.73
10	.038462	4.62	10	(5.38)	15.35
11	.025641	3.08	10	(6.92)	8.43
12	.012821	1.54	10	(8.46)	(.03)[2]
Totals		$119.97[2]	$120	(.03)[2]	

Note: Although it is still called the Rule of 78, for loans of more than one year and/or other than monthly payments, the denominator is not 78. In the case of a one year installment loan with payments every other month, the de- nominator would be 42, the sum of 2, 4, 6, 8, 10, 12. Lenders will say they use the Rule of 78 to compute your *rebate,* which makes it sound like you are getting something back. Instead, they are simply figuring the amount of interest you will not now have to pay because it is interest they would have earned in the future.

[1] .153846 is obtained by dividing 12 by 78. The figure for month 2 is obtained by dividing 11 by 78; the next by dividing 10 by 78, and so on.

[2] Error of three cents is due to rounding of product—$119.97 should be $120.00, and the two .03 figures should be zeroes.

terms available. The credit grantor must provide the consumer with complete and comparable information concerning the cost of loans and installment purchases, including both the total cost in dollars and the annual percentage rate. Total cost includes interest, investigation fees, credit life insurance premium, and so on. In 1970 this Act was amended to prohibit the issuance of unsolicited credit cards and to set the maximum liability of a cardholder for unauthorized use at $50. In 1975 additional amendments were made. Some of the major provisions of the amendments were to prevent errors and expedite their correction on credit bills and to prohibit discrimination based on sex or marital status in the granting of credit.

Firms which offer credit cards or revolving-type credit must credit payments to your account the day payment is received. They must mail your bill at least 14 days before payment is due. They must send a detailed explanation of your rights and responsibilities either twice yearly or send a brief explanation with each bill; also when you request it or complain of an error. Your written inquiry must be acknowledged within 30 days and resolved within 90 days. The credit grantor will forfeit the first $50 in dispute if the proper procedures are not followed. Any error must be corrected and any associated charge removed from your bill. You must be notified of such an action. If the lender is correct, he must explain why. While a dispute is in progress, the lender must refrain from trying to collect the amount in dispute, closing your account, assessing a charge, making threats to make an unfavorable credit report on you, or deducting money from some other account of yours.

You have the right to cancel a credit transaction within three days of signing it if a lien on your house is involved, unless the credit is for the purchase or construction of a house.

You may file a complaint by writing—not telephoning—your creditor within 60 days of the first billing. Your letter must contain your account number, a description of the error, the dollar amount, and your complete return address. You cannot refuse to pay for faulty or improper merchandise or service if the price is $50 or less, or if you live more than 100 miles from the creditor. These restrictions protect the seller. Your option under these circumstances is to return the merchandise.

Banks, finance companies, department stores, and other lenders must make credit equally available to all creditworthy customers without regard to sex or marital status. This part of the Act is aimed primarily at women. In the past, even if a married woman was responsible for the payment of the couple's bills for 40 years, she had no credit record. If her husband died or she got a divorce, a lender considered her an individual without a credit record, making it impossible, or nearly so, for her to get credit. On top of that, creditors sometimes would not consider either alimony or child support as income. (Needless to say, having an income is a prime prerequisite for getting credit!) When a married couple applied for credit, they might be asked about their plans for having children, and the wife's income might be ignored.

Today creditors must establish a "credit identity" for a married woman so that, if she should be widowed or divorced, she will have a credit record. If such a woman is denied credit, reasons must be specified. A woman's income must be considered, regardless of the source, and a couple cannot be refused credit on the basis of their childbearing plans. Credit can't be automatically terminated by divorce or being widowed.

In the past some banks took away people's credit cards when they reached 62 and gave people a lower credit rating because they were elderly. Now they can do neither, but they can lower an elderly person's credit *limit* because of his age.

If you believe that you have been discriminated against by a retail store or consumer finance company, you should complain to the Federal Trade Commission, Equal Credit Opportunity, Washington, D.C. 20580.

As you may recall from Chapter 3, leasing is an alternative to borrowing. Early in 1977 another amendment to the Truth in Lending Act went into effect covering leases of four months or more for which your total contractual obligation is under $25,000. The leasing of an apartment is not covered. The property you are leasing must be described and you must receive all pertinent facts and figures. This includes: total amount of any payment (i.e., security deposit, advance payment, trade-in-allowance, etc.); your obligation to pay official fees, registration, certificate of title, taxes, and their total amount; the number, amount, and due dates or periods of payments, and the total amount of money involved; an itemized list of all other charges; and, a description of any security deposit you must give to the leasing company, clearly linking this deposit to this lease. A warranty or service statement must tell you of any express guarantees and who is responsible for maintaining or servicing the leased property and what this includes. You must be told the kind and cost of any insurance included in the lease agreement. Penalty and option clauses must be complete. The same is true of the liability statement. When can you terminate the lease? What will be the cost? Do you have an option to buy the property at the end of the lease? What, if any, is your liability for a difference between the estimated value of the property and what the property can be sold for at the end of the lease?

TYPES OF CREDIT AVAILABLE

Whenever you use a charge or credit card or use an installment plan to purchase something, you are using consumer sales credit. When you borrow money through a personal installment loan, single payment loan, or a check-credit plan, you are using consumer cash credit. By far, most American families use one or both forms of consumer credit. Currently, consumers are using more than $200 billion in installment borrowing. This amount, which sounds so very large, should, however, be put into perspective. Consumers have $1.2 trillion salted away in deposits in banks, savings and loan associations, and credit unions. Thus, consumers, as a group, are hardly insolvent! The most rapidly growing segment of consumer credit is bank credit cards. Their rapid growth and the recent introduction of bank debit cards leads some to speculate that the long heralded cashless/checkless

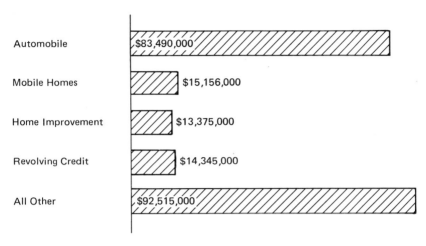

FIGURE 4–1. Consumer Installment Credit by Use, April 1978. (Federal Reserve System, *Federal Reserve Bulletin,* June 1978, A42.)

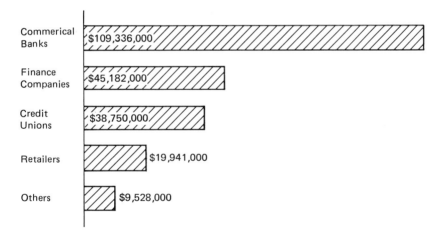

FIGURE 4–2. Consumer Installment Credit by Source, April 1978. (Federal Reserve System, *Federal Reserve Bulletin,* June 1978, p. A42.)

society may finally be upon us. Figure 4–1 shows the composition of consumer installment credit in recent years, while Figure 4–2 shows who granted it.

Bank *debit cards* differ from bank *credit cards* in that, while the latter means you are billed for your charges, the use of a debit card means that your bank debits your account for your purchases. Some savings and loan associations have a similar plan: They install a computer terminal in a retail store and, through it, your account is debited for purchases made in that store. You may also have a savings and loan association pay, via debiting your account, regularly recurring bills such as your mortgage payment or a utility bill. Credit unions are also beginning to move into this field, and recently the nation's largest stock brokerage firm began testing a system whereby customers who have left funds with this brokerage will be issued a bank credit card which permits them to borrow up to 50 percent of the value of the securities in their accounts. Other credit card issuers also allow you to borrow money via use of their cards.

A third kind of card you may obtain, assuming you are very creditworthy and live in one of the areas where it is offered, is one which you can show to merchants or others when you write a check to them. This card certifies that your checks are guaranteed up to some limit.

Revolving credit is, perhaps, the most insidious form of consumer credit. This form of credit is likely to lead to continuous indebtedness and, therefore, the continuous paying of a relatively high interest rate. *Consolidation loans* are probably the greatest snare and delusion in consumer finance. Many families consolidate their debts over and over again; thus, pyramiding both their debts and their interest costs. Often, the misuse of revolving credit is the main factor leading to the taking out of a consolidation loan. Revolving credit obtained via the use of a charge card is the type credit most easily misused.

Consumer Sales Credit

The three basic types of credit offered by retailers are the *open* or *charge account,* the *installment account,* and the *revolving account.* Each of these has a counterpart in consumer cash credit. In order to obtain any of these, you must sign a *credit agreement,* which protects both you and the creditor. *Read this agreement carefully before signing it.* Ask about anything you are in doubt about. Note what action the creditor will take if you pay late, miss a payment, or fail to complete the payments. Find out what, if any, down payment is required. Find out if you can pay in advance and whether or not you will receive a refund of credit charges on the prepaid amount. Only pay charges stated in this agreement, as they are all you are bound to pay. Deal only with reputable retailers. Be wary of high-pressure types.

Charge Accounts. You open a charge account by entering into a general contract with a retailer. The retailer agrees to allow you to purchase merchandise up to some limit in exchange for your agreement to pay for it when billed or pay interest on the unpaid balance. These are also called *open accounts*.

The *regular* or *30-day charge account* differs very little from paying cash. You promise to pay in full within 10 to 20 days after the billing date. You pay no finance charge if you pay in full within the allowable period of time. Most people open such an account for convenience. They do not have to carry cash around to make purchases, and they only write one check a month for several purchases. If your credit rating is poor, you cannot open such an account. Retailers generally will not open such an account for a young person with no credit history who has only been employed for a short period of time.

When you buy merchandise on an open account, you sign a charge purchase sales slip, which indicates when the purchase took place, what was purchased, and what the sale price was. Title to the merchandise then passes to you. The merchandise is not specific security (the merchant has no claim on it) for the credit; thus, it is not repossessable by the merchant if you fail to pay. The merchant does, however, have a legal claim against you for payment of the amount on the sales slip and finance charges for late payment.

Although some retailers will permit it, it is not a good practice to fail to pay in full on time and, thus, treat this account like an installment plan. When you do purchase something from a retailer on an *installment plan,* you do not obtain title to the merchandise, so it can be repossessed if you fail to make a payment. Payments are made monthly, biweekly, or weekly in equal amounts. Usually full payment is completed within two years. The installment sales account which is established by a written contract between you and the retailer is called a *conditional sales contract,* which means you own the item once it is paid for. Generally, this plan is used to finance furniture or appliances, that is, relatively expensive items. Increasingly, however, it is being used for "soft goods" like clothing.

The *revolving* or *optional revolving* account combines features of the 30-day and installment accounts. Like the 30-day accounts, you are issued a *charge card* which entitles you to purchase whatever you wish. Under an installment plan, a separate agreement is made for each purchase. This is not true for the revolving charge account. Like the installment account, there is a credit charge, and full payment is accomplished by a series of partial payments. If you are less than an excellent credit risk, this is the only kind of charge card you can get. How much you can charge is limited. If the retailer's experience with you is favorable, you can have this limit raised. The retailer may automatically raise your limit if you have been making your payments in full on time.

The agreement you sign for a revolving charge account requires that you pay any amount you are allowed to charge over the limit on your account within 30 days. If you do not pay, your entire balance becomes due and the usual monthly payment provision is halted.

The optional revolving account is actually a 30-day charge account that you have the option to use as a revolving account—you simply do not pay the account's balance in full on the billing date. By doing this, of course, you incur a financing charge. Retail credit usually costs at least 18 percent per year! Thus, it pays to go to a lender who charges less, as many do, and borrow enough to pay off what you owe a retailer rather than to continue to owe the retailer.

Credit Cards. The credit cards issued by retailers can only be used to purchase merchandise and services from the issuing merchant. Oil companies also issue credit cards, and while originally they could only be used to buy from them, in recent years some travel-related businesses have agreed to accept them. At the time this took place, oil companies were rather aggressively pursuing credit card business. This situation has changed dramatically recently.

The five major credit cards are American Express, Carte Blanche, Diners Club, Master Charge, and VISA. The first three are called *travel and entertainment cards.* Originally they could only be used to buy airline tickets, pay hotel and restaurant bills, and so on. You used them when you went to the far coast or Europe. They were what you used when your Aunt Minnie came to town and you wanted to impress her with yourself and the big city by elaborately wining and dining and entertaining her.

Recognizing that most retailers could not afford to offer 30-day or revolving charge accounts, banks began signing up small- and medium-sized retailers for cards that the banks offered. Most bank card systems failed, and today Master Charge and VISA dominate the market. To expand their business, the cards systems have entered the travel and entertainment field, and their cards compete effectively with the travel and entertainment cards. All of the "big five" cards can be used abroad. To counter this trend, the travel and entertainment card companies have moved into retailing, but they have invaded their competitors' "home turf" less extensively than their own has been invaded. Until recently retailers offering their own credit cards have generally refused to honor any "outside" cards. Now some honor both their own cards and a few outside bank and card-company cards. A few retailers have dropped their own cards and only honor outside cards.

American Express, Diners Club, and Carte Blanche earn their income via the annual fee a holder must pay for the card and from discounts they charge participating restaurants, hotels, and other merchants. (The seller is remitted less than the customer is billed. This is called discounting.) Customers should normally pay no interest, as they are expected to pay in full promptly when billed. Thus, users of these cards are motivated by convenience rather than substantially deferred payment. For some, a major benefit provided by their credit card is the records its use produces. These can be used either to make claims to your employer for reimbursement or as supporting documents for deductions on your income tax form.

Not surprising, in light of the fact that they have vast deposits of money to lend, is the fact that banks do not expect you to pay in full by the due date. Bank credit cards are free. There is no membership fee, as is the case with the travel and entertainment cards. (Neither retailers nor oil companies charge for their cards; nor do other, smaller issuers such as airlines and rent-a-car companies.) Banks charge for their service via discounting participating merchants' receipts, in other words, banks retain a percentage of the sales price of every item purchased via use of their card.

VISA, formerly BankAmericard, is owned by its issuing banks in proportion to the volume of their card sales. Interbank Card Association sponsors Master Charge. Unlike VISA, it is a nonprofit organization whose member companies simply share costs and revenues. Each member company is profit-seeking. Master Charge is the larger system, but VISA has recently been growing more rapidly. Together their business approaches $40 billion a year. Master Charge has 41.5 million card holders in the United States. VISA has 33.7 million. In some European countries, an American credit card has the largest market share. Because of a Justice Department refusal to allow either system to prohibit its member banks from issuing the cards of the rival system, recently more and more banks have begun offering both cards. Some predict that a single system will emerge from this.

To banks, people who promptly pay their bills in full are a problem. Unlike the T & E (travel and entertainment) card systems, the bank systems are not designed for convenience. They are designed to lend money, either through being used for revolving credit or being used to obtain a money loan. To offset the drain caused by "convenience" users, some banks have started charging these card holders—one bank charges them 50 cents a month.

American Express currently charges an 18 percent penalty and cancels accounts which are long overdue. It allows extended-payment balances on airline and tour tickets, however. Its charge for this balance is 1 percent per month. Carte Blanche charges 2½ percent per month on an amount 60 days overdue. It offers extended-payment balances on airline tickets and certain gifts. Its charge for such a balance is 1½ percent per month. Diners Club charges 1 percent per month on payments 30 days past due and on extended-payment travel tickets. Unlike American Express and Carte Blanche cards, your Diners Club card can be used to obtain a cash loan. All three T & E cards cost $20 a year.

Both Master Charge and VISA charge 1½ percent per month on balances not paid by the due date. Both also offer cash loans to card holders on demand. The amount that can be borrowed this way, however, is limited.

Many issuers today charge interest, not on the end-of-the-month balance, but on the average of amounts owed each day during the billing period. This, of course, raises their return. (Recall that a 1½ percent monthly rate is an 18 percent annual rate.)

Even though you can now limit your loss through fraudulent use of your credit card to $50 by immediately notifying the issuer of the card, in writing, of its loss or theft, you should take care to avoid either of these mishaps. There is no reason to throw away $50, and someone using your card can cause you a lot of other trouble.

Consumer Cash Credit

You may obtain a cash loan in order to purchase something or to refinance the payment of your existing bills. In the latter case it is said that you are acquiring a *consolidation loan*. A cash loan, of course, may be repaid in either one lump sum or via a series of periodic payments, which may or may not be of equal size. When the last payment or payments are larger than the others, the loan is said to be a *balloon loan*. Generally, the larger consumer loans are of the installment type, as few people can pay off a large loan in one lump sum comfortably. Installment repayment also reduces risk for the creditor and raises the effective rate of return earned.

There are a variety of sources of consumer cash credit. Such financial institutions as commercial banks, consumer credit companies, savings and loan associations, and credit unions provide *consumer financing*. You may also borrow from a life insurance company if you have one of their whole life policies, and, of course, you can borrow from friends and relatives. In some states there are mutual savings banks and industrial loan companies that provide consumer financing. (Their name means that they loan to industrial workers, not industry.)

Commercial Banks. You can obtain *single payment loans, personal installment loans, passbook loans, check-credit plan loans,* and *credit card loans* from commercial banks. Commercial banks are the dominant financial institution in consumer lending (see Figure 4–1). More than three-quarters of the consumer loans made by banks are of the installment type. They provide nearly one-half of the nation s consumer installment loans, and they are the largest single holders of noninstall-

ment consumer credit; yet, their main lending business is commercial.`
Some of their commercial lending, however, is indirectly consumer
lending, as banks purchase the notes of consumers from various dealers
in commodities who have sold goods to consumers at the retail level
or provide consumer services.

When you borrow from a bank you often sign a credit agreement called a *promissory note,* which acknowledges that you have
received a cash loan from the bank and agree to certain repayment
terms. If you fail to fulfill the terms of this agreement, the bank has
the legal right to force payment through a court order within the
limits of your income and property. If the loan is *secured,* the credit
agreement will note this fact and describe the property offered as
security. Property pledged to one creditor cannot be used to compensate another creditor unless the secured creditor is first paid what
he is owed. A *collateral note* provides the lender with either real or
personal property (negotiable stocks, bonds, savings or life insurance
policies, etc.) as security for the payment of the debt. A *chattel
mortgage* transfers title to personal property to the lender as security
for the payment of the debt. In many cases, if the debt is not repaid
according to the credit agreement, the lender has the right to repossess
the mortgaged property, which may be an automobile, household or
personal property. In lieu of collateral, a lender may demand that
someone *cosign* your note. This means that if you do not pay, he is
obligated to pay the debt. Another option is a wage assignment,
which should not be confused with wage garnishment. Wage assignment means that the lender may collect a certain percent of your
wages from your employer. If a loan is unsecured, it is called a *signature loan.* Such loans go to the best credit risks and are generally
small in size, which further reduces the risk of the lender.

The loan agreement may contain what is called an *acceleration
clause.* This gives the lender the right to demand immediate payment
of the entire unpaid balance if one or more installments are overdue.
A *prepayment privilege* gives you the right to make payments in
advance of their due date and possibly provides for a refund of credit
charges proportionate to the amount prepaid. A *default charge* is a
charge made because a payment is made after it is due. A loan agreement may also contain a requirement for life, disability, and/or
property insurance. These provisions are not limited to bank lending.

A *passbook loan* is one where the bank establishes a passbook
account for you from which you can withdraw funds as needed. The
funds in this account earn interest, but they do so at a lower rate than
you pay for the loan. This type of loan is appropriate when you are
not going to spend all the proceeds of the loan at once. Until you use

the funds, you pay less for them (on a net basis) than those you have withdrawn to use.

A *check-credit plan loan* is handled by associating a line of credit with a checking account. A *line of credit* is an amount of money which, over some given period of time, the bank promises to lend you on demand. The most common form of check-credit plan is the *overdraft account*—a prearranged, automatic line of credit activated whenever you write a check for more than you have in the account. These loans are usually paid on a revolving basis. They can be paid via ordinary deposits to your account or by separate loan payments. The latter is the more common. The *check guarantee card* plan method identifies you as one who can write an overdraft on your checking account. Some banks issue guarantee cards to preferred customers who have no overdraft arrangements. These simply serve as identification. Yet another method involves the bank giving you a special checking account which is drawn upon by using special checks. Some banks provide predenominated checks similar to traveler's checks.

Banks provide three types of credit cards. A bank can offer its own card, but few banks take this route, because they cannot gain a large enough volume of business to make it pay. A bank is more likely to offer a card by entering into a licensing or franchise agreement under which it becomes a participating or associate member with a group of banks, or acts as an agent of the group. The third alternative is to offer another bank's card. The most popular arrangement is offering a card via a franchised program which issues a nationally known credit card.

The cost of bank loans is lower than that of some other lenders because banks take fewer credit risks; they utilize a low-cost source of loanable funds—deposits; and, they deal primarily in large loans, thus administrative costs are low per dollar loaned. This low-risk policy means that if you need a small amount of money and are not an excellent credit risk, you aren't likely to get a loan from a bank. If, however, you are a good credit risk and need a relatively large amount of money, a bank is likely to lend you the money you need, and, because banks usually charge at least as low a rate as do other lenders, you should certainly look into borrowing from a bank.

Banks also offer financial counseling and will handle credit transactions confidentially.

Savings and Loan Associations. Most states and the federal government confine the savings and loan associations they charter to lending only for purchasing or improving a home. Generally, they are competitive with banks and, if this is the type of financing you need, you should see what kind of deal they will offer you. They offer mortgage and passbook loans like those offered by commercial banks.

Credit Unions. Automobile loans dominate credit unions' loan portfolios. Credit unions specialize in relatively small personal installment loans for the acquisition of durable goods. While they may make a small loan on an unsecured basis, they usually require collateral or a cosigner for larger loans. Normally they lend only to members and often repayment is made via payroll deduction. They offer a variety of repayment schedules.

The interest rate you will pay a credit union for a loan is likely to be lower than you can get anywhere else. The problem is that you have to be able to join a credit union and want the type of loan they will make. The risk and expenses of a credit union are far lower than are a bank's, so they can afford to undercut this relatively low-cost lender. In recent years, the possibility of membership in a credit union has been extended to more and more people, and credit unions have won the right to offer more types of loans. If this trend continues, credit unions will become a more likely place for you to go for a loan.

Consumer Finance Companies. These companies will lend to people who cannot obtain loans from deposit-type financial institutions. They will make personal installment loans to people who do not have established credit ratings, and they are more likely not to require security. They also make relatively more small loans than do other lenders. The rate they charge varies with the size of the loan. How much they can lend is limited by law, but they offer a variety of repayment schedules and rapid processing of loan applications.

Because they take greater risks, make relatively small loans, and must borrow the funds then lend (often they borrow from banks), it is normally more expensive to obtain a loan from a consumer finance company than from some other source. Many of the loans made by consumer finance companies are made because the borrower has no other choice. Sometimes, however, borrowers fail to realize that they have other, perhaps better, options. In part this may be due to the relatively aggressive pursuit of customers by these institutions.

Consumer finance companies are willing to make loans to pay off your accumulated debts, which are called *consolidation loans.* Such a regrouping of debts can reduce your current total outgo and give you time to get a fresh start. There is, however, the danger mentioned earlier, that this will be done over and over again, pyramiding both debt and interest cost. Such a loan likely carries a very high interest rate.

Consumer finance companies design the repayment schedule to

fit your income. They are, like banks, providers of financial counseling and confidential credit transactions.

Insurance Companies. Because they take no risks, insurance companies can offer you a very low-priced loan if you are one of their policyholders and have a whole life policy with a cash surrender value. Since the insurance company deducts the amount of the loan from the value of the policy benefit if you die or if the policy matures before you repay the loan, they do not demand that you repay the loan; and they, therefore, levy no penalty for failure to pay. You can repay the loan when and if you want to. You do, however, have to pay the interest on the loan. The interest on this loan does not indicate the full cost of tapping this source of credit.

Other Sources. Paying off your bills with a *second mortgage* on your home or dealing with a so-called *loan shark* are two expensive ways to go into debt. In the latter case you are dealing with lenders who operate outside the law. They have no license and charge more than the law allows, that is, they charge a usurious rate of interest. A *pawnbroker* may charge you no more than would a consumer finance company, but you run the risk of losing the item pawned because you can't pay on time. Today there are so few pawnbrokers that they are not an alternative for many people.

HOW DO YOU GET CREDIT?

The credit grantor is mainly interested in your ability and willingness to pay. This is measured largely by the amount and stability of your income and your character. Your character is largely determined by your reputation. The most important facet of your reputation is your previous record for repayment of credit. This is why it is often so difficult for young people or older people who have never obtained credit to get credit.

The things that a creditor wants to know about you can be classified as either relating to your *character, capacity,* or *capital. Character* refers to personal attributes such as honesty, trustworthiness, sound judgment, and a sense of responsibility. *Capacity* refers to your financial position. What kind of job do you hold? Is the job secure? How much does it pay? *Capital* refers to what possessions you have that could serve as collateral for a loan.

Generally a credit-granting firm will ask a *credit bureau* for a report on you. From the records of merchants, financial institutions, and those of the government which are open to public inspection, credit bureaus obtain financial information about you. The most important information they have is your repayment record.

In the past people were turned down for credit and never knew the reason. Sometimes the reason was not valid. Concern over this situation brought about the passage in 1970 by Congress of the Fair Credit Reporting Act. This act gives you the right to demand a report on the substance and source of the material a credit bureau has on file about you and to correct any errors in this information. If the material is correct but can be interpreted in two different ways, you have the right to insert your interpretation in your file. A merchant or lending institution is also required by this act to inform you as to why your request for credit was denied. If you find that you were denied credit because of a credit bureau report, you should demand a report on your file from this bureau within 30 days of being denied credit because this report will then be free of charge.

When you apply for credit you can expect to be asked where you are employed and how long you have been employed by your current employer. You can also be expected to be asked what your position and income are. What, if any, income does your spouse receive? Do you own or rent your home? Have any judgments been recorded against you? How long have you lived at your present address? Do you have any bank or other deposit accounts? Do you have any credit cards? Do you have a telephone?

At least in part because they are more objective, and thus have removed any hint of discrimination against minority groups, sophisticated scoring systems are being used increasingly by banks and finance companies to rate credit applicants. By correlating the characteristics of previous credit recipients with their repayment records, lenders have devised scoring systems whereby they assign you so many points for each relevant characteristic. You must score some minimum number of points in order to obtain credit. Your occupation can be used to illustrate how this system usually works. If you are a professional or supervisory worker, you will probably receive more points than would a proprietor of a small store or a farm worker. A homeowner would do better than a renter. Being on the same job longer would increase your score; so would being at your current address. Having a telephone would raise your score. Having credit cards or bank accounts will also raise your score. Having outstanding loans will lower your score.

If you are persistent, you can sometimes get a credit turndown reversed. Before arguing for a reversal, however, you should find out exactly why you were turned down. You need to know if the decision was based on incorrect information and/or information which can be seen in more than one way. Was some relevant, favorable information ignored? Are you an exception to a general rule? For example, homeowners are generally better risks than tenants. If, however, you are a well-paid engineer living temporarily in an area where most homeowners are very low-income people, you may be the better credit risk.

Amendments to the federal Equal Credit Opportunity Act forbid credit discrimination on such grounds as race, color, religion, national origin, and age. These amendments have affected scoring systems in a variety of ways. The Federal Reserve Board, which enforces the act, has ruled that no one over 62 can be given a lower score because of age. Marital status has also been eliminated from scoring. Clearly, if you think this act has been violated in turning you down, you should complain to the Federal Trade Commission.

Your credit rating is very important to you—make sure that yours is good. Try hard to make all payments on time. If you see that you can't do this, go to the creditor and try to work out something. Don't just sit back and let a repossession take place. Most creditors will go that last mile with you if they are convinced you are doing your best to repay them. It's worth the effort! If your credit rating is good you have borrowing power. In an emergency this can be a lifesaver!

CASES FOR DISCUSSION

Case 1 Wanda Crawford was driving to work and listening to the radio when she heard a bank advertisement. The announcer said that this bank will send you a monthly statement which will cover your checking and savings accounts and your line of credit. Having all of this on one statement seemed like a great idea to Wanda, so she moved her accounts to this bank. What do you think of Wanda's behavior? Why?

Case 2 Doug and Amelia Ashley were killing some time before a movie started by window shopping in the shopping mall where the theater was located. They stopped to watch a demonstration of an elaborate vacuum cleaner which, by adding a variety of attachments, could be used to clean almost anything in a house. The demonstration was very impressive, so they asked about the credit terms if they bought it. The saleswoman told them it was a great buy.

Today, she told them, there's no down payment required, tomorrow a down payment would be required. For only $18.75 a month for two years they can, she told them, purchase the vacuum. That sounded great to Doug and Amelia, and so they signed a conditional sales contract right then and there, even though it made them late getting to the movie. What do you think of their behavior? Why?

Case 3 Chris Sturtevant is really keen on stereo music. He has saved $100 towards buying one. Chris makes $150 a week after taxes. He has visited two stores and found that both carry a component outfit he'd like to have. One store wants a $100 down payment and monthly payments of principal and interest of $65.33 for one year. The other store only wants a $50 down payment, but it wants $74.67 a month for one year. Which is the better deal? Why?

Case 4 Wade Roberds was about to sign a conditional sales contract for a new bedroom suite when he remembered that his bank makes consumer installment loans at a stated rate of 10 percent a year. The sales contract also carries a stated rate of 10 percent. The contract also requires a $50 down payment, and interest is figured monthly on the unpaid balance. His bank uses the Rule of 78. It also requires monthly repayment. Which of the two alternatives is the best? Why?

Case 5 Tom Schmidt is 36. His wife Karen is 32. They have two children, Pam, age 8, and Carlton, age 3. When they married, Karen worked as a telephone installer, but she hasn't worked in the last eight years. Tom sells road-grading equipment, and his annual income varies between $13,000 and $18,000 a year. Tom has to travel extensively over the three western states in his territory. Because the children are so small, the Schmidts only vacation is usually a once-a-year trip to a California beach resort. Other than one department store charge card, they have no credit cards. Tom thinks they should get either an American Express, Carte Blanche, Diners Club, Master Charge, or VISA card. What do you think?

Should Paul, Karen's younger brother who is a college senior with a part-time job, do the same? Why or why not? What about Tom's father Martin, who is head of an American firm's European division? Why or why not?

Case 6 Denise Witcher has discovered that two department stores she likes equally well do not have the same APRs on their charge accounts. She has always heard that smart people are interested in the APR; not some other rate. Thus, she has decided to open an account at the store with the lowest APR. What do you think of her behavior? Why?

Case 7 Five years ago Imogene Hamiter bought a pair of tennis shoes for $25. Fourteen month later she threw them away. She bought them on a revolving credit plan. Items like this are all she buys using this account. For the past 5 years her average unpaid balance has been $25. Do you see anything to criticize about her buying habits?

Case 8 Right after they got married Eddie and Debbie Gustafson completely furnished an apartment on credit. Before they finished paying for most of it, Debbie had to quit work to have a baby. They fell behind on their bills because of the resulting 50 percent decline in their monthly income. After they had received several notices about their living room furniture, collectors began visiting them. They simply wouldn't answer the door. They bought the furniture on a conditional sales contract. You are a friend of theirs, and they have just told you all this. How would you advise them? Would you criticize their earlier behavior? Why?

REVIEW QUESTIONS

1. Why can't you enjoy any standard of living you wish by using credit?
2. How should you go about deciding what to save for and what to buy on credit?
3. What is the difference between consumer sales credit and consumer cash credit?

4. What is the APR?
5. What are some of the major rights federal law has given consumers?
6. Compare and contrast consumer installment sales credit with installment cash credit.
7. What is the basic difference between a regular or 30-day charge account and a revolving charge account?
8. What are the sources of consumer cash credit?
9. Compare and contrast banks and consumer finance companies as sources of loans.
10. What is an overdraft account?

YOUR PLAN: CHAPTER 4

The following are some basic do's and don'ts of credit which you should follow.

1. Don't use consumer sales credit before finding out what terms you could get on consumer cash credit, because it is likely to be cheaper and may have other advantages also.
2. Don't use credit until you have considered dipping into your savings or waiting until you can save enough to make a purchase.
3. Don't buy an item on credit when the item's lifetime is less than the credit period.
4. Don't assume more debt than you can reasonably pay out of your current income.
5. Don't deal with a creditor whose reputation is not good or not known.
6. Don't buy on credit if you have no savings. If you do, an emergency can ruin you because you have no savings and have used up all or part of your borrowing power.
7. Don't use credit to buy things you don't really need.
8. Don't let credit turn you into a spendthrift. (This means you must be aware of how much you are spending!)
9. Don't let your account become delinquent.
10. Don't use credit unless the benefit from having the item acquired justifies the cost of the credit used. (Keep up with how much you are paying annually for credit.)
11. Shop around for credit.
12. Talk with your creditor if you run into difficulty in paying on time.
13. If you can do so without a penalty, repay early.

14. Don't buy on credit rather than with cash because it is easier or makes you feel important.
15. Return the item rather than let it be repossessed.
16. Know both the cash and the credit price of an item. They may differ.
17. Know both the dollar cost and the APR of the credit.
18. Sign a contract only after you are sure you want to go through with the deal. Don't depend on the salesperson tearing it up if you change your mind.
19. Pay off your charge accounts as rapidly as possible rather than just paying the minimum payment required.

Questions you should answer before you sign a conditional sales contract:[1]

1. Is a downpayment required? A larger down payment can help you cut the cost of the credit. Beware of borrowing the down payment from a second lender. This means two payments instead of one.
2. What is the size of the payments? Are they all the same size? Watch out for a balloon payment plan. You may be able to afford the smaller payments, but not the larger final payment or payments.
3. Does your home serve as security? If so, the seller should give you a cancellation form. The Truth in Lending Act allows you three days to change your mind and rescind.
4. What happens if you repay in advance? Is there a resulting saving in finance charges?
5. What happens if you miss a payment? Is there a penalty charge? Does the entire debt come due? If so, when? Immediately?
6. What happens if you default? Are there collection charges? Are there storage or court costs? Can you later reclaim the item? If it's sold, but this doesn't cover what you owe, do you have to pay the difference?
7. What happens if either workmanship or merchandise is faulty? Is there a limit for your complaints? To whom should you complain? (Today, even if your installment contract is sold to another company, you have recourse

[1] This material was largely adapted from Lynch, Jeanette M., and Kelly, Eleanor M., "Shopping for Credit Can Save You Cash," *The 1974 Yearbook of Agriculture,* Washington, D.C.: U.S. Department of Agriculture, 1974, pp. 298–302.

on the holder of your contract.) What satisfaction can
the creditor provide?

8. Can you move the purchased item from the state?

9. Is insurance involved? Is it on you or the item? What kind
is involved? Who collects? Can you get cheaper coverage
from your own insurance company or some company
other than the one the creditor wants to use?

10. What, if any, rights do you waive? Avoid signing a statement that work has been completed on an item received
when it hasn't been, because if it never occurs, you have
no recourse.

11. Is the item an add-on to a contract? Think twice before
you add an item to an existing contract. A missed payment can mean you lose all the items even though you
have paid for the first ones.

12. Be sure that the contract states exactly what the salesperson has promised. If it isn't written in the contract,
it is not binding.

13. Make sure you understand the terms of the contract.
Make sure all blanks are filled in *before* you sign so that
something cannot be added later.

Providing Yourself with Transportation

OBJECTIVES

When you have completed this chapter, you will have accomplished the following:

1. Know how to go about selecting an automobile.
2. Be familiar with the types of automobiles available.
3. Learned how to evaluate a used car.
4. Know how to negotiate with a dealer.
5. Know where to look for an automobile.
6. Know how to sell an automobile.
7. Learned how to finance the purchase of an automobile.

Other than a home, the largest purchase most people make is that of an automobile. For renters, an automobile is most likely their largest single purchase. The relative importance of the purchase of an automobile is understated by simply comparing its price with that of a house. You may, for example, keep your $40,000 house for 20 years, but you will probably replace your $4,000 automobile in four or five years. Some people swap cars every two or three years. Thus, it is highly likely that you will buy several cars for every house you buy.

Of course, it is not necessary for you to buy a car. You can lease a car, or you can do without one. If you live and work in a congested, downtown location, the cost of operating a car is greater than for other people, and your need for a car may be less. The cost of parking a car in a congested, downtown location is very high, and public transportation may both be convenient and meet your needs. If so, you can do without a car. Other people, however, find a car, or several cars, an absolute necessity. There may be no other way for them to get to their jobs. Some jobs require that you use your car for the job. Other members of your family may need a car and it may be impossible to arrange your schedules so that one car will serve everyone's needs.

SELECTING A CAR

The first steps in buying a car are determining how much you can afford to spend on it and when you should buy it. Clearly you should sell your present car and purchase another one when the operating costs of your present car have risen so high that the cost of buying another car would be justified by the lower operating costs associated with the replacement car.

The prices of both new and used cars fluctuate during the year; thus, once you have chosen the year in which you will make the purchase, you must determine when within that year it is best to make the change. The demand for new cars is usually greatest just after they come out; so this is not a good time to buy a new car. As a rule, in the fall prices will be high because of the high level of demand. On the other hand, this is likely to be a good time to buy a used car, because the appeal of new, new cars depresses the demand for used cars. Generally, the best time to buy a new car is in the late summer, when dealers are trying to move out their stock of this year's model in order to make room for next year's, which will come out in the fall. New car prices are likely to be higher in the spring than in the winter because many people buy a new car just before going on a vacation. The used-car market also picks up in the spring for the same reason.

Special circumstances can either emphasize or alter this seasonal pattern. If the auto industry expected a good year but had a bad one, dealers may be vastly overstocked in July and August, causing prices to be abnormally low. A strike in the late fall may so reduce the supply of cars that prices are very high in the winter. A shortage of new cars will also cause the price of used cars to rise. A new car received very poorly by the market may be selling at a bargain price before Christmas.

If you can accurately predict the automobile market, you should contact our auto manufacturers because they will pay a lot for this information. For years they were convinced that Americans would not buy small cars in large numbers, so they continued to turn out big cars only to find themselves losing a tremendous number of sales to foreign makers of small cars (see Figure 5–1). This problem began

FIGURE 5–1. Sales Trends by Car Size (*U.S. Industrial Outlook 1977*, U.S. Dept. of Commerce)

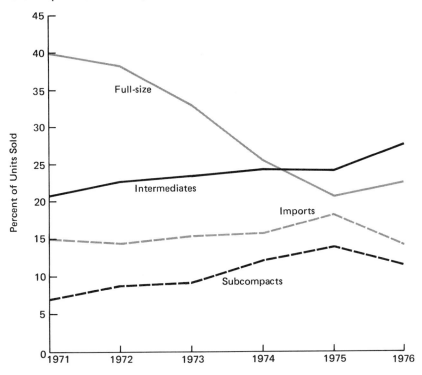

Categorized by wheelbase: Subcompact — 100" and under.
Compact — 101" to 111"; Intermediate — 112" to 119".
Full-size — 120" and over.

Estimated

before the energy crisis, which initially intensified the loss of business to foreign small-car manufacturers. So, American makers added smaller cars to their lines, stepped up small car production, and reduced their production of large cars. They ended up with vast stocks of small cars and not enough big cars to meet demand, as, after years of buying smaller, Americans began buying larger!

New or Used?

One cannot say that it is always more economical to buy a used car than a new one, or vice versa, for a variety of reasons. One reason is illustrated in Figure 5–2, which shows that the prices of new cars relative to old cars' varies over time. Another reason is that cars change over time; thus, seldom are you really considering buying a car that only differs from others only as to age. Another reason is that there is greater uncertainty about the operating costs of a used car than a new one. In other words, while the used car may be the better buy if it is in good shape, you cannot determine with a high degree of reliability when this is the case. Of course, a new car may be a "lemon," but because of the warranty on a new car, the dealer or the manufacturer will bear the cost of the flaws. There is much less like-

FIGURE 5–2. The Rise in the Price of an Automobile, Used and New 1954–1974 (U.S. Dept. of Commerce, Bureau of Economic Analysis, *Business Statistics*, Washington, D.C., May 1976, p. 43)

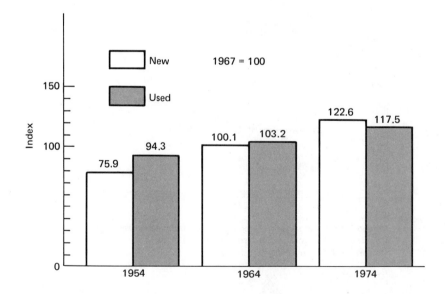

lihood that a new car will be a "lemon" than is the case with a used car, which has a lesser warranty or no warranty.

People seldom buy a car on a purely rational basis. Even when buyers think they are buying a car rationally, they may actually be buying for emotional reasons. They may say they are buying a small foreign car for economy, when what they are buying is an image, just as their neighbor does when buying an expensive, high-powered sports car because of its connotation of youth and vigor. The small car may be poorly made and mechanics who work on it may be poorly trained. It might guzzle gas like a larger car, and nobody may be able to fix it. Dealers who handle this line may be few and overworked. They may be located many miles from some customers. Thus, when a customer has a problem with his car, he may have to drive many miles for service and leave the car for more than one day. If it is poorly made, he may frequently be without his car, because it will often need repairs. Parts may have to be mailed to some dealers, because many dealerships are underfinanced and can't carry a large stock of repair parts. Complaints to a foreign manufacturer may fail to get results, because American sales are of minor importance. Foreign firms often only sell their excess production in America. If you try to sell such a car, you may find that it has depreciated far more than would an American car. The best deal the owner may be able to get is to trade it in for another car of the same make. If the car is involved in an accident, the driver is more likely to be hurt and the repair costs will likely be higher. (It is much easier to do major damage to very small cars.)

The purpose of the preceding discussion is not to argue that you should not buy a small car or a foreign car. Its purpose is to argue that you should not buy an economy image. *If you want economy, you should get economy; not an economy image.* A small, foreign car may get excellent gas mileage and be well made. Dealers may be well stocked and their mechanics well trained. The car's resale value may be high. Another purpose of the above is to point out that the cost of a car is the product of many factors and that a car may not be all it's cracked up to be in the public's eye.

Clearly, some people must select a used, rather than a new car. A new car simply will not fit into some people's budgets. Some people will never find a new car economical because of the tremendous depreciation that occurs the minute you drive it out of the dealer's showroom. It simply isn't worth it to some people to pay this much simply to be a car's first owner. Other than, possibly, status and a new car odor, all the new car buyer gets for the money which is lost as soon as he takes possession of the car is the security of knowing the car hasn't been mistreated.

Decide on Your Objectives

Before choosing a car, you should decide what it is that you are buy-ing. A woman who is buying warmth and convenience will buy a quilted, nylon coat. A woman who is buying good looks and envy will buy a mink coat, which probably provides less warmth, can't be washed, and weighs far more. Why do you want a car? Transporta-tion alone? Transportation and other things? Other things only? In short, what needs are you seeking to satisfy by buying a car?

Are you buying a second car which will only be used to drive around town to buy groceries, take the children to school, and so forth, or are you buying a car you will use in your job as a salesman who covers four states and has bulky sample cases? Do you live in Cut Bank, Montana or Miami, Florida? Snow tires are a must in the former, and air conditioning, most think, is a must in the latter. Undercoating is useful in both places. They put salt on the roads in Montana, and there's salt water around Miami. How many people are going to be riding in the car? Can or will all drivers use a manual transmission? Are some of the riders children?

In buying a car you must compromise between your *desires* and *practical reality*. You may want a little sports car, but you can't afford two cars, and you have six children to haul around. The appearance and degree of performance and comfort you want and how you will use your car determines what trade-offs you will have to make to stay within your budget.

Resale Value

As has already been observed, predicting the automobile market is a risky venture. Some cars are exceptionally popular when they are introduced, but they are not very popular as used cars. In other cases, the exact reverse is true. Sometimes a car is popular both as a new and an old car. Other cars are never popular. Popularity greatly affects price. General economic conditions and supply also affect price. Prices of a given make, model, and year car vary significantly depend-ing on the car's appearance, condition, mileage, and extras, such as automatic windows and FM radio.

It is cheaper to have a car in good condition by regular mainte-nance rather than to get it into good condition by a major overhaul just before selling it. Historically, certain makes and body styles have held their value better than others. What things hold their value well does, however, shift somewhat over time. Luxury options do not hold their value well, but some basic options do. A "stripped" car is a drug on the market. In recent years it has been very difficult to sell a car with a manual transmission. It is also very difficult to sell a used car without a radio. Power windows, however, will add little or nothing to the value of a used car. Some people will actually avoid such a car, since breakdowns are likely and will cost a lot of money.

Fuel Economy

While fuel economy did not used to be considered by many buyers, higher gasoline prices and the anticipation of even higher ones has placed fuel economy at the top, or near it, of many people's list of needs. The federal government is requiring that cars use less gas in the future. How you drive and where you drive are important elements in fuel economy. Jack-rabbit starts, for example, waste fuel. Gunning your engine while waiting for a red light also wastes fuel. A smaller car takes less fuel to move it around than does a larger car. Engine size, type of transmission, size of tires, read axle ratio, optional equipment, and weather will also affect the gas mileage you get. Unfortunately, there is a trade-off between fuel economy and emission control.

Body Styles and Sizes

Available are the two-, three-, and four-door sedans; the two-door hardtop; the two- and four-door pillared (roof supported in middle) hardtop; the station wagon; the sports car; the van or bus; and, the light truck. The two-door sedan is the lowest-priced car in a given line. It is sturdy and least subject to body squeaks as it ages. The four-door sedan, however, is easier to get into and out of, but it is more subject to squeaks and drafts as it ages.

The hardtops hold their value better than do sedans and have a better side view, but they are less safe, due to their less rigid construction. (The top is more likely to cave in if the car turns over.) It is also a bit easier for a thief to break into a hardtop. Any four-door car is less safe for a child than a two-door, because children in the rear seat have access to door handles. (This problem can be avoided with special equipment.)

The station wagon is a highly useful all-purpose vehicle. It is versatile, rugged, and adaptable. It has a good resale potential. It is noisier than sedans, however, and it is harder to heat or cool. It is also more likely to squeak and rattle as it ages, and it costs more to buy. It is more subject to theft of items left in it, as they can always be seen since there is no trunk space.

Styling and performance are the two main attractions of a sports car. Sports cars are relatively high priced and will cost more to insure, repair, and keep full of gas. They are more likely to be stolen and cannot carry many passengers, particularly in comfort.

Vans or buses offer the most enclosed space in the least amount of body. They are versatile, all purpose passenger and cargo carriers. They are relatively inexpensive to operate. They are relatively high priced and are more subject to theft than a standard model.

Light trucks are multipurpose vehicles particularly appropriate for rural families. They are also good commercial vehicles. They can carry a few passengers, but their open cargo area means that theft is easy and uncovered cargo may be damaged by bad weather.

The four basic car sizes available are standard, intermediate, compact, and subcompact. The dimensions of each of these varies between makers and over time. In the 1970s, for example, the standard size cars of some makers has shrunk back to their much smaller size in the 1950s. All body types are not available in all sizes. Hardtops, for example, are available only in the larger sizes. The intermediate-priced lines usually offer the most body types. Luxury lines only offer two-door bodies. (Since two-door bodies look better, the top of the line only offers this type body.)

Options

You need to be particularly careful in selecting options. The dealer's profit margin is much higher on options than on the rest of the car. Thus, you pay relatively more for options. What is optional equipment on the cheaper lines may be standard equipment on a more expensive line. To get you to buy options you otherwise wouldn't, a dealer may offer you a "package" of options at a reduced price over buying them singly.

Options can be classed as comfort (reclining seat, air conditioner); nonfuel-using convenience (interval windshield wipers, remote-controlled outside mirror); fuel-using convenience (power steering, power brakes); safety (day/night rearview mirror, power door locks); antitheft (antitheft alarm, spare tire lock); appearance (vinyl roof, special trim, wheel covers); fuel saving (engine low vacuum warning gauge); transmission (rear axle ratio); heavy-duty suspension system (springs, shock absorbers, stabilizer bars); and engine size and type (cubic-inch displacement and 6 cylinder, V-6, or V-8). The lowest-priced standard-equipment engine will offer the lowest performance, but it will give you the greatest fuel economy under normal conditions. (Pulling a trailer over mountain roads, of course, is not a normal condition!)

The manual shift transmission is the cheapest to use and repair, but most people today prefer the easier-to-use automatic transmission, which eliminates the need for a clutch. Automatic transmissions are standard equipment on most American cars.

The standard equipment rear axle ratio is the one most suitable for the average driver, and it costs the least. If you are going to carry heavy loads and/or drive in hilly country, another ratio is more efficient. Another ratio is also appropriate if you are going to drive through a lot of snow or on unpaved roads. A heavy-duty suspension system is needed if a car is to carry heavy loads without sagging. An automatic load adjuster is also an option appropriate for those who will carry heavy loads.

PURCHASING YOUR CAR

Purchasing a Used Car

You can save hundreds of dollars by buying a used car. You don't, of course, have all the choices available to you that a new car buyer who orders the car has, but many new car buyers just buy from among what a dealer has in stock. As is the case with any car purchase, your cost exceeds that painted on the windshield. There are taxes, title fees, license plates, and insurance. In the case of a used car there may also be some minor repair costs. With good care, an automobile can provide you with satisfactory service even when it has 100,000 miles on the odometer. Sometimes you can go well over 100,000 miles.

Possibly the best way to acquire a used car is to let a neighbor, friend, or relative know you are interested in buying their car when they decide to replace it. This is a car that you know something about. Obviously, you make this offer only if you know they take good care of their car, and it is the body style, size, and so on, that you need. If they trade in their car for a new model instead of selling it, all they will get is its wholesale value, which is several hundred dollars below its retail value. Thus, you can pay them a good bit more than what a dealer would give them and still get a car at well under what you would pay at retail. The major drawback to buying this way is that you get no warranty. If your credit is not good, you will also have more trouble borrowing to finance the purchase than if you dealt with a dealer.

Both individuals and dealers advertise used cars in newspaper classified advertisements. When buying from a stranger you need to be wary of ending up with a stolen car or one that is about to be repossessed. Find out as much as you can about the seller, and check

with the state motor vehicle office for ownership information on the car.

New car dealers are a source since they receive older cars traded in on new ones. Generally they sell the worst of these to wholesalers, keeping only the later models which are in reasonably good condition to sell. Their prices are fairly high, but they can be bargained down. Usually they provide a warranty, which may be as long as 12 months or 12,000 miles. Usually, however, their warranty covers only the *drive train*—engine, differential, transmission, and related parts—and it does not run very long.

Another alternative is an independent used car lot—a lot not associated with a new car dealership. A high-volume used-car dealer may offer financing and insurance. Usually, however, you can do better by obtaining these on your own. Prices are generally lower at the high-volume lots than on little lots tucked away here and there. Small lots, however, deal in a wider range of cars than do large lots. Inexpensive cars are to be found on the very small lots. The medium-sized lots generally stock better quality cars, but their cars will cost more. It pays to visit several lots before buying. Always keep in mind that a car lot is not a one-price retailer, that is, cars will be sold for less than the prices posted.

Car rental companies periodically sell their older cars to make way for new acquisitions. Some of them recondition these cars; others offer them as they are. A few give a standard 12-month, 12,000 mile warranty for the entire car. Some companies with fleets of cars will give their employees the option of buying them when the company disposes of them. These cars must be taken as they are without a warranty. Public auctions of automobiles are another source of a used car, but you really need to know cars to take the risk involved in buying in this manner. You are at a competitive disadvantage at these auctions because many bidders are wholesale buyers of automobiles.

Certain years are not good years as far as buying a used car is concerned. For example, 1973 and 1974 were the years when pollution control equipment was still new, and these cars had very low gas mileage and high engine wear. Models which appeal to the type of person who is likely to give a car a hard time (i.e., sports cars) are not good used car buys.

If you are not a good judge of cars, it is a good idea to take someone shopping with you who is. Examine the car carefully for rust spots, including those that have been painted over. Sight down the sides, hood, and trunk for waves and ripples which indicate the car has been in a wreck and poorly repaired. By turning the steering wheel, look into the fender wells for rust and corrosion. Check the tires for wear and cracking on the inner sidewalls—abnormal wear indicates a tire problem. Look under the car for deterioration, rust, and corrosion. Look under the hood. Do the hoses and wires appear to be in good condition? Don't be fooled by the fact they have been wiped clean. Does the battery look old? Is it covered with encrustation? Check the trunk. Is there a spare tire and a jack? Is the condition of the trunk good? After driving the car, look for coolant leaking from the radiator, oil dripping from the sump or transmission, wet spots or hydraulic fluid around the brake lines, and so on. Drive the car at various speeds and note how it handles. How does the engine respond to pressure on the accelerator? Try the brakes. Do they grab? Does the car stop in a straight line? Are there any strange noises? Does blue smoke pour from the exhaust? Run over some rough road; this way you can test the suspension system and differential. If the car has an automatic transmission, check the dipstick while the engine is running. If the fluid is dark and smells burned, the car may have transmission trouble. Check the inside of the car for wear and tear. Don't buy a car with holes in the dashboard (indicating it is a former police car or taxi) because these cars have received rough treatment.

To play it very safe, hire a good mechanic to look over a car you are considering buying. Don't buy a car with structural flaws. To get an idea of about what you should pay for a used car, you can look at one of several guide books which list, by area, retail and wholesale prices. They also indicate how much a car's price will be increased by certain options such as air conditioning or a vinyl roof. Guides you can find at financial institutions which make auto loans are *N.A.D.A. Official Used-Car Guide, Black Book Official Used-Car Market Guide, Red Book Official Used-Car Valuation,* and *Kelley Blue Book Market Report.* You can also check the classified ads in your local paper to see what people are asking for similar cars.

Purchasing a New Car

In purchasing a new car you are interested in both the deal and the dealer. Obviously, you are interested in the deal—how much the dealer wants for the car. If you are wise, you will also be interested in the dealer. Does he have a good service department? Inquire around to see what kind of reputation he has (your local Better Business Bureau can help). Are cars serviced rapidly, satisfactorily, and at a reasonable cost? (You can learn a lot by just hanging around the service department a while and observing what goes on.) Is the dealership located conveniently to your home and/or place of work? Does the dealer have a habit of making estimates well below what ends up being charged? Do ex-customers say the dealer drags his feet on warranty claims? Does he guarantee the work he does? Does he have the equipment and trained personnel necessary to handle anything that might go wrong with your car? If he farms out work, are the firms he deals with reliable? (Dealerships often do not do everything that can be done to a car. Sometimes they do not do body work. They may not work on air conditioners, radios, or radiators. Dealers in small towns often don't do enough business to justify doing all repair and body work.)

A dealer will always want to arrange for you to finance your car through him and trade in your old car for the new one. He wants to do this because he expects to make a profit on both the financing and the sale of your old car. If you pay cash for the new car, he only makes a profit on the sale of the new car. (Dealers normally do not finance your car purchase themselves; instead, a financial institution they work with is actually the credit grantor.)

The following hypothetical situation will illustrate how they generally go about selling a customer on trading in their old car for the new one and why this may not be to the customer's advantage. Say you tell a dealer you want to buy a car whose sticker price is $3600. (Federal law requires that a sticker on the car tell you its total cost and the cost of each optional feature on it.) The dealer tells you that he will come down $200 on the sticker price and give you $1400 on the trade-in of your car; thus, you will have to pay or finance $2000. Since you know that your car would probably sell on a used car lot for about $1300, you may be delighted with the deal. He's giving you a generous price for your car and coming down from his price of $3600 it seems.

You wouldn't be so delighted if you knew that for payment in cash he would sell the new car to you for $2800, and that you can sell your car to a used car dealer for $1000; thus, the net cost of the new car will be $1800, as contrasted to the $2000 you will pay if you trade in your old car.

There is a minimum price a dealer will accept for a car. Say his minimum cash price is $2800. If you ask to trade in a car he thinks he can sell for $1300, then the dealer knows he wants to get at least $1500 from you. So, he simply reduces the sticker price by some amount and raises the trade-in price of your car by some amount to produce, at a minimum, a $1500 difference between these two figures. Unless you bargain hard, he will not likely settle for only a $1500 difference. If you are impressed with the very generous trade-in figure and the fact that he has come down from the sticker price, you probably will not bargain hard. He hopes to buy your old car for, say, $800 and sell it for $1300. All this $500 is not profit, of course, as it will cost him something to sell your car, and he may have to fix it up. It will cost him far less to fix up your car than it would you; thus, it is not wise to buy the new car for cash and sell the old one yourself after having paid to fix it up if much work is required to fix it up. (Used car dealers don't have repair facilities; thus, the most they will give you for a car in need of a lot of work is less than what, by hard bargaining, you may be able to get from a new car dealer.) You can sell a car in good shape yourself for more than a used car dealer will give you, because he will not give you the car's retail value. He will only pay you its wholesale value, which is much less.

A good strategy is to find out what the wholesale value of your car is and tell the dealer you will pay cash for the new car. Then you get his cash price. Go to several other dealers and get their cash prices. Before getting a price from a dealer, you should mention the lowest figure you have gotten up to this point so that he will know he has to beat it to get your business. Subtract the value of your car from the lowest price and say, for no less, you will trade in. Some people prefer to say they are going to trade in and finance with the dealer, hoping to get the price of the car down because of all the money the dealer expects to make on the trade-in and financing; then they tell the dealer they will buy the car for cash and not trade-in. Beware of making up some low price and saying some dealer offered it to you. If it is ridiculously low, he will know it.

Even if you are not sure about exactly which car you want, always obtain a price for the same car and options for each dealer, otherwise, you will not end up with comparable prices. Pick a car you are sure is very near what you will want. Assuming everything besides price is satisfactory, buy from the dealer who offers the lowest price. Once you have gotten the lowest price, ask how much he would reduce this by if you trade in your old car. If he doesn't reduce it by its wholesale value, you know you should continue to bargain.

No salesman is going to be happy to be faced with a hard bargainer. He may get pretty frosty when you tell him, politely, that his price is too high; that you can do better elsewhere. If this frost bothers you, you can eliminate it by agreeing to pay more for the car than you could get him to agree to accept, but is his happiness worth that much to you?

The financing that a dealer will arrange for you often is not the cheapest available. If your credit is good, you can likely do better by borrowing the money elsewhere. Try your bank. The insurance the dealer will arrange may also not be the cheapest, and it may not suit your needs. *Do not let a dealer pressure you into accepting his financing and insurance arrangements.*

If you do finance your car through the dealer, insist on knowing the total price of the car. Don't simply ask how much a month. Don't sign a contract without reading it. Don't sign a contract with blank spaces in it. Be cautious about cosigning a note for someone else who is buying a car. If he or she doesn't pay, you will have to. If you don't, the auto lender can claim your house and/or furniture. A minor has to have a cosigner.

Whether you are buying a new or a used car, insist on having a title certificate signed over to you, and check to see that the motor number and body number on it match those on the car. When buying a used car insist on getting the receipt given the previous owner when its tag was bought. You will need this to get a new tag; it shows that taxes have been paid on the car; and the seller will certify he has transferred ownership to you by filling in the appropriate spaces on this form.

It is rare to find exactly the car you want on a dealers' show-room floor. There are two reasons for this. There are thousands of combinations of options, colors, body styles, and body sizes. A dealer can't possibly stock them all. Dealers also tend to stock cars with far more options than are initially desired by many customers. They hope that you will be so anxious to get a new car that you will agree to take one off the floor rather than ordering and, thus, you will accept and pay for some extra options. To avoid the time and expense of ordering a car to your specifications, a dealer may come down in price. If you insist on ordering a car from a dealer who has a very substantial inventory that is not moving very rapidly, you can count on him offering you a better price than he has previously given you if you will buy from his stock. If you want a lot of options, this is very likely an excellent deal.

If you really need a car fast and the dealer who offers you the best price does not have the car you want, you have an alternative other than taking what he has or buying what you want at a higher price from another dealer. Dealers can and do swap cars. There are also businessmen who arrange such swaps.

FINANCING A CAR

If it is a matter of indifference whether or not you own the car you drive, there are two ways to finance a car. You can either borrow and buy it, or you can lease it. It will cost you more to either borrow and buy or lease a car than to buy it with your own money because, by paying cash, you eliminate the financing charges associated with both borrowing and leasing. Financing through a car dealer is normally the most expensive way to borrow the money you need to buy a car. The situation in the fall of 1975 was typical: The annual percentage rate for a three-year new-car loan from one finance company was 13.17 percent. (Most finance company loans are those handled through dealers.) At commercial banks a similar loan cost 11.25 percent. At credit unions the cost was 10.54 percent.

Some people mistakenly think that they must finance through the dealer. They are unaware of the fact that bank loans are available or think that only businesses and rich people can borrow from a bank. This is not true. Anyone with a regular job held two years or more, who is not already overburdened with debt repayment and has a good credit rating, can get a bank loan, even if no collateral other than the car being financed is offered.

Car dealers will try very hard to get you to finance through them. If you offer to pay cash, they may try to sell you on financing instead. The reason for this is not hard to understand. A dealer must immediately pay the automobile manufacturer for the cars he stocks. He does not normally have enough funds to pay for them all; thus, he borrows the funds he needs to finance his stock from a sales finance company, agreeing to repay it by turning over to it the loan agreements signed by the people he sells cars to on credit.

In simplified form, what happens is this: The dealer borrows $3600 from the sales finance company to buy a car. The dealer sells the car for $4000. The customer makes a down payment of $400 and borrows the rest from the dealer at, say, 8 percent a year. The terms of the loan are that the loan will be repaid in equal-sized installments paid monthly for the next 36 months. The size of these installments is computed thusly: $3600 is multiplied by .08 and the result is divided by 12 to obtain the monthly interest payment. The size of the principal payment is obtained by dividing $3600 by 36. Therefore, the total monthly payment is $124. A total of $4464 will be paid for the car: $124 × 36.

By turning these payments over to the sales finance company, the dealer repays his $3600 loan. The sales finance company probably borrowed the $3600 from a bank! Thus, it is usually really a bank that is financing a car purchased on credit, regardless of who issues the credit to the customer.

The Real Cost of the Loan

In the real world, of course, a dealer doesn't borrow for one car at a time, and the down payment doesn't just happen to reduce the loan size to exactly what the sales finance company is owed for each car in the dealer's inventory. Note that two profits are made: one on the sale of the car for more than it cost and the other on lending the customer the money needed to buy the car. Note also, that the effective rate of interest paid by the car buyer is well in excess of 8 percent annually, because interest is paid on the full amount borrowed, rather than on the declining balance.

For only one month is the outstanding balance of the loan $3600, but interest every month is based on $3600 ($24). For the first month the customer has $3600 in borrowed funds. Then he pays $100 (plus $24 interest), reducing the size of the principal loan to $3500. The next month the size of the loan falls to $3400. After one year the outstanding balance has fallen to $2400. If you add up the outstanding balance at the beginning of each of the first 12 months and divide by 12, you will obtain the average size of the loan over the first year: $3050. For a loan whose average size is $3050, the customer is paying interest of $288 a year (.08 × $3600). Thus, the effective annual interest rate the first year is 9.4 percent, that is, $288 divided by $3050. The effective annual interest rate will be higher in years two and three because the average size of the loan will be lower: $1850 and $650. Thus, the effective annual rate for the 36 months will be much higher—15.6 percent ($288/$1850).

The federal Truth-in-Lending Act requires that a lender or other creditor state interest charges, no matter how they are calculated, as an effective annual interest rate. This is called the *annual percentage rate.* It also requires the lender to disclose an itemized list showing the dollar cost of interest and any other charges you will have to pay, such as a service charge or premium for credit life insurance, a credit investigation fee, registration fee, and so on.

The dealer may require that you pay for credit life insurance in order to finance the car. This is simply a term life insurance policy payable to the holder of the loan, whose diminishing size is adequate to cover the unpaid balance of the loan if and when the debtor dies before the loan is paid off. The dealer is quite anxious to get you to take out this policy because he gets a finders fee from the insurance company. It is likely that you can take out an adequate policy at a lower cost.

In addition to investigating alternatives other than financing through the dealer, you should also investigate several of the alternative sources since, even within one city, interest rates can vary among the same type of financial institution.

Leasing a Car

There are two reasons for leasing rather than borrowing and buying a car. Leasing could be the cheapest way to obtain auto transportation, and leasing makes your life simpler—property taxes, maintenance, and selling the car are the lessor's problem. In order to compare the cost of leasing with the cost of borrowing, you will have to compare the monthly lease with the monthly interest charge on your loan plus depreciation, taxes, and maintenance on a monthly basis. (Depreciation is the cost of the car less its value when sold prorated over the years you will own the car. You will, of course, have to estimate how much you will sell the car for and how long you will keep it.) This method of calculation ignores the time value of money, but, generally, this is a reasonable procedure when comparing financing a car by borrowing via a loan agreement providing for equal-sized periodic repayments with leasing via a firm lease. (The time value of money refers to the fact that a dollar received today is worth more than one received, say, a year from now, because you would lose the interest on the dollar if you don't get it now.)

There are two types of leases available for the financing of a car. They are the *firm* and the *open-end leases*. In the case of the firm lease, you know what your periodic lease payment will be. In the case of an open-end lease, you only know what size payment you will make up to the last one. The size of the last one depends on what the lessor determines is the market value of the car at the end of the lease period. The open-end lease is like a balloon loan where all payments are equal-sized but the last, except that, whereas the last balloon payment is larger than the others, the last lease payment may be either larger, smaller, or the same size as the other lease payments. The lower the market value of the car, the higher will be the last lease payment. Lessees can protect themselves from an underappraisal of the value of a car by having the lessor agree to sell the car at the appraised figure.

Whether you lease or borrow and buy can affect your taxes and, thus, your decision as to which route to take. This is seldom a factor, however, in the case of a consumer acquiring a car for personal use.

Some people say it is better to pay cash for a car than to finance it by either borrowing or leasing because it is cheaper. Others argue that it is better to finance than to save up the cash needed, because you get the car sooner, and having it sooner is worth the cost of financing. In addition, they point out, in a period of inflation, the true cost of financing is less than the interest rate on the loan or the like portion of the lease payment since the value of the dollar is declining. (Your lease payments will also include a profit to the lessor and the return of his investment in the car which he does not get by its sale.) In other words, though the interest rate is, say, 8 percent, the lender doesn't increase his purchasing power by 8 percent as a result of being repaid, because the dollar buys less than it did when the loan was made. Conversely, the borrower doesn't reduce her purchasing power by this much in paying the interest. Presumably, however, many lenders are savvy enough to raise their interest rates sufficiently to cover anticipated inflation.

SELLING A CAR

The best thing you can do when trying to sell a car yourself is to take a page from the book of a successful used car salesperson. Does the used car dealer who really moves cars show dirty cars covered with rust spots and an engine buried under oil and dirt? Does the oil on the dipstick look like soot? Are the whitewalls dark gray? Does the car cough and sputter when it's started? Is every hinge squeaky? Does the exhaust pipe rattle or drag on the road? Does the windshield washer have water in it? Are the windshield wiper blades worn out? Is the price set on the car just plain ridiculous? Is he keeping the fact he has a car for sale a deep, dark secret, depending on you to seek it out? If the dealer does advertise, are you kept in the dark about the essential facts about the car? Of course not! So, don't you either!

For both your own protection and the buyer's, check with your state's Department of Motor Vehicles and find out how you go about transferring title. Either the buyer or you may need to get a safety inspection of the car made before it can be registered. You should insist on either cash, a certified check, or a cashier's check. Notify your insurance company that you no longer own the car. Don't spend a lot of money fixing up the car—you will not be able to raise its selling price enough to justify this expenditure. Think twice about selling your car to a relative or close friend unless you are very certain that they will be satisfied with the deal in the future.

SHOULD YOU DRIVE OR GO SOME OTHER WAY?

Some people think that it is always cheaper to drive a car than to fly. For a short trip when several people will share a car and accommodations, driving is cheaper, but for one person to go, say, across the United States, it is much cheaper to fly. One reason people think it is cheaper to drive is that they forget that it takes up to ten times longer to go by car as by plane. Thus, a five-hour flight can easily take four days by car, since you don't drive 24 hours a day. Therefore, you are going to have to pay for food and lodgings you wouldn't need if you flew. Another reason people think driving is cheaper is that they fail to consider depreciation on their car and any operating costs other than gasoline.

In comparing driving with flying, consider whether or not you will need transportation at your destination and what this will cost. How much more would this cost than using your own car at your destination? Would it cost more? How much would it cost to rent a car, use public transportation, hail a cab?

Minimizing the cost of flying is very difficult. There is not one fare for flying from point X to point Y. Instead, there are a variety of fares. The most common variances in the fare between two given cities depend on what time of day or what day you will fly. Another important reason for a variance is whether or not you are flying as part of a group. How long you will be gone may also affect the fare. (This requires that you buy a round-trip ticket.) As an experiment, the author once called several airlines (and one of them more than once) and asked for the fare between two cities at approximately the same time of day on a given day. The situation was a bit complex. There were no direct flights, and there were two ways to make the trip that were about the same distance. Several airlines served these routes. No two fares quoted were the same, even from the same airline, and the difference between the lowest and the highest was substantial! Others have had the same experience.

Going by bus or train are also alternatives. You can usually save money by going by bus; of course it will take far longer than if you fly. Yet, you will see more of the country. Train fares, however, may exceed airline fares, and the trip takes longer. Many cities are not served by passenger trains. Buses serve far more cities and towns than do their competitors, but, because of this, they often stop very frequently. The level of service and comfort also varies between the various modes of travel. Trains seem to receive the most criticism.

CASES FOR DISCUSSION

Case 1 Karol Kopernigk was discussing with Gail Lovvorn the feasibility of him buying a car. He had just finished listing the expenses associated with owning a car when she interrupted him to point out some costs he had ignored. "What about," she said, "the loss of the saving you would obtain by using a car pool instead? What about all the money it takes to build and maintain the roads for your car? If everyone used the subway, we wouldn't need these roads. What about all the illness caused by the exhaust from cars? What about the medical bills from accidents? And what about the higher land costs caused by using so much land for roads and garages?" Karol agreed that these are costs caused by automobile use, but he wondered how and if he should consider them. How would you advise him? Why?

Case 2 Marion Rainwater is a college junior. Her parents are paying her tuition, and she pays for her clothes by working part time and in the summer. She has saved up $1000 and wants to buy a sports car. She earns $60 a week during the school year and twice that amount during the summer. After graduation she plans to get married and obtain employment as a surveyor. She wants a sports car because she likes the way they look, how they handle, and she wants her friends to envy her. If you were her fiance and she came to you for advice, what would you tell her?

Case 3 Buddy, a car salesman, has just pointed out to Fred Tsukahara the fact that he can save $30 by buying a package of options rather than buying them singly. If he does so, he will get two more options than he had intended to get. Buddy has also offered to knock off $90 if Fred will buy a car he has in stock rather than ordering. In addition, he will let Fred have the wheel covers on the car, which normally cost $80 apiece, for $40, which is what Fred would have paid for the cheaper ones he would have ordered. How would you advise Fred? Why?

Case 4 When Robert and Jill Guynn were living in an apartment and had no children their subcompact car suited them fine. Now, however, they feel they must make a change because they have two children and a third is on the way. They live about 20 miles from Robert's job as a telephone repairman. Jill sometimes works from her home as a telephone solicitor for a photography shop. Together they make about $12,000 a year. Several times they have borrowed a friend's pick-up truck to haul gardening supplies, furniture, and so forth. Robert thinks they should trade-in their car for a pick-up truck. How would you advise them? Why?

Case 5 When Ross Brady was a junior college student he

bought a used van and really enjoyed it. Now he is a loan officer in a small town bank and is married to Jean, who is a church secretary. Jean thinks they should get rid of the van. She prefers a new, standard-sized car with power equipment. Ross prefers a sports car, but really sees no reason to make a change. The Brady's have no children and live in an apartment. They use their car for vacations. They have asked you to arbitrate. Assuming they make about $15,000 a year, how would you advise them? Why?

Case 6 Eliot and Bea DeVillier are in their mid-forties. They have two teenage children, a boy and a girl. They have a 3-year-old, two-door sedan. Bea doesn't work. Eliot earns $13,000 a year. Their house is nearly paid for. Eliot needs the car to go to work in. Bea drives him to work and picks him up so that she and the children, who both drive, can use the car. The family is constantly in an uproar over who is going to get to use the car. The DeVillier's are camping enthusiasts and have a small trailer they use for this purpose. Often their son stays home, and he complains of feeling trapped. He thinks the family needs a second car. His father says they can't afford it and that the high insurance premium he pays so his son can drive is one of the reasons why they can't afford another car. How would you advise them? Why?

Case 7 Maria Gonsalez has just taken a job as an electrician for $7000 a year. She has just finished an electrical technology course at vocational-technical school, and is still living at home with her parents in the inner city area of a major metropolitan area. The business where she works is 15 miles away in the suburbs. Maria cannot get there by public transportation. She has $300 saved up for a car. Her father will give her another $100. Maria wonders where she should shop for a car; what kind of car she should buy; how should she finance it; and how should she go about avoiding being ripped-off? How would you advise her? Why?

REVIEW QUESTIONS

1. What is the first step in buying a car?
2. Why do you need objectives in order to properly select a car?
3. Give examples of how your objectives influence your selection of a car.
4. What are the advantages and disadvantages of buying a used car?
5. What are the advantages and disadvantages of buying a new car?
6. How should you evaluate a used car?
7. How do you go about getting a good price?
8. What are the advantages and disadvantages of trading in your old car on a new one?
9. Why do you suppose the government requires that automobile loan contracts state the annual percentage rate?
10. Why should you shop around for an automobile loan, and where do you look?
11. How would you decide between leasing and borrowing to finance a car?
12. How would you go about selling your own car?

YOUR PLAN: CHAPTER 5

**Questions you need to answer
before shopping for a car:**

1. How much can you afford to spend on a car? (Consider both the total amount and the monthly amount. Consider both the cost of acquiring the car and operating it. Consider the car's resale value.)
2. What needs do you have that can *only* be satisfied by a car?
3. What other needs do you have which could be satisfied by a car?
4. How much comfort and performance do you want?
5. Will you use this car for family vacations?
6. How many people will ride in the car on long trips?
7. What will be carried in the car?
8. Will the car be used to tow anything?
9. Will the car be used for business purposes?
10. Will it be used as an all-purpose car?
11. Will it be a second car?
12. How many miles a year will it be driven?

13. Will most driving be in highly congested conditions?
14. Will it be used for commuting to work?
15. Will it have to be parked a lot where space is at a premium?
16. Will small children be riding in it?
17. Will young people be driving it?
18. Will it be driven in exceptionally hilly country or in flat country?
19. Will it be driven in extremely cold or hot country?
20. Will it be driven over poor roads or off of roads?
21. Will it be driven near the ocean?
22. How skilled are those who will drive it?
23. Is your budget so tight that operating costs must be held to a minimum?
24. Is driving just a necessary evil to you, or are you a person who really enjoys driving and wants a highly responsive car?
25. What options would be nice but could be given up if necessary to hold down cost?
26. Which options that you want are essential and have a good resale value?
27. Will the car be parked where theft is a serious problem?
28. Will a handicapped person drive the car?
29. Are you a member of a credit union?
30. Can you borrow money on your life insurance policy?
31. Is your credit rating good?
32. Can you pay cash for the car? If not, what size down payment can you make?
33. If you will be getting rid of a car you now own, what is the likelihood that you could sell it yourself? How much might you sell it for?

How to Use Your Answers

Obviously, a car must fit into your budget and meet those of your needs which can only be met by a car. (A two-seat sports car will not meet your needs if you plan to take a family of six on vacation in it!) Some cars do not have adequate space to carry very much luggage, sports equipment, groceries, and so on. This, if you plan to haul around much, sports cars will not do. Certain types of cars and engines are not appropriate for hauling heavy loads—hauling heavy loads requires some special equipment. Only a specially made vehicle will be satisfactory for driving off the road. Special equipment is needed for using a car in extreme conditions. (Tinted glass and air conditioning are great in the desert, but if you live in Alaska your special needs will differ!) Some cars are not very safe for children. Insurance for young men, which is more costly than for other people, is extremely high if they drive certain models, and certain models are more expensive for anybody to insure.

You may not be able to afford all the features you want; thus, you must have a set of priorities so that you can reduce cost by deleting features. If a driver, through lack of knowledge or a handicap, cannot handle a manual transmission and manual brakes, you will have to get an automatic transmission and power brakes. If you must keep operating costs to a minimum, certain cars will be more satisfactory than others. For example, a small car will use less gas. Spare parts for an expensive and not very numerous model car will be costly.

Certain cars and accessories are particularly attractive to thieves because they are easy to steal. Mag wheels, tape decks, and CB radios are good examples. A manual transmission is tiring when driving in heavy traffic, and a large car is more difficult to maneuver in heavy traffic and tight parking spaces than is a small car. A small car is less safe in an accident than is a larger car. Power steering improves maneuverability but lowers gas mileage. Repair frequency and its cost varies among makes, models, and accessories. Many accessories are relatively expensive to buy and maintain, and they increase resale value little or not at all.

If the uses to which you will put a car are too disparate, it will be better to buy two cars rather than one, assuming you can afford to do so. If you can afford one new car, you can afford two used cars. If a car is simply a necessity to you, you should stick to entirely practical requirements in selecting a car and accessories. A used car will likely be satisfactory. If this is not the case, you should admit this and decide how much you can afford to spend to satisfy your desires.

Buying a car on credit through a dealer is likely not to be the least expensive way of financing a car. If your credit rating is good, it is virtually certain you can do better elsewhere. The cheapest source of financing is probably going to be a credit union or borrowing on your life insurance policy. Since rates vary between lending institutions, you should shop around. If you do not belong to a credit union and have no cheap loan available via borrowing on the cash surrender value of your life insurance policy, or you don't want to so reduce your insurance, a commercial bank is likely to be your best bet.

Investments in Real Estate

7. Know how to finance a home purchase.
8. Be familiar with the different types of mortgages.
9. Know how to sell a house.
10. Be familiar with the following terms:

condominiums	warranty deed
cost plus contract	sales contract
fixed price contract	conventional mortgage
points	variable rate mortgage
shell home	second mortgage
urban homesteading	insured mortgage
title insurance	purchase money
closing costs	mortgage
	escrow

Some people think real estate is the best investment you can make. Unlike stocks and bonds, land's value will not drop to zero. And, as they say, since God isn't making any more of it, if you didn't pay far too much for it, eventually its value will rise as the population grows. In addition, you can live on it. This is not true of stocks and bonds.

As is the case with every other investment, all the characteristics of investment in land are not good. *It is one of the least liquid investments you can make.* For a few dollars a year you can rent a safety deposit box to store stocks, bonds, and jewelry in and forget about them. You can't forget about a piece of land or a building—you have to pay property taxes on them, you probably need liability insurance, you will need fire insurance on a building, and you may have to pay paving assessments. If utility service is available on the property, you will have to pay a minimum bill. If the property is in the city, it may require you to keep the property from becoming an eyesore or a place for muggers to lurk.

INVESTMENT IN RAW LAND

An investment in undeveloped or raw land is the most speculative kind of investment in real estate you can make. To be successful in investing in undeveloped land, you can't follow population growth, you must be ahead of it. If you are successful, the rewards can be tremendous. You will earn the highest rate of return on your investment if you utilize as much borrowed money as possible, but this will greatly increase the risk you take. (If, say, a recession hits, the bottom may fall out of real estate, and you will be faced with the choice between selling the land at less than it takes to pay off the loan or risk paying interest for years before you can get a decent price. In 1974, for example, the real estate industry went through its worst bust in 40 years. The once-glamorous real estate investment trusts were largely either bankrupt or near it. Those who suffered the most were very highly *leveraged,* that is, a very large portion of their funds were borrowed. They found themselves paying up to 16 percent for some of the money they had invested, and they couldn't sell the property.)

The value of raw or undeveloped land usually doesn't rise steadily year by year. Instead, its value rises in spurts generally associated with the general level of economic activity in the nation and in the community in which the land is located. Prices rise rapidly once development is anticipated in the vicinity. Thus, you need to invest before others see development on the immediate horizon.

Getting ahead of population growth is a matter of educated guessing. If you study the growth patterns of many cities you are likely to find some useful clues for predicting where future growth will take place. Highways, for example, clearly foster growth by making an area accessible. In the case of limited access highways, however, only areas near interchanges may be much benefited. Natural barriers such as mountains, oceans, rivers, swamps, and deserts block growth. Places of employment, schools, and shopping centers promote growth.

You can't know enough about a city, town, or county if you plan to invest in land; thus, *it's best to invest at home,* where you are most familiar with housing growth patterns the political scene, and commercial and industrial growth patterns.

The value to you of a piece of undeveloped land depends on what you anticipate selling it for and how far into the future this will occur. Between the time you buy and sell the land you will have to pay property taxes. You should pay different prices for pieces of land with the same anticipated selling prices if one will be held longer than the other. You should pay less for the land held the longest in order to compensate yourself for the additional taxes you will pay and the longer time you have to wait to get the proceeds from selling the land.

What you can sell land for depends on how it can be used. If a piece of land can be used both for grazing cattle or building a shopping center, its value will be greater than land that can only be used as pasture land, as a cattleman will not pay as much as will the shopping center developer.

Zoning affects the potential of a piece of land. Many people have bought land planning to develop it commercially only to find that it is zoned residential, and, except perhaps at great cost, they can't get it rezoned. Land zoned for offices and stores usually has the greatest potential. Land zoned for apartments ranks next, followed by industrial, one-family homes, and farms.

The possible uses to which land can be put will depend on, among other things, its location relative to roads, railroads, airports, and utilities such as ˙electric, gas, water, and sewerage. Of course, after you buy the property, you can make it possible for the land to serve new purposes by adding the missing facilities, but this may cost a very large amount of money. (You can pay the electric utility to run lines to the property. You can try to persuade the local government to build a road to it by offering to pay part of the bill and playing up the fact that a big industry which will pay a lot of taxes will likely build on the land if it is served by a road.)

Because land costs you money as long as you hold it, you should try to find ways to generate an income from it. If nothing else, unless it's in a desert, you can grow trees on it and sell lumber. Maybe you can lease it to a farmer who will put it in crops. Maybe hunters will pay to hunt on it.

You often can sell a piece of land for more if you sell it piecemeal, that is, subdivide it. (There may be nobody willing to buy all the land for one house, and, if there is, they may not pay as much as 50 people will pay for 50 sections of it to build 50 houses on.) You may sell the land for an even greater price if you build the houses yourself. This is because you will also earn a profit on the houses. You can obtain a higher total price for building lots by selling the worst pieces first, as once some houses are built and people are in them, people will pay more for the remaining lots, particularly if they are the most desirable.

Before buying land, you should consider whether or not the nation is headed into prosperous times or a recession. *Land prices rise faster than prices in general do in boom times, but they fall faster in recessions as a rule.*

Obviously, you should take the precaution of seeing land before buying it! You should also talk to people who have lived in the vicinity for a while. Many people who haven't taken this simple precaution have discovered, to their horror, that their land is either under six feet of water half the year or is in the middle of a desert 200 miles from the nearest town, which boasts one filling station and a population of 25! You should also learn to recognize a flood plain when you see it.

HOW ABOUT BEING A LANDLORD?

So-called slumlords have given landlords a bad name. People forget that landlords provide many people with living facilities far better than what they would have if they had to buy property. People, too, often ignore the extremely high property taxes in some cities, rent control in New York City, and irresponsible, destructive tenants whose behavior forces rents up and discourages landlords from making improvements.

The fact that the federal government has long made owning apartments a tax loophole rather than a pure investment has also helped give landlords a bad name, since if all an apartment is to its owner is a tax loophole, it is more likely to be poorly built and maintained. But, even if all past landlords were bad guys, you don't have to be.

Renting houses or apartments is less risky than investing in undeveloped land, but it is not likely to make you a lot of money fast. In addition, a good deal of your time is required to oversee the property. One night you may be roused out of bed because all the toilets are overflowing. The next day an important business meeting of yours may be interrupted by the announcement that there's a fire in one of the units—one of your tenants fell asleep in bed with a cigaret. That night one of your tenants may pack up and move, leaving the rent unpaid. To remind you of him, he may tear up the apartment. If you hire someone to manage the property for you, you may find he or she spends more time in the local bar than trying to collect rents or seeing to it that repairs are made.

Even if you have enough money to go into renting in a big way, it may be better to start small. This way you are not risking much while you learn the business. One way to start is to acquire a duplex or small apartment building and live in it yourself. If you don't have much money, this is a way to accumulate the funds to go into renting on a large scale.

The major problem in investing in single-family houses, duplexes, or small apartments is that a vacancy for a few months may wipe you out. Thus, small-scale renting is best where the demand for rental units is so high that it is unlikely you will long have a vacancy, and you think it highly likely you can eventually sell the property at a good profit. Another problem you will face is that the return from the units will not likely be high enough to hire an electrician, a plumber, and so on, so you will have to do a lot of the maintenance work yourself. In some places competition will force you to offer tenants expensive frills like tennis courts, swimming pools, playgrounds.

It is important that you carefully pick tenants and that you purchase well-built units. Destructive tenants you can do without, and there is no point in making the apartment easy to damage. Local antidiscrimination laws may preclude you from refusing to rent to families with children, even though many firmly believe that apartments will more likely be damaged by families with children and/or

pets. (Pets may also leave an odor that is difficult, if not impossible, to get rid of.) Renters are notorious for not taking as good care of their housing as do owners. If your units are not well built, repair and maintenance costs may eat up your profits or force rents so high that you cannot fill all your units; thus, you make no profit. Like motel owners, the apartment owner should furnish units so that they are difficult to mess up, and furnishings should be so cheap that it is not costly to replace them.

BUY OR RENT?

It has long been thought by many in the United States that it is best to own your own home. As a result, many people do. In recent years, however, the advantage of buying over renting is increasingly being questioned. In large part this is the result of the exceptionally great increase in the cost of the average home. Today the average new home costs over $50,000, a price most families probably cannot afford. Figure 6–1 shows how rapidly the cost of owning a home has risen. It shows this cost has risen more rapidly than has rent. Table 6–1 illustrates the rapid rise in home prices. As would be expected, the cost of buying an old home has risen right along with the cost of a new home. Home mortgage loan interest rates have reached unusually high

FIGURE 6–1. Annual increase in Cost of Home Ownership* and Rent. (U.S. Dept. of Commerce, Bureau of Economic Analysis, *Business Statistics,* May 1976, p. 42 and *Survey of Current Business,* May 1977, p. S-8. Washington, D.C.) 1954, 1964, 1974, and 1977**

* Includes home purchase, mortgage interest, taxes, insurance, and maintenance.

** January 1977. All other figures are annual averages.

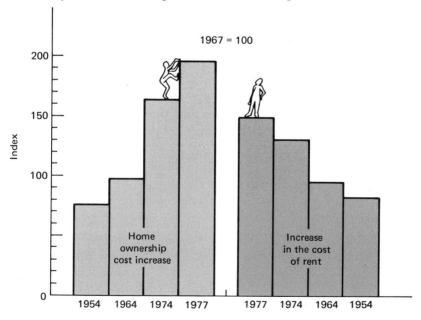

TABLE 6–1   New One-Family Homes Sold, by Sales Price

	Number of Homes (Thousands)				Percentage Distribution			
Year	Under $30,000	$30,000– 39,999	$40,000– 49,999	$50,000 and Over	Under $30,000	$30,000– 39,999	$40,000– 49,999	$50,000 and Over
1965	476	55	13	6	87%	10%	2%	1%
1966	347	59	15	8	82	14	3	2
1967	353	72	21	11	76	16	5	2
1968	325	97	28	16	71	21	6	3
1969	281	94	34	19	66	22	8	4
1970	333	79	35	19	73	17	8	4
1971	436	132	53	37	66	20	8	6
1972	426	170	70	52	59	24	10	7
1973	257	192	96	76	42	31	15	12
1974	141	176	96	87	28	35	19	17
1975	110	174	127	133	21	32	23	24
1976°	78	166	167	225	12	26	26	35

Source: Bureau of the Census and Department of Housing and Urban Development.
Note: Components may not add to totals due to rounding.
° Preliminary.

levels in recent years, as is shown in Table 6–2. Maintenance and repair costs have also exploded. Yet, despite the high cost—which is causing some to question the traditional wisdom that you should own rather than rent—single people, who seldom used to buy homes, now frequently buy a home. They see a house as a good investment and as a provider of a more pleasant style of living.

The reasoning that lies behind many people's belief that it is better to buy than rent is shown by the following hypothetical example: Suppose someone using $5,000 of her money and $25,000 of borrowed money (borrowed for 20 years) buys a home for $30,000. This person expects to rent it out and keep it for the rest of her life, leaving it to her children. This person, of course, doesn't know when she will die. To earn a return, this person must first cover, through the rent charged, the $30,000 investment, the interest on the loan, maintenance and repair costs, and property taxes. It is difficult to keep a rental unit filled 100 percent of the time. Since one can reasonably expect the unit to be empty part of the time, the rent on the unit should include a return to cover anticipated vacancy time.

The rent a landlord charges annually will be figured by adding profit to total cost and dividing by the number of years over which she expects to realize this money. If you rent this house from the landlord, and you plan to live in it for the rest of your life, which matches his, how should your total renting expense compare to what it would have cost to buy the house on the same basis the landlord did? Clearly, on the basis of the information given, you would come out ahead by buying, as you would avoid paying a profit to the landlord and covering his vacancy costs. In addition, you would gain because rent is not a tax-deductible expense, but interest on a loan to buy a house is. (The 1976 increase in the zero bracket amount, formerly called the standard deduction, greatly reduces this advantage for homeowners, since paying for a house will not necessarily enable one to itemize deductions, because they are less likely to exceed the zero bracket amount.) The homeowner can also deduct property taxes. On the other hand, the landlord, but not the homeowner, can deduct depreciation on a house. The homeowner also loses the interest that could have been earned on the down payment on the home if he had rented instead. The fact that the landlord can depreciate the house may lower the rent on it, and the renter gets to keep his money in an interest-bearing account, rather than having to put it into a down payment. Clearly, whether renting or buying is superior depends on the magnitude of all these amounts plus a few other factors.

Some of the costs and benefits of buying and renting are not measurable in monetary terms. Often, for example, a renter is not responsible for maintenance or repairs, though, through his rent, he pays for the maintenance and repairs on an average unit. The renter simply calls the landlord and tells him to see to getting repairs made, but the renter may still be waiting for the repairs to be performed long after the homeowner has gotten them done! If the renter is unhappy and the lease is up, he can simply walk off at no cost. (If he breaks his lease, he usually loses a deposit, the size of which varies a good deal.) The homeowner has to find someone to buy the house and, if a fast sale is a must, its sale may occur at a loss. Selling a house involves other monetary costs too. Part of the family may have to go ahead and move because a family member has a job elsewhere. Another family member may have to remain behind to sell the house. Living costs of a family will be greater if the family is split up. Of course, the whole family can move, leaving the house in a real estate agent's care. With no occupants, however, the house is a likely target for vandals. As long as it remains unsold, too, property taxes will have to be paid.

Frequently a homeowner who is still paying off the loan on a house can get the mortgage lender to let a buyer assume this loan. If, however, the homeowner has paid back a large part of this loan, he still has a problem. He may have a lot of money invested in the house, say, $20,000 or more, and very few buyers will be able to pay him this much money. Not being a financial institution, the homeowner is not keen on giving some stranger credit; besides, he needs the money to spend on another house to avoid borrowing and acquiring an unnecessary interest cost. Thus, the buyer will have to get the lender to increase the size of the mortgage so that the buyer can borrow enough money. The interest rate on this additional money may be higher than on the original amount. Other similar houses may be on the market whose owners do not have so much equity in them, and so the buyer will buy one of these instead, because when these owners took out their mortgage loans, interest rates were less than today's, which is what the additional money will cost. The only way to keep the buyer from doing this is to sell at a lower price in order to offset the higher interest charge the buyer will have to pay for the house whose owner has a lot of equity in it. This hurts the owner's pocketbook!

Sometimes you have no alternative but to rent. Financial institutions will not lend you the full value of a house you want to buy. You must make a minimum down payment. This down payment may be much more money than you have. Many young people run into this problem; thus, they must rent. Young people sometimes, too, prefer to rent because of the social life it provides them and the facilities it makes available: tennis courts, swimming pool, game room, and so on, typically found at large apartment projects. They may also like living close to a lot of people their age. In addition, upkeep on a house and yard would restrict a social life they value highly.

If you want to live in the center of a large city in order to partake of downtown activities or reduce commuting time, an apartment is often the only alternative. Increasingly, however, *condominiums* are an alternative to a downtown apartment. These are multiunit buildings where each unit is owned by its tenant. It may be built like an apartment or be row houses. Through fees paid to a management company, maintenance, repairs, and various facilities are provided. Most condominiums, however, are too high priced for most people. The main danger involved is the possibility of the management company going bankrupt. Another danger is that you will have more difficulty selling the unit than you would with a house.

A major advantage of home ownership is that you will have more *predictable long-term shelter expenses* than will renters. You know what your monthly mortgage payment is. Rents may be increased at the end of every lease period, which is usually one year. Homeowners have *inflation protection* because the market value of a house rises along with other prices; often faster. Unfortunately, the same is true of construction and interest costs (see Figure and Table 6–2). Due to interest ceilings on savings accounts, renters' returns on their savings will not keep up with inflation unless they invest them somewhere less safe than a savings deposit. Home ownership is least likely to be advantageous to people who move quite frequently because a loss on sale is likely to occur at least once.

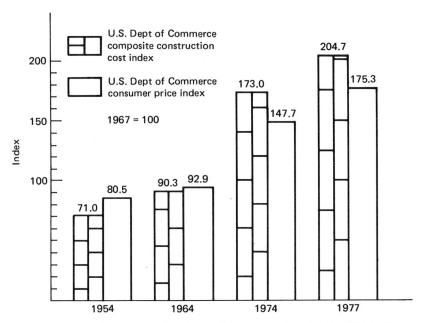

FIGURE 6–2. The Rise in the Cost of Construction, 1954–1977 (1967 = 100). (U.S. Dept. of Commerce, Bureau of Economic Analysis, *Business Statistics,* May 1976, p. 54 and *Survey of Current Business,* May 1977, p. S-10. Washington, D.C.)

TO BUILD OR NOT TO BUILD?

Once you decide to obtain a home, you must decide whether or not to build it yourself. Sometimes you may have no choice. In some small towns there may be no suitable homes on the market.

Land prices could also decide the issue. In large, rapidly growing metropolitan areas the cost of land is very much higher than it is in other parts of the nation. By buying blocks of land, perhaps in advance of rapid growth, developers are able to buy land for a much smaller price per acre than you can. Thus, you may pay less for the land if it is under a house than for a similar empty lot. Elsewhere, developers' cost advantage is smaller; thus, you may buy a lot and build on it yourself. Buying a lot gives you more choice.

While some people will hire a general contractor and not see him or the work he is doing until the house is complete, few people are willing, or should be, to take this much risk. Thus, building a house is likely to take up a lot of your time.

There are two types of contracts you may sign with a contractor: *cost plus* and *fixed price.* You probably will choose the cost plus if you

TABLE 6–2   Home Mortgage Interest Rates

Period	Conventional Loans, on New Homes, Effective Interest Rate
1965	5.81%
1966	6.25
1967	6.46
1968	6.97
1969	7.81
1970	8.45
1971	7.74
1972	7.60
1973	7.95†
1974	8.92
1975	9.01
1976	8.99
1976:	
January	8.99
February	8.93
March	8.93
April	8.92
May	8.97
June	8.89
July	8.97
August	9.02
September	9.08
October	9.07
November	9.05
December	9.10

Sources: Federal Home Loan Bank Board; Federal Reserve Board; Moody's Investors Service.

† New series.

think it is likely that the contractor will be able to shave costs; thus, you want to share in this cost saving by having him charge you what he spends plus some percent of this amount for a profit. This is also the type of contract that contractors favor, since it assures them of a profit. If they have plenty of business, contractors may refuse to sign a fixed price contract.

With a cost plus contract there are several ways you can lose money. The most flagrant is simply for the contractor to double-bill you, that is, charge you twice for the same thing. He may also accept kickbacks from suppliers and subcontractors for looking the other way while they pad their bills. He may also buy more materials than needed for your house, bill them all to you and use the excess on a house he is building on a fixed price contract or one he is building speculatively.

The advantage of the fixed price contract is that you know how much the house is going to cost you. (Table 6–3 shows how difficult it is to estimate the cost of building a house.) The main problem with this kind of contract is that the contractor may try to increase his profit by using cheap, inferior materials and working on it only when he has no other work to do. Thus, in such a contract you should specify the materials he is to use and check to make sure that they are used. You should also set a completion date. If possible, you should get a clause which penalizes him if he misses this date written into your contract.

Another problem with the fixed price contract is that the general contractor, who is the one you sign a contract with, may hire cheap and incompetent subcontractors. There is also a greater likelihood of the general contractor going bankrupt, leaving you with a partially built house, because it is possible for him to lose money on this kind of job.

In the contract between you and the general contractor you should *get him to take the responsibility for paying all bills;* otherwise, you may pay him and then find he hasn't paid the bills, then you will have to! Workmen and/or suppliers he owes will slap a *lien* on your property to make sure you do!

Deal with a contractor you believe is honest and who has good judgment. To find out about him, talk to people he deals with: suppliers, workmen, customers, and savings and loan association officers. Before hiring him, look at homes he has built. Look at some he is building so you can see what's behind the wallboard! Since the best builders usually confine themselves to commercial buildings because

TABLE 6–3 Percentage Change in Cost of Selected Building Materials

Material	1972	1973	1974	1975	1976†
Hardwood Lumber	14.5%	69.3%	−22.7%	−12.9%	33.5%
Southern Pine	10.1	28.6	−18.5	10.1	28.5
Douglas Fir	17.3	29.4	−15.3	19.6	25.6
Plywood	12.3	25.5	−10.3	13.9	19.3
Millwork	5.1	15.1	2.0	7.4	11.7
Plumbing Fixtures	2.0	7.8	24.0	1.3	9.5
Gypsum Wallboard	0.4	7.5	14.2	−3.4	8.0
Building Board	2.5	12.0	1.0	8.6	7.7
Asphalt Roofing	0.0	6.6	47.7	5.0	5.2
Heating Equipment*	2.5	2.0	22.1	4.5	5.2
Concrete Products	3.7	5.5	20.3	7.0	4.9
Paint	2.0	8.8	25.8	5.2	4.2
All Materials	5.0%	11.7%	16.5%	6.0%	8.7%

Source: Department of Commerce.

* 12 months ending November.

the return is greater, you are likely not to have complete confidence in your general contractor and the subcontractors, even though they are the best available. Thus, you will want to check out their work regularly and you must know what to look for. Read up on building and look at the houses under construction and talk to building craftsmen.

Selecting the house plan best suited to your needs which you can afford usually occupies a lot of time. It may cost ten times as much to hire an architect to draw a plan as it would cost to buy an already drawn plan that you and the contractor can alter if it doesn't quite suit you. Before hiring an architect to draw a plan, look at some of his work and talk to the people he has built for. Talk to more than one architect. Talk to contractors who have built houses designed by the architect you are considering hiring.

Architects' main weakness is that they may tend to be artists more than engineers. Their services are most justified for very expensive homes where looks count for a lot and the greatest amount of knowledge is needed to draw a plan which is acceptable.

If you can do the work of electricians, plumbers, carpenters, or what have you, and you have the time to spare, you can save a lot of money by doing some of the work on your home yourself. The purpose of so-called shell homes is to allow you to save by doing much of the work yourself. In some places, however, you must have a license to do some types of construction work, and you must be familiar with the appropriate codes governing this type of work. If you are familiar with the people in the building trades, building material suppliers, and building materials, you can serve as your own general contractor and save a lot of money by doing the hiring and buying yourself. Do not do this unless you are sure you can handle it—few can. Also, is it worth it? Will it take up time you could use to make more money than you save by doing it?

If your financial resources are small, you should build what is called a "basic" home, that is, one which is modest in size and features: no extra baths; no family room; no extra-large windows. You might also look at a recent innovation: kit-type homes. With these homes, you are provided all the materials and instructions for putting them together. Everything that requires special skills is done at the factory.

Building your own home will occupy a lot of time via visits to building supply stores to select the things which will go into the building of your home unless you pay an architect and an interior decorator to do all this for you. The architect will also supervise the general contractor for a fee. This is, however, rather expensive, and these people's taste may differ from yours. Decorators working for department stores will be the most reasonable, but some people think other decorators usually do better work.

If you have a choice, you should not build your home unless it is very important to you to have the house exactly like you want it, and you are willing and able to devote a substantial amount of time to this project! You will also need to be a patient individual—very patient! You will have to deal with workmen who promise that they'll be out the next day "for sure." You'll wait for hours and they won't show. Days or weeks later, they will, after numerous, increasingly hostile calls from you, show up with innocent, mistreated, expressions on their faces.

If you enjoy creating things and have the right set of interests and abilities, building a home will provide you with a lot of satisfaction and a feeling of accomplishment, otherwise, you will simply rue the day you got yourself into this frustrating hassle.

In designing a home there are many pitfalls for you to avoid. A wall of glass looks great, but even if double-pane glass is used, the heat loss in the winter and the air-conditioning loss in the summer will be terrific. A cathedral ceiling looks great, but your roof will then be less well insulated, and you may have as much or more air space to heat and cool above the 8-foot level as below it. An open staircase is striking in appearance, but in the summer you will find your second-floor air conditioning flowing down it, and, in the winter, your first-floor heat will rise up it. A wood house looks charming, but if it is painted, you may not find what it does to your pocketbook charming as you repaint it every few years or chase termites out. If you live in a dry climate, a grass fire may make you wish you had a brick home with an asbestos roof rather than a wood house with wood-shingled roof. If you live in a very wet climate, building your house just off the ground can lead to mildew all over everything. A steep roof is a good idea where snow fall is heavy. Wide eaves will reduce your air conditioning bill. Large windows facing south will help heat your house in the winter. Large windows facing north will run up your heating bills. Heavy drapes and shades will help insulate your home.

False economies are a pitfall easily fallen into. A good roof costs much more than the cheapest roofs available, but in terms of cost per year of service, the good roof may be the cheapest. With some flooring materials you run into the same situation. With bricks, however, all you get when you buy expensive ones is, hopefully, better looks. Plastic pipe is much cheaper than copper, but while you will likely never have trouble if the water pipe to the water main is copper, if it is plastic you are likely to be out digging it up looking for a leak in only a few years. Plastic pipe for the drains in your home, however, is satisfactory. Copper water pipes should certainly be used for your hot water. An enclosed carport costs more, but it will insulate your house somewhat and add to its looks and resale value. It will also pay off if you later decide to expand the house via adding the carport to your living space since it is much cheaper to build originally than to add later. A concrete driveway costs more, but it is more durable than asphalt and will add to the value of the house.

The land for your home to be built on should not be selected casually. An odd-shaped lot may be hard to resell. The type of home you want to build may not be suitable for certain lots, at least not without a lot of dirt being hauled in and moved around, which can lead to water and sinkage problems. Will someone's backyard adjoin your lot on the side? This may reduce the value of the property when you sell it. If you are going to use a septic tank, some lots will not do. You don't want a lot that water is going to sit on after grading, or flow across in a raging torrent. You don't want to locate in a flood plain. If you have to have a well, don't locate on top of a mountain of rock. (When buying a lot on which you need to drill for water, get a clause in the contract with the seller that says it is void if you are unable to find water.)

Is the lot large enough? Does it have access to a road or street? Can utilities be obtained? At what cost? Is it zoned properly? Does the seller have clear title to it? If it is likely mineral-bearing, will you get the mineral rights? Are any abandoned mines under it? What public services are available? What taxes have to be paid? Is it located conveniently? Are there any restrictions on what you can build on it? Do you like the neighborhood? Is it near shopping areas and other places you go frequently?

Beware of buying land that a developer has advertised heavily and employed a lot of salesmen to push, as the land is likely overpriced to cover the cost of all this! Be sure that any facilities the developer promises are promised in the contract, and that he has made provision for paying for them. Look at places he developed earlier.

BUYING A READY-BUILT HOUSE

Relative to the lot on which a house is built, you are interested in the same things the person buying a lot to build on is. You are interested in whether or not the house will adequately suit your needs and whether it is reasonably priced and the price is one you can afford. Before looking at any houses, decide exactly what you want in a house and how much value you place on each desired item. The reason for assigning values is because you are not likely to find a house with everything you want—each house will lack something. Which flaws do you most want to avoid? This can only be determined if you have assigned priorities. Knowing exactly what you want will help you avoid being overly impressed with good features of a house that are not important to you. It also helps avoid making an impulse purchase.

The condition of the house is of vital importance. Don't buy a house in poor condition and plan to fix it up unless its price is extremely low and/or you will do a lot of the work and enjoy doing it. It is much more costly to get the same work done fixing up an old house than to do the same thing building a new one. Many people are not in a good position to judge the condition of a house. If you doubt your ability to judge a house's condition, make out a mental list of the people you know and decide if there's one who could judge the condition of a house, and invite him or her to look at a house you have tentatively decided to buy. You can also hire someone to do this.

Try to talk to some of your potential neighbors if you are considering buying an old house. One of them might let slip the fact that termites swarm out of the house in the spring, or the owner is always pumping water out of the basement. Also try to talk to the owner when the realtor is not around to coach him. Try, too, to look at the house without either the realtor or owner at your heels distracting you. (Take someone with you assigned the job of keeping the realtor busy.) If the realtor fails to tell you of some significant flaw in the house, you have legal recourse against him should you buy the house and find out about it. If the house has been added to, make sure that the addition is legal.

You should test all the appliances and plumbing fixtures. See who produced them. Is it a good company? Is there a warranty? Note workmanship. Do windows and door frames join properly at the joints? Do doors and windows open and shut properly? (With an old house you shouldn't be as demanding as with a new one, as all houses settle some and wood expands and contracts over the years.) Do the windows allow drafts? Can plumbing fixtures' water supplies be cut off, and can this be done conveniently? Can the house's water supply be cut off? Conveniently? Is the furnace large enough? Is the house adequately insulated? If the house is new, is the lumber seasoned? (Lumber needs to be dried out before it is used.) Is the electric service adequate? Are there enough electric outlets? Is the hallway large enough to get your furniture down it? Are the rooms large enough so that your furniture will not look out of proportion? Can you use the furniture you plan for each room in the room? Is the kitchen conveniently arranged? Are there enough floor supports and roof supports? Any signs of a leaky roof or basement? Are there any cracks indicating excessive settling of the house? Any sign of termites? Is the house likely to get termites, that is, has it been termite treated and does wood touch the ground or come near to it? Are floors durable in areas of hard wear? Have good quality materials been used?

An inexpensive way to obtain an old home is through the urban homesteading program. By agreeing to fix up an abandoned house and living in it for at least three years, you can buy the home for $1! This is usually a federal program handled through city government. Low-interest loans are available for making necessary repairs.

BEING CAREFUL PAYS OFF

Builders are likely to vent the hood over the range into the attic. As a result, some homes have burned down because a fire on the range was sucked into the attic, which was full of grease. Venting automatic dryers into some part of the house creates a fire hazard by causing an accumulation of lint. Not venting gas appliances can cause an explosion or death or illness from breathing the gas. Faulty wiring—wires of insufficient capacity or short circuits—can and has caused houses to burn down. People have been seriously injured because steps are too steep, had no hand rails, or were heavily padded. Bathtub injuries are extremely common, and they can be reduced by having a nonskid bottom surface. Painted concrete floors are slippery, particularly if wet, and they are often wet due to the condensation painting them causes.

Being careful in buying or building a house can save a life—yours and your family's! In addition to avoiding hazards, you can take positive, preventive steps. Today good fire alarm systems are priced in the reach of all but the destitute. Inexpensive fire extinguishers are also on the market. (Because different type fires require different treatment, you will need more than one type of extinguisher.) Various devices for bathtubs and steps are available to make them less risky. Protective devices for electric outlets to keep children from sticking things in them are also available. You can also buy protective screens for fireplaces which are extremely reliable. (To avoid loss of heat or air conditioning up a chimney, you need a damper in it. A glass screen in front of the fireplace is also a good idea.)

You should also protect yourself from theft. Sliding glass doors are attractive and allow for a style of living you may enjoy, but they can be a cinch for a thief to get in through. With the best protective devices, they are no match for a solid wood door with no windows in it and a strong deadbolt lock. No matter what you do, you can't make it impossible for a thief to get in, but usually thieves will pass up a house which is hard to get into for another which is easier to get into. In addition, many home burglars are teenage boys who are not experienced at breaking into houses, and they may be stopped by protective devices. You can install very sophisticated alarm systems that will defeat most thieves, but these are very costly. Remember that no house is burglarproof. If what you have in your house can be easily replaced, insurance may be far cheaper than protective devices.

You should be cautious about using burglar bars. If they can't be removed easily from the inside, they may trap you inside in case of fire. Also consider whether you are making your windows more secure than your door or vice versa. A house is only as safe as its weakest point makes it. Doors which cannot be opened from the inside except with a key are dangerous, as they may cause you to be trapped in a fire.

You also need to protect yourself legally. It is not uncommon for people to find that they have built a house on a piece of property they do not own. Either the seller did not have clear title to the land, or not enough care was taken to properly locate the land being sold. A developer may tell you he is selling you this lot, which is lot number 43, but if you go down to the county courthouse you may find that the lot he showed you is number 44. Surveyors can make mistakes. The developer's surveyor may not agree with yours or a neighbor's. Besides getting yourself a good surveyor, you should take out insurance to protect yourself against attacks on your claim to the property. A good rule to follow is not to depend exclusively on someone else to take care of you or yours.

LEGAL ASPECTS OF HOME OWNERSHIP

When you buy a house there are three things you should obtain: *a sales contract, a warranty deed, and title insurance.*

When you have tentatively decided to buy a house and want to make sure that someone else doesn't buy it or bid up its price, consider signing a sales contract. Signing *sales contract* will cost you a small percent of the sales price or simply a small amount of money. If you do not buy the property, you lose this money unless your failure to buy was for a reason specified in the contract as being an acceptable reason for not buying. (A common reason is that the buyer cannot get a mortgage loan. Another typical reason for voiding the agreement is that the seller turns out not to have clear title.) You should make sure that anything that would make you not want to buy is stated in the sales contract as a reason to void it. The sales contract is a legal agreement. It normally includes the sales price; identifies the property; promises you a warranty deed; tells when you will get possession (the previous owner may need time to move out); what appliances, drapes and so forth are included in the sale price; when you will be responsible for paying the property tax or a portion thereof, and so on. The money you pay to get this contract is called *earnest money.* No contract is valid unless the seller receives some form of consideration for the rights or property being sold.

In the *warranty deed* the seller of the property warrants that he has a good and salable title to the property being sold. A *quit claim* deed does not give you this warranty. The warranty deed may specify just what property rights the seller is transferring to the buyer and include protection for the buyer in case the seller grants something he is not entitled to. The seller normally guarantees that he has the right to transfer title to the property, and, if it turns out that this is not the case, the buyer has the right to take action in court against the seller to recover any loss suffered as a result. The seller may promise that any deficiencies in the wording of the transfer of title that show up later will be corrected. The seller may also specify any outstanding claims on the property or that there are none. It is likely that the buyer will be given both possession and title forever. (Sometimes possession is not taken. Sometimes, too, one does not buy all the rights associated with having title to a piece of property, as when one purchases the land less mineral or water rights.)

You should have your deed *recorded.* This means that the clerk of the county or parish in which the land is located is notified of the transfer of title and records it in the county records. If there are two successive transfers of title to a piece of property and only one is recorded, the holder of the recorded deed is granted title to the property, unless fraud can be proved. Thus, as soon as you get a deed, you should visit your county clerk.

Most people consider title insurance a must. If you are getting a mortgage loan to buy the property which is insured by the Federal Housing Administration (FHA), you must have this insurance. Savings and loan associations also normally require title insurance before they will give you a mortgage. Even though you have a lawyer do a *title search* and the title is found to be clear, it is not certain that it is clear. In a statement, the lawyer will point out that the title is clear only so far as he could determine from the records in the local courthouse. *Title insurance* protects those who have money invested in the property —you and your lender—against any claims against the property not turned up in the title search. You cannot get title insurance without a title search. Since their risk is so low, title insurance companies charge very little for their policies, and the policy is paid for in one payment.

If you ask a savings and loan association, the source of most home mortgages, if it will lend to you, it will not tell you until you pay for a title search. Then, if you decide not to deal with them and go to another lender, he will likely demand a second title search, which you have to pay for. Therefore, you should not agree to a title search until you know enough about the lender's terms to decide if you wish to deal with him.

SELECTING A REALTOR

A realtor or broker is an agent of the buyer or the seller or both. Like all agents, they cost money. They may or may not be worth it. Most people use real estate brokers in buying or selling a home, but you don't have to use one. You may use one because you think she will be able to sell your house for enough more than you could to more than cover her cost, or, if you are buying, she will reduce the price of the house enough to cover her cost. You may use her because you don't think you can handle the deal by yourself or don't have time to do it.

The realtor seeks out buyers for sellers and sellers for buyers. Instead of looking at 50 houses on your own, only ten of which come close to meeting your needs, you will only see the ten houses that interest you if you go to the realtor, because she knows what is on the market that meets your specifications. Instead of you escorting 50 people through your house, only ten of whom it comes close to suiting, you will escort only those ten through if you use a realtor, because she knows who is looking for what.

When you employ a realtor, your property is said to be *listed* with his or her agency. There is a termination date to this listing. The listing agreement is difficult to break, so don't sign it unless you are satisfied with its terms and have confidence in the realtor. If the property is not sold during this period of time, you can switch realtors then. Once you have listed a house with a realtor, you must pay a commission if the house is sold during the listing period even if the realtor had nothing to do with making the sale. Therefore, if you have a potential buyer in mind, contact him before listing your home. It is possible to arrange a *multiple-listing agreement* whereby several real estate firms list your house.

A realtor provides you with advice. How much should you offer to sell or buy a house for? When should you try to sell or buy? Who should you borrow the money from to buy a house? Realtors will also work to get you the best loan terms available if they are good at their jobs. They usually will advertise your home for you.

HOW MUCH SHOULD YOU SPEND?

An old rule of thumb is that *you should not spend more for a house than 2½ times your annual earnings.* The savings, life-styles, and future income of families with the same level of income varies so much, however, that this rule is only a very rough guide. The poorer a family is, the larger is the percent of their income accounted for by housing expenses. Lower-income families can expect to spend at least one-fifth of their incomes on housing. The lowest income families will spend considerably more than this. High-income families will spend probably no more than 15 percent.

You have to be concerned both with the total and the monthly cost of the house. Few people can buy a house outright; instead, they have to borrow most of the necessary money via a mortgage loan. *The longer the period of time you have to repay this loan, the less will be your monthly payment of principal and interest to the lender, but the larger will be your total payment to the lender.* This is illustrated in Tables 6–4 and 6–5.

The reason a longer-term loan involves a higher total payment than one of shorter duration is that you have to pay more interest, because you're using the money longer. You should never forget that if you lower the size of your monthly payment by agreeing to a longer-term debt, you are increasing the total cost to you of the house. Some offset to this is provided if the loan period is an inflationary period, as this enables you to pay off the loan with "cheaper" dollars than those you borrowed. You will also add to the cost of the house by agreeing to a higher interest rate than you could have obtained if you had looked around more or made a larger down payment. (In June 1977

TABLE 6–4 Monthly and Total Payment on a $40,000 Mortgage

Term (Years)	7% Rate		8% Rate	
	Monthly	Total	Monthly	Total
10	$464.44	$55,732.80	$485.32	$58,238.40
20	310.12	74,428.80	334.58	80,299.20
30	266.13	95,806.80	293.51	105,663.60

TABLE 6–5 Monthly Payment on a $60,000 Mortgage

Term (Years)	6% Rate	7% Rate	8% Rate	9% Rate
10	$673.69	$696.66	$727.97	$760.06
20	438.56	465.18	501.87	539.84
30	369.44	399.19	440.26	482.78

the Federal Home Loan Bank Board reported that the average home buyer receiving a savings and loan association home mortgage loan was making a 25 percent down payment.)

If the maximum down payment you can make is a very small percent of the price of the house, you had better pass up the house! People who make very small down payments rather frequently find that they cannot afford to make the required mortgage payments. You should, however, avoid making too large a down payment and not having enough money left, therefore, to cover lawyers', surveyors', appraisers', and architects' fees; recording fees; insurance fees and closing charges on the loan; and insurance and taxes on the house. By putting up more than the minimum down payment required to get the loan, you will reduce both the interest rate charged and the amount borrowed, which is why you get the lower rate.

Don't make the mistake of thinking of your monthly mortgage payment as the only cost of owning the house. This is simply the cost of repaying the money you borrowed to get the house. (Included in your monthly payment to the lender may be a premium on a life insurance policy you took out to pay off your loan if you die before the loan is paid off.) By buying the house, you lose the interest you could have earned on the down payment if you had rented and kept this money in an interest-bearing account. You also acquire a variety of expenses. There are taxes to pay. You must repair and maintain the house and keep up the yard. Thus, what you spend per month on the house may substantially exceed the mortgage payment. You should hesitate to spend more than 25 percent of your monthly income for all these things.

How much you should spend for a house depends on a wide variety of things. Its value depends on demand and scarcity. Table 6–6 illustrates the wide fluctuations in the supply of new houses. The demand for a given type of house will vary with its location. Even within one large city or metropolitan area there may be a several thousand-dollar price differential between neighborhoods. This is caused by status differences or the proximity of some place or activities. Scarcity—a lack of available houses—usually occurs in an area whose population is growing so rapidly that houses can't be built fast enough, or in an area of no growth in the recent past. In the latter case, few will be built until demand clearly has picked up. Because higher-than-average incomes often accompany rapid growth in its early stages, demand is also likely to be very high in a rapidly growing area; thus, prices are likely to very high.

Within a given neighborhood, the value of a house varies with age, condition, appearance, and size. Centrally air conditioned homes will sell for more than like homes with window units, because better

TABLE 6–6   New Home Construction in the United States 1962 to 1976

	Type of Dwelling (Thousands of Units)		
	Single-Family	Multifamily	Total
Average 1962 to 1970	898.2	538.7	1436.9
Average 1971 to 1973	1197.4	954.0	2151.4
1971	1151.0	901.2	2052.2
1972	1309.2	1047.4	2356.6
1973	1132.0	913.3	2045.3
1974	888.1	449.6	1337.7
1975	892.2	268.2	1160.4
1976	1162.8	376.9	1539.7

Source: U.S. Bureau of the Census, Construction Reports, Series C-40.

results and appearance are achieved with the former than the latter. If an owner spent $3000 to put in a swimming pool it may be reflected in a higher market value for the house, but $3000 spent on better quality materials which are hidden behind the wallboard will not affect the price the house will sell for. This is the cause of one of the major problems in buying rather than building a home. Knowing most people will pay for things which show and are showy, developers spend money on these things, which often, like the pool, add to operating expenses, while the things that don't show, like insulation and plumbing, would reduce the operating and repair expenses if the money was spent on them. Improvements you make to a house seldom will increase the house's resale value by as much as they cost.

People in the real estate business believe that large closets and plenty of storage space increases the value of a house. Location on a corner lot and not being the most expensive or least expensive house in the neighborhood increases the value of a house. Restrictions on leaving campers and boats in the front yard or putting up shabby storage buildings also increase the value of a house. Schools and stores being nearby, but not too near, also raise the value of a house. If mobile homes are allowed, the value of nearby houses will be reduced. Nearness to an unsightly or odorous industry greatly reduces the value of a house.

The fact that a house is in what is considered "the" neighborhood to live in will cause it to cost significantly more than a like house elsewhere. If you have no interest in snob appeal, it is questionable whether you should buy a house in such a neighborhood. While you may get the money back when you sell the house, you are not likely to get much more than you paid for such snob appeal, and you may not get it back, as after a few years some other neighborhood will likely become the in place to be.

Never pay more for a house than it is worth to you. Remember that buying a house isn't like shopping in a department store. There is no one price policy. The seller is very unlikely to initially ask you for the lowest price he is willing to take. Your best guide as to how much to pay is to find out what like houses in the same vicinity or equally desirable area have been selling for recently. Don't agree to pay more than this.

WHAT ABOUT A MOBILE HOME?

While in some communities mobile homes are about as popular as the plague, and, thus, they are banned, mobile homes account for most of the inexpensive housing available. Mobile homes are the cheapest form of housing to buy and to maintain, but they also have the lowest resale value. After ten years their value is usually nil.

Actually, calling them mobile homes is misleading, as most are placed permanently on a foundation. Thinking that living in a mobile home is like living in a closet is also a bit off, since today you can buy two units and put them together to form a small house, which is placed on a foundation like a conventional home. A double-wide mobile home often looks very much like a conventional dwelling and may be financed with a regular home mortgage. (Mobile homes are usually financed like an automobile.)

Mobile homes are especially attractive to people who expect to move frequently, because the time and expense involved in selling one house and finding another is eliminated. Of course, it will cost you to move a mobile home.

Mobile homes have some significant disadvantages in addition to their low resale value. They cannot be placed just anywhere. You are much more restricted as to where you can locate one of them than you are in the case of a conventional house. Most mobile homes are in mobile home parks, where there is little privacy and high noise levels. Storage space is nonexistent; fire is a real danger; and high winds are a major hazard. A high wind that would have no effect on a conventional house can destroy a mobile home and kill its occupants. Wind is such a danger that it is suicidal not to tie a mobile home down. While the required down payment on a mobile home loan is low, the interest rate, except on double-wides, is higher than for a conventional house.

Another form of relatively inexpensive housing is a modular or prefabricated house. The bad early experiences some had with this type of housing in the past gave this type of building technique a poor reputation (most construction is done in a factory and assembled by the contractor on the site). However, the industry has now worked out most of its early problems, and today even very expensive homes contain many factory-constructed components. In heavily unionized areas you may find that you can't get workmen to deal with prefabricated homes, since much less labor is needed to build houses this way, and the unions are trying to preserve jobs. Some companies, however, as was mentioned earlier, are selling housing kits that you may be able to put together yourself with some help from family, friends, and casual labor. Where a license is required to do the work, however, you may have to hire a union worker. (This is commonly the case for electrical and plumbing work.) In buying any housing of this type, you need to be sure that it will meet local building requirements, as this is often a problem. If it doesn't, bringing it up to standard may be extremely expensive.

HOW TO FINANCE A HOME PURCHASE

To protect themselves, those who lend to people to buy houses require the borrower to give the lender the right to take possession of the property if repayment of the loan is not made—this is called a *mortgage loan*. Because a house is the largest single investment most people make, the mortgage loan is the largest single obligation most people take on.

Mortgage loans are made by savings and loan associations, commercial banks, mortgage companies, insurance companies, pension funds, and individuals. These sources will give you a mortgage loan for purchasing either a new or an old house, though they prefer the former. If you are going to build a house, you must first get a *construction loan,* which usually comes from a commercial bank, and, when the house is completed, pay this loan off by getting a mortgage loan. Obtaining a loan for a "shell" home is difficult. Often the seller of the "shell" home has to finance it in order to sell it.

Mortgage lenders charge different rates; thus, you should shop around. Interest rates on mortgage loans also vary over time; thus, you should hesitate to take out a mortgage loan when rates are very high unless the advantage of a lower interest rate will be offset by higher materials and labor costs in the future when interest rates are lower.

In addition to taking out a mortgage loan, you can assume someone else's mortgage if you are buying an old house. You can do this when the seller has a mortgage that hasn't been paid off, and the lender's O.K. to transfer the loan to you is obtained. (If you sell a house like this, be sure that the lender releases you from the loan, otherwise, you will end up paying if the buyer doesn't!) If you don't

have enough money to pay the seller the amount invested in the house
—his equity—you can take out a *second mortgage* loan on the house
for the amount you are short. The cost of it is likely to be twice what
the first mortgage costs, and it will not likely be for more than five
years.

The total cash outlay you will make when you buy a home is not
simply the sum of your down payment, return of the principal of the
mortgage loan, and the interest on this loan. Because some states and
mortgage loan insurers limit interest rates on mortgages, lenders obtain
the rate of return they wish to earn by charging what are called *points*.
This means that if you borrow, say, $20,000, if 6 points are being
charged, you will only get $18,800, which is 6 percent less. You will,
however, repay the $20,000, and interest will be computed on this
amount. Thus, the effective cost of the mortgage will be increased by
the charging of points. (Enough points are charged to enable the
lender to earn the going market rate of interest on like loans.)

You will also have to pay *closing costs* when you buy a house.
They include property taxes, fire insurance, title insurance, credit life
insurance, appraisal fee, credit report fee, survey fee, legal fee, lender's
processing charge, recording fee, termite-proofing cost, and the cost
of the title search. (Your closing costs may vary from this list, which
is simply typical.) You may be able to negotiate some of these costs.
Many critics have attacked closing costs as being highly inflated. On
even a relatively low-priced home they can run over $1000.

Sometimes a borrower will some day find that he is capable of
making a higher monthly mortgage payment that he had thought he
could. Because it would mean quicker repayment of the loan, the borrower's interest cost would be reduced. Some lenders will not allow
the borrower to pay off the loan faster without levying a penalty
charge. You should try to obtain the right to speed up repayment of
the loan without a penalty being levied, as this penalty may be rather
large. Another way to lower your interest cost is to refinance the house,
i.e., replacing the existing mortgage with a new, cheaper one. Today
some mortgage lenders offer mortgage loans whose early payments are
lower than later ones. This helps young people who expect their income
to grow. It also makes early repayment more advantageous.

There are three major types of mortgages: *Federal Housing Administration insured loans, Veterans Administration insured loans,* and
conventional loans. In order to make it easier for people to obtain
mortgage loans, the federal government will, if certain conditions are
met, insure that the lender will be repaid. This is done through the
Federal Housing Administration and the Veterans Administration. You
will have to pay a fee for this insurance. Because repayment of principal and interest is guaranteed, the lender is more likely to lend and

to do so for a longer period of time and at a lower interest rate. You will pay a one-half of 1 percent annual premium that is based on the unpaid balance of the loan for this insurance. The FHA will not guarantee a mortgage larger than a certain amount.

An FHA-insured loan may run up to 35 years. The minimum down payment required is very low. Like many government programs, there can be a lot of red tape involved and it may take a very long time to get the loan processed. Before the FHA will insure a mortgage loan, it has to assure itself that certain standards of construction, livability, and location are met by the house being purchased. The borrower must meet certain credit and income requirements also.

As you probably assumed, Veterans Administration (VA) insured mortgage loans are only available to veterans. Up to 100 percent of the appraised value of a home can be borrowed if the lender is willing. The VA sets a maximum allowable interest rate on any loan it will insure. In order to qualify, a person must have served in the armed forces during certain time periods set by Congress and meet certain credit and income requirements. To get a VA guarantee, the price the veteran agrees to pay for a home cannot exceed the appraised value. The appraisal value of a home is determined by professional appraisers. More than one estimate is obtained. Double-wide mobile homes built to engineering standards set by the Housing and Urban Development Department are eligible for a VA guarantee.

The fact that you can obtain a government guarantee on your loan does not guarantee that you will be able to get a loan. When interest rates on noninsured mortgages, called *conventional mortgages,* rise above the ceiling of FHA and VA guaranteed loans, it becomes difficult for one wishing to have a loan insured to get one because of the relatively low interest rate allowed on these loans. Lenders may, while the FHA and VA look the other way, make the loan because they raise the effective rate of interest by charging points. The points may be borne by either the borrower or the seller of the home via altering the house's price.

A conventional mortgage exposes the lender to more risk than do the insured ones. These loans are, as a result, shorter in duration than the insured ones. Many states prohibit a conventional mortgage lender from lending more than 75 percent of the appraised value of a house. Some savings and loan associations in other states may lend up to 90 percent. (The selling price of a house may exceed the appraised value of the house; thus, a mortgage loan for a very large percent of the appraised value of the house doesn't mean you borrow that much of what you need to buy the house.)

A conventional mortgage loan is usually the easiest and fastest kind of mortgage loan to get. Savings and loan associations are generally the most liberal conventional mortgage lenders.

If your family's income is no more than 95 percent of the median income in your area, the federal government's Section 235 program will provide you with a mortgage at an interest rate well below the going rate on conventional mortgages. The Farmer's Home Administration also offers a subsidy program for low-income people in small towns and rural areas. The interest rate on mortgages under this program may be as low as 1 percent. During the 1977 fiscal year this government agency made more than $52 million in housing loans.

Home buyers will often be asked if they wish to add to their mortgage loans the cost of such major appliances as a refrigerator. Before agreeing to this, consider that, while the term of 'the loan may be 25 years, the life of the appliance is much less. It doesn't make much sense to be paying for something long after it is worn out. It would probably be better to borrow the money elsewhere for a shorter period of time, because, even if the interest rate is higher, total interest paid may be less due to the much shorter loan period.

Lenders get upset when the current rate of interest on mortgage loans is well below what they are paying on deposits. Homeowners get upset when the current rate of interest on mortgage loans is much lower than what they are paying on mortgage loans they took out years ago. A solution to some of the problems of both the lender and the borrower is the *variable rate mortgage loan,* whose rate varies with the current one. The only problem is that lenders don't want to make them when the current rate is well above its usual level, and borrowers don't want to take them when the current rate is well below its usual level, because each wants the future rate to cause the mortgage loan's rate to change in their favor. (If rates are now above their usual level, they will likely fall in a few years and vice versa. The change will help one party and hurt the other.)

To protect your family, it is a good idea to take out credit insurance which will pay your mortgage loan payments if you are disabled and unable to work or die before the loan is repaid. This protects both you and the lender, and this latter fact should help you get the loan and/or get a lower interest rate. If interest rates drop significantly and you can repay your mortgage early without penalty, you should consider doing this by taking out a new mortgage.

SELLING A HOUSE

You may be able to save 5 to 6 percent of the sales price of your home by selling it yourself rather than using a broker. To do this successfully, you will have to learn much of what a broker knows. You will need to know how to price a house, finance a home purchase, be a good salesman, and write a good advertisement.

You have already read that the best guide in pricing a house is to determine what like houses have sold for recently. You must determine what this figure is. Mortgage lenders and the FHA and VA, however, will require an appraisal of your house by professional appraisers to set its fair market value. This determines how much money they will lend or guarantee, respectively. You should select an appraiser who is a member of either the Society of Real Estate Appraisers or the American Institute of Real Estate Appraisers.

Check with the holder of your mortgage and see if he will let a buyer of your home assume your mortgage and if he will release you from the mortgage. Find out all the conditions involved: amount of the loan, interest rate, points, and down payment.

Prospective buyers will want to know or will be impressed by a variety of facts about the property: price; number of rooms and baths; shower or tub; neighborhood; post office, taxes; how to get to; room sizes; dining area or dining room; family room; built-ins; heating; air conditioning; pool; patio; porch; size and condition of yard; nearness to schools, stores, major highways, and any other place of significance; age; single- or two-story; type of construction; fireplace; insulation; type and age of roof; finished basement; separate apartment for elderly parents or grown children; and any other special features.

Newspaper advertisements should be imaginative and as complete as you can afford. Don't appear too eager to sell. Set your price higher than you will accept so that the buyer can get you to come down in price. Leave the buyer alone to look over the house and talk with friends and relatives who come along. Consider sharing the expense of a broker with the buyer. Have prospective buyers make an appointment to see the house so that you will be prepared to show the house when they come. Have both the house and the yard looking good. Talk about both the good and bad points. If you don't mention some bad point you know about, this makes the sale fraudulent if the matter is significant. Don't get angry if the buyer criticizes some feature of the house. You may sell a hesitant buyer by throwing in an appliance, drapes, or rugs not initially included in the deal. It is usually easier to sell a home while you are still living in it, and this protects it from vandals. An empty house looks less attractive than an occupied one. Some people, however, do feel that they are intruding on a family if it is still living in a house. Try to dispel this feeling if you detect it.

A mortgage lender will not lend a buyer the entire sales price. He will lend some percent of its fair market value. If the buyer doesn't have the remainder as a down payment, the deal will fall through. Some avoid a down payment by signing two sales agreements: a larger one to show the lender and another, lower one, which will be honored by the buyer—*don't do this*. Federal law prohibits making a false statement in applying for a government-insured loan. State and local laws also often prohibit this practice.

Sometimes a buyer will ask for a *purchase money mortgage*. This is a mortgage made by the seller. No third-party lender is involved in the deal. The seller is the mortgage lender. Many people do not wish to take the risk involved in being a mortgage lender, so this doesn't happen very often.

Clearing title and obtaining a loan takes time. How can the two parties trust each other to carry out each party's side of the deal? One way to handle this problem is via *escrow*. The seller will deliver to a third party (a lawyer or a financial institution) a deed with instructions that it be delivered only when all conditions specified by the seller, including delivery of the money, are met. You should insist on picking the escrow agent, because this agent can favor one party or the other.

CASES FOR DISCUSSION

Case 1 Sid is a fireman in a large city and he and his wife, Billie, now live in an apartment. Their rent, including utilities, is $325 a month. Sid earns $12,500. Billie works as a receptionist and earns $6,500. They want to start a family, but want to buy a house first. They have $3,000 in a savings account. They pay $250 a month on their two cars. They have found a house they like for $38,000. Mortgage lenders are asking for 8½ percent for 20-year mortgages with a 20 percent down payment. For 9 percent they can get a 30-year mortgage. How would you advise them? Should they buy this house? How should they finance it? Why?

Case 2 Eddie is willing to go along with his wife Anita's desire to purchase a $50,000 house in the best neighborhood in the small town they live in. Eddie is vice president of one of the local banks. They have a 5-year-old son. Eddie makes $20,000 a year with the bank. Anita doesn't work. The house is adjacent to the country club which Anita thinks they should join. So does Eddie's boss. Eddie would prefer a less-expensive house so that they could afford a cabin on a nearby lake as a weekend retreat. They have $4,000 in stocks and $3,000 in a savings account. What would you advise them to do? Why?

Case 3 Harry is a 28-year-old construction worker. He has been in this business since he finished related training at a vocational-technical school eight years ago, and he is now a journeyman. Some years he is in-between jobs for several months; frequently he can't work because of bad weather. Often he has to move because he has an out-of-town job. Sometimes he just rents a room, spending the weekends at home with his wife Pat. Pat is a bookkeeper. Their frequent moves have reduced what she can earn because she can't get seniority. Together they average about $16,000 a year. Sometimes, however, they may have to make do on $9,000. Harry would like to buy a $15,000 mobile home and have Pat quit work and travel with him. If he buys this mobile home, Harry thinks he could get more and better-paying jobs. They have $2,000 in a savings account. They pay $100 a month on one of their two cars. How would you advise them? Why? Come up with recommendations based on varying assumptions about Pat's views about quitting work, their plans regarding children, and so on.

Case 4 Vickie is a dental hygienist making $8000 a year. She finished junior college only two years ago, so she only has $500 in savings. She has been reading about how a lot of single people are now buying houses. She lives in an apartment. Her car is paid for. Her grandmother recently left her $5000. She wonders if she should buy a house, and, if so, how much she should spend? She also wonders how to go about picking one, and how to go about financing it. How would you advise her? Why?

Case 5 Judy, who has one more year of college to go, has just finished putting her husband, Scott, through law school. He's just joined a law firm at $11,000. Judy plans to quit her job, which pays $7,000, to return to college, where she would continue as an English major. She plans to teach English in high school. Scott wants to buy a home, but Judy thinks it would be better for them to rent. They are undecided about where to live—Scott's job prospects are best in a large city, Judy's are better in smaller towns. Scott doesn't intend to stay with the firm he is now associated with because he wants to go into practice for himself. Judy's parents would lend them the money for a down payment up to $6,000. They have $2,000 in savings. How would you advise them? Why?

Case 6 Alex's mother keeps trying to get him to marry and settle down, but he has no intention of tying himself down or taking on any more responsibilities. Since Alex, who is 32, is a good tool and die maker, he would have little trouble finding a well-paying job if he decided to quit the one he has. He normally makes more than $20,000 a year. He used to go to Las Vegas every few months to gamble. Now he's stopped doing that because he nearly always loses money. He wants to make a lot of money fast so he can retire early. He's heard that real estate is a good way to make a lot of money. He has a good credit rating and $10,000 in stocks and bonds, whose return he is not happy with. He lives in an expensive apartment complex. His car is paid for. How would you advise him? Why?

Case 7 Tim and Lynn are, respectively, junior and senior in college. Both work part time, collectively making around $6,000 a year. They get help from both sets of parents. Tim hopes to go into social work. Lynn plans to be a medical technologist. Because Tim has just turned 21, he is entitled to the funds in a trust his grandfather established. He wants to take the $12,000 and invest in a mobile home. He says he is tired of paying rent, because he has nothing to show for it. Including utilities, they now pay $225 a month in rent. Lynn would prefer to invest in a house, perhaps an older one, because they are cheaper. How would you advise them? Why?

Case 8 George is a brick mason making $9,000 a year. His wife makes $3,000 with a newspaper route. Their oldest son is in the army. Their younger son is in his last year at a local junior college. He has a job lined up as a draftsman and plans to move soon into an apartment. George grew up on a farm and would like to return to one when he retires in ten years. He and his brother have found a small farm they would like to buy for $40,000. They would rent out the farm until they retire. (George's brother retires in five years.) George has $4,000 in the bank and his credit is good. He is paying $285 on the mortgage on his present home. It has ten years to run. The house would now sell for about $28,000. His wife, Becky, will go along with George, but reluctantly. Both are in good health, but they have no medical insurance. How would you advise them? Why?

REVIEW QUESTIONS

1. Why is undeveloped land the most speculative type of real estate investment?
2. Discuss the relative merits of investing in undeveloped property and rental housing.
3. What are the major problems involved in building a house?
4. Discuss the relative merits of building and buying a house.
5. When would a mobile home be a person's best choice?
6. Compare and contrast renting with buying a home to determine what is best for you.
7. Doesn't the fact that renters do not pay property taxes and may not be responsible for repairs and maintenance mean that renting is cheaper than owning a house? Why or why not?
8. How do you decide what a house is worth?
9. Should you make as large a down payment as is possible? Why or why not?
10. What factors determine the size of your monthly mortgage payment?

11. What is a second mortgage? Is taking one out likely to be wise?
12. What is involved in financing a house purchase?
13. In Southern California's Orange county, the average price for a single-family home in 1977 was more than $107,000 —twice the national average. Often lotteries were held to determine which of hundreds of prospective home buyers would get to buy the houses available in a new development. Why do you suppose this situation existed? Is this likely to become more common in the future? Why or why not?
14. Do you think a variable rate mortgage is a good thing for the home buyer? Why or why not?
15. Describe the three major types of mortgage loans.
16. How should you go about selling a house?
17. What are the pros and cons of being a landlord?

YOUR PLAN: CHAPTER 6

You should answer these questions
before deciding to invest in a house:

1. How much can I afford to spend per month on housing?
2. How much do I have for a down payment on a house?
3. Based on the above information and current interest rates, what price can I afford? (Subtract monthly operating expenditures from what you can spend in order to get what you can spend on the mortgage!)
4. Am I adverse to doing yard work?
5. Am I adverse to doing minor maintenance and repair work?
6. Do I have any skills that could be used in building a house?
7. What do I want in a house?
8. Can what I want in a house be obtained for what I can afford to pay?
9. Would I be satisfied with something less than what I want if I can't afford what I want? What would this be?
10. Would I rather live in an apartment if I can't get what I want in a house?
11. Do I greatly dislike living in multiunit housing?
12. Is my credit rating good?
13. How much more money am I willing to pay in total to get my monthly mortgage payment down?

14. Can I afford to spend the time necessary to build a house?
15. Am I unhappy and/or dissatisfied unless everything is done just as I want it?
16. Am I impatient?
17. Can I make my mind up and keep it made up?
18. What do I know about building a house?
19. Do I highly value my privacy and peace and quiet?
20. Do I think the people I would like best live in single-family houses?
21. Can I reasonably expect to move frequently?
22. What, if any, differences are there between my answers to these questions and those of members of my family who live with me?

You should answer the following questions before investing in real estate as an income-generating investment:

1. Do I like to gamble, or do I strongly dislike it?
2. Have I the patience to wait many years to discover if a gamble has paid off?
3. Do I have the knowledge and judgment necessary to make reasonable forecasts about real estate values?
4. How much time and effort am I willing to put into this endeavor?
5. Is my credit good?
6. How much do I have available to invest?
7. Can I afford to tie my savings up for many years and, perhaps, lose them?
8. Can I earn the kind of return I'm looking for in real estate?
9. Can I handle the problems a landlord has to face?

How to Use Your Answers

Obviously, the first thing you must do is decide how much you can afford to spend on housing. Then there is the matter of deciding what kind of housing you can obtain for this much money. You can live in a single-family house, a multifamily house, or an apartment. You can either rent or buy. If you buy, you can buy an already constructed new or old house or you can build a home. Your monthly cost and your total cost over a number of years will vary with the type and quality of housing selected and the cost of any borrowed funds utilized, which varies with the rate of interest and the length of the loan period.

If you own your home (and sometimes when you rent), you will be responsible for maintaining both the house and the yard. Are you willing to take on this responsibility? The cost of building a house can be reduced if you do some of the work yourself. Can you? Do you have the necessary skills and knowledge?

Only by building your own home is there much chance of you having exactly what you want. How important is this to you? Some people can hardly bear living in multifamily housing because of the lack of privacy and the noise. In the case of mobile homes, you lack both of these, even though you are not in a multiunit dwelling, if you locate in a mobile home park.

Building your own home is quite time-consuming and requires a great deal of patience. Do you have both? Many decisions are required in building a home; frequently changing them can be quite costly.

Renting is most favorable when you do not plan to stay in one place a long time. There are a variety of costs associated with buying and selling a home, and, if you are frequently doing this, the total amount spent can be substantial. A house may take many months—ever over a year—to sell at an acceptable price or even at a very low price. In the meanwhile, your money is tied up. Real estate is a very illiquid investment.

If you feel that people like yourself do not live in single-family homes, you are not likely to be satisfied living in one. If status is important to you, some types of housing are out. Living in a mobile home doesn't, for example, impart much status, but if your income is rather low and/or you have to move frequently, it may be your only financially possible alternative.

What you can afford depends on your savings, your income, and how much you can borrow. How much you can borrow depends on your credit rating. You can lower your monthly payment on a loan by stretching out the loan, but this will add to your total cost. If you cannot afford what you want, you have to decide what is the least undesirable alternative. If, for example, you can't afford a new house, would you rather buy an old house or live in an apartment?

An investment in real estate may be made either to provide you with a place to live or to provide you with an income. An investment in undeveloped land is very risky, but may be very profitable. It is likely to take many years for this profit to develop. In the meantime your money is tied up in something which will be generating expenses—property taxes at a minimum. Thus, you should find a way to get the property to generate an income while you hold it. You may lease land to a farmer. If the property has housing on it, you can rent it. Being a landlord will take up a lot of time and present you with a variety of problems. Finding new tenants once the old ones have left and repairing and maintaining the buildings and collecting the rent will take up a lot of your time. Do you have it? Can you handle the problems? If you have only a few units, risk is rather high, as a relatively few, short-term vacancies can break you.

Losses through investing in real estate, at least in the short-run, are fairly likely. Can you bear them?

PLANNING FORM 1
Determining How Much To Spend Monthly on a Home

1. Family annual income:

   salaries ____

   bonus, com-
   missions, etc. ____

   interest, divi-
   dends, etc. ____

   other ____

   Less total of:

   income taxes
   (withheld), social
   security, pension
   fund, other ____

   Net annual income ____

   Monthly income
   (net annual
   divided by 12) ____

2. Family annual expenses:
   (excluding housing)

   food ____

   clothing ____

   home furnishings ____

   church and charity ____

   insurance ____

   education ____

   medical ____

   transportation ____

   entertainment ____

   taxes (not with-
   held) ____

   debt payment ____

   other ____

   Total annual expenses ____

   Monthly expenses
   (annual divided by 12) ____

3. Available for housing costs:

   Monthly income ____

   (Monthly expenses) ____

   Difference ____

   (Savings monthly) ____

   Difference (positive)
   available for
   housing.*

   * This has to cover:

   mortgage payment or
   rent, utilities, repairs,
   maintenance, home or
   apartment insurance,
   property taxes.

PLANNING FORM 2
Checklist for Comparing Houses

Assign a number to each house and write in the appropriate number by each characteristic that house meets best.

_____ location (convenience)

_____ location (type neighborhood)

_____ down payment (size)

_____ price

_____ term of mortgage

_____ interest rate

_____ monthly payment

_____ closing costs

_____ property taxes

_____ deed restrictions

_____ floor plan

_____ repairs needed

_____ appearance (interior)

_____ appearance (exterior)

_____ number of rooms

_____ size of rooms

_____ number of bathrooms

_____ heating system (size, quality, type)

_____ cooling system (size, quality, type)

_____ closets (size, number)

_____ appliances (which, quality, etc.)

_____ basement or crawl space (adequate, dry)

_____ type house (one- or two-story, etc.)

_____ lot (shape, drainage, size, etc.)

_____ workmanship

_____ landscaping

_____ construction (type)

_____ materials (quality)

_____ electrical service (amount)

_____ plumbing fixtures (quality, condition)

_____ water heater (size, quality)

_____ lighting fixtures (size, number, quality)

_____ water supply (dependable, safe)

_____ sewerage (type, adequate)

_____ fire protection

_____ linen closet

_____ kitchen (layout, size, appliances available)

_____ pantry

_____ porch or patio

_____ laundry facilities (location, adequate)

_____ dining rom or area (size, location)

_____ carport or garage (size)

_____ roof (quality, age)

_____ insulation (type, amount, location)

_____ driveway (size, type)

_____ attic (usable, quality construction)

_____ fireplaces (safety, adequate)

_____ windows and doors

_____ flooring (durable, looks)

_____ termite-proofing

_____ special features (pool, etc.)

_____ doors (solid, fit)

_____ locks (doors, windows, type)

_____ repairs required

_____ alterations required

_____ other

Investing in Securities

8. Be familiar with what mutual funds have to offer investors.
9. Be familiar with the different types of debt securities.
10. Know how to invest through stock options.
11. Be familiar with the various methods for determining which stocks to invest in.
12. Be familiar with the following terms:

trading on the equity	churning
par value	intrinsic value
discount or premium	technical approach
mortgage bond	random walk theory
municipal bond	diversification
margin call	open-end fund
covered option	closed-end fund
put option	sinking fund
call option	load or no-load funds
short-selling	callable
dollar-cost averaging	

The game of professional investment is intolerably boring and over-exacting to anyone who is entirely exempt from the gambling instinct; whilst he who has it must pay to this propensity the appropriate toll.
　　　　　—JOHN MAYNARD KEYNES, *noted English economist*

Why do I rob banks? Because I enjoyed it. I loved it. I was more alive when I was inside a bank, robbing it, than at any other time in my life. I enjoyed everything about it so much that one or two weeks later I'd be out looking for the next job. But to me the money was the chips, that's all. The winnings. I kept robbing banks when, by all logic, it was foolish. When it could cost me far more than I could possibly gain.
　　　　　—WILLIAM (WILLIE) SUTTON, JR., *noted American bank robber*

I have known a lot of investors who came to the market to make money, and they told themselves that what they wanted was the money: security, a trip around the world, a new sloop, a country estate, an art collection, a Caribbean house for cold winters. And they succeeded. So they sat on the dock of the Caribbean home, chatting with their art dealers and gazing fondly at the new sloop, and after a while it was a bit flat. Something was missing. If you are a successful game player, it can be a fascinating, consuming, totally absorbing experience, in fact it has to be. If it is not totally absorbing, you are not likely to be among the most successful, because you are competing with those who find it so absorbing.

—GEORGE ("ADAM SMITH") GOODWIN, *American financial writer*

Some people like to take chances. Others don't. Some may be compulsive gamblers who destroy themselves just as surely as an alcoholic may. Other people wouldn't put a nickel in a slot machine even if they were multimillionaires and could, therefore, easily afford to lose it or were paupers and badly needed the possible $10,000 payoff:

The most important thing to know about securities investment is whether or not you have the temperament and ability required to invest successfully. If you are lacking somewhat in ability, you can hire others to help you invest, but there is nothing you can do about having the wrong temperament.

Why should you consider investing in securities? You should consider doing so because the federal government, for many years, has held down the return individuals can earn on money in savings accounts. In recent years the return on money in savings accounts has not even covered, before taxes, the loss in the value of the money in the account caused by rising prices! The returns on corporate stocks and bonds and government securities have not always exceeded the rate of inflation either, but these securities have done better than have saving accounts, and there are no government-set ceilings to prevent them from doing better in the future.

Another reason for considering investing in securities is the fact that, after you retire, there is no limit on how much income you can earn on securities without your social security payments being reduced.

For some people investment in securities provides them with their only opportunity to earn a substantial amount of money. You can't make a lot of money with a savings account. Investment in real estate is not practical for many people, because it would tie up too much money over too long a period of time. In addition, a real estate investment also generates constant expenses, such as property taxes, for as long as it is held. It also needs to be managed, and usually many years must pass before much money will be made. A much lesser amount of money and time invested in securities can be equally or more productive.

PROFIT AS CAPITAL'S WAGE

In some parts of the world food is produced on government-owned land; automobiles are manufactured in government-owned factories, and barbers cut hair in government-owned shops. In the United States, however, most goods and services are produced in the private sector, that is, productive resources are privately rather than publicly owned. As a result, Americans enjoy money-making alternatives not available to most of the people in the world.

When a car is sold for more than it cost to pay the automobile workers who built it, those who supplied the materials and utilities used, and those who loaned the automobile company money to pay its bills on time, the car is said to have been sold at a profit. This profit, after taxes are paid to the government, belongs to the owners of the automobile company. Through annual profits the company's owners hope to ultimately get back more money than they have invested in the firm. Thus, they plan to earn a return just as you do when you deposit money in a savings account at a bank and later withdraw a larger amount because interest has been credited to your account. (The bank can pay you this interest because it lends automobile companies and other businesses some of the money you deposit. Thus, by making a deposit in a bank, you are indirectly lending money.)

In communist countries, where the government owns all productive resources, all profits go to the government, rather than only a part of them in taxes, as is the case in the United States. If one of our privately owned companies does not earn a profit, it will eventually go out of business, since its owners will not wish to (and normally can't afford to) bear continual losses. If government-owned, a company, for political reasons, might be allowed to continue to exist despite continual losses. This can take place because tax receipts from privately owned firms or some of the profit from other government-owned companies can be used to cover its losses. If the government does not subsidize such a company, the company will wither away due to a lack of funds to replace facilities as they wear out or become obsolete. *Just as wages enable workers to keep working, profits keep capital working.* (Capital refers to plant and equipment which is acquired with owners' funds.)

Americans each have two money-making options: They can sell their personal services or they can invest, directly or indirectly, in resources which produce a marketable product or service. Unless you are given money by someone else, the money you need for investment will have to be earned by working for a salary or wage. The money you invest will come from that part of your income after taxes which you do not spend on consumption: food, clothes, shelter, entertainment, transportation, and so on. Income after taxes is called disposable income.

You can earn a return on that part of your disposable income which you do not consume either by lending it to others who, in turn, use it to acquire productive resources, or you can acquire the productive resources yourself. In this latter case you are the owner of a business; in the former case your debtor is the owner. You can do either of these directly or indirectly.

An example of direct lending is if you give a friend $500 on the condition he return you $550 a month from now. He, in turn, decides to use this money and $100 of his own money to buy the materials necessary to make 400 sandwiches. (Each sandwich costs him $1.50 to make. This cost includes compensation to him for his own time.) He then sells these sandwiches for $2.00 each in the college dormitories. He will gross $800, enough to pay you your $550 ($500 plus 10 percent interest); get back his $100, and earn a $150 profit. This means he will earn a 150 percent rate of return on his investment of $100 ($150 divided by $100).

He could then repeat the process on a larger scale. He could again borrow $500 from you and use this and his $250 to buy $750 worth of materials for sandwiches. With this amount of materials he could make 500 sandwiches ($750 divided by $1.50). He would gross $1000 from selling them. His profit would be $200 ($1000 less $550 less $250) for an 80 percent rate of return on his investment ($200 divided by $250), a 47 percent reduction in his rate of return.

He could have avoided lowering his rate of return by increasing the size of the loan by the same relative amount his investment increased by, that is, from $100 to $250. To do this he would borrow $1250 and return $1375 to you, which would provide you with the same 10 percent rate of return. He would then be able to make 1000 sandwiches, which he would sell for $2000, giving him a profit of $375 ($2000 less $1375 less $250). This $375 provides him with a 150 percent rate of return on his $250 investment.

On the other hand, you could have gone into the sandwich business yourself with your $500, rather than lending to him so he could go into this business. For $500 you could have obtained the materials for 333⅓ sandwiches. You would gross $666.67 from selling them for $2.00 each, giving you a profit of $166.67, which would provide you a 33.3 percent rate of return on your investment of $500.

INVESTING IS RISKY

Before deciding that you would rather be a borrower than a lender because the fellow who borrows from you to finance a sandwich-making business makes a higher return than you will even if you use this money yourself to go into the sandwich business, consider the fact that he takes a lot more risk than you would. If he can't sell the sandwiches, he still has to pay you your $550. The law requires that borrowers repay loans; it doesn't require that people buy what others want to sell them, that is, consumers are not required to provide sellers profits. Thus, if he can't sell the sandwiches, he will have to sell his car or do whatever else he can do to try and pay you. (If you are a smart lender, you will make sure he has an alternative way to pay before deciding to lend to him.) Unless he can't come up with the money, you will get your $500 back. If you run the business yourself and can't sell the sandwiches, you have lost $500.

Lending to a business is risky, but owning one is more risky. It is safer to earn a return on your money by lending it to a business rather than acquiring an ownership interest in it. As a result, you will normally earn a lower rate of return from lending than owning, because businesses will not have to offer potential creditors as high a rate of return as they will potential owners in order to obtain funds from them.

As the sandwich-making example illustrates, a business can increase the rate of return earned by its owners by borrowing money; thus, most businesses borrow money regularly. This is called *trading on the equity* or *leverage.* (Your creditor earned 150 percent on his investment. With only your funds, you earned 33.3 percent doing the same thing.)

INVESTING THROUGH SECURITIES

There are several ways you can become an owner of a business. If a firm has only one owner, it is called a *sole proprietorship.* This firm's debts are treated as the personal debts of its owner; thus, the owner may have to sell his home in order to pay a business debt. If a firm has several owners, each of which, or several of which, are personally liable for its debts, it is called a *partnership.* Partly because of their personal liability for the partnership's debts, most owners of such businesses, as do most sole proprietors, work in the business. Most people, however, do not want to, or are in no position to, run their own business. Yet, some would like to invest in a business. Because there is also a *corporate* form of organization, it is possible to invest without incurring a personal liability for the business' debts, managing it, or incurring the other drawbacks of a partnership. (Even if you are a partner with limited liability, being a partner has some risks: if a partner dies or wishes to withdraw from the firm, that business firm ceases to exist. This is not the case for owners of a corporation. They can simply will or sell their ownership position to another. Divided authority can also cause problems for partners.)

The most the owners of a corporation can lose is what they invested in the business. Shares of stock are securities provided to those who own the corporation. A *security* is a piece of paper which specifies the rights of ownership. A security is issued to you in exchange for money.

A corporation can only issue a specified number of shares without the approval of all current shareholders. Each like type of share gives its owner an equal claim on the firm's assets and earnings. Usually, if there are, say, 50,000 shares *outstanding* (issued, i.e., purchased), each share entitles its holder to 1/50,000th of after tax profits or, if the firm is liquidated (sold), 1/50,000th of the sale price *after all creditors are paid,* including the tax collector.

A few corporations offer what is called *preferred stock.* The holder of such stock is entitled, if it is earned, to a payment of a fixed or limited size called a *dividend.* If the firm is sold, the holder of a preferred share is entitled, if it is available after creditors of the firm are paid, to the return of his investment in the firm.

All corporations offer what is usually called *common stock. The holder of such a share is not entitled to any given-sized payment, nor is any payment guaranteed.* Common stockholders are entitled to all profits after taxes once preferred stockholders are paid their dividends. If the firm is sold, any excess of proceeds over creditors' and preferred stockholders' claims is divided among common stockholders. Thus, there is no limit to how high the return on common stock may go.

Each share of stock has what is called a *par value.* This does not represent what the share is worth to the buyer of the share. Largely for tax purposes, states require that a par value be set, and corporations set this value with tax problems in mind; not the value of the right to receive dividends or payment upon the sale of the firm, and it is clearly these rights which determine the value of a share of stock. The value of a share depends on the amount of anticipated earnings accruing to the holder.

The fact that a corporation has earned a profit does not mean that dividends must be paid to its owners. A corporation may retain its earnings—keep the funds rather than paying them out to stockholders. Firms should retain earnings only if this will increase their owners' long-term return from owning the stock. If a firm retains earnings, and, as a result, its earnings rise, the price of the owners' shares should rise. If a corporation paid out its profits, its owners would have to pay personal income taxes on this additional income. A gain on the sale of stock will be taxed at the capital gains rate rather than the rate on ordinary income, which is higher.

Owners of shares of common stock control the corporation via their right to elect the board of directors of the corporation. This board sets all corporate policies and appoints its chief officers. Just as the number of shares you own determines what proportion of profits after taxes you are entitled to, so, too, does the number of shares you own determine how many votes you may cast for members of the board of directors.

In addition to stock, which is called an *equity* security, corporations offer *debt* securities called *bonds*. A *bond* is a security which entitles its holder to a series of equally spaced, fixed interest payments which will be paid until the bond's maturity, at which time the par value (face, maturity value) of the bond will be paid. Bonds are unlike stock in that they do have a maturity—termination—date. (Figure 7–1 shows recent investment in stocks and bonds.)

If you buy a bond with a maturity value of $10,000 and an annual interest payment of 10 percent, you will receive $100 annually until the bond matures, at which time you will receive $10,000. Most bonds provide for quarterly interest payments. Bonds may sell for more or less than their maturity value. When this happens, your effective rate of interest will not equal the rate stated in the indenture. An *indenture* is a contract between the issuer and the buyer. If you buy at a *discount* —less than maturity value—the effective rate of interest is higher

TABLE 7–1   How Stockholdings Are Changing

	January 1970	Percentage of Total	January 1977	Percentage of Total
	($ billions)		($ billions)	
Decline in Stock Holdings				
Individuals	$582.1	66.9%	$508.6	53.2%
Mutual funds, investment companies	$ 51.3	5.9	$ 48.9	5.1
Rise in Stock Holdings				
Bank trust funds	$ 84.2	9.7	$103.2	10.8
Private pension funds	$ 61.4	7.0	$109.7	11.5
Foreign investors	$ 26.9	3.1	$ 61.4	6.4
Foundations	$ 20.0	2.3	$ 27.1	2.8
Insurance companies	$ 27.0	3.1	$ 51.6	3.2
State, local retirement funds	$ 7.3	0.8	$ 30.1	3.2
College, educational endowments	$ 7.6	0.9	$ 10.4	1.1
Mutual savings banks	$ 2.5	0.3%	$ 4.4	0.5%
Total	$870.3	100.0%	$955.4	100.0%

Source: Securities and Exchange Commission, 1977.

Note: Investment company shares held by other institutional groups are counted twice, by amounts of $4 billion in 1970 and $10 billion in 1977.

than the stated rate. The reverse is true if you buy it at a *premium*—above the maturity value. The market price of a bond is expressed as a percentage of its maturity value. Thus, a $1,000 bond selling at 98 would sell for $980.

In addition to promising bondholders a periodic interest payment and another payment at the maturity of the bond issue, the issuing (borrowing) corporation often offers security or *collateral*. A common practice is to promise that if the corporation fails to make an interest payment and/or redeem the bond at its maturity, the ownership of certain real estate will pass from the corporation to its bondholders. Such a bond is called a *mortgage bond*.

Other corporate assets (property owned) may also be offered as security, or the corporation may promise to set up a fund called a *sinking fund*, which is a fund created by the corporation by periodically setting aside funds until there is enough to pay off the bond issue at its maturity. Such provisions reduce the risk you take when you purchase a bond. As a result, corporations do not have to offer as high an interest rate when selling these bonds as they would bonds offering buyers no security. If a bond does not offer the bondholder some type of security, it is called a *debenture bond*. Corporations also offer bonds which, in the future, under given conditions, can be converted into stock. They are called *convertible bonds*. A rise in the value of the stock makes conversion attractive, that is, a $1000 bond might, for example, be exchanged for stock now worth $1200.

Rather than you having to keep a close eye on the bond-issuing firm and hiring a lawyer if a problem arises, each bond issue has a *trustee* whose responsibility is to look out after the interests of the bondholders.

GOVERNMENT SECURITIES

Federal, state, and local governments do not offer equity securities, but they do offer negotiable debt securities. State and local securities are particularly attractive because the interest earned on them is exempt from federal taxation. All these securities are usually called *municipal bonds*. Their tax exemption is most important to people with high incomes and, therefore, a high marginal tax rate. If, for example, your marginal tax rate is 50 percent, an 8 percent tax-exempt return would be equal to a 16 percent return subject to tax. If, however, you have borrowed money to make any investment other than your home, you may lose all or part of the interest you pay as a tax-deductible expense if you own municipal bonds, because the loan will be assumed to be financing your municipal bond holdings.

Federal securities are also attractive, but for a different reason. *Short-term, direct debt of the federal government is, for all practical purposes, risk free.* Direct federal debt is that issued by the government itself rather than by its agencies. Direct federal debt is backed both by the government's power to tax and its power to print money—pretty strong backing indeed! Federal agencies' debts are not guaranteed by the federal government, but most investors doubt that the government would allow its agencies to default.

Long-term federal debt is a bit more risky than short-term, because the market price of this debt can vary more due to its longer life. *The price a debt security sells for varies inversely with changes in the interest rate buyers seek.* (When one buys a $10,000 bond for, say, $9,500, the effective rate of interest exceeds the stated rate, which is earned when $10,000 is paid for the bond, because you get interest on $10,000, rather than on the $9,500 you have invested, and you are returned $10,000 rather than $9,500!) Over a long period of time interest rates will change many times; thus; so will a bond's price.

Government securities never provide the buyer with collateral; thus, if a government should default on its debt, you cannot lay claim to any of its property. Many state and local debt securities are, however, secured by a promise to apply certain tax revenues or income from some project like a toll road toward paying principal and interest. The latter is the more risky of the two, as the project being financed may not produce enough revenue to cover the bond issue.

Until recent years great confidence was placed even on local obligations backed by nothing more than the moral obligation of the issuing state or local government. The default of New York City on some obligations has radically changed this!

Federal, short-term securities, such as U.S. Treasury bills, are extremely liquid, that is, they can usually be sold very quickly with very little or no loss. (These are securities; not dollar bills.) Because of the resulting high degree of safety, these securities pay a relatively low interest rate. Thus, people often hold these securities, not as an investment, but as an alternative to holding money, which earns no interest. Buying these securities is a way to earn money on funds which you will soon need to spend.

SPECULATION OR INVESTMENT?

You have to choose between holding a share of stock or a bond and earning dividends or interest, respectively, or selling the security for more than you paid for it. In some cases the choice between selling and holding is easy to make. There may be virtually no market for the security; thus, selling it would mean taking a big loss. For some securities, there is no market.

If you buy securities with the intention of only incidentally collecting dividends or interest, you are said to be a speculator. One who plans to quickly resell a security for more than was paid for it is often depending on fickle, mob psychology, a frail reed to depend on; thus, such a person is called a speculator. In contrast, the investor is one who holds securities for a relatively long period of time, intending to benefit, not from short-term price movements, but from earning dividends or interest, as the case may be. In the case of stock, the investor also hopes she will benefit from a permanent increase in the price of the stock.

Most speculation is in common stock. This is because the price of a share of common stock can rise more than can the price of a bond because of the unlimited return possible on common. Since the speculator takes more risk than does the investor, if speculation is to persist, speculators must average earning a higher rate of return than investors do. In recent years, stock speculation has been much less common than in the past. It is no coincidence that recently there was a unique relationship between bond and stock yields. The former were higher! This situation also reduced total investment in stock (see Figure 7–1).

There are many ways for you to speculate. You can speculate by borrowing some of the money you use to buy stocks. This is called buying on *margin*. (The federal government prevents you from borrowing all of it.) Clearly this adds to the risk you take because, if the price of the stock falls enough, you cannot repay the loan by selling the stock. The smaller the percent of your money in the stock, the smaller is the price decline necessary to prevent repayment of the loan by selling the stock. Even though you think its price will eventually rise, you may have to sell the stock at a loss in order to pay off the loan on time or meet a *margin call*, that is, the lender wants partial repayment early because the value of the loan's collateral, the stock, has fallen.

Another way to speculate in stock is to sell someone an *option* to buy stock from you in the future (at a set price, usually today's) that you don't now own. You are gambling that the price of the stock will, until the end of the option period, remain below the option price; therefore, the option buyer will not exercise his option. The option buyer is counting on the reverse happening; then he can buy the stock from you for less than he can resell it. You will have to buy the stock at better than the option price in order to deliver it to him. There is no limit on how much you may lose on such a deal because there is

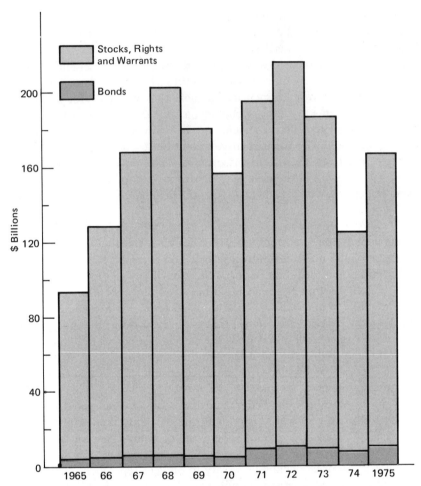

FIGURE 7–1. Market Value of Securities Traded on All U.S. Stock Exchanges, 1965–1975. (U.S. Securities and Exchange Commission, Washington, D.C.)

no limit to how much you may have to pay to get the stock. This maneuver's attractiveness is that if the option is not exercised, you have earned money without making any investment!

Clearly, it is much safer to sell an option to someone to buy stock from you that you already own. This is called selling a *covered option*. If the stock's price doesn't rise above the option price, you will still have the stock and be entitled to dividends, and you will be richer by the amount charged for the option! If the price of the stock rises above the option price, you only lose this gain. Agreeing to sell stock in the future at the option of the buyer is called a *call option*.

You can also sell an option to someone to sell you stock in the future at a fixed price, usually today's. This is called a *put option*. The buyer is hoping to avoid a loss on a stock he owns whose price he thinks will fall. If it does fall, he will exercise the option to sell it to you at the higher option price. You don't think the stock's price will fall; thus, you will simply earn a fee if you are right; otherwise, you will take the loss.

The popularity of both types, but particularly the call option, has grown enormously in recent years, and they are traded on some exchanges. A major reason for the popularity of options is that it takes far less money to invest in options than it takes to invest in stocks, and your yield is higher. (A share of stock may cost, say, $80, but a call on it may sell for $10. If the stock's price rises above the option price by, say $6, the buyer of the call can probably sell it for about $16, providing himself a nice rate of return on his $10 investment!)

A very speculative maneuver is to sell—not just agree to sell—stock you do not own for future delivery. This is called *short-selling*. As when you sell a call, you are counting on the price of the stock falling, that is, you hope to buy for delivery in the future at a price below what you sold the stock for.

A conservative investment strategy is *dollar-cost averaging*. You do this by periodically, like every month, buying a fixed dollar amount of stock. Thus, when prices are low, you obtain more shares than when prices are high. In this way you buy stock at an average price below the average price of the stock over the period of time you were buying. Thus, you are more likely to be able to sell at a gain.

THE MECHANICS OF INVESTING

Most people buy stocks and bonds through a *broker*. A broker usually acts as an *agent* for either a buyer or a seller of securities. He or she seeks someone willing to buy or sell you a security. He or she can buy or sell you the security himself or herself. If he or she does this, he or she is acting as a *dealer*. Brokers also provide investment advice.

Perhaps the most common mistake people make in dealing with a broker is ignoring the fact that his interests sometimes conflict with yours. If he is a party to a sale (i.e., he is the one buying from or selling to you), he has the same conflicting interests any other party you are selling to or buying from has. Also remember that when a broker is trying to talk you into buying from or selling a security to someone other than himself, he is generating a commission for himself in the process. When a broker talks you into buying or selling unwisely, he is said to be *churning* your account.

Obviously, people with securities to sell can simply look around for someone who wants to buy these securities, but this is not very often done. Banks can also handle some security transactions. U.S. Treasury securities can be purchased directly from a Federal Reserve Bank.

If a corporation is quite financially sound and there is a large and active market for its numerous securities, the firm can have its securities *listed* on an exchange such as the New York or American Stock Exchanges, both of which also deal in bonds. You must go through a broker to utilize the services of an exchange. *Stock exchanges do not deal in a security until it has been issued (sold) by the issuing corporation.* Stock exchanges only handle the securities of listed firms and all public sales of listed securities must first be offered on the exchanges. If your broker does not have a *seat* on an exchange (a membership), he or she will have to deal with a broker who does in order to utilize the exchange's services. This adds to your cost. The exchanges serve as a central market for those wishing to buy and sell corporate securities. Via an exchange, buyers and sellers are brought together faster and more cheaply than otherwise would be the case. The prices at which transactions take place on an exchange are made available throughout the nation very shortly after the transactions take place. These prices are an important piece of information for the investor.

Securities transactions which do not take place at an exchange are said to take place in the *over-the-counter market*. All initial sales of a security (i.e., they are sold by the issuer) take place in this market. Although a few corporations sell their securities directly to the public, most sell through brokers. Subsequent sales of nonlisted securities by their holders are also over-the-counter transactions. Listed securities may also move in this market.

The National Association of Securities Dealers has, in recent years, established a network of telephone and teletype wires linking various member brokerage houses, and these brokers are able to provide stiff competition to the exchanges. A variety of recent actions by the federal government's Securities and Exchange Commission has also reduced the competitive advantages, attained via monopoly practices, formerly enjoyed by the exchanges.

Thanks to action by the Securities and Exchange Commission, brokers no longer can get together and set minimum commissions for handling transactions. Thus, you should shop around for a broker both on the basis of ability and fees charged. Whichever broker you deal with, you will have to pay a relatively higher commission for a small than a large transaction. Because of this fact, it is very difficult for the small investor to successfully speculate via frequent buying and selling stock because brokers' commissions often will eat up all but an unusually large price change. Odd-lot dealers offer the individual the best deal.

DECIDING WHEN AND WHAT TO BUY

What and when you buy and sell depends on when and what stocks you can buy for less than they are "worth" or no more than they are worth, and when and what stocks can be sold for more than they are "worth." But how does one measure the "worth" of a share of stock? You could simply say that what something is worth is what someone else will pay for it and, thus, dismiss the subject of valuation, but not if you plan to deal in stock! Clearly, you need to know why people will pay you what they will, because you need to predict what they will pay.

There are many views of how people determine the value of a share of stock. Several have a psychological basis. The *intrinsic value* theory, however, postulates that "real" factors determine a stock's value. The psychological view of how a stock's price is determined can, perhaps, best be explained by example: Often, in the past, two or more persons would acquire, largely with borrowed money, some low-priced stock in a near moribund corporation. They would buy and sell this stock between themselves at an ever higher price. This would attract the interest of speculators, who would rush to buy the stock. The perpetrators of this con game would then sell out their holdings to these speculators, and the price of the stock would plummet.

Why did these speculators buy this stock? The companies involved were invariably ones few people had ever heard of. Nothing about the companies had changed except who owned a lot of their stock, and these people kept their position secret. It is obvious that the reason speculators bought the stock is because its price had risen. They hoped that this would continue long enough for them to make a profit.

If you operate on a psychological basis, you will try to figure out what the crowd will do and get ahead of them in buying and selling. In other words, if you think people are going to decide a stock's price will rise, you buy it now before their buying bids its price up. If you think they are going to decide a stock's price is going to fall, you sell now before their selling causes its price to fall. If everyone followed this policy, then, to be successful, you would have to predict what everyone else is going to predict everyone else is going to predict!

Those who follow this theory say that the concensus view of market trends is always wrong. Thus, what you should do is not follow the concensus. The concensus view is wrong because everybody doing the same thing to make money prevents anyone from making money.

Chartists are stock market analysts who utilize this type of approach. They study charts showing price changes in stocks over time and try to find patterns that they think foretell future prices. This is called a *technical approach.*

What causes something to have value? Suppose I picked up some pine cones and offered them to you. Like stocks, the pine cones probably have no value to you in use. You can't eat or wear them. They are not art objects. In short, they have no value to you unless you can sell them to someone else, who, in turn, would buy them because he could sell them to someone else, and so on. Clearly, something can't be sold unless somebody, somewhere wants it, not to sell, but to keep, or people think some such person or persons exists. If they don't exist, ultimately this will be discovered and the price will drop to zero.

Why would anyone want to hold a share of stock? Obviously, the answer to this is because of the dividends they will receive. Your home provides shelter. Your car provides transportation. *What you get out of owning stock is a monetary return.* Stock is an earning asset, and it is a relatively liquid earning asset—it can be sold quickly, often without substantial loss. It is convenient to hold some of your wealth in a liquid form, and it is certainly better to earn a return than not to. Thus, one often chooses not to hold all liquid wealth in the form of cash, since it earns no return.

It is the *earning power* of stock that causes it to have value. An increase in that earning power causes its price to rise; thus, stocks provide the holder with two types of returns: dividends and capital gains. Stocks also provide speculators (gamblers) with a medium other than real estate, sports betting, and so forth.

People who accept the intrinsic value theory believe that, at least in the long run, what determines the value of a stock is the size and timing of the issuing firm's anticipated future earnings and the risk associated with these earnings. They believe that in order to predict earnings, you need to study the firm's financial statements, markets, competition, plans, and managers. You would buy a stock, according to this theory, when projected earnings justify a market price higher than its current price and sell when the reverse is true, because you would anticipate that ultimately the market will realize that the stock is, respectively, under- or overvalued. When this happens, prices will rise or fall, respectively. Some studies support this view; they indicate that, in the long run, stock prices do reflect future earnings adjusted both for risk and how far in the future they lie.

In recent years some academicians have done mathematical studies of the stock market which indicate that the stock market is a *random walk*—one can no more predict fluctuations in a stock's price than predict what number will come up on a "fair" roulette wheel.

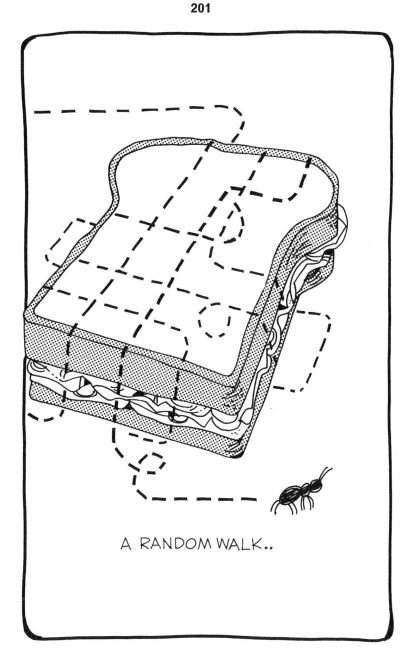

A RANDOM WALK..

Studies show that over the long run individual investors, as a whole, have lost money in the stock market. In contrast, institutional investors have, as a whole, made money. Studies indicate, however, that no institutional investor has consistently done better than the market as a whole, that is, no institution's dividends and capital gains have been greater than those achieved by the average share in the long run. This is the result one would expect if the random walk theory is true. Some observers, however, dispute this work.

If the random walk theory is true, the best an investor can hope for is to do as well as the market does in the long run. This is done by buying and holding some of every stock available in the market. How much of each stock to buy depends on what percent of the total available shares this stock accounts for. Because there are so many stocks in the market, doing this is extremely expensive; thus, it is not possible. An alternative is to randomly select the shares you will buy from all stocks traded in the market. It is very likely that such a group of shares will very closely mirror the performance of the entire market, as below-average performers you happen to pick will, in the long run, be offset by above-average performers you will pick. In other words, over the long run you are unlikely to select relatively more "bad" than "good" stocks using a random selection process.

If you do not randomly select your stocks, one or the other of the groups (better- or worse-than-average performers) will very likely be overrepresented, and, according to the random walk theory, you are just as likely to over represent the worse performers as the better ones. Some argue, however, that, while you can't accurately pick winners, you certainly should be able to pick likely losers, and eliminate them from your portfolio. Therefore, your portfolio of stocks would perform better than the market as a whole.

MUTUAL FUNDS

The main things mutual funds offer you are *diversification,* which reduces risk, and professional managment of your securities portfolio. A mutual fund takes the money it gets from selling its own shares of stock and invests it in stocks, bonds, or other securities. By collecting the funds of many people, the mutual fund is able to invest in many more different companies' securities than would any of its investors. This reduces risk because it is much more likely that the stock of, say, five companies will decline in value at the same time than it is that the stock of, say, 500 will decline simultaneously.

In addition to offering diversification, mutual funds hold out the hope that you will earn a higher return because mutual funds engage professionals to determine when and what to buy and sell and, presumably, they can do a better job than most people. Because they deal in large blocks of stocks, they can also obtain lower brokerage commissions than can an individual. Studies show that the average fund hasn't, over the long run, beat the market average, but it has beat the individual investor. Transaction costs—trading costs—seem to have been the chief factor preventing achieving the market average.

Because some studies have shown that, in the past, randomly selected groups of stock bought and held would have outperformed the average mutual fund, a few mutual funds have been converted into so-called index funds, and some new funds have started as index funds. An *index fund* follows an investment strategy dictated by the random walk theory. Index funds try to match some index of market performance. Few funds take this route. Some of the funds that do simply invest part of their money in this way.

A mutual fund may be either a load or a no-load fund. It may be either open-end or closed-end. The *no-load* fund employs a few salesmen and does little or no advertising. A *load fund* has a number of salesmen and advertises extensively, and, as a result, levies a charge when you first invest in it. A no-load fund does not levy this charge. A *closed-end fund* is one which can only issue a limited number of shares. An *open-end fund* can issue an unlimited number of shares. Some observers think the poor performance of some open-end funds is due to the unrestrained growth this led to.

A closed-end fund's shares can be sold by the investor like any other stock. This is not true of an open-end fund's shares, which can be liquidated only by being redeemed by the mutual fund. Thus, with a closed-end fund you risk being unable to sell your shares when you want to. On the other hand, the investor in an open-end fund, which can sell an unlimited number of shares, risks his or her fund acquiring funds faster than it can increase its earnings; thus, reducing earnings per share. Another risk of the open-end fund is that there will be such a flood of redemption requests that they cannot be met.

No-load funds have performed as well as load funds, but it is difficult to find a no-load fund. About 90 percent of mutual fund investors are in load funds.

There are all kinds of mutual funds, and new types keep springing up. Some invest only in stocks, others invest in both stocks and bonds. Some invest only in government securities, while others invest only in the safest stocks—the so-called *blue chip* stocks. Some mutual funds invest in stocks expected to show large capital gains. Others invest in those expected to pay high dividends. Thus, you should be able to find a mutual fund that follows an investment strategy you agree with.

HOW TO SELECT BONDS

In recent years corporate stocks have been widely discarded as a road to easy riches. (The figures in Table 7–1 suggest that the recent poor performance of stocks is driving the individual investor from the market.) Thus, it may be a good time to get into stock, since one doesn't make a lot of money very often by doing what everyone else is doing!

(Stocks are not overvalued when few are buying them!) Nonetheless, the reaction of many has been to switch to the bond market. They seem to have decided that, if you can't have riches, you might as well at least have safety. Bond yields have also been usually high.

In addition to the poor performance of stocks in recent years, there was also the debacle of the real estate investment trusts. Options and commodity futures contract are very complex. All this played a role in the bond market assuming a much greater importance than ever before. Yet, investment in bonds is not without its problems. Bonds may be callable and, thus, if interest rates decline, your high-yielding bond will be *called*—redeemed before maturity by the issuer. (You should protect yourself from this by paying less for a callable bond than you would pay for a noncallable bond.)

Corporate bonds are usually sold in multiples of $1000. It is rare for a bond to be denominated as low as $1000; therefore, the small investor can obtain more diversification with stocks because, on the average, they cost far less per share than a bond.

The small investor can avoid the rather stiff sales commissions on small bond transactions by buying bonds only when they are originally offered, as no sales commission will have to be paid. (Bonds are initially offered by their issuer—the borrowing firm. Buyers from the issuer may resell them. Such sales involve sales commissions. The fewer bonds involved, the relatively larger is this commission.)

Before buying a bond you should consult one or both of the bond rating services: *Moody's* or *Standard and Poor*. Good sources of investment information for either the bond or stock buyer are: *The Wall Street Journal, The New York Times, Barron's, The Commercial and Financial Chronicle, Business Week, Forbes, Fortune, Standard and Poor's Outlook, Moody's Stock Survey*, the *Value Line Investment Service*, and *Wall Street Transcripts*.

The opinions of the rating services may differ, so it is probably a good idea to consult both. Bonds that merit one of the top four ratings are called *investment grade* securities. This means there is virtually no speculative element involved in investing in them. Those bonds rated seventh or more are predominantly speculative.

WHICH KIND OF SECURITY SHOULD BE INVESTED IN?

Your needs and objectives determine what kind of security you should invest in. You invest in securities rather than putting your money in a savings account because you need to earn a higher return. Table 7–2 shows how your return may vary depending on what you invest in. (Shown are various representative groups of securities.) It also illustrates how returns vary over time.

TABLE 7–2   Bond and Stock Yields Percent: 1950 to 1975

Class	1950	1955	1960	1965	1970	1975
Bonds						
U.S. Government[1]	2.32%	2.84%	4.01%	4.21%	6.50%	6.98%
Municipal (Standard & Poor's, 15 bonds)	1.98	2.53	3.73	3.27	6.50	6.89
Municipal (Bond Buyer, 20 bonds)	1.90	2.49	3.51	3.28	6.34	7.08
Corporate, by years to maturity:[2]						
5 years[3]	1.90	2.70	4.73	4.29	8.10	7.70
10 years	2.30	2.80	4.60	4.33	8.00	8.00
20 years	2.48	2.95	4.55	4.35	7.60	8.35
30 years	2.58	3.04	4.55	4.37	7.60	8.35
Corporate (Moody's Investors Service)	2.86	3.25	4.73	4.64	8.51	9.46
Industrials (40 bonds)[4]	2.67	3.19	4.59	4.61	8.26	9.25
Railroads (29 bonds)	3.10	3.34	4.92	4.72	8.77	9.39
Public utilities (40 bonds)	2.82	3.22	4.69	4.60	8.67	9.88
Stocks						
Preferred (Standard & Poor's, 10 stocks)[5]	3.85	4.01	4.75	4.33	7.22	8.36
Common (Standard & Poor's):						
Composite (500 stocks)	6.57	4.08	3.47	3.00	3.83	4.13
Industrials (425 stocks)	6.69	3.97	3.36	2.94	3.62	3.96
Railroads (15 stocks)	6.55	4.82	5.72	4.33	6.22	5.92
Public utilities (60 stocks)	5.78%	4.57%	3.89%	3.24%	5.81%	8.74%

Source: Except as noted, U.S. Bureau of Economic Analysis. Monthly data from *Survey of Current Business.*

[1] For 1950, average yield on taxable bonds due or callable after 15 years; thereafter, on those due or callable in 10 years or more. Data from Board of Governors of the Federal Reserve System.

[2] For 1950, estimated yields prevailing on highest grade issues in first quarter of year; thereafter, in February only. Through 1955, from National Bureau of Economic Research, New York, N.Y.; thereafter, Scudder, Stevens & Clark, New York, New York, N.Y.

[3] More than usually liable to error.

[4] Number of issues as of January 28, 1974; number varies for earlier years.

[5] Yields based on number of stocks and determined from average of median yields as follows: 1950 to 1965 (Sept. 8), 14 stocks, 8 yields; beginning September 9, 1965, 10 stocks, 4 yields. Issues converted to a price equivalent to $100 par and a 7 percent annual dividend before averaging.

You invest in securities rather than real estate because it is difficult to sell real estate quickly without taking a big loss, and you have to pay property taxes whether or not the property is generating any income. You invest in securities rather than commodity futures contracts because they are less risky and require less specialized knowledge.

The need for a steadier income is probably the main reason for selecting preferred stock or bonds rather than common stock. With these fixed-income securities you can make reliable estimates of each year's return over a long period of time. (While, normally, preferred stock dividends and bond interest are not greater than the dividends on common stock, in recent years the yield on these securities has often been higher. This has not been offset by higher capital gains on common stock, which would be expected.) Greater safety of principal is another reason for selecting fixed-income securities. Risk is less than with common stock because preferred dividends and bond interest are more likely to be paid than are common dividends, and these securities' price fluctuations cover a narrower range. In addition, if the issuing firm fails, fixed-income securities have a prior claim on the proceeds from the liquidation of the firm's assets.

Bonds are selected in preference to preferred stock because they are less risky. Unlike preferred dividends, interest must be paid at fixed points in time. The principal amount must be returned if this is possible. All bondholders have a prior claim on the proceeds of liquidation of the firm's assets in case of bankruptcy over preferred stockholders. Some bondholders have a specific asset pledged to them in case of bankruptcy. If the proceeds of liquidating this asset do not cover what bondholders are owed, the proceeds of liquidation of unpledged assets go to cover their remaining claim before preferred stockholders get anything.

Common stocks are chosen over bonds and preferred stocks because of the higher return possible via either holding the stock or speculating with it. Over the very long run, common stocks would have provided you with a much higher return than either preferred stock or bonds. Common stocks have traditionally been seen as protection against inflation. The logic behind this belief is that as prices rise, profits and, therefore, common's dividends will rise. Recent experience, however, suggests that common stocks only protect you against moderate inflation.

INTRASTATE SECURITIES

Corporations which plan to sell stocks and/or bonds to persons who are residents of more than one state will, unless very few securities are involved, have to register these securities with the U.S. Securities and Exchange Commission. This registration protects the potential investor because a variety of conditions have to be met before a security issue can be registered, and these conditions cannot be met by an outright con artist. A large amount of financial data has to be provided the SEC, and much of this data will have to be provided each potential investor in what is called a *prospectus*. A variety of other useful data, including a warning, if appropriate, that the security is highly speculative, also has to be included in the prospectus.

If, however, a security's sales are to be restricted to one state, the issuing corporation does not have to register with the SEC. Each state has security laws that a corporation has to meet, but they are usually less strict than are the federal security laws. Supervision is also often more lax. Thus, it is more risky to buy a security that is not registered with the SEC. Selling an unregistered security is more difficult because there is a limited market for them. Unregistered securities, therefore, are likely to sell at lower prices; thus, only a few dollars' increase in price will produce a much greater rate of return on your investment than is the case, as rule, with registered securities. This is simply another of the many examples of how the return and risk of investments is inversely correlated.

Another correlation frequently found in investing is the one between greed and loss. Many investors won't quit when they are ahead— they wait too long to sell and so they sell at a loss. Another common mistake is an unwillingness to admit you have made a mistake; thus, you hold a security until it becomes worthless, rather than cutting your losses when it becomes evident you have a "dog." You must, however, be careful to distinguish between this and too easily becoming discouraged and selling an eventual winner.

CASES FOR DISCUSSION

Case 1 Joe Clay has come to you for advice. He tells you the following story. Joe is a motorcycle enthusiast. A few months ago he was at a motorcycle race and met a fellow who introduced himself as Barney Weil, a partner in a motorcycle dealership. He told Joe that a mechanic who works for him has designed a motorcycle using largely aluminum and fiberglass parts that could revolutionize motorcycling. It could be quickly and inexpensively produced and would be exceptionally fast. The problem is that Weil, his partner, and the mechanic need money to develop the idea. Joe, who has $10,000 in savings, expressed interest in seeing the mechanic's drawings and talking with him. Weil invited him and several others interested in investing in the motorcycle, which would be assembled from parts supplied by various manufacturers, to meet with the mechanic, Bill Norman. Joe was impressed and decided to buy 250 shares at $20 each in a corporation Weil had obtained a state charter for. A building was rented and Norman began assembling a prototype, working in the evenings and on Saturday. Recently Joe was approached by Weil, who told him expenses were running ahead of what had been expected, and asked if he would be willing to buy two or three hundred more shares. What advice would you give Joe? Why?

Case 2 Your local television station has been running a lot of advertisements for some thrift notes that pay 9.25 percent interest. The ads are run several times a day and feature several well-known football players. Several friends have mentioned them to you, remarking on what a great deal it sounds like. This is a lot more than you can make on a savings account, they point out. It's almost as much as you can expect to make on most stock in the long run. Only residents of your state can invest in the notes. You decide to talk to one of the company's representatives. You ask how they can afford to pay such a high interest rate, and she tells you that they are investing the money they get for the notes in second mortgages. Should you invest in the notes? Why or why not?

Case 3 Assume your father is 50 years old. He is in a first-level supervisory position with the U.S. Post Office. He makes $18,000 a year. You are the youngest of three children. He has made no plans for retirement but he has a government pension plan. He will have paid up the mortgage on his home in five more years. He bought it 15 years ago for $22,000. Similar homes in this area are selling for around $40,000. He has $8,000 in a savings account. Your mother doesn't work. He asks you what you think he should do to try to assure himself and your mother adequate retirement income to maintain their current standard of living and do some traveling. Should he invest in stocks? Bonds? A mutual fund? What stocks? What bonds? What type of mutual fund? Why?

Case 4 Bart Gumpert is the most conservative fellow you have ever known. He has worked hard for several years in the job he got right after he finished college. He manages a small, fast-food outlet, which is part of a national chain. He likes his work and is pretty good at it, but it is obvious he will probably never do much better than he does now. Bart grew up poor, and he has a burning desire to be rich. He believes that you will never get rich by working "for the other guy," but he is afraid to go into business for himself. Thus, he has decided that the stock market is the only answer. He respects your judgment and would like to hear what you think he should do. He makes $13,000 a year and has saved $4,000. His only child is 6 months old. Presently his wife, a secretary, doesn't work.

Case 5 Your grandmother left you some electric utility stock that could be sold for $5,000. You recently got married, and your spouse wants you to sell the the stock so the money can be used as a down payment on a house. Both of you work for modest salaries. You plan to have a family. Both of you have company pension plans and Social Security. You have $1,000 in a savings account. You are both looking for new jobs which, unlike your current jobs, require a college degree, something the two of you have recently acquired. If you get the type of jobs you are trained for, your combined annual earnings will be approximately $20,000. Your new employers will probably be partnerships which do not have employee pension plans. In the new jobs, you expect after ten years to be earning nearly twice as much as when you started, not considering inflation. What should you do? Why?

Case 6 Pat Slovik was the most adventurous girl in your high-school class. After a tour of duty with the army, which sent her to Europe, she took a job with one of the wire services in Europe. A vacationing TV executive met her at a party and gave her a job at a local TV news show as an on-the-air newscaster. The job had more glamour than pay, but it gave her exposure and she landed a network job. Now she is making big money, and a broker says he can multiply it several times in the stock market. He knows of several small companies in the electronics industry which he thinks have great prospects. Their products are good, and the market in recent years was very receptive to the stocks of high-technology firms. Her mother has told you all about this and the fact that she plans to warn her daughter against following the broker's advice. She wants you to help her. What would you advise? Why?

Case 7 Shelia MacDonald makes $8,000 a year as a home economist for an electric utility. Her husband Bob is an accountant making $15,000. Bob's father is a foreman in an automobile assembly plant. He thinks investing in stocks and bonds is for rich "Wall-Street types." Shelia's father is a physician and has invested in stocks and bonds for years. He has advised the MacDonalds to regularly invest some money in "blue chip" stocks and top-rated bonds in order to provide themselves with security in their old age and a source of funds to finance a college education for the children they plan to have. Bob's father says to put their money in savings bonds and savings accounts. Who's advice should they follow and why?

REVIEW QUESTIONS

1. Why is investing in stocks more risky than investing in bonds?
2. What kind of needs are best served by investment in bonds?

3. What kind of needs are best served by investment in stocks?
4. In what ways is preferred stock like bonds? Like common stock?
5. What is the difference between the investor and the speculator?
6. How does one go about speculating in the stock market?
7. What do you think determines the market price of a share of stock?
8. What are the advantages in investing in a mutual fund?
9. What is the reason for diversifying your investment in stocks?
10. What investment strategy does the random walk theory suggest?

YOUR PLAN: CHAPTER 7

**Questions you must answer in order
to decide whether to invest and how
to invest in stocks and/or bonds:**

1. How dependent am I upon investment income?
2. How much money can I afford to invest?
3. How much money can I afford to lose?
4. How much risk am I able and willing to take financially and temperamentally?
5. Am I patient enough to pursue long-term goals?
6. How much do I know or am likely to learn about investing in stocks and bonds?
7. What needs will an income from such an investment serve?
8. What investment strategy do I agree with?
9. How can I carry out this investment strategy?
10. Is the risk I am willing to take in line with the return I want to earn, or must one take more risk than this to earn the return I desire?
11. Am I temperamentally suited to speculate?
12. Will I give up investing if I suffer some losses?
13. Will my immediate family support me in investing?
14. What will I do if my investments go sour?

How to Use Your Answers

Your attitude toward investment is influenced by how important it is to you. If you do not need investment income very badly and do not like the idea of investing, the situation is quite different than if you did badly need this income, but did not like the idea of investing. In the first case you probably shouldn't invest, but you may have to in the second case.

You should never invest so much money that you do not have enough left to handle regular living expenses: food, clothing, shelter, recreation, insurance, and savings. The inclusion of savings may surprise you, but it would be difficult to successfully invest if you must periodically liquidate your investments in order to handle emergency expenditures.

You should not invest when the maximum possible loss is more than you can afford. You should not invest or not invest in certain ways if investing or certain investments will result in constant worry. Impatience and successful investing don't go together. You don't need a broker churning your account to ruin you if you are going to churn it yourself by constantly buying and selling when you don't get fast results. It is highly likely that it will take several years for your investments to show a good return. Can you bear to wait?

Unless you are quite knowledgeable, you are unlikely to be a successful investor—you will be competing with many people who are quite knowledgeable; many of whom are in a better position financially and informationwise than you are. Your only solution to this problem is to hire someone to make investment decisions for you. Paying someone, of course, will reduce the return you earn. Are you willing to trust someone else's judgment?

What you should invest in depends on more than what return you want to earn and how much risk you are willing to take. It also depends on what your needs are. If, for example, you need a steady additional source of income, bonds are better than stocks. Bonds are also better if you do not wish to take much risk. Your return, however, will probably be less over the long run. You may have to scale down your earning anticipations if you are not willing to take the necessary risk.

If you love to gamble, a mutual fund that only invests in government securities or corporate bonds is not appropriate. It would be like playing hearts when you could be playing poker. Mutual funds of this type are for people who want to play it safe. Direct investment in stocks is appropriate for those who like to gamble. Your method of investment should suit your personality.

Since successful investment is a long-term process and some losses are likely, there is no sense starting if you will quit as soon as you lose some money. It is risky to invest if your husband or wife is violently opposed to investing because this is likely to cause you to either push too hard for results or to be too cautious in order to prove, respectively, that you can earn money or that you won't lose money.

Never start anything without planning an escape. Things don't always pan out right. There are good and bad ways of getting out of a bad situation. Plan a good one.

Commodities: The Fastest Game in Town

OBJECTIVES

When you have completed this chapter, you will have accomplished the following:

1. Know what commodity futures contracts are.
2. Be aware of the risks associated with speculation in commodities contracts.
3. Know why your potential return in commodity futures contracts can far exceed that of stocks.
4. Know how to hedge.
5. Understand the difference between futures contracts and forward contracts.
6. Know what offsetting is.
7. Know what arbitrage is.

8. Understand the difference between a long and a short contract.
9. Know what a commodity option is.
10. Know how to go about participating in this market.
11. Be familiar with the various trading philosophies.
12. Be familiar with the following terms:

spot price	liquidating sale
standard contract	fundamental approach
margin	technical approach
commodities	volume
exchange	moving average method
round turn	

Sophisticated speculators with a substantial amount to invest who crave fast action, high leverage, and the chance to make a lot of money quickly, will find commodity futures contracts far more to their liking than common stock. Speculation in the *commodity futures markets* involves betting on whether or not the price of certain commodities will rise or fall from a given level. While speculating in commodity futures is very risky, some agribusinessmen and farmers use commodity futures to reduce their overall risk. They do this by *offsetting* an anticipated loss in the value of inventories of commodities they hold with gains made by betting with people who have the opposite view of the future. (If they lose a bet, this is offset by a gain in the value of an inventory.)

Price fluctuations in commodities make those in the stock market look tame by comparison, and the use of much more leverage greatly magnifies the impact of given price fluctuations on the commodities speculator as compared to the stock market speculator. The risk involved in investing in commodity futures is so great that they most certainly cannot be considered a prudent use of your funds. (That old risk-return trade-off again!) Such a use of your funds usually cannot be treated in a passive manner, as when you buy and hold stock for many years. Assuming you do not take a "know-nothing," random walk approach, to wisely invest in commodities requires much more specialized knowledge than is required to invest in stock.

Because of the high degree of risk and the specialized knowledge required to intelligently invest in commodity futures, until recent years these markets were not considered suitable for the average investor; thus, no effort was made to promote such investment. The below-average performance of the stock market over the last decade and the much better performance of the commodity markets, however, caused brokers to reexamine their policy vis-a-vis the commodity markets. As a result, many of them have begun promoting investment in the commodity markets for those well-heeled investors who, if they invested in stocks, would be looking for substantial and rapid price appreciation. Like investors in commodity futures, this type of stock investor is simply betting on future prices, but he does, unlike the speculator in commodity futures, acquire an income-generating asset in the process.

Economists do not consider commodity futures an investment; whereas, they do consider the purchase of stock from the issuing corporation an investment. (Investment, economists say, increases the economy's productive capacity.) The economist would classify acquiring a commodity futures contract as gambling. This is why some people are leary of engaging in commodity trading. Yet, life itself is a gamble. Everyone gambles, whether he or she wants to or not. On the other hand, this does not mean one should not minimize or limit gambling.

THE MECHANICS OF COMMODITY TRADING

On the surface, speculating in the commodity markets may seem no different from playing "the numbers" (sometimes called "the bug"), except that it is legal. There is, however, no logic to the numbers game. It is simply a chance process. In contrast, *commodity prices are largely determined by supply and demand.* Comparing the numbers game with the commodity markets is like comparing picking what number will turn up when a roulette wheel is spun with predicting the price a given car will sell for two months from now. However, some argue that commodity prices are, for practical purposes, identical to roulette numbers, because one can't predict fluctuations in them. (This will be discussed later.)

Among the commodities in which you can speculate are live cattle, corn, cotton, Ginnie Mae certificates, gold, live hogs, frozen pork bellies, silver, soybeans, sugar, 90-day U.S. Treasury Bills, and wheat. (Ginnie Mae certificates are debt securities issued by an agency of the federal government.) Speculation on these and others is carried out on several exchanges and privately. Originally, only commodities in the usual sense (i.e., cotton and wheat) were traded. Because the marketing of agricultural commodities is centered in the Midwest, this is where most commodity exchanges are located. The successful promotion of commodities markets speculation by brokers, including both those who used to deal only in or largely in stocks, and those who always dealt in commodities, has largely accounted for the recent addition of trading in securities such as Ginnie Mae certificates and 90-day U.S. Treasury bills. People who are used to buying and selling securities often find these to be the most attractive commodities in which to speculate because they only have to switch from buying a security (which means they are betting on a profit by selling it for more than they paid for it, or by selling it short), to simply betting that a security's price will rise or fall. This bet is made through what is called a *futures contract*. You either buy a contract in which you agree to accept delivery of a fixed quantity of the commodity at a fixed future date at a fixed price, or you sell a contract in which you agree to deliver a fixed quantity of the commodity at a fixed future date at a fixed price. Very rarely is delivery made. If the contract price is less than what the commodity can be bought for at the time of delivery, the buyer and seller may simply cancel the contract via the seller of the commodity, paying the buyer the difference between the contract price and the *spot price* (current market price of the commodity.) This, of course, is what the buyer would earn by paying the contract price to the seller and taking delivery of the commodity and selling it for the higher, spot price. It is also what the seller would lose by buying the commodity at the spot price so as to make delivery and collect the lower contract price. (The buyer would pay the seller if the spot price was lower.)

Most commodity market speculators lose money on most trades, but, when they make money, they may make a very lot of money, and they do so in a very short period of time. In three months they often may make, say, a 25 percent return on their money. This is an annual rate of 100 percent! Sometimes a fortune is made overnight.

THE DIFFERENCE BETWEEN SPECULATION AND HEDGING

You *speculate* when you sell a contract in which you promise to deliver a commodity in the future that you don't currently own and will never deliver. You also speculate when you buy such a contract and don't accept delivery. You *hedge* when you sell a contract in which you promise to deliver a commodity in the future which you do currently own, whether or not you make delivery. You also hedge when you buy a contract in which you promise to buy a commodity in the future which you currently hold a stock of, whether or not you accept delivery. If delivery is not made, hedging involves speculation.

Say you are a farmer with his fields full of not-yet-ripe wheat. If it was ready for market, you could sell it for $40,000 because the spot price of wheat is $4 a bushel, and you have 10,000 bushels. The spot price when you are ready to sell may be more or less than $4. Suppose that you think that it will be $3. Because you expect price to fall, you might sell a futures contract promising to deliver 10,000 bushels at $4 a bushel at the time when you will be selling your crop. (The buyer of your contract, of course, expects the price to rise.) Suppose you are right and the spot price is $3. Rather than taking delivery at $4 a bushel and selling at $3 a bushel, it is easier and cheaper for the buyer to simply pay you $10,000 and cancel the contract. You sell your wheat for $30,000. Thus, your winnings and the sale of your wheat nets you $40,000. *By entering into a futures contract, you lock in the current spot price. You shift the risk of a change in the spot price onto the speculator.* (If the price had risen to, say, $5 per bushel, you would still have net proceeds of $40,000. You would sell the wheat for $50,000 and pay the buyer $10,000.) *There is a cost to avoiding this risk.* You give up the benefit of a price increase

Now, let's suppose you are a flour miller who buys wheat. You bought your current wheat inventory of 10,000 bushels for $4 a bushel. You are concerned that you will have to pay $5 a bushel to replace this inventory. Thus, you buy a futures contract from a speculator who promises delivery of 10,000 bushels at $4 a bushel. Suppose that at the time of delivery the spot price is $5. The speculator will cancel the contract by paying you $10,000, which is what he would lose by buying at $5 to sell to you 10,000 bushels of wheat at $4. You would replace your inventory at a cost of $50,000, for a net outlay of $40,000. Thus, you have locked in the current spot price for your future purchase, just as the farmers do for their sales.

Since the farmer and the miller had opposite forecasts of future price changes, they could have done business with each other and let delivery take place. When this occurs, the contract is simply said to be a *forward contract*. A futures contract is merely a form of forward contract where neither party actually plans to deal in the commodity being traded. (Much commotion was caused in the potato futures market when a trader, who believed that the spot price was being rigged by those he had contracted with, failed to cancel his contracts, but was unable to buy enough potatoes to make delivery by the due date.)

When you speculate or hedge in commodities like sugar and cotton, you are betting on changes in the price of these commodities per pound. *When you speculate or hedge in commodities like Ginnie Mae certificates and Treasury bills, you are betting on changes in interest rates.* If you buy a $1000, 90-day Treasury Bill for $980.39 and hold it until is it redeemed 90 days later by the Treasury, which will pay you $1000, you have earned a 2 percent quarterly rate of return. This is an 8 percent annual rate of return. If, instead, you had sold this bill in the market for $986.92 after holding it for one month, you would have earned a 0.67 percent monthly rate of return. This is an 8 percent annual rate of return. If, however, buyers demand more than an 8 percent annual rate of return—interest rates change—one month after you buy the bill, you will not be able to sell it for as much as $986.92; thus, you would earn less than 8 percent. If you think that interest rates will rise, you can hedge against the loss you would suffer by selling before the maturity of the bill by entering into a futures contract. You would sell your promise to sell at $986.92 one month from now. Thus, if bills are then selling for, say $984.00, the buyer will pay you $2.92, which, when added to the $984.00 you get when you sell the bill you hold, will provide you with an 8 percent annual rate of return on your investment of $980.39.

Ginnie Mae certificates are debt securities issued by the Government Home Mortgage Association to finance their purchase of home mortgages from the financial institutions (such as savings and loan associations) that made them. This is a federal agency, and the mortgages it buys are insured by the government; thus, these certificates are of extremely low risk. Treasury bills are, for practical purposes, riskless. Fluctuations in the prices of these securities, therefore, reflect only changes in investors' desired rate of return on a virtually riskless investment; not changes in their estimate of the risk involved in holding these securities, which would cause them to demand a different rate of return.

LIMITING YOUR LOSS

Suppose you have agreed to sell 10,000 bushels of wheat three months from now at $4 a bushel. A month after you make this contract, the spot price of wheat rises to $5 a bushel and you think it will continue to rise over the next two months. You can limit your loss to the $1 a bushel it currently stands at by entering another contract in which you agree to buy 10,000 bushels in two months at $5 a bushel. Your original contract was a *short contract,* that is, you agreed to sell. You limit your loss on it by making an offsetting *long contract*—you agree to buy. (The reason why this offset is not total is because this is likely to be the case: If you earlier agreed to sell at $4, and the price has risen to $5, and you think this rise will continue, it is very unlikely anyone will agree to sell to you at $4. The current spot price is likely

the lowest figure you can obtain.) To understand commodity futures trading you must keep in mind that going short is selling and "going long" is buying.

Suppose that three months after entering the original contract the spot price rises to $6. You will lose $2 on each bushel in the original contract, but you will make $1 a bushel on the second contract. Thus, you have limited your loss to the $1 per bushel level it stood at one month after you made the first contract. Now suppose that, instead, the spot price fell to $3. You would make $1 on the first contract, but you would lose $2 on the second contract. Thus, even if your price expectation is wrong and price falls rather than rises, your loss is still limited to $1. *You can also use offsetting to lock in a profit.*

Spot and futures prices move together because of arbitrage. Because a rise or fall in one is soon reflected by the same movement in the other, you cannot expect to completely offset the loss you have, to date, experienced on a contract. Instead, as illustrated above, you can only expect to limit it; hopefully, to its current level. *Arbitage* refers to the process by which the prices of a given commodity in different markets are held in line, that is, variances are explained by transportation costs in the case of spot prices and by storage costs in the case of spot and futures prices. For example, if corn is selling in New York for $3.50 a bushel and for $3.00 a bushel in Chicago, and it costs $.25 to ship a bushel of corn from Chicago to New York, you can make a profit of $.25 a bushel by buying in Chicago and selling in New York. You would pay $3.00 to buy in Chicago and $.25 to ship it to New York, where you would sell for $3.50. People buying in Chicago to sell in New York will increase demand in Chicago and increase supply in New York. The former will raise the price per bushel in Chicago, and the latter will lower the price per bushel in New York. This process would come to a halt once the price difference between the two cities was reduced to $.25. In other words, if people in New York decide to increase their use of corn, raising its price in New York, this will cause people in Chicago to ship corn to New York, which will raise its price in Chicago until there is no profit in shipping corn to New York.

This same process works in the futures markets. In the futures markets variances between futures prices and spot prices are based, not on transportation, but storage costs. If, for example, the spot price of cocoa is $1 a pound, and its futures price three months from now is $2 a pound, and it costs $.50 to store cocoa three months, people will buy cocoa at $1 and store it for delivery at $2, since later they will make a $.50 profit per pound. The resulting increase in demand for cocoa will raise its spot price, and the increasing demand for long positions (offers to sell will proliferate) will lower the futures price; thus, reducing the spread between spot and futures prices. People will stop buying futures with the intent of making delivery once the variance between spot and futures prices doesn't exceed storage costs. Clearly, therefore, people dealing in the futures markets must be aware of the cost of storing commodities.

THE KNOWLEDGE REQUIRED
FOR COMMODITY TRADING

A good bit of knowledge is necessary to intelligently select which commodity futures to acquire. Unintelligent investing in futures markets is prohibitively risky. In the stock markets it is often wise to rely heavily on the judgment of others. This is not the case with the futures markets—you need to treat commodity investment like a business.

Much of the information you need can be found in various newspapers and financial magazines. Both *The Journal of Commerce* and *The Wall Street Journal* report on all the major commodity markets every day. If you are investing in farm commodities, you will need to read the various federal government reports on them, such as crop forecasts. If you are speculating in cocoa, which is grown abroad, you will need to keep up with foreign crop forecasts. If you are speculating in a metal such as copper, you will need to keep up with production, scrap, and consumption figures published by governmental and private sources. Since this is an international market, you will need figures from around the world. Through agricultural support programs, tariffs, and so on, governments affect the prices of commodities. Therefore, be familiar with all government programs that affect prices. If you are speculating in futures in foreign currencies, you need to be familiar with worldwide monetary policy and foreign trade statistics. If you are speculating in stock market futures—actually put and call options— you will need the information described in Chapter 7. Currently *commodity options*—options on commodity futures contracts—are not available in the United States, but they are traded abroad. Thus, if you go this route, you will need to be familiar with another country's laws. (Commodity options, are in effect, a bet on a bet!) A *commodity option* gives the purchaser the right, but not the obligation, to buy or sell a futures contract at a fixed price for a certain period of time. Options are more appropriate for the small investor than are futures. Commodity options cost less than do commodity futures contracts, and while the commodity futures buyer may have to put up more money because the price of the commodity falls, the option buyer pays a one-time premium plus a commission.

Because of the large amount of data you need to intelligently speculate in commodity futures contracts, many commodity speculators are professionals, that is, speculating is their business, or their business exposes them to the information they need to speculate. For example, if you buy oranges for a frozen orange juice company, it makes sense for you to speculate in frozen orange juice futures rather than in plywood. Let the plywood salesman speculate in plywood. One of the

advantages of commodity speculation is that you can make use of
information you have which, if you used it in stock speculation, might
be ruled as being inside information which it is illegal to use in buying
or selling stocks.

THE COMMODITY EXCHANGES

The largest American commodity exchange, and one of the largest in
the world, is the Chicago Board of Trade. The nation's commodity
exchanges in 1970 handled around 27.2 million contracts worth an
estimated $145.3 billion. By 1976 annual volume had reached 73.7
million contracts valued at $819.9 billion. Over that same period of
time the stock exchanges were in the doldrums. Clearly, speculative
activity, on an unprecedented level, had switched from stocks to
commodities.

To acquire a commodity futures contract you can go to a broker.
Most stock brokers also deal in commodities, and some brokers only
deal in commodities. A *standard contract* is utilized which calls for
delivery of a set amount of a given grade or type of commodity. In
the case of agricultural commodities, you are allowed to substitute
other grades, but this entails a specified price differential. This contract
is cleared through the clearinghouse of the exchange, which becomes
a third party to the contract. The clearinghouse assures payment and
delivery to the two parties involved. (The two parties have no contact
with one another.) *One of the major advantages of dealing through
an exchange is that your bet is guaranteed.* The exchange also gives
you more liquidity than you could obtain via private transactions.

You have to make a deposit called the margin with your broker.
The *margin* is money which will cover any loss your broker might
incur if he were forced to liquidate your contract. If, during the life of
the contract, price changes enough so that the margin doesn't cover
the loss if your position was liquidated, the broker will ask for more
margin. Initially, margin seldom runs more than 10 percent of the
value of the contract; so, leverage is great. (Note the similarity of
terminology in the stock and commodity markets.)

The commodity exchanges are regulated by the Commodity
Futures Trading Commission. Its role and powers are comparable to
those of the Securities and Exchange Commission's in regard to the
stock markets.

SELECTING A COMMODITY BROKER

The first thing to do is inquire about the reputations of a commodity
brokerage firm and its brokers. Do both have extensive experience in

commodity futures? How much and what kind of information will they provide you? How well have their former customers fared? Do they have a reputation for efficiently and accurately executing orders? Do they cover the markets you wish to trade in? Are they interested in and have experience with the individual speculator? Are their beliefs as to the appropriate method of trading in line with yours? Will they provide you with the amount of assistance you desire?

SELECTING A COMMODITY

In order to select a commodity or commodities to trade, you must first know something about each alternative. There are so many commodities to choose from among that only a few will be considered here. They are pretty representative of all those available. Those not discussed or not previously mentioned include: boneless beef, lumber, milo, coffee, silver coins, platinum, oats, eggs, soybean meal, rye, cottonseed oils, and wool. Note that some of the commodities are related to one another. Cottonseed oil, for example, is a by-product of cotton; thus, the supply of cottonseed oil is determined by the supply of cotton. The markets for soybeans, soybean meal, and soybean oil are also related. Soybean oil and cottonseed oil compete with one another. Soybeans compete with some meats. Silver coins can be melted down into silver. Most corn is used to feed livestock. Beef and pork are substitutes for one another. Copper and silver are mined jointly.

Wheat

The harvesting of winter wheat begins late in May in the Southwest and then progresses northward. By July the harvest has reached the northwestern wheat fields. By this time some of the spring wheat belt is starting to be harvested. Prices usually decline from May until a low is reached in the July-to-August period. Prices reach a peak in winter or spring. The United States and Canada are the world's largest wheat-exporting nations. A large part of these nations' crops are sold abroad; thus, price is greatly influenced by foreign demand. New crop futures decline in anticipation of the replenishment of supplies. The United States government frequently holds very large stocks of wheat and, thus, can substantially affect prices. (Figure 8-1 shows the volatility of wheat prices!) Over time the size of these stocks changes substantially.

The four basic grades of wheat are No. 1 Northern Spring Wheat, No. 2 Hard Winter Wheat, No. 2 Red Winter Wheat, and No. 2 Yellow Hard Winter Wheat. Most wheat futures are traded on the Chicago Board of Trade, the Minneapolis Grain Exchange, and the

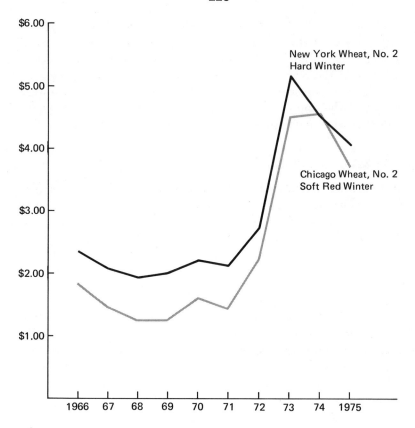

FIGURE 8–1. Wheat Flour Prices: Chicago and New York, Average Price per Bushel, 1966–1975. (U.S. Dept. of Commerce, *U.S. Statistical Abstract 1976*, Washington, D.C.)

Kansas City Board of Trade. The Commodity Exchange Act limits the amount of wheat futures that can be carried at one time. Large contracts must be reported to the Commodity Futures Trading Commission. The exchanges set price limits beyond which trading during a day may not take place. The regular or standard contract is for 5000 bushels. Each exchange sets a minimum commission per "round turn" and a minimum margin per contract. (They do the same for the other commodities.) A *round turn* is a purchase and its liquidating sale or the reverse. The delivery months for wheat futures are March, May, July, September, and December. The seller of a wheat contract may be an elevator company, a grain dealer, a miller, a farmer, a speculator, or some other person or organization involved in the wheat business.

Silver

Silver comes out of the ground as a by-product of copper, lead, and zinc. For this reason, the production of silver is more dependent on the prices of these metals than on the price of silver. It is traded as dust, coin, and bullion. The United States consumes almost half of the world's silver. America's number one user of silver is the photographic industry. For many years consumption has exceeded production. These deficits are covered by hoarders. Once a big stockpiler of silver, the United States government no longer has a vast hoard to cover this deficit and so hold down silver prices.

In recent years silver has been one of the most actively traded commodities. Like gold, silver has long been held in metallic form as a hedge against hard times and as a way of speculating. It is far cheaper to speculate via silver futures than by holding silver, and you can enjoy a high degree of leverage with futures. The silver futures market is participated in heavily by both industrial users and speculators. Silver is used by the electronics and jewelry industries as well as by the photographic industry. Industrial demand is expected to grow and production is expected to continue to fall below demand.

In forecasting the price of silver you must consider a wide variety of factors. You must forecast copper, lead, and zinc prices. You must determine whether new technology will increase or reduce the use of silver. You must estimate the size of silver hoards and what price will bring them to the market. You must forecast whether political and economic conditions will raise or lower the size of hoards. What effect will monetary conditions have on silver demand?

Soybeans

Soybeans are one of the most volatile and actively traded commodities. Soybean futures are traded by growers, processors, exporters, and speculators. As is the case with all crops, the supply of soybeans is greatly affected by weather. The United States is the world's largest producer of soybeans. This crop is normally harvested early in the fall. While soybeans have long been a popular cattle feed in the United States, only recently have Americans eaten them, and they are only used as an extender. The Japanese, however, have long considered soybeans a staple in their diet, and they import large quantities of soybeans from the United States. Soybeans and soybean products compete with a wide variety of other foodstuffs. They are a source of protein. Technologies for turning soybeans into textured vegetable protein to be used in combination with meat or alone to simulate various meats, such as bacon and sausages, are progressing rapidly.

Corn

This is America's largest crop and it is the most actively traded commodity future. Both commercial and speculative trading is heavy. The corn market is generally less volatile than the soybean market. Most corn is used to feed animals, but much corn, either directly or as oil or starch, is consumed by humans. Corn is the most common food additive. It is grown throughout the United States.

Pork Bellies

This is the part of the hog that is turned into bacon. It is one of the most volatile commodities. The price of pork bellies is tied to the supply of hogs, people's consumption of bacon, the stored supply of pork bellies, and the price of corn (which is used to feed hogs). Slaughter begins in early October.

Foreign Currencies

Speculators in foreign currencies are betting that the value of one or more foreign currencies will rise or fall in value in relation to other currencies over a given time period. Most currency speculation goes on through a network of large banks, and the small, individual investor cannot participate. He or she can, however, participate in foreign currency speculation indirectly via futures contracts traded on the floor of the Chicago Mercantile Exchange. The required margin is lower than is the case for most other commodities. This market is, however, rather thin, that is, you may find it difficult to find a buyer or a seller when you want one. It differs from other commodity markets in that it is not governed by supply and demand in the same way. The amount of money in circulation is largely government determined, and its maximum size is set by the government. A complicating factor is that central banks of the world's nations manipulate the exchange rates between the world's currencies for both political and economic reasons.

Matching Commodity with Speculator

Clearly some commodities' characteristics are such that they are not appropriate for some people. Some require too much money; some involve too much risk; others require too much specialized knowledge.

Because of your interests, experience, job or profession and/or contacts, some markets are more suitable for you than others. All commodity trading requires steady nerves, but trading in some commodities requires particularly steady nerves! Any commodity trading also requires a lot of time, but some commodity trading requires an enormous amount of time! Are your nerves very steady, and are you willing and able to devote a great deal of time to trading?

TRADING PHILOSOPHIES

There are two basic approaches to commodity trading. They are the same two that are found in the stock market: *fundamental* and *technical*. Many traders utilize some aspects of both approaches, which is also true of the stock market. One can, of course, trade without method. Most prefer to do otherwise because *traders as a whole lose in the commodities market*. Whatever one person wins, another loses, and all "players" must pay commissions; thus, total costs exceed total returns for the market as a whole. Without a method, one's trading would be random, and results in the long run would mirror the market average, which is to lose. This is a major difference between the commodity and stock markets. You can buy a share of stock, collect dividends for several years, and sell it to someone who does the same. It isn't necessary that one party lose, as is the case in the commodity markets.

Commodity trading, like stocks, can follow a *psychological approach*. Those who subscribe to this approach assume that commodity prices are a phenomenon of social psychology. Therefore, prices would go up when people are feeling "bullish" and down when they are feeling "bearish." (*Bulls* are optimists. *Bears* are pessimists. Bulls buy. Bears sell. These terms are also used in the stock market.) To make money would, then, require that you sense the mood of the people in the market. Some believe that instead of the mood of the "mob" determining prices, it is the mood of a few. To believe that prices are determined by social psychology, one must believe that prices are not affected by economic and political factors. It is, however, widely believed that prices are affected by these factors, mainly economic factors.

Clearly a drought that cuts a crop in half, or good weather that increases crop size by 50 percent, will outweigh, respectively, even the most bullish and bearish moods. Changes in supply can and does change price. The fact that most observers think economic factors are the main determinant of prices does not mean that psychological factors do not, at least sometimes, affect prices.

The Fundamental Approach

The fundamental approach is founded on the belief that prices are determined by the forces of supply and demand. Evidence of the validity of this belief is the significant correlation between prices and the ratio of consumption to available stocks (beginning stocks plus current production). If you follow this approach, you predict price by predicting consumption and stocks.

In general, economists regard commodity markets as markets that are largely competitive, ones in which untrammeled competition allows prices to find their equilibrium—where supply and demand are equal—according to the laws of supply and demand. Futures markets are seen as being close approximations of *perfect competition*. In a perfectly competitive market no single buyer or seller can significantly influence price by his activities or inactivity. Prices can move in any direction, and prices always reflect all price-influencing information, since this information is available immediately to all market partici-pants. (You can't buy, say, wheat at a too-low a price because you, but not wheat sellers, know about a drought which will shrink wheat stocks in the near future.) If commodity markets are *efficient*—perfectly competitive—price changes will move in a random fashion, that is they are a *random walk*. Studies indicate that commodity price changes are substantially random.

The Technical Approach

As is the case with the stock markets, technicians are those who believe that they can predict future prices by looking at charts that show previous market activity. These charts show a variety of patterns, such as a "V-top," "rounded bottom," "head and shoulders," and "neck-line." Implicitly, this is a psychological approach. Chartists, however, are not concerned with the cause of the patterns, only with what they portend for the future. Charting is purportedly an empirical method. The test of a chartist is his or her track record. There are no track record studies available.

Other Methods of Forecasting

One fairly popular method of forecasting is based on the amount of trading that is going on in a futures market. This can be measured in two ways—One way is called open interest, the other is volume. *Open interest* is one-half the number of open contracts (i.e., contracts in force and not offset). If you and someone else sign a new futures contract, open interest increases by one. Offsetting reduces open interest. *Volume* simply refers to the number of transactions, without regard to their consequences for open interest. In addition to being used for predictive purposes, these figures measure the liquidity of the market. A rise in futures prices is thought to be more likely to continue if volume and open interest increase. A decline, too, is thought to be more likely to continue if these activity indicators rise.

The logic behind open interest is that if it rises, new shorts and longs are coming into the market. If price is rising, it is assumed that the buying pressure of the longs exceeds the selling pressure of the shorts. Presumably, the assumption is that more of the same will occur; so a bandwagon effect is assumed. Thus, this, too, seems to be a psychologically based method, or it is believed that some real economic factor is being gradually perceived by market participants.

Another method is the *moving average method,* of which there are several variants. To use this method, you must first calculate a moving average of closing (end of day) prices. When a futures price is above this figure, you go long; when it is below, you go short. It is somewhat similar to dollar-cost averaging in the stock markets. Neither involves predicting; both are mechanical. Neither is concerned with why prices change; both assume the market is a random process and exploit this fact to put you "ahead" more often than you are "behind."

As is the case with the stock markets, the acceptance of the random walk theory as explaining price changes means that you should diversify your investments or, in this case, your bets. You are just as likely to pick a "bad" as a "good" commodity; so, take advantage of the law of large numbers and end up, by having "good" and "bad" bets offset one another with the performance of "average" bets. You take advantage of the law of large numbers either by dealing in every commodity proportionately or by selecting commodities randomly. If your random selections cost more money and expose you to more risk than you can afford, you will, in order to follow this method, have to join a fund or form an investment club, which is a partnership formed for the purpose of pooling funds for investment.

The *funds* which deal in commodities are actually limited partnerships. Limited partnerships are partnerships in which all partners do not have unlimited liability. Having unlimited liability is, of course, risky. The fund's managing partners have unlimited liability and are compensated by the limited partners paying them management fees and a share of profits. You can obtain information about such funds in *Commodities* magazine. These funds follow a variety of trading methods, so inquire about how they make their trading decisions.

CASES FOR DISCUSSION

Case 1 Vic Gamadanis is in business with his father. They run a small appliance store which offers a repair service. In junior college Vic took a business program. Vic makes $10,000 a year. He is married and has one child. He rents the house he lives in. Before he got married, he worked for an American engineering firm abroad, and he was able to save $6,000, which he still has, along with $2,000 more he has saved since. Vic has just read *The Commodity Futures Game* by Teweles, Harlow, and Stone. By combining supply availability and usage figures and comparing them to the highest price recorded on the July contract between March 1 and the expiration date of that contract for a number of years, the authors have created a forecasting model for soybeans. They show that by using their model in the past, one could have made significant profits. Vic is all set to jump into soybean futures. How would you advise him? Why?

Case 2 Knowing that you have studied the commodities markets, Dewey Andrews comes to you for advice. Dewey is a wheat farmer. He's thinking of going into wheat futures. He's read that "spreading" is a good to minimize your losses. To spread you might buy one wheat contract for delivery next March and sell one wheat contract for delivery next May. Why, he says, would this minimize his loss? (Reread the material on wheat.)

Case 3 Elizabeth Bankston is not one to take chances. For a college professor, she has an excellent salary and usually makes an equal amount via consulting. She has never before considered the commodity markets because of the risk involved. Recently, however, she read an article in a business magazine about a "sure thing," grain arbitrage. The article told of arbitrage between contracts and between commodities. The secret of the first is knowing storage costs of the grain in question. The secret of the other is knowing the usual spread between such competing crops as wheat and corn (to feed livestock). You profit by finding a too-large spread in prices. How would you advise her? Why? Would your advice differ if she was employed by a grain elevator company? Why?

Case 4 John McClure recently received an interesting telephone call. The caller, whose name sounded vaguely familiar, described the huge gains that have been made in the past in sugar, copper, and other commodities. The safest way to trade in these commodities is, he says, through options. He offered to send John an options information kit and invited him to a seminar at a major hotel in John's city. The options involved are, he says, traded on the London exchanges, which are very reputable. Established American brokerages are, he adds, prevented by law from trading these wonderful securities, but his firm can do so because it deals directly with London. Thus, it eliminates the cost of a middleman. To show John how good his firm is, he offers to send him a bank statement. How would you advise John? Why?

Case 5 Margaret Collins is taking a college course in agribusiness. She has been assigned to write a paper on futures markets' impact on commodity prices. Do they increase or reduce the amplitude of commodity price movements? How would you advise her to argue? Support your position.

REVIEW QUESTIONS

1. Why are commodity futures a risky investment?
2. What is the difference between using commodity futures for speculation and hedging?
3. Is hedging costless? Why or why not?
4. How can someone who holds stocks of commodities use commodity futures to lock in a profit or loss resulting from a change in the value of his holdings?
5. What are commodity options?
6. If someone warns you against going short on orange juice during the Florida freeze-threat season, what trading philosophy are they following?

7. What are the major differences and similarities between the stock and commodity markets?
8. Explain how margin provides you with leverage.

YOUR PLAN: CHAPTER 8

**The following are do's and
don'ts of commodity trading:**

1. Don't invest in commodities unless you are willing to take a lot of risk and hanker for fast action. Determine what is your objective: action or profits.
2. Only invest money you can afford to lose. (You can lock in a loss at an acceptable level.)
3. Practice on paper before actually making any trades.
4. Study the markets and each commodity before investing.
5. Settle on a trading philosophy.
6. Hold back some of your funds available for commodity trading to handle possible calls for more margin.
7. Expect to make mistakes.
8. Start with domestic rather than foreign commodities (i.e., most production and sale is in the U.S.).
9. Unless you invest through a fund or investment club, don't invest in more commodities than you can keep well informed about, unless you have a "know-nothing" view of the market.
10. Start small.
11. Check carefully anyone you turn to for advice and/or brokerage services.
12. Deal only with someone who agrees with your trading philosophy.
13. Look for arbitrage possibilities. (They appear and disappear quickly!)
14. Don't act on hot tips.
15. Don't try to play daily price fluctuations—you'll spend too much in commissions.
16. Beware of taking small profits, but letting losses mount up, hoping for a change.
17. Don't pyramid, that is, don't use your gains to date on a contract to go into another, etc. The risk of this is fantastic.

Things Both
Enjoyable and
Marketable

OBJECTIVES

When you have completed this chapter, you will have accomplished the following:

1. Be aware of the advantage that investment in tangibles has over securities vis-a-vis depressions.
2. Be familiar with the determinants of value for each of the investment media discussed.
3. Be familiar with the sources of the various tangible investment media.
4. Know where to seek the knowledge required to intelligently invest.
5. Understand the various risks you take in investing in tangibles.

A few people prefer to invest in things which, unlike stocks and bonds, provide them with both monetary and nonmonetary benefits. Often the investment aspect of these things is not the major reason for their purchase. Your home, for example, is probably bought mainly for the shelter it provides, rather than a profit on resale. Other investments, such as old coins, antique furniture and automobiles, paintings, gems, stamps, and gold are purchased for a variety of reasons. You may enjoy the beauty of a fine, old painting. Restoring a long-neglected old car may be your favorite hobby. Collecting antique furniture or old military weapons may be one aspect of your interest in history. You may like to wear jewelry.

A particular attraction of this type of investment is that, in addition to the joy of looking at it, displaying it, and assembling a complete collection of it, one can also protect oneself from being completely wiped out by a depression. For, while the value of stocks and bonds can drop to zero, the value of these investments will not drop this far; yet, many earn a return in the long run as high as that earned on stocks and bonds. *As a group, these investments are, however, much less liquid than stocks and bonds.*

Although in 1977 stocks as a whole were just a little more valuable than they were in 1966, gems continually advanced in price over this period with no real setbacks (which was certainly not the case with stocks!) and many experts think this trend will continue. Gold, however, after rising to nearly $200 an ounce, plummeted to below $105.

Like investing in securities, investing in collectibles can produce tax advantages. If, for example, you donate your collection to a non-profit organization, you will get a tax deduction equal to its current value, which may be well above what it cost you, perhaps years ago, to acquire it.

If there are any common denominators to investing in collectibles, they are that considerable time, money, and expertise is usually necessary. Learning the ins and outs of the relevant markets is time consuming, and it often takes many years for significant price appreciation to take place. Collecting paintings by old masters or antique automobiles requires more money than the average person has, and though people of modest means can collect stamps, they usually cannot afford those most likely to appreciate substantially. (Of course, the large investor also has the advantage in the stock and bond markets too.) It often takes great skill to distinguish between the genuine and the fake collectible and between poor and high quality items. One can question, however, whether it takes any more skill than it does to select good stocks to invest in.

For the person of modest means to earn a large return on this type of investment, it is essential that he or she be exceptionally astute and diligent in spotting value overlooked by others. (This is also the case in the stock market!) Being just plain lucky helps too!

DIAMONDS AND OTHER GEMS

Whether or not you are a girl, diamonds can be your best friend. Diamonds have long been a popular investment medium because they are seen as being good protection against both inflation and depression and are a way to pass wealth, illegally, from generation to generation without taxation. Women have always found them to be a very attractive form of ornamentation, and so have some men. Few weddings, even during depressions, take place without a diamond ring being slipped on the bride's finger. In times of prosperity diamond sales rise significantly. The constant demand for diamonds and the fact that supplies are limited and quite tightly controlled, mean that prices are unlikely to fall. (One company, DeBeers Consolidated Mines of South Africa, controls an estimated 85 to 90 percent of world diamond production.)

Before you rush out to buy diamonds, however, you should know about the one big fly in the ointment: Individuals generally must buy diamonds at retail and sell them at wholesale. Thus, you pay a retailer's substantial markup when you buy, but you do not reap the same when you sell. This is the result of the tight grip of a few on the supply and marketing of diamonds.

A good diamond for investment purposes will probably cost over $5000. The vast majority of the diamonds you see on women's fingers are not good investments. They may even be simulated diamonds!

In addition to diamonds, you can invest in sapphires, opal, spinel, tourmaline, emeralds, rubies, amethysts, and various lesser-known gems. Synthetics of some of these are available but are not good investments. The chief reason for the high value of fine gems is scarcity, and it seems that they are destined to become relatively more scarce as discoveries of new gem deposits become increasingly rare. Known diamond deposits may be depleted within 40 years.

Determining Value

A diamond's value is determined by its color, clarity (lack of flaws), weight (measured in carats), and cut. Colorless diamonds are worth far more than are yellow ones. There are 23 color gradations, and they vary subtly. A flawed diamond has little value; very few diamonds are completely flawless, just as few are "blue white," a widely misused term. Even if it is a clear and colorless diamond, if it is poorly cut it has little value. It may be impossible to recut it, and recutting will waste some material. The few people able to do this work are also very expensive workers! For a large, exceptionally good stone, however, recutting may greatly enhance its value.

A diamond's setting has no effect on its value; settings can be changed and the setting itself has relatively little value. The quality of any gem cannot be determined by the naked eye. Synthetics, altered stones, and fakes can only be detected by a professional gemologist in most cases. A reputable dealer will supply a buyer a certificate of authenticity. When you sell, having documentation on your gem is crucial to getting a good price. Therefore, get documentation before buying. A jeweler can send your diamond to the Gemological Institute for certification of its grade.

If you do not deal with a reputable dealer and do not have the gem appraised by a trustworthy professional, you run a high risk of being sold a stolen or bogus diamond or one of a lesser quality than claimed. Frequently the lower quality is due to a natural flaw in the diamond or a chipped place.

A reputable dealer may try to sell you a beautiful piece of jewelry whose price is largely based on its setting. Settings will not appreciate much. It is better to put your money into a better diamond rather than into a lesser diamond with an elaborate setting. The number of diamonds in a setting also is not important. You just end up paying a lot of money for a lot of diamonds, each of which has little value. You should comparison shop among several jewelers since their prices for a given quality stone may vary.

If gems are purchased with cash and no record of the transaction is made, you can, quite illegally, use them as a method of avoiding estate taxes, since they are easily concealed. People who do not seek to avoid taxes also find gems a convenient and safe way, valuewise, to pass their wealth on to their children. This convenience, however, poses a danger. Gems are very attractive to thieves because they are very portable and are usually hard to identify. Gems should be kept in a very safe place and be insured. This costs money, and, of course, you earn no offsetting interest on gems. Through a diagram of its flaws, it is possible to "fingerprint" a gem so that it can be identified.

Where To Buy

Retail jewelers are a numerous and well-known source. They are also often the most expensive source. Settings frequently account for a large part of the price of their gems. Most jewelers will have a fairly wide selection available, particularly major dealers in large cities. Small-town jewelers will have a smaller stock and are unlikely to carry gems of investment quality in their stock. Jewelers' sales are unlikely to provide you with a bargain because there is no reason for a jeweler to sell gems at a loss. There is always a wholesale market open to dispose of stock if the jeweler needs money fast.

Estate sales and auctions are another source of diamonds and other gems. Some think that this is a good place to get a bargain. Often, however, the people handling the sale are quite knowledgeable about gems. These sales usually attract professional gem buyers who know what the gems are worth. Brokers can be hired to buy and sell for you. Their fees may be less than the retail markup and a good broker can provide you with expert advice. Rockhounds, as gem collectors are called, often organize gem shows as part of their hobby. (Don't let their hobby status fool you though, as they are usually pretty well informed about current market prices!) It is at such shows that you have your best chance of finding unusual stones such as andalusite, iolite, and scapolite. The shows also provide you a place to sell gems without paying an intermediary.

WORKS OF ART

Art can be one of the best investments in the world and provide you with a rewarding hobby at the same time. The key to obtaining a high rate of return on an investment in art is *quality, rarity,* and *significance.* It is best to have several thousand dollars to invest, as well as time and a personal interest. *Like all commodity investments, art is sensitive to economic conditions.* If keeping up with inflation is your main goal, this is an attribute of value to you. If, however, protecting yourself from the effects of depression is your major goal, art is not a very good investment. This is because art prices tend to go up more rapidly than does the economy, but they also go down more rapidly.

Art is largely a long-term investment. It is not a very liquid investment—it is often difficult to sell quickly without a large loss. Seldom can a large gain be made in a very short period of time. The sources of investment in art are dealers and other collectors. In addition to dealers and collectors, prices are influenced by museums, who are large buyers and trend setters. Unlike securities markets, art markets aren't regulated by the government, and this provides both opportunities and risks.

Unlike many other investments, art provides much more than a monetary return. In collecting art one often learns something about history and gains something that can be displayed with pride and derive aesthetic pleasure from.

How to Collect

One cannot become a successful art collector overnight. It takes a great deal of time to learn enough about art and those who buy and sell it to be able to invest wisely. Of course, you do not have to personally buy and sell art. You can hire someone to do it for you. It is difficult, however, for one totally ignorant of the field to successfully select a person to do this. Using an intermediary will add to the cost of investing. If, however, her expertise is far superior to yours or what you can acquire, hiring her is your best move.

You should be wary of advertisements in magazines or received through the mail proclaiming the splendid investment potential of some reproductions. Reproductions are not going to become valuable unless they are designed by the artist (preferably by hand) and only a limited number are made.

Prints

Prints, once snubbed by those who collected paintings, are rapidly growing in popularity as an investment medium. One major reason for this is that the price of a good print is well below that of a good painting; thus, prints make art collecting possible for people whose incomes are not large enough to invest in paintings. Today a fine collection of prints is almost as much a status symbol as a fine collection of paintings.

There are a large number of dealers in prints. Modern reproduction methods provide a high quality product, but the value of a print is determined by the name of the artist, the subject, its rarity, and its condition.

An artist's reputation in another medium is not closely correlated with the value of his or her prints. Fads are not uncommon in prints and are dangerous to succumb to. Beware of poor quality prints and restrikes—reruns using the original plates. The more often a plate is used, the poorer the results and the less rare is the print.

Prints may be either originals or reproductions. *Originals* are prints made from a medium on which the artists themselves have made the drawing. A *reproduction* is a copy of the work. The former is by far the more valuable.

Inspect catalogs and visit galleries before buying prints. Consider specializing in one artist's work or a school of artists. Buy only what you like; buy signed prints; deal only with reputable dealers. Know what you are doing before bidding at an auction. Be wary of buying a page torn from an art book. Buy only limited editions put out by living artists, otherwise a living artist can flood the market with later works.

Determining Value

Originality and uniqueness give art value, but they do not guarantee it. Availability and demand determine value, and demand is determined by a host of factors, among which originality and uniqueness are simply two of the more important. Some art works of little artistic merit are valuable simply because of the artist who created them. Often the identity of the artist is the main determinant of the work's worth. Works of greater artistic value may have little value on the market. The size, subject matter, condition, and date of execution also affect the demand for a work and, thus, its price.

The art market is so vast that many advise that you specialize in one segment of it, such as English pastoral paintings of a given period, American folk art, jade figurines from China, and so on. This enables you to really become an expert and acquire a collection whose value is greater if it is sold as a whole rather than piece by piece. In contrast to a specialized one, an unspecialized collection will not bring a higher price if sold as a whole than if sold piece by piece. On the other hand, an unspecialized collection is a less risky investment. (That risk-return trade-off again!) Tastes change rapidly, and this will adversely affect the specialized collector far more than the unspecialized collector, who is unlikely to hold only pieces that have gone out of favor.

How to Buy

You can learn what you need to know by reading art auction catalogs, visiting galleries, attending auctions, reading scholarly books, reading art investment publications, and taking art appreciation courses.

There are several investment strategies open to you. One is to carefully, over a long period of time, buy the best you can afford. Another strategy is to buy works currently out of favor (i.e., inexpensive) anticipating that they will return to favor. This is the more risky approach, but your possible return is much higher. A close relationship with a dealer is another possible, shorter-range strategy.

A dealer can get you discounts or tip you off about promotions and museum purchases that may make an artist's work scarce. You can also try to stay ahead of the market, as would someone who had anticipated that people would start collecting photographs. (Photography is a relatively new art form. Both black-and-white and color pictures are being collected.) Beware of buying just after some works have become very popular, as it is likely that prices are at a peak they will not reach again for many years, if ever.

A major problem with art collecting is that clever art forgers can fool even many experts. The best protection is to deal only with well-established dealers and auction houses. A dealer can be asked to write on the bill of sale that the work is by a certain artist—not just signed with a certain name—along with a description of the work. You can ask for the names of previous owners and check with them. If the artist is alive, you can check with him. If not, his family may be helpful. Always look carefully at the work, and hesitate to buy it if you don't like it, as it is hard to buy wisely things you don't like. Nonetheless, some people have made money investing in artwork they themselves did not like. However, if you like it, you can at least enjoy it if you can't sell it.

THAT PRECIOUS YELLOW METAL

Gold sent men on the arduous and dangerous trek to California and Alaska. Men have lied, cheated, stolen, and killed for it. The Spanish destroyed an ancient Indian civilization and enslaved its people to obtain it. Today men spend years and take terrible risks to bring gold up from Spanish treasure ships sunk hundreds of years ago. Africans in South Africa toil in deep mines for it. In India, one of the world's poorer nations, a vast hoard of gold is held by its citizens. Much of it is worn by Indian women. Instead of investing in stocks and bonds and so making possible additional production, they put all their excess money into gold because they believe that only gold can be depended on to maintain its value in hard times. (History gives them some grounds for this belief!)

The secret of the yellow metal's fascination to mankind has long been debated without agreement. It is this fascination with gold over the centuries that has convinced people of its safety as an investment. Everyone wants it because everyone else wants it; thus, it is always valuable.

Because it was desired and convenient, once it was alloyed to give it hardness, gold was used as money at an early date. When paper money came along, issuers promised to hold gold so that those with paper currency could exchange it for gold. Only in this way could people be induced to hold paper instead of gold.

Today all you can exchange for paper money is more paper money or coins that contain no gold and are worth less in the metals market than they are as money. (Their lower value as a metal is what keeps them in circulation!)

Determining Value

Gold used to have value both because of the demand for it as a money and as a commodity for use in jewelry, dental work, and industry. Today, while nations hold some gold, international payments are not normally carried out via the use of gold as once was the case. There are no gold coins produced for use as money. You might expect, therefore, that the value of gold would, like the value of iron, be based entirely on its value in use, that is, for making the steel in cars. If this was the case, investment in gold would not differ from an investment in any other commodity. However, this is not the case. Why? The following example will explain.

Suppose you lived in a barter economy. In order to buy something in such an economy you have to exchange something the seller wants for the item that you want. You would quickly realize that this method of exchange wastes a lot of your time because you have to search for someone who has what you want and who wants what you have. You may have to make a lot of previous trades to get what he wants. You might get a bright idea for a way to avoid all this time-consuming activity. You might suggest to the seller that he accept a piece of paper from you that says "I owe you," say, fifty pounds of flour. If he agreed to accept your I.O.U., he might then talk someone into trading your I.O.U. for something he wants. This person, in turn, might use your I.O.U. to make a purchase, and the process might go on and on. "Hey," you would tell yourself, "this is great. All I have to do is write out I.O.U.'s to get anything I want." (Some governments have fallen into this way of thinking!)

As your I.O.U.'s pile up in other people's hands, and their goods pile up in yours, they are going to begin to ask themselves why they should allow this process to continue. They're not producing goods in order to consume pieces of paper. So, they are going to demand that you redeem all those I.O.U.'s—you end up wiped out, and they end up short-changed.

So-called gold bugs, people who invest in gold to the exclusion of most anything else, anticipate that governments will print too many I.O.U.'s—their currency. Other nations will demand gold from them in exchange for their currency because this is a convenient way to gain commodity redemption. This demand for gold will increase its price, and the gold bugs will prosper.

Why Buy Gold?

James Dines, a financial consultant who is a well-known gold bug, says that "People who buy gold aren't looking for income. People are buying gold because they are terrified by what they see around them."[1] What they see is a future financial crash of the 1929 genre.

An investment in gold is usually made to protect oneself against the loss of wealth that a financial disaster would cause for holders of paper assets (i.e., securities). In a period of widespread fear of financial disaster gold prices often rise, enabling those who buy early in the panic and sell before it collapses to make a lot of money. Thus, one may also speculate in gold. (In recent years the gold speculator has been able to do better than the gold investor.)

Instead of buying gold directly, one can buy stock in a gold mining company. This has certain advantages over buying gold, such as cheaper storage, as it is cheaper to store stocks than gold. Gold is also attractive to thieves. Stocks, too, generate a return—dividends— while gold generates expenses—storage and insurance. You will also benefit more from an increase in the price of gold if you hold gold mining stocks rather than stocks of gold. Say a gold mining company spends $15 to produce gold it sells for $25. If gold's price rises to $35, shareholders' profits have doubled, but a gold owner who bought at $25 has only experienced a 40 percent gain, that is, $10 divided by $25. On the other hand, although gold's value will not fall to zero, the stock's value can. (Poor management can drive the mining company into bankruptcy, reducing its worth to zero.)

Another alternative is to invest in gold coins. The value of gold coins is based both on their gold content and their value as coins. Gold content is measured in carats; "pure" gold is 24 carats. Coin values are based on collectors' fancy, rarity, condition, date and mint marks, and whether or not they are part of a complete set. Because of their value as coins, it is less risky to invest in gold coins than gold. Because of the cost of melting gold coins down, it is more profitable to buy and sell gold than to buy gold coins and sell gold via melting the coins down. (U.S. law prohibits you from melting down its coins.)

[1] "Investing in Gold: Five Sides of the Coin," *Money*, September 1974, pp. 33–37.

Beware of buying gold coins with a low-gold content that are sold at the same price you can get a higher-gold content coin.

CURRENCY

Many of us have at one time or another collected coins, if only to save unusual coins we receive as change. The long-term trend of the value of coins has been up; thus, over a number of years you are likely to make money by investing in coins if you do not buy over-valued coins.

The Red and Blue guide books by R. S. Yeoman are the "bibles" of coin collecting. (The red-colored guide has retail prices; the blue, wholesale. Both are entitled *A Guide Book of United States Coins.*) Do not assume that you will be able to either buy or sell at these prices —they are simply estimates of prices at retail and wholesale. You have the same problem with coins that you do with diamonds: You buy at retail and sell at wholesale. However, supply and marketing are not tightly controlled as is the case with diamonds.

Pitfalls

In recent years many governments have made a lot of money by minting attractive, *proof sets* of coins (one of each denomination, none of which has been circulated) packaged in fancy cases and priced well above their value. Private mints are doing the same thing.

Periodically coin-collecting fads arise naturally rather than being created by public or private mints turning out handsome coin sets. (The coins struck by private mints are not legal tender, that is, they aren't money.) The Kennedy half-dollar craze is an example of a spontaneous fad. So many Kennedy half dollars were struck that there is not even a remote possibility of people alive in the 1960s living long enough to see them become valuable. Yet, so many have been hoarded that these hoarders have almost driven the once popular half dollar out of circulation.

Because coins are unidentifiable, they are attractive to thieves. Thus, take precautions to safeguard them. Counterfeits and forgeries are not unheard of, so only deal with a reputable dealer. Hesitate to deal through the mail; the seller can just take your money and disappear. Be wary about buying on the basis of rumors that the U.S. Treasury is going to stop circulating a coin. Facts about Treasury plans not known to many others can enable you to make some money, but you are not likely to get such information.

Determining Value

There is no relationship between a coin's face value and its market value if it is a collector's piece (see Table 9-1). Simply being old is not enough to make a coin valuable unless it is, perhaps a thousand years old, which usually means it is very scarce. Newer coins may be more valuable than older coins. There is a vast difference between the value of a given coin if it has never been circulated than if it is well worn (see Table 9-2). The uncirculated coin is more valuable. The most valuable coin is one in *mint condition*. Its condition is perfect. A difference in where a given coin was minted can make a vast difference in its value. The date on a given type of coin can also make a great difference in its value.

TABLE 9–1 Sampling of Uncirculated Coin Prices, 1966 and 1977

Type	1966	1977	1966–1977 Average Annual Percent Change in Price
Large cent, coronet type; 1820 large date	$ 55.00	$325.00	18.0
Nickel, 1937D; 3-legged var.	180.00	375.00	7.0
Dime, Liberty-seated; no stars on obverse; no drapery from elbow; 1837 small date	200.00	250.00	2.0
Quarter, Washington-type; 1945D	1.35	5.50	14.0
Half dollar, Barber or Liberty-head type; 1911	27.50	460.00	29.0
Silver dollar, peace-type; 1922D	5.00	27.50	17.0
Three-dollar gold piece; 1865	500.00	3700.00	20.0
Five-dollar gold piece (half eagle); Indian head type; 1914S	55.00	425.00	20.0
Columbian Exposition half dollar (Chicago); 1893	4.00	20.00	16.0
Confederate 1861 half dollar (Scott token, obverse)	110.00	190.00	5.0
Mormon five-dollar gold piece; 1849	$725.00	$3500.00	15.0
Average annual rate of change of these coins' prices			15.0

Source: R. S. Yeoman, *A Guide Book of United States Coins,* Racine, Wis.: Western Publishing Co., 1966 and 1977 annual editions.

TABLE 9–2   Comparison of Investment Value of Coins
by Type and Condition,* 1966 and 1977

Winged, Liberty-head of "Mercury type dime. **

Year and Condition	1966 Price	1977 Price	Percent Change between 1966 and 1967
1926:			
Good	$ .35	$ .65	86.0
Very good	.55	.85	55.0
Fine	.95	1.00	5.0
Extra fine	2.50	4.00	60.0
Uncirculated	10.50	25.00	38.0
1926D:			
Good	.75	.75	0.0
Very good	1.25	1.35	8.0
Fine	2.25	2.25	0.0
Extra fine	9.25	15.00	62.0
Uncirculated	45.00	105.00	133.0
1926S:			
Good	3.00	5.75	92.0
Very good	5.75	8.00	39.0
Fine	9.50	11.50	21.0
Extra fine	45.00	70.00	56.0
Uncirculated	$150.00	$700.00	367.0

Source: R. S. Yeoman, *A Guide Book of United States Coins,* Racine, Wis.: Western Publishing Co., 1966 and 1977 annual editions.

* There are no "proof" prices for the coins selected. Between 1966 and 1977 a class
called "very fine" was established between "fine" and "extra fine."
** Quantity minted: 1926, 32,160,000; 1926D, 6,828,000; 1926S, 1,520,000.

Rarity is usually the dominant element in determining a coin's
value. Buffalo nickels, for example, which have an Indian head on the
other side, usually sell for modest amounts, though this is several
times their face value of five cents. (These coins were last minted in
1938). Yet, you will have to pay around $200 to buy some of these
coins minted in 1937, because these buffalo nickels have a buffalo with
only three legs showing. Some others are worth even more due to even
more rare variations.

Assure yourself of a coin's rarity before buying it. This way you
can avoid the big shock of finding after you buy a coin that someone
holds thousands of them and, thus, by selling, can greatly reduce your
coin's worth. (You can find out how many coins of a given type were
ever struck, and how many were struck each year in the "Red" and
"Blue" guide books, but not where they are.) It is safer to deal in
American than foreign coins. There is greater interest in the United
States in its own coins, and American money is among the more
valuable monies in the world.

Before buying a coin, compare the offering price with that listed in one of the many coin catalogs available. It is best to also price the same coin at several dealers. Dealers who are part of a nationwide teletype system can obtain for you bid and asked prices from all over the country on a daily basis.

Study the history of coinage before beginning to collect. Then you will know what is meant by the words *mint marks, pure, fine, standard, sandwich, milling, commemorative issues, reverse, dies, devices, proofs,* and so on. To increase your chances of success as a coin collector, you may decide to specialize: gold coins, ancient Roman coins, American coins prior to the Revolution. This will help you become an expert on some coins and have a related, and, thus, more valuable collection.

There are a number of books, magazines, and newspapers available in this field. There is a national organization of collectors, and it and local groups hold shows regularly. (Some of the books make claims you would be well advised to be skeptical of.) At the Smithsonian Museum in Washington you can see every piece of money ever issued by the U.S. government. The Smithsonian also has a good collection of Confederate money.

Paper money is much less often collected than are coins. Partly this is due to taste. In addition, paper money is a fairly recent innovation and is not very durable. The government quickly withdraws worn paper money from circulation and destroys it. A piece that escapes this process may be very valuable. Basically the same rules that apply to coins apply to paper money. However, in the case of paper money the quality of the engraving and coloring have a significant effect on value. Signatures and pictures also affect value.

POSTAGE STAMPS

Don't sell stamp collecting short because it is so often a child's hobby. Coin collecting is probably exceeded only by stamp collecting in terms of popularity. In terms of possible gain, stamp collecting is probably a bit more lucrative. Stamps are more likely to be worth several hundred thousand dollars!

Probably the most well-known example of a collector striking it rich is the person who discovers a 1918 U.S. airmail stamp. All of these have a value well over their face value because of the newness of airmail then, but some are worth thousands of dollars because they were printed upside down. (The government tries to avoid circulating such errors and today will reprint those they discover after they are in circulation so as to reduce their value.) Governments cut themselves in on the money to be made on stamps by printing special stamps which will appeal to collectors. These are unlikely to be very profitable to the collector unless he has them all. Some small nations make a lot of money by printing beautiful stamps for collectors. No one uses these works of art for mailing a letter!

Postage stamps have traditionally been a hedge against inflation because, historically, their prices have held up better than most investments'. On the other hand, a stamp collection is nice to have around in hard times unless people all over the world are affected. If foreign markets are not affected, you can sell your stamps abroad, since the stamp market is worldwide.

Stamps' values are very large relative to their size. They are easy to store and transport. Since they are not identifiable, they are attractive to thieves. Stamps should be stored in a safe place, such as a safety deposit box.

Determining Value

Like paper money, the demand for stamps is related to their appearance. How fine is the engraving? How good is the color? What picture or artwork appears on the stamp? Often stamps are really art, as reproduced on them are works of art. Sometimes the artwork was commissioned just for the stamp. The condition of a stamp also greatly influences its price. Lack of cancellation marks, tears, creases, and no thin spots normally increases a stamp's value. To protect them, stamps must be kept in a dry and dark place; otherwise, they may fall in value. On occasion a stamp's value is greatly increased by being on a letter which went through the mail, perhaps, to someone like George Washington. The stamp itself in this situation may be worth little. Typographical errors or lack of glue or perforations can also greatly increase a stamp's value. The nation issuing it also affects its value. The first stamps of a new nation and the stamps of a defunct nation are likely to be valuable compared to other similar stamps. As is the case with coins, rarity is a key ingredient of value.

How To Buy

Just as when buying coins, beware of counterfeits and get more than one price quotation. Check stamp catalog price quotations. Study stamp collecting before becoming a collector; consider specializing.

Cheap packets of stamps that are widely advertised are unlikely to be bargains. Those who package the stamps aren't going to give away a valuable stamp. They will keep it for themselves. Whole sheets of newly issued stamps are not likely a good buy, although a whole sheet of a rare stamp is extremely valuable.

As is the case with gems, higher-priced stamps are more likely to appreciate than are low-priced stamps. Deal only with reputable dealers. (Dealing with others is a big gamble.) Check on a dealer through the American Stamp Dealers Association in New York City or with one of its chapters elsewhere.

Like gem and coin collectors, stamp collectors hold shows at which you can buy and sell stamps. Shops specializing in stamps exist and so do stamp departments in department stores. Dealers in stamps often also deal in coins. Many catalogs are available.

RARE BOOKS AND MANUSCRIPTS

Rare books and manuscripts can sell for hundreds of thousands of dollars! Collecting and investing in rare books, manuscripts, maps, autographs, and like items is booming. This is, however, certainly no field for the amateur. Very, very fine points can turn what would otherwise be a very valuable book into one of little value. Simply being an edition lacking an errata page or a fly leaf can drastically reduce a book's value. Being rebound can too.

The extreme scarcity of very old books makes them valuable, but they are usually too costly for most people to invest in even if one doesn't have to compete for them with a museum (which may be financed by a government). For people of modest means, buying a first edition of a new book and getting an author to autograph it is the best bet. (Authors often travel around the country signing their books.) Most of these books will not become very valuable, but you have little invested, and some will appreciate substantially. (You can always read them!) Books of no great rarity will decline in value by a substantial amount in a recession or depression. As is the case with other collectibles, there are fashions in literary collectibles. You need to anticipate these. Purchases should be the result of study: not hunch. Stay in the area or areas you know best rather than scattering your investments.

In addition to rarity, a book's value depends on importance, beauty, and condition. Is it the first edition of Darwin's first book or a work by someone nobody has ever heard of on an unimportant subject? Is it illustrated? How well? By whom?

Original papers outlining history-making events can be quite valuable, and in recent years their value has grown rapidly. Therefore, look for old editions of professional journals. The first published works of any famous person are likely to be a good investment. Autographed copies by the author, particularly if a dedication is included, may increase a book's worth. First editions of classics are valuable. Ancient, handwritten maps and documents are often extremely valuable.

A relatively new collector's item is comic books. Those of the 1930s and 1940s are the most sought after. A complete set is much more valuable than a similar, assorted group of comics. Condition is very important; so is the character involved. The cost of most comics is low enough for even those with modest incomes to collect; yet, the rise in value can be great on a relative basis.

ANTIQUES

Americans seem to be fascinated by everything old, whether it be butter churns, barbed wire, or old plows. Wall telephones, duck decoys, wash pots, scrub boards, irons, toy trains, mail order catalogs, stained glass windows, Coca-Cola trays, round piano stools, brass bedsteads, coin banks, tiffany lamps, patent medicine bottles, toys, Kentucky long rifles, and Confederate belt buckles have all been or are popular. Sometimes an antique is not even very old. Soon after collecting the originals becomes popular, you can usually buy a copy, which is usually inexpensive but sometimes can be quite costly. It is not unusual for a collectible to start a new fashion fad, as was the case with brass headboards for beds. *Copies usually have very little investment value.* Copies are sometimes passed off as originals, so you can pay far too much for them.

When an item becomes popular its price can increase hundreds or thousands of times. Often one fad leads to another. For example, there is now a catalog to guide you to all the Coca-Cola-marked items you can buy, and this all started with a tray-collecting fad.

The type of items discussed so far are not likely to be very profitable investment media because their popularity is likely to be short term and unpredictable. Who can predict when one of the millions of mundane things used in the past will become popular? But, if you do, you can make a lot of money! The major sellers of antiques of all kinds are Christie's and Sotheby Parke Bernet, British firms with New York subsidiaries.

Guns

Old rifles and pistols, and edged weapons too, have long been collected. While any collector's item may be as much a hobby as an investment, if not more so, gun collecting is one of the more hobby-oriented

collector's items. Guns are a hobby that can develop into an investment. Gun collectors are often hunters, target shooters, or military history buffs. Some people like to restore old guns (which they can then sell at a profit), and many of these people would do it even if they didn't make a profit. Great care must be taken in restoration. As much of the original finish and parts must be kept as is possible; otherwise, value will decline.

Gun collectors often buy and sell privately, but they also buy from antique stores and those sporting goods stores that deal in antique guns. Gun collectors regularly hold shows, and some buying and selling takes place there. A gun's value depends largely on its popularity and the quantity available. Who made or used them or where they were used also affects their value.

If your time and knowledge is limited, have a reputable expert do your buying and selling for you. She'll save you more than she costs. There are many catalogs, books, and magazines to guide you. Look at guns for sale and those in the many museums that display guns.

Obviously guns, particularly modern ones and powerful military models, are attractive to thieves. Gun collectors usually do not publicize their collections for this reason. Gun collections should be insured and kept locked, with a record of their serial numbers kept elsewhere. Firing pins should be removed to prevent them from being accidentally fired and to make them less attractive to thieves. Special care must be taken to avoid their falling into the hands of children.

Many laws affect firearm owners. Federal law prohibits the ownership of some types of weapons. Local laws often prohibit firing a gun or concealing one on your person. You may have to register your guns or obtain a permit in order to legally possess them.

Reproductions of all the most popular weapons are available. Their value is not great and is unlikely to rise significantly. Some people collect books, paintings, and prints related to guns in addition to or instead of collecting guns. Some gun collectors also collect various military relics. Some people collect edged weapons. Reconditioning and firing old weapons and recreating battles is also popular.

Furniture and Related Items

Here is an investment that can be both lucrative and functional. Furniture and related items can double in value in only a few years' time. The ever-popular nature of these items and their limited supply makes an investment in them a good hedge against inflation. Unfortunately, both big gains and losses are possible. The value of furniture is determined by age, condition, and style. If a famous person owned it, its value will be enhanced. Some styles stay popular for many years. Others are only popular for a short period of time.

As is the case with guns, you have to be on your guard against modern imitations. Verify the date of manufacture and the name of the maker. Study the many catalogs available. Consult with experts. Consider specializing.

The value of silver pieces, pewter, cut glass, snuffboxes, dishes, candelabras, pottery, porcelains, and so forth, is determined somewhat like works of art, which they often are. Beware of paying the price of sterling silver for silver plate. As in the case of furniture, you are concerned with the extent of repairs and restorations. Is anything missing? Is it the best example available?

One may, of course, find a very valuable antique in their grand-mother's attic, but it is more likely that you will find one in an antique store or at an auction. The price they charge will probably not be low enough for you to earn a large return quickly. Unless you are absolutely certain you know what you are doing, *do not refinish antique furniture —this can drastically reduce its value.*

It may take many years for a piece to gain appreciably in value, and in the interval its value may fluctuate a lot due to changes in taste. You must not panic and sell. Those pieces most immune to taste changes are, on the average, the higher-priced ones, since sellers are generally aware of this immunity.

Touring the backwoods looking for old couples who don't know the value of their furniture or an antique store run by ill-informed rustics is likely to be unproductive. Sometimes you can get a better price in the big city where people don't think they are getting a bargain and so bargain harder. In addition, competition is greater, and this keeps prices down. If you can keep your head, you can often do better at an auction than at a dealer's store.

Automobiles

Antique cars are booming in popularity and prices have risen spec-tacularly. Those with the time and know-how to take an old car and recondition it have, in the past, sometimes made a very large profit on a small investment. Today, however, even a car in very poor condi-tion may sell for a pretty good price, as people are today usually aware of reconditioning possibilities. As is the case with many other antiques, modern imitations are available, but, unlike many other reproductions, these are expensive and so don't exert much downward pressure on the price of the real thing. "Replicars" will not appreciate in value as much as will the originals. Like guns, operability is an important ingredient in value. If a car is the first example of some new technology its value is enhanced. If it is the last car of its type its value is also enhanced.

The antique car market is centered in clubs, regional and national car meets, auctions, and periodicals' advertisements. Prices at auctions are likely to be unrealistically high. (Some car auctions are held by art galleries!) There are a number of antique car museums and books you can look at to learn about antique cars. *Hemmings Motor News* is a bible of vintage car information.

Needless to say, an antique car is normally an expensive investment, particularly if it has been restored or needs none, which really makes it valuable! A good way to start is to buy a low-priced vintage car with restoration potential and restore it yourself. Restoring a car will cost you a good deal even if you do it yourself. If you pay someone else to do it, it may cost up to $20,000. Parts are hard to obtain and are expensive. The work is difficult and requires a lot of tools. Replacement parts may have to be fabricated. By doing your own work, you may be able to halve the cost of restoration, but it will probably take years to recover this cost. Storage and maintenance of several cars will be expensive.

There are three major collectible car categories: antique cars, classic cars, and milestone models. *Antique cars* are vintage cars, that is, very early cars like the Model-T Ford and earlier. *Classic cars* are designated by the Classic Car Club of America and include late 1920s and early 1930s Cadillacs, Lincolns, Packards, Mercedes, and Rolls-Royces. *Milestone models* are designated by the Milestone Car Society. These are 1950s models chosen on the basis of engineering, performance, styling, innovation, and craftsmanship. There are 125 models currently listed.

As is the case at any auction, be sure you know the facts about the autos being auctioned so as not to be carried away by the auctioneer's spiel. Beware of shills—people who bid up the price and then disappear—having earned their pay from the auctioneer. When buying from a dealer, treat the purchase just like one from a used-car dealer.

An antique car's value is dependent on its condition, its age, the popularity of the model and make, and its original cost. Age has little effect; model very much. If a very famous person has owned the car or it was involved in a famous event, its value will be greater than a like car without these features. Rarity also affects value. If the maker is not in business anymore, this can favorably affect value. The fact that the car is propelled by other than a gasoline engine will affect its value.

Perhaps the most inexpensive way to get into automobile collecting is to buy a car you think will become a milestone. Your profit will be greatest if the car's condition is not too good and you can fix it up yourself.

Other Modes of Transportation

Trucks, airplanes, trains, and ships are collected, but only by a few people since the cost is high. These are also very illiquid investments. Maintenance and storage costs are high; large losses are possible. Often owners of such items rent them out to movie companies, advertisers, or charge admission to see them. Most are in museums. Sometimes people organize clubs to collect and maintain such items, as the case with the so-called Confederate Air Force.

Unique Items

Some people collect old printing presses. Others collect baseball uniforms. Some collect theatre posters or musical instruments. Others collect radios or cameras. Someone, somewhere, probably collects anything you might name. Few of these collections, particularly if they are unspecialized, are worth what they cost. Very few bring their owner a profit. However, there are noteworthy exceptions to the general rule. It is said that some baseball cards sell for $4,000 apiece and that some people make $20,000 a year dealing in these cards.[2]

There is no organized or unorganized market in many of these items. If, therefore, you decide to collect the socks of every player in the National Football League, you will probably be on your own! You might strike it lucky with some unusual collection. If you collect handsome, handcarved merry-go-round horses, maybe an amusement park with an old-time theme will buy them. If you collect one of each thing a company puts out, maybe it will buy your collection to start a company museum. Nonetheless, it is a way-out gamble to engage in this kind of collecting. About the best you can reasonably expect is a picture in the local newspaper if the collection is very big and unusual plus a spouse unhappy about all the space and money your collection requires.

Whatever you are collecting, there are some general rules you should follow:

GENERAL INVESTMENT RULES

1. A plentiful item is not very valuable—you want to collect something rare.
2. Age and value are not directly correlated.

[2] "Baseball Card Investors, Not Just Kid Stuff Any More," *Time*, August 22, 1977, pp. 54–55.

3. Condition is an important determinant of value.
4. Alterations should not be made except where operability is important; then alterations should not alter original appearance.
5. Uniqueness increases value.
6. Don't buy unless quite knowledgeable about the market or have the help of someone who is.
7. Beware of counterfeits, altered items, and imitations.
8. Don't invest unless you will not need the money for many years.
9. Do not invest in fads.
10. Specialization will likely increase value, but it also increases risk.
11. Demand is substantially determined by taste.
12. Protect yourself against theft. By serial numbers, photographs, and so on, keep a record of each item.
13. Select carefully who you deal with.
14. Don't bank on doing better than you would with your money in a savings account.
15. Insure your collection.
16. A good collection is worth more than the sum of its parts, that is, the parts relate to one another; adding to each's value.

CASES FOR DISCUSSION

Case 1 Phil Wiley has been a philatelist (stamp collector) since he was a teenager and discovered that his great-great-grandfather was a Confederate postmaster. He joined the Confederate Stamp Alliance and has specialized in Confederate stamps, particularly Confederate blockade covers. His wife resents the time and money he spends on his hobby. "What a waste," she tells friends. How would you advise this couple if they came to you as an arbitrator?

Case 2 Wade Domengeaux has worked for the gas company for 30 years. He had only been on the job a few years when he started collecting old gas meters. He has a garage full of gas meters now. Some date back to the early days of the industry. He has almost every meter ever produced by one old company. He is very proud of his collection, and he thinks it is quite valuable. He makes $20,000 a year, is married, has one married daughter, and twin sons starting college. His home is nearly paid for. He has $4,000 in a savings account and a company pension plan. He plans to continue his collecting, which, considering he travels a lot to find meters, probably averages costing him $1,000 a year. How would you advise him?

Case 3 Amelia Somers was an art history major in college. She worked awhile as a secretary before marrying Greg. Now she stays at home and takes care of their two small children. Greg recently received a raise, and now earns $14,000 a year. Amelia and Greg rent a house inexpensively from her parents, but have only managed to save a couple of thousand dollars. Amelia wants to start collecting paintings. Since you are so knowledgeable, Greg sends her to you for advice. Should she? How should she go about it?

Case 4 Tom Koch's family suffered a lot in the Great Depression, and he heard a lot about their hardships as he grew up. Tom is an accountant who regularly deals with firms in financial trouble. He is alarmed over current government monetary and fiscal policy. Tom is determined never to be broken by hard times as were his grandparents. He wonders how to protect himself. He is 25, single, and has $5000 in the bank. He rents an apartment and owns a car. He's thinking of marrying Yvette Martin, who makes $9000 a year working in a department store's travel agency. People have suggested antique cars, paintings, and gold to him as good investments. How would you advise him?

Case 5 Sonia Sheehy holds a B.A. degree in English and a teaching certificate, and has a well-paying job as a buyer for a national department store chain. She has about $10,000 in savings. She has always saved by buying savings certificates from the local savings and loan association. She's greatly disturbed by the fact that the interest she receives after taxes doesn't even cover inflation. She is not willing to risk her money in the stock market—she has never been a gambler. She won't even play bingo. She is 32 and has no marriage plans. Friends have suggested she invest in gold. How would you advise her?

Case 6 Mary Ann Knutson is determined to be a millionaire by the time she is 35. She's now 23 and has just received a master's degree in business administration. She's had mainly part-time jobs up until now and is currently in an executive training program at a large bank. Mary Ann has $25,000 left her by her grandfather. Initially she had planned to put it in stocks, but the stock market's recent performance doesn't look good enough to make her a millionaire in ten years. She has come to you for advice.

REVIEW QUESTIONS

1. What is the difference between rare and unique?
2. Why should an entire specialized collection sell for more than you could get by selling each item by itself?
3. Why does one take more risk via a specialized collection rather than generalized collecting?
4. What advantages does collecting art or antiques have over investing in stocks? What disadvantages are involved?
5. Why collect rather than putting this money into a savings account?
6. What factors generally play a major role in determining the value of a collector's item?
7. When would investing in gold be a good idea?
8. If you could be taken back in a time machine to 1925 with $200,000 to buy collectibles with, what would you invest in? Why?
9. What is the difference in the steps you take in investing in diamonds and in buying them simply as jewelry?
10. How can you protect yourself from buying a forged or stolen painting?

YOUR PLAN: CHAPTER 9

**Questions you must answer
before deciding to collect:**

1. Can you safely invest any of your money in a collector's item? (Collector's items are very illiquid, i.e., one often

cannot sell them quickly without taking a big loss on the sale. Thus, when investing in collector's items you must use funds you are sure you will not later need on short notice.)

2. Do you have any use for the items collected, and can you provide safe storage for them?

3. Do you have the time and interest necessary to engage in collecting?

4. Do you have the necessary knowledge of the item to be collected and its market to do your own investing?

5. Are you willing to trust someone else to invest for you?

6. Is your main objective in collecting appropriate? A hobby that could be profitable? Protection against inflation? An investment whose worth will not decline without limit? A sideline business? Something to enjoy as well as earn a return? To possibly earn a higher return than could be earned on securities?

7. Is the unit price of the average item to be collected low enough so that you will not have to tie up all your money in only one or a few items and, therefore, risk losing everything due to a few poor selections?

8. Would it suit you better to acquire a specialized collection or a mixed collection, which is less likely to be adversely affected by changes in taste, but is not as likely to appreciate greatly?

9. Are you able, psychologically and financially, to absorb the loss of your investment?

10. Can you afford the upkeep, storage, and insurance costs involved?

11. If you plan to make a large profit, are you prepared to spend the enormous amount of time and money necessary?

12. Will collecting better serve your investment goals than would other types of investment, or help you achieve them in combination with other forms of investment?

How to Use Your Answers

Your answers to these questions rather obviously determine whether you should become a collector, what you should collect, how you should collect, and the appropriate type of collection. As your financial condition changes over the years—hopefully for the better—and you gain in knowledge and experience, the answers to some or all these questions may change, if so, you should adjust your behavior appropriately.

Being Your Own Boss

6. Be familiar with the various methods of financing a business.
7. Know how to estimate the amount of financing necessary.
8. Be familiar with the following terms:

assets	trade credit
liabilities	factoring
owner's equity	accrual accounting
current assets	cash accounting
fixed assets	balance sheet
cash budget	income statement
capital budget	

Some surveys have indicated that today's college students are less likely to consider going into business for themselves than students were in the past. Yet, running your own business is currently one of the "in" things for a young person to do. Many of the same people who, a few years ago, were dropping out in protest against middle-class America, are today dropping into small businesses. They are attracted by the same things that have always attracted people to running their own businesses: independence, a chance to put your ideas into operation, control over your destiny, and an opportunity to create that is seldom enjoyed by one who is not some type of artist.

About 95 percent of all the businesses in the United States can be classified as small. There are few products or services which are not produced by the small business sector of our economy. In our free market economy, anyone who wishes to can start his own business, and every year a lot of people take the plunge. Your chances of getting rich are far greater working for yourself than working for the other guy.

Some people get rich by going into business for themselves; most, however, do not. Most giant corporations were once small businesses, and, in a few cases, the same person who started these companies guided them into the giant category.

If you were working in a shoe store and got an idea for greatly increasing the store's business, your boss might think you were nuts and tell you to get lost. If you owned the store you could try out your idea and reap all the benefits it might generate. Even if you worked for someone who did use your idea, you might not be rewarded or not receive a reasonable reward. Your boss might end up with all the credit for the idea. Your coworkers, out of jealousy, might become cool, discouraging you from continuing to be an idea person.

Many, if not most, small businessowners get much more out of their business than money. Of course, you may be thinking, they get problems! This is true, yet, without problems one cannot achieve the self-satisfaction and pride that arises out of solving problems. The price of achievement is struggle.

Running one's own business is particularly attractive to people who do not like to be subjected to authority and control. Undoubtedly, this is a major reason why some of the antiestablishment youth of the sixties have gone into business for themselves. But, this escape from authority and control, like everything else in life, has a price, and this price is responsibility. If you have any employees, and few businesses are so small that they don't, this responsibility is not for yourself only.

Of course, it is naive to think that one can really escape authority and control. Every businessperson is subject to many local, state, and federal laws and regulations and demands of creditors, customers, and workers which cannot be ignored.

If you run a restaurant, the city health inspector may come by and tell you that you will have to close down unless you install a tile floor. A man from the Occupational Health and Safety Administration may drop in to tell you to install protective devices on your meat cutter and to hang fire extinguishers on the wall. A woman with the Wage and Hour Law branch of the U.S. Labor Department may come by to warn you that you will have to start paying your employees more for overtime. The city building inspector may tell you that you will have to make expensive repairs to your building. The city tax office may send you a higher property tax bill.

Your meat supplier may tell you that you are going to have to pay him something on your bill or he will halt deliveries. You may be begging the air conditioning repairman to come fix your unit. The bank may call to say your loan will not be renewed unless you improve your cash flow. Customers may be staying away in droves because, unlike your competition, you don't have a salad bar. A customer may be suing you over a foot injury she suffered when she stepped on a fork on the floor of the restaurant. Her lawyer may say she will settle out of court for a bundle. Your waitresses may threaten to quit unless you supplement their tips.

AM I THE TYPE?

One study of the owners of small businesses concluded that five characteristics were associated with success, both financially and otherwise. These characteristics are *drive, thinking ability, human relations ability, ability to communicate,* and *technical knowledge.*

A person with drive displays initiative and persistence. He or she is a responsible person with good enough health to function at a high level of activity. This is a thinking person—an original and creative thinker, excelling at analytical thinking. He or she deals with other persons effectively, is tactful, sociable, cooperative, and cheerful, and emotionally stable. Such a person is able to communicate effectively both in writing and orally. Communication, of course, is a two-way street, so he or she is a good listener. This is a person who is very knowledgeable about the product or service being produced and effectively uses this knowledge.

Many of those who organize a business are highly ambitious. This is a good thing, because if the business is not to go under, the small business owner must be willing to put in long hours. For the owner-manager of the small business, which includes most owners of small businesses (because their owners find it necessary to manage them), going home and forgetting the business is a fatal mistake. (Most owners manage their business for financial reasons as well as to enjoy some of the other benefits they started the business to enjoy.) To be a manager, you must be a leader. The job of the manager is to *plan, organize, control, coordinate, and staff the business.*

As the owner-manager of a small business, you will be responsible for acquiring and spending funds; thus, you will be keeping financial records and making financial decisions. You will be deciding where to locate the business and what to sell at what price. You will be deciding whether to advertise; how much advertising to do; where to advertise; and, what type of advertisements to run. In order to control costs, you will have to decide what costs should be. You will have to hire, supervise, and fire workers.

Clearly, to do all these things with maximum efficiency requires a great deal of knowledge. Much of this knowledge can most efficiently be learned via a formal education; some must be acquired by experience! It is true, of course, that in the past many successful businesspeople had little education. However, today this happens much less often.

The so-called uneducated, but successful, businessman of the past didn't fail to get an education because he thought an education was a handicap. He didn't get it because a formal education was not so easily obtained then as now. And though he had little formal education, he was not uneducated. He knew a great deal in at least some essential areas.

Although an education is very important, this certainly does not mean that you can do without experience. To start a business with absolutely no relevant experience is generally very foolhardy. Success then depends on luck. Yet, people who would scoff at the idea of attempting brain surgery without either a medical education or experience will blithely go into business for themselves sans education and experience, and, as a result, the "patient"—the business—dies. Of all new businesses started, about one-third are discontinued within a year. Fifty percent are discontinued within two years. Around two-thirds have left the scene within five years. After that the failure rate drops sharply. *Too many people make the mistake of thinking that because anyone can start a business, that anyone can make a go of it.*

The foregoing may have led you to think that only a real superman or woman can succeed. This is not true. Weaknesses in a few areas, if not too great and offset by great strengths in other areas, will not prevent you from being successful.

HOW TO DECIDE WHAT BUSINESS TO ENTER

You can't make money selling snowshoes in Florida! The first step in deciding what business to go into is to decide what product or service there is a demand for that is currently not being adequately served, either because it is not available or available in an inadequate quantity, or it is unsatisfactory in some way.

Do not believe that if you build a better mousetrap that people will beat a path to your door. A better mousetrap has been produced, but what people were willing to pay for a better mousetrap was less than it cost to make them! You must determine *(1) if there is an unmet need and (2) if you can satisfy it at a low enough cost.* Failure to consider one or both of these factors has beaten many small businesses even before they opened their doors for business.

Given that you find several unmet needs that you can serve at a low enough cost, you normally should select the one you think will be the most profitable. The fact that you do not like a business or lack interest in it is likely to mean that you will not find it to be very profitable, even if demand is very high and costs low. Even if your lack of enthusiasm doesn't cut profits, you may prefer to make less money and do something you like and are knowledgeable about. Beware, however, of sacrificing too much profit—maybe all—in order to do something you like.

If all the other factors are equal, pick the business you know the most about or, if the business you really have your heart set on isn't the one you know the most about, learn enough to make this the case before you start your business. The more you know about a business, the greater is your chance for success. A good way to learn about a business is to work for someone else in the business. This has often been the path followed by successful small businessmen and women.

Working for someone else can provide you with appropriate skills and knowledge because the business is similar, the same, or complementary. An example of the first is working for the Internal Revenue Service and then setting up a tax service. An example of the last is working in a grocery store and then going into grocery wholesaling. Sometimes even experience in a totally different field can pay off handsomely. Maybe, for example, you work in sales; then you set up a small manufacturing firm. All your competitors are production-oriented types. They just push the stuff out the door and count on it selling itself. With your sales background you revolutionize the industry. You go out and sell the product. Because of your selling efforts, your sales zoom, while your competitors' slump. You have increased the scope of the knowledge needed to succeed in this industry. You are a creative thinker and, as a result, are successful!

How do you find an unmet need? That is a difficult question to answer because there are so many possible ways to do this. Perhaps a few examples will serve.

You live in desert country. To brighten up things, you scoop up some dirt and put it in a window box in which you plant flower seeds. Every morning you water them. You get some wonderful flowers. That dirt seems to be good to grow things in! You get the dirt analyzed and find it is great for growing a lot of things. You check with the state geologist and find there's a good bit of water underground in your area. You read everything you can get your hands on about well digging and irrigation. You visit well diggers. Maybe you work for one. You learn the business. You find out how much it will take to go into this business and what your costs would be. You figure out what people could grow in the desert if they had water, and what they could sell it for. Could they pay a price for the water that would give you a profit? If so, and you can get up the money to go into business, you are off and running!

In a department store you notice some scarves signed by the person who designed the pattern printed on them. You start thinking of all the artists that it must take to design all the patterns you see in stores. You think about how some patterns popular when you were young or when your parents were young are now back in style. Then you remember that your grandfather ran a mill way back yonder and you still have his sample books. Couldn't you offer these patterns to cloth producers at a lower cost than they would pay an artist to come up with a new design; yet, still make a nice profit? And you could keep this up by scrounging around for more old patterns! (Before you rush out to get into this business, you should know that someone has already thought of it!)

You are visiting another city to buy merchandise for the store you work for. You stop in an ice cream shop for some ice cream and notice how the children from a nearby school pile in when school lets out, and so do the people coming out of the nearby movie theater. At home there's a similar location without an ice cream shop, and there is a small building for rent there now. You rush home; rent the building, and you're off!

Creative people see the same things other people see, but they see them differently. The noncreative person would simply say, "What a desolate place!" "I wish I could design scarves like that and make all the money that guy does!" "I wish all those noisy kids hadn't come in!" He sees problems rather than opportunities.

HOW MUCH MONEY DO I NEED?

Before you can decide how much money you will need to start a business, you have to identify what you will need money for.

You will need money both for working capital (current assets) and fixed assets. *Current assets* are things like cash, checking account balances, customer I.O.U.'s (accounts receivable), and inventories of materials, supplies, and merchandise. *Fixed assets* are things like furniture and fixtures, equipment, buildings, and land—items you normally hold for more than one year. In addition, you will need money for legal fees; state organizational taxes; the expenses of starting, such as paying rent in advance and utility deposits; advertising; and, operating expenses such as wages and utilities which will have to be paid before revenues start coming in.

Many new businesses fail because their organizers didn't consider the fact that it might be only after several months, or at least several weeks, after operations commence before any cash revenues will be received. Workers are likely to demand their wages before sales are made or, because they are credit sales, collected. Before a product can be manufactured you may have to pay for the materials used in it. (Later, after you are successful, you may be able to purchase them on credit terms long enough for you to sell the items produced with these materials.)

Don't forget about yourself! It is surprising how many owner-managers forget to pay themselves a salary. If you worked for someone else, you would get a salary. Thus, if you work for yourself, you should get a salary too. Of course, since you are the owner of the business, you will also, hopefully, reap a profit, which is a return on the money you have in the business, not a reward for your labor. You will certainly need the salary to live on until the profits start rolling in, and, often, this takes a year or more.

If you don't consider a salary for yourself as an expense of doing business, then you are not likely to charge a high enough price for the product or service you are selling to provide yourself with a salary. For example, suppose you list the following needs for cash during the first year of operating of a wig shop:

Interest	$ 4,000
Rent	36,000
Merchandise	80,000
Utilities	6,000
Workers' salaries	34,000
	$160,000

Suppose you expect to sell 8000 wigs if your selling price is $21.50. At this price you would cover the above expenses and clear $12,000 before taxes. Suppose you put up $100,000 as your investment in the business. The $12,000 would represent a 12 percent return on your money, and this sounds good. Suppose, however, that you quit a job which would now pay $16,000 before taxes in order to run the wig shop. Many owner-managers have made exactly this kind of mistake, but have gone around bragging about that 12 percent return on their money, which is so much more than they used to get in the bank, which paid 6 percent. Yet, if they had left the money in the bank, they would be making $6,000 on it and $16,000 from their labor, for a total of $22,000, as compared to the $12,000 they earn from the wig shop!

If you had included a salary for yourself in the list of expenses, you would have seen that $21.50 is not a high enough price. At a higher price, of course, you would sell fewer wigs. As a result, it might not be possible for you to match your earnings in your old job plus your earnings on your savings by running the wig shop. If this is the case, do not invest in the wig shop. If, however, at a price of $45.50 you could sell 4000 wigs, you would gross $22,000 for yourself. If demand at 45.50 is greater than 4000, you would certainly be interested in the possibility of opening the wig shop. If demand was any less than 4000, you wouldn't.

The amount of money you will need, of course, will vary with the type of business you go into. An examination of the experience of similar businesses is your best guide as to how much money you will have to spend. Once your business has been in operation a while, your own experience will be the best guide.

In addition to the type of business, the level of sales will also affect the amount of money needed. Operating expenses usually vary rather closely with variances in the level of sales. The amount of fixed assets needed varies with the anticipated average or maximum level of sales. For example, the cost of goods sold will probably be nearly doubled if sales are doubled. More facilities are required to produce a higher rather than a lower level of output only if the difference between these levels is great enough.

WHERE AND HOW DO I GET THE MONEY?

Before you decide where and how to get the money, decide how you are going to organize your business, since this affects where and how you get the funds necessary to start your business.

Most businesses, particularly small ones, are organized as *sole proprietorships*—the business has only one owner. Many small businesses are organized as *partnerships,* that is, the business has more than one owner. In a *general partnership,* all the owners participate directly in the management of the business. The share of the firm's revenues that goes to each partner depends on the size of the partner's investment and the amount of personal services provided. Both the sole proprietor and the general partner have *unlimited liability;* that is, the owner's personal assets are subject to claim by an unsatisfied creditor of the business. In a *limited partnership,* at least one partner has limited liability and no voice in the management of the company. Unlimited liability is probably the most serious drawback of these forms of organizations. They are, however, relatively easy to form and comparatively free from government restrictions. They are not subject to the federal income tax, though all wages, salaries, bonuses, commissions, and profits paid out by them are subject to the personal income tax, which is paid by the recipient of the money.

Retail shops, filling stations, barber shops, beauty parlors, auto repair shops, and so on, are frequently sole proprietorships. While all of these are also sometimes partnerships, partnerships are most common in the professions, particularly law and public accounting. Both forms are also common in medicine, real estate, and insurance, but are least often found in manufacturing. This is because manufacturing usually requires a much larger amount of financing than these types of businesses can acquire. Many manufacturing firms, most large firms, and all giant firms are *corporations.* Unlike the other forms of organization, the corporation is a legal entity like a person, except that it has no individual-type rights. Like a person, it pays income taxes. It can sue and be sued. All of its owners have limited liability, and they do not manage the company directly. Instead, they elect a board of directors, which determines general policies and hires the people who will manage the company. (Owners can be hired as managers.)

Because they participate directly in management, a partnership with many thousands of partners is impractical. The corporation faces no such problem. There is no practical limit as to how many owners it can have. The corporation, therefore, can acquire a lot more equity (owners' money) than can the other two forms of organization. The other types of business organizations cease to exist once an owner dies. The corporation's life is unlimited. Because of all this, under a given set of circumstances, lenders are far more willing to lend to a corporation than to one of the other forms of organization.

A corporation is more difficult to organize. It pays taxes on its profits, and so do its owners when they receive what is left. If a firm's income is rather low, the owners' tax bill will likely be less if if the firm is not incorporated. If the amount of income is high, the reverse is true.

If you wish to remove your money from a sole proprietorship or partnership, it will normally be much more difficult to do than if you wished to get your money out of a corporation. In the case of the sole proprietorship, you have to sell the business. In the case of the partnership, the business will have to be dissolved and either sold or another partner or partners will have to invest the money necessary to buy you out. (They can, if they wish, form another partnership and continue in business without you.) If, however, you own *shares of stock* in a corporation, you can simply find someone to buy them from you. You could remain a manager or other type of employee of the corporation even after you sold out your ownership position.

There are some other forms of business organization, such as joint stock companies, trusts, and cooperatives, but they are far less common than are these three.

Your first source of funds is yourself! Friends and relatives are also frequently a source of funds for small businessmen or women. (Be careful! Money has broken up a lot of families and friendships.) In order to sell a business to you, the owner of a business you are buying may accept a note from you for part or all the selling price. If you take the *franchising* route—you own the business, but operate it as though it was a part of a chain. The franchiser may finance you or help you get financing.

By taking on partners, you can get equity money from them. By incorporating, you can sell shares and get, probably, more equity money this way. If you are a retailer, you may be able to get suppliers to provide you with inventories on a credit basis. This is called *trade credit*. As a manufacturer, you may also be able to get suppliers of equipment to provide you with needed equipment on a credit basis. It will be easier to get trade credit, under given conditions, if you incorporate. You may also be able to get a bank loan. This, too, is more likely if you incorporate.

Most small businesses make do with four sources of funds: *owners, trade creditors, short-term bank loans,* and *mortgage loans.* Their major source of outside financing is trade credit and short-term bank loans, with the former usually being by far the larger and most frequently used. Some small businesses make use of *factoring.* If you factor your customers' accounts, instead of waiting until they come due and collecting these accounts receivable yourself, you have turned over the right to collect these accounts to a factor for an immediate payment of an amount smaller than what he expects to collect from your customers.

You may be able to obtain financing from small loan companies, commercial credit companies, sales finance companies, and insurance companies. If you cannot get a loan from a private source, you can go to the Small Business Administration, an agency of the federal government, that may lend you the money you need or participate in a loan with a private source that otherwise would not lend to you or would not do so at a reasonable interest rate. If you need long-term funds, which the Small Business Administration doesn't provide, you can go to a Small Business Investment Company, a private company supported by federal legislation. It provides both equity and long-term debt funds.

The Small Business Administration also provides advice and counseling and government contracts for the goods and services produced by small companies. The Small Business Investment Companies will provide managerial services.

In obtaining funds from sophisticated investors and creditors it will be necessary to have well-prepared financial statements showing your firm's recent performance, current position, and projected future position. The minimum financial statements required would be your current income statement and balance sheet. The *income statement* shows your revenues and expenses over one accounting period, which is normally a year (see Exhibit 10–1). The *balance sheet* shows your assets, liabilities, and owners' equity at the end of the accounting period (see Exhibit 10–2). An *asset* is a piece of property or a right to receive payment which you own. When accrual accounting is used, assets are shown at their original cost less, in the case of fixed assets, such as buildings and equipment, accumulated depreciation. If accrual accounting is used, expenses are recorded when they occur; not when money is spent; thus, the cost of a fixed asset is, via an annual reduction in value called *depreciation,* shown as an expense over its useful

EXHIBIT 10–1

McGOUGH MANUFACTURING COMPANY[1]
Income Statement
For the Year Ended December 31, 19—

Net Sales			$669,100
Cost of Goods Sold:			
Finished goods inventory, January 1, 19—	$ 69,200		
Cost of goods manufactured	569,700		
Total cost of goods available for sale	$638,900		
Less: Finished goods inventory			
December 31, 19—	66,400		
Cost of Goods Sold			572,500
Gross Margin			$ 96,600
Selling and Administrative Expenses			
Selling Expenses:			
Sales salaries and commissions	$26,700		
Advertising expense	12,900		
Miscellaneous selling expense	2,100		
Total Selling Expenses		$ 41,700	
Administrative expenses:			
Salaries	$27,400		
Miscellaneous			
Administrative expense	4,800		
Total Administrative Expenses		32,200	
Total Selling and Administrative Expenses			73,900
Net Operating Profit			$22,700
Other Revenue			15,300
Net Profit Before Taxes			$38,000
Estimated Income Tax			12,640
Net Profit (After-tax Income)			$25,360

[1] A fictitious company

EXHIBIT 10–2

McGOUGH MANUFACTURING COMPANY[1]
Balance Sheet
December 31, 19—

Assets

Current Assets:			
Cash		$20,000	
Accounts Receivable	$40,000		
Less allowance for doubtful accounts	3,000		
		37,000	
Inventories	$45,000		
Less allowance for inventory loss	5,000		
		40,000	
Total Current Assets			$97,000
Fixed Assets:			
Machinery	$20,000		
Less allowance for Depreciation	4,000		
		$16,000	
Buildings	$28,000		
Less allowance for Depreciation	6,000		
		22,000	
Land		12,000	
Total Fixed Assets			50,000
Total Assets			$147,000

[1] A fictitious company.

EXHIBIT 10–2 *(Continued)*

Liabilities and Equity

Current Liabilities:

Accounts payable	$20,000	
Notes payable	30,000	
Accrued liabilities	6,000	
Allowance for taxes	4,000	
Total Current Liabilities		$60,000
Equity:		
Capital stock	$50,000	
Retained earnings	37,000	
Total Equity		87,000
Total Liabilities and Equity		$147,000

life. In other words, the balance sheet value of an asset is reduced each year by an amount which is shown that year as depreciation expense on the income statement even though the entire cash expense occurred when the building was purchased. (Land is not depreciated.) Depreciation differs from most expenses shown on the expense statement because it does not involve a current cash outflow. The cash outflow occurred when the asset was purchased. At that time it showed up as a reduction in the cash account, but did not show up as an equal-sized expense of the accounting period in which the asset was purchased. The use of depreciation is one of the chief differences between *cash accounting*, which only shows cash inflows and outflows, and *accrual accounting*, which produces a much more meaningful picture of a business' financial position, because it associates both expenses and income with the year in which they were incurred or earned.

The name *balance sheet* comes from the fact that the total value of assets is equaled by the sum of total liabilities and total owners' equity. The amount of the owners' equity will rise from one accounting period to the next if the income statement for that period shows revenues exceeding expenses, and that that profit was not paid out or withdrawn by the firm's owners.

Liabilities represent amounts owed to creditors such as trade creditors and banks. *Owners' equity*, of course, shows how much the firm's owners have invested in it by making payments to it or allowing earnings to be retained by the firm. *Assets* are things owned, such as inventories and buildings, which are tangible, and things such as cash, which is an intangible asset. Assets also include intangible assets that are rights, such as accounts receivable, which give you the right to collect money.

Creditors are very much interested in what your financial performance and position will be in the future. Thus, they may ask for *pro forma* income statements and balance sheets. These statements show what you expect your financial statements to look like in the future. A potential short-term creditor may also wish you to draw up a cash budget. A *cash budget* shows the cash inflows and outflows you expect to result from operating the business over the next month, few months, or a year. A potential creditor may also wish to see a capital budget. A *capital budget* shows what you plan to invest in fixed assets during the following year or several years.

Potential creditors are interested in how well the firm has handled its debts in the past. Has it paid them off in full and on time? Since a new firm has no credit record, it is more difficult for it to borrow money. Lenders will then be particularly interested in the credit record of the firm's owners. They will also evaluate their character and ability to manage the business.

SHOULD YOU BUY AN EXISTING BUSINESS?

Just as you may get a bargain in buying an old house or a used car because the seller needs money very quickly and very badly, and so will give you a good price, you may get a real bargain by buying an existing business. You also avoid going through the start up period, i.e., equipment, stock, etc., has already been accumulated. In addition, you may be able to continue relationships with customers, suppliers, and creditors that the former owner established. The former owner, too, may give you a lot of useful advice.

The main danger is that the seller may mislead you about the business's value, leading you to pay too much. He may have been a bad businessman and established a poor reputation for the business which you will have to overcome. The stock he sells you may have been poorly selected, and you will have to sell it at a loss. The business' location or its facilities may be poor.

In deciding what to pay for a going business, you are not interested in what the seller paid for the business' assets. What would it cost you to replace the building, furniture and fixtures, etc., is what you are interested in. What you can sell the inventories for also interests you. How much is the location worth? How much is any customer loyalty to the business worth?

You are buying the business to make a profit, thus, *you are interested in anticipated revenues and expenses and what you are willing to pay to gain the resulting profit.* This depends on what rate of return you believe you must earn. Keep in mind the fact that under your management revenues and expenses might not be what they have been under the seller's management.

You can find businesses for sale in newspaper want ads or you can go to a business broker, who brings together people who want to sell businesses with those who wish to buy. He will probably charge a fee of around 10 percent of the selling price, which is likely to be from $30,000 to $40,000 at a minimum, though it may be much less or much more.

WHAT ABOUT FRANCHISING?

Franchising is not a new idea, but its current great popularity is. A *franchise* is simply an agreement between a franchisor and a franchisee in which the former gives the latter the right to sell a product or service using the franchisor's name, reputation, selling techniques, and possibly other services for a fee. A franchisee may make an initial payment to the franchisor and periodically pay a percent of the gross sales to the franchisor. He may also agree to buy supplies from the franchisor, and may have to pay part of the cost of national advertising, or pay for services provided by the franchisor, such as training employees.

There are a number of advantages to franchising. The franchisor has experience that you would have to acquire the hard way. Franchisors can provide you with financial assistance directly and indirectly. They may give you credit, and their name will help you get credit from others. They provide an already developed consumer image and goodwill with proven products or services. Franchisors will provide you with completely designed facilities, including layout, equipment, and displays, and will provide an operating plan and a financial records system. They will assist you in picking a location for your business, which is a major factor in retailing. Most franchisors provide training for both managers and workers, and their nationally-known name will bring you customers you otherwise would not get, particularly in the case of people not living in the vicinity. By being part of a chain, you will enjoy the lower prices granted bulk buyers. If you want to get out of the business, the franchisor may help you dispose of it; even buying it themselves as a company-owned outlet.

Being a franchisee, however, does have some drawbacks. You

lose some of the usual advantages of being in business for yourself. The business has the franchisor's name on it, and you must follow his or her rules, and these rules may be quite specific. Inspectors may come by periodically to see that you are toeing the line, and, if you aren't, you may lose your franchise. You can buy some supplies locally or add a local dish if you are running a restaurant on your own, but you will not be able to if you are a franchisee. Because you are a franchisee, you may be unable to respond quickly, or even at all, to the actions of your local competitors. For example, a competitor may cut price, but you can't, because each unit in the chain must charge the same price. Another problem is that you will have to share your profits with the franchisor, and sometimes his cut is unreasonable. Also, other of the chain's outlets may perform badly, and their reputation may rub off on you.

Franchising is dominant among automobile dealerships and fast food outlets, and there are few areas in retailing without any franchising. Franchising is very important, too, in service industries such as rug cleaning, termite proofing, dry cleaning, roofing, and so on. Other fields where franchising is important are: motels, rentals and leasing, vending machines, tree services, travel agencies, beauty and slenderizing salons, cosmetics, dance studios, employment services, lawn and garden care, swimming pools, nursing homes, pet shops, printing, and signs.

You can often find franchising opportunities in daily metropolitan newspapers. Trade publications will often include advertisements for a franchise in that trade, and there are also publications devoted exclusively to franchising. The federal government publishes a list of franchisers. Franchisers also hold exhibitions in major cities, and there are franchise marketing agencies and consultants who will help you obtain a franchise.

THE PITFALLS AND DRAWBACKS

The major pitfalls of going into business for yourself are: lack of experience, lack of money, wrong location, inventory mismanagement, too much capital going into fixed assets, poor credit-granting practices, taking too much money out of the business, unplanned expansion, and having the wrong attitudes. *The major cause of failure is insufficient funds to keep the business going during the first critical months of operation.*

The major drawbacks of being in business yourself are the same as those that plague the farmer—you are tied down, your risk is great, and your responsibilities are heavy.

THE NEED FOR AN OBJECTIVE

You cannot make rational decisions unless you have some objective toward which the decision is to take you. Without an objective, any decision is as good as any other. Presumably you go into business to accomplish some personal objective or objectives; thus, the objective or objectives of your business decisions should be in line with obtaining your personal ends. What this personal objective is makes a lot of difference. If being the boss and controlling everything in the business is more important than making more money, you may choose not to allow the business to grow beyond a certain size, even though more money would be made by expanding further, because this would mean taking on partners and not controlling everything yourself.

CASES FOR DISCUSSION

Case 1 Running a restaurant is a risky business, but Dean Bradshaw has wanted to since he was 17. In line with this goal, he chose to major in business administration in college. Then he took a management trainee job with a major department store. He spent three years with them as a department manager, where he learned about everything from personnel management and unit-buying control to unloading trucks. He also learned to budget and bring in a profit. Then he worked as a district office manager for a manufacturing firm, where he learned about inventory control, manufacturing, and distribution. By this time he and his wife, who worked as a model, had saved up enough money, they thought, to start a restaurant.

Having observed the growing interest in ethnic foods and being friends with a couple that run a Chinese grocery store, Dean and his wife, Linda, who studied restaurant management in college, have decided to open a 60-seat restaurant featuring Chinese foods called The Dragon. Though not very keen about Chinese food, the Bradshaws are familiar with it. To play it safe, however, they formed a partnership with their friends who run the grocery store. Their lawyer, however, advises them to incorporate. She says this will reduce their risk.

They have leased a building which formerly housed a clothing store. It is located in the business district of an affluent surburban section of a large city. Other restaurants are nearby. None of them specialize in Chinese foods. The nearest residences are condominiums, which are largely inhabited by elderly people. Dean and Linda, with the help of friends, have decorated the restaurant in an oriental style. They have both quit their jobs to devote full time to the restaurant. They have $10,000 to invest; their partners have $5,000.

They estimate that monthly sales will average $8,700; cost of sales $3,000; total operating expenses $5,007, which includes salaries for themselves and their employees, insurance, depreciation, advertising, utilities, rent, supplies, employee withholding and unemployment fees, and sales tax. This would give them a net profit before income taxes of $693. They estimate that start up costs, part of which they have already spent, will be $13,592. This includes fixtures and equipment, utensils, initial advertising and lease payment, licenses, opening inventory of food, wiring, plumbing, utility deposits, signs, furniture, and decorating. What do you think of their plans? How would you advise them to proceed?

Case 2 Phyllis Kawashima has just received a degree in mechanical engineering technology. Her family's income was too great for her to receive financial aid, but her parents found putting her and her brother through college more than they could afford. Thus, Phyllis worked part- or full time all the way through college. First she worked in a fast-food outlet, but for the past two years she has worked in a pet store. Originally she took the job because it was available and she likes animals. A couple of months ago she was thinking of leaving this job when she graduated, but then she realized she didn't want to quit. She realized that she would like to make running a pet store a career.

Phyllis is ambitious. She doesn't want to remain a rather low-paid assistant all her life. She wants to own a pet store. In fact, though she thinks it is really an impossible dream, she would like to run a chain of pet stores. But how, she wonders, can she ever achieve even the goal of owning even one store? How would you advise Phyllis?

Case 3 Louis Erlich majored in music at college for two years. Then he dropped out and, for the past two years, has been playing in a combo that plays at fraternity parties and the like. Louis isn't making much money, and he has decided that he will never amount to much as a musician. He just doesn't have the talent, and he hates all the travel. For the past few months he has been acting as the business manager of the group and, to his surprise, he enjoys this work. What he would really like to do, he now believes, is open a theatrical agency. He can't decide what he should do to start working toward this goal. How would you advise him?

Case 4 Cory Sokolov began college as a mathematics major. He didn't do well and ended up only getting a junior college degree. He really didn't know what he wanted to do when he finished college. His first, short-lived job was as a life insurance agent. For the next few years he sold tires in a tire store. He recently took a job as assistant manager of a tire store in a medium-sized city. He got married a year and a half ago and now has a two-month-old son. Cory is fed up with working for someone else and he wants to go into business for himself.

His neighbors are always complaining about being unable to get various repairs and maintenance work done around the house and having to do it themselves. When they do get someone, they have to wait a long time before he or she shows up; the work is often inferior, but it costs a lot. This has given Cory an idea he is all fired up about. He has $2000 he can invest, and his wife's brothers will probably lend him another $5000. He could sell his second car for $2400. He would use the money to start a repair service which would handle such work.

Cory lives in a city of 275,000 people. Another 400,000 people live within a 50-mile radius of this city. Other than some groups of teenage boys who do odd jobs in their neighborhoods, Cory can discover no one who provides a similar service, and Cory, of course, would have men working for him who could do work that the boys don't, such as repair small appliances, do wiring, and so on. How would you advise Cory?

Case 5 Margaret Harris was a college student majoring in marketing when she met and married Stan. She quit school and worked as a groundskeeper so Stan could finish college. Eventually she planned to return and finish, but five years went by and she didn't get around to it. Except for working every spring for the Internal Revenue Service when they take on extra help, she hasn't worked since her marriage. They have no children. Four months ago Stan was killed in an automobile accident. Margaret collected a $25,000 life insurance policy on Stan and wants to use it to start a record and tape shop. She is looking at a free-standing building on a major highway leading into the city and a store in a large shopping center. How would you advise Margaret?

Case 6 Alfred Kessler received a business administration degree with a specialization in economics three years ago. He has been working as a loan officer in a bank since then. Because his mother runs a restaurant, he has been exposed to the restaurant business all his life. After a taste of another kind of life, he has decided that he likes the restaurant business better. He has $4,000 saved and his mother would lend him $15,000. He is torn between setting up a restaurant that would offer a general menu and opening a franchised fast-food outlet, hoping to ultimately run two or three of them. He is also wondering if he should run it as a sole proprietorship, partnership, or corporation. He lives in a metropolitan area of about 1 million. How would you advise Alfred?

REVIEW QUESTIONS

1. What abilities do you need to manage your own business?
2. How should you decide what business to go into?
3. How do you determine how much money you need to start a business?
4. What do the balance sheet and income statement show? Why is this information important?
5. What are the major advantages and disadvantages of the various forms of organization, that is, proprietorship, partnership, and corporation?
6. What are the advantages and disadvantages of franchising?
7. How can you go about raising the money you need to start and operate the business?
8. How should you determine how much to offer for an existing business?
9. Why go into business by buying out an existing business?
10. What are the advantages and disadvantages of being your own boss?

YOUR PLAN: CHAPTER 10

**Questions you should answer before
deciding to go into business for yourself:**

1. Do you have the proper personal qualifications to run a business?
2. Have you considered your weak points and taken steps to improve them or found an associate whose strong points compensate for them?
3. Have you considered what you would like to do?
4. What business or types of businesses do you know the most about?
5. Is there an adequate demand for the product and/or service you are thinking of providing?
6. Would it be better to work a while for someone else, gaining experience before striking out for yourself?
7. How much competition would you face and how would you handle it?
8. Are general business conditions good now?
9. Are business conditions good in the line of business you are considering going into?

10. What is the typical rate of return in the line of business you are considering going into?
11. How much will you need to invest to go into the line of business you are considering?
12. Is the rate of return you would earn, in light of risk, as good as you could do otherwise?
13. Have you estimated the first year's cash inflows and outflows?
14. Have you obtained the prices of the equipment and supplies you will need?
15. Have you located sources of supply?
16. Have you determined how many employees you will need and what they will cost?
17. Have you allowed for some funds to handle emergencies?
18. Have you determined how much money you can invest at a maximum?
19. Do you know how much credit you can get from suppliers?
20. Do you know where you can borrow money?
21. Have you talked to a banker about your plans?
22. Do you need a partner or partners?
23. What form of business organization would be best?
24. Have you talked with a lawyer about your plans?
25. Have you identified your potential customers?
26. What do you know about your potential customers' buying habits and income?
27. Are potential employees available?
28. Is a suitable location available?
29. Are appropriate facilities available at the proposed location?
30. Have you estimated future profits for several years?
31. Are these profits adequate?
32. Have you considered buying an established business?
33. If you are considering buying an established business, has a lawyer checked the seller's title to be sure it is clear?
34. Have you checked out the seller's claims?
35. Have you compared the seller's offering price with what others would give you and what it would cost you to start from scratch?
36. Have you considered a franchise?
37. Have you investigated to discover what franchising arrangements are available?

38. Have you worked out a financial record-keeping system?
39. Have you made cost estimates?
40. Have you devised a system to control costs?
41. Have you decided how to train and compensate employees?
42. Do you plan to sell for credit and, if so, on what terms?
43. How will you set prices?
44. Have you checked with the proper authorities to find out what, if any, licenses are necessary to do business?
45. Do you know what police and health regulations may apply?
46. Will you be subject to interstate commerce regulations and, if so, which ones?
47. What kinds and amounts of insurance will you need?
48. What taxes will your business be subject to?
49. How will you handle employee withholding taxes?
50. How will you handle sales taxes?
51. Have you planned an adequate record system for making out your tax forms?
52. Have you set goals and sub-goals for your business?

How to Use Your Answers

Several purposes are served by these questions. Should you go into business for yourself, and, if so, what kind of business is best? You should carefully choose the form of organization because this will affect your ability to raise money and your control over the business. Due to financial needs or a lack of knowledge or ability on your part, you may not be able to choose the sole proprietorship form of organization. You may choose the corporate form simply because of the lesser risk you then will be taking.

You can go into business etiher by starting from scratch on your own, obtaining a franchise, or buying out an existing business. Each option has both advantages and disadvantages. Conditions will determine which is best for you.

You go into business to earn a profit. The business cannot continue to exist unless it is profitable. Thus, you must estimate the cost of investment, revenues, and costs in order to determine whether or not to go into a given business. Revenues depend on the demand for the product, the price charged, and the competition you face. Price must cover all costs, such as rent, supplies, utilities, and also a return on your investment and a salary for yourself, assuming you work in the business, which is usually necessary.

Managing a business involves planning, organizing, controlling, coordinating, and staffing. You must decide what is involved in performing each of these functions and how you will carry out each one.

PLANNING FORM 1

Estimating Start-up Costs

Start-up Costs*	Credit	Cash	Total
Fixures and equipment	——	——	——
Decorating and remodeling	——	——	——
Installation of fixtures	——	——	——
Starting inventory	——	——	——
Deposits with public utilities	——	——	——
Legal and other professional fees	——	——	——
Licenses and permits	——	——	——
Advertising and promotion for opening	——	——	——
Accounts receivable (to replace stock sold on credit basis)	——	——	——
Cash	——	——	——
Other	——	——	——
Total estimated start-up costs	——	——	——

* These costs are paid only once when you start the business.

PLANNING FORM 2

Estimating Monthly Expenses

Monthly Expenses	Credit	Cash	Total
Salary of owner manager	____	____	____
Other salaries and wages	____	____	____
Rent or mortgage interest	____	____	____
Insurance	____	____	____
Advertising	____	____	____
Delivery expense	____	____	____
Supplies	____	____	____
Inventories	____	____	____
Telephone, postage, etc.	____	____	____
Other utilities	____	____	____
Maintenance	____	____	____
Legal and other professional fees	____	____	____
Miscellaneous	____	____	____
Total Monthly Expenses*	____	____	____
Payments to creditors (principal and interest)		____	
Advance payments		____	
Total Monthly Cash Outlay		____	

* Add this to start up costs to get total initial outlay to begin business.

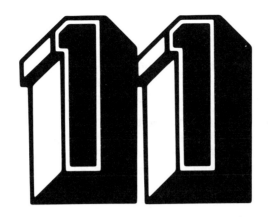

Tax Planning

7. Know how to compute your federal income taxes.
8. Be familiar with the following terms:

personal income taxes	assessed value
excise taxes	millage rate
estate and gift taxes	unearned income
1040 and 1040A forms	schedules
withholding	depreciation
corporate income tax	deductions
progressive taxes	adjustments
proportional taxes	zero bracket amount
regressive taxes	gross income
property tax	adjusted gross
sales taxes	income
joint return	taxable income
income averaging	tax credit

There are only two things you can't avoid, they say—death and taxes. Yet, the news media for years have told us of millionaires who paid no tax on their income, and that the middle class pays relatively more in income taxes than do the rich. The rich, they say, are allowed to escape paying taxes via Congressionally created tax loopholes. Others argue that these people are simply utilizing wise provisions of the tax code that are designed to promote certain socially beneficial activities by providing a monetary incentive to engage in them.

As a result of a mutitude of complaints about abuses of the tax system, in 1976 Congress passed a Tax Reform Act. This massive piece of legislation contained 250 provisions, including many long-sought reforms. The effectiveness of these reforms cannot yet be determined. It is certain, however, that the number of legitimate *tax shelters* has been reduced. A tax shelter is an investment that enables you to avoid paying taxes on some of your income. One of the most popular of these in the past was a limited partnership which invested in real estate. The partners would put up some money and then borrow many times as much money on a nonrecourse basis, that is, the limited partners would not be individually responsible for repaying the loan. Frequently this money would be invested in building and operating apartments. The interest on the borrowed funds would be repaid well before it was due so as to create a loss for the partnership in that expenses, including interest, would exceed revenue. Then the partners, who would have income from other sources, would protect some of this income from taxation by matching it with the "losses" on their real estate venture. These partnerships also took advantage of rapid depreciation to further increase their "losses," i.e., they would, over a very short period of time, recognize the cost of apartment buildings as an expense of the business rather than spreading their cost over the life of the buildings, which is more realistic. Once they had used up all available interest and depreciation expense, they would sell the project to some other limited partnership, which would do exactly the same thing—recognize expenses rapidly enough to exceed revenues. If the selling partnership made a profit on the sale, it would be subject to a lower tax rate than the one they would have paid on income recognized as being generated from operating the apartments.

LIMITATIONS ON TAX SHELTERS

The Tax Reform Act of 1976 sought to eliminate tax shelters of this type by limiting the deductions a taxpayer could take to the actual amount of money being risked in the venture. (Since the loans were nonrecourse, the limited partners were not at risk for this amount.) In addition, it broadened the scope of what is called the *minimum tax,* which is designed to force everyone to pay some taxes on income from investments. Real estate investments, however, were exempted from the at-risk provision. Thus, the at-risk provision only affects oil and gas drilling, absentee farming, sports franchises, motion picture production, and equipment leasing. Yet, it was real estate shelters that were the main impetus for the reform movement!

Real estate shelters, however, were affected by provisions prohibiting the deduction of prepaid interest and the levying of a tax on the profit made when the project is sold, which serves to offset taxes previously lost due to the use of rapid depreciation.

Tax policy, as you probably already suspected, is a very controversial subject. The tax code is very complex, and it is constantly being changed. If you have ever wrestled with an income tax Form 1040, you know that simply filling out a tax return is no picnic. You may have been tempted to send in some tea bags (remember the Boston Tea Party?) after you found out how much you owed. (Someone has sent in tea bags; another sent in his shirt.) Because we have a progressive federal income tax—the more you make, the larger is the share of your income taken by the government—and inflation, the amount the average taxpayer pays has gone up every year both absolutely and relatively. State and local taxes have also been rising very rapidly. Clearly, then, taxes are a major financial problem.

TABLE 11–1   Gross National Product and Income
(Billions of current dollars)

	1974	1975	1976
Total	1412.9	1528.8	1706.5
Personal consumption expenditures	889.6	980.4	1094.0
Gross private domestic investment	214.6	189.1	243.3
Net exports of goods and services	6.0	2.0	7.8
Government purchases of goods and services	302.7	338.9	361.4
Total in 1972 dollars[a]	1217.8	1202.1	1274.7

Source: Board of Governors of the Federal Reserve System, Washington, D.C., *Federal Reserve Bulletin* (January 1978), p. A52.

[a] These figures show real GNP, that is, what GNP would have been if prices had not risen after 1972. Current dollar GNP reflects both an increase or decrease in real national output and in the prices at which this output sells. Note that although the current dollar value of GNP rose from 1974 to 1975, there was actually a decline in real GNP, which is shown by eliminating the effect of the rise in prices from 1974 to 1975.

A significant share of national income is consumed by local, state, and federal governments. (see Table 11–1.) Nearly everybody pays income taxes. Everybody pays some type of tax. Because the tax code is not neutral as to the timing and source of one's income, how much tax you pay on a given long-term income can vary substantially depending on when it is earned and where it came from. *Tax planning* enables you to minimize the amount of tax you pay on a given level of income. This is entirely legal. *Tax evasion, not tax avoidance, is illegal.* The law does not say that you must arrange your affairs so as to pay as much as possible to the government. However, any act engaged in with the sole motive of avoiding taxes can be disallowed by the tax-collecting agency involved. In other words, *avoiding taxes cannot be the only benefit you enjoy from the act taken.*

You must have a basic knowledge of our tax system in order to formulate a tax strategy. If your situation is very complex, you will likely need the help of one or more tax specialists. Just to decide if you need help or not requires some knowledge of the tax system.

THE HOW AND WHY OF TAXATION

The fundamental purpose of taxation is to provide the government with the money it needs to finance its activities. In all the sound and fury over who should pay and how much should be paid, this essential fact often tends to be ignored.

Many people think that the government both provides too few benefits and collects too much in taxes. In other words, they either do not think the tax system is efficient, or they expect something for nothing. (If someone gets something for nothing, someone else is getting nothing for something!) *A fair tax system is one that is both efficient and equitable.* The problem in designing such a system is that there is wide disagreement as to what is fair, efficient, and equitable taxation.

Efficiency refers to more than just the ratio of taxes collected to the cost of collection, because the power to tax is the power to destroy. Taxes can destroy jobs and reduce the level of output, and, thus, the standard of living. Taxes can also take away the incentive necessary for growth and progress.

Taxes reduce individual purchasing power, which reduces business sales. This, in turn, destroys jobs. Through taxation, unequal before-tax incomes can become equal (or less unequal) after-tax incomes; thus, removing the incentive a higher-than-average income gives for a better-than-average performance. Can the government spend the tax money so as to provide benefits great enough to replace these losses to society? If taxation is efficient, it will, at a minimum, cover these costs.

Measuring the costs and benefits of taxation is a difficult and controversial subject. For example, the benefits of a new post office may be fairly obvious and a good way for a politician to get votes, but it is not clear what society has given up to get the new post office. What would the tax money used to build the post office have been used for if the money had been left in the hands of the taxpayers? What benefits would these expenditures have provided?

Equity, as you would expect, refers to the fairness of a tax. A question arises, however, as to what is fair? Some people say that to be fair a tax should be *proportional,* that is, if a person earning $10,000 pays $1,000 in taxes, then a person earning $100,000 should pay $10,000 in taxes. Others say that taxes, to be fair, should be *progressive* —the larger your income, the relatively, as well as absolutely, larger is your tax bill, that is, maybe you would pay $40,000 on $100,000. A progressive tax is justified on more than one basis by its supporters. One justification is called the *benefit principle.* This postulates that the protection the government provides the wealthier person is worth more simply because the wealthy person has more property to be protected than does the poor person. It is also argued that the very fact one is wealthy means that the government is doing more for you than for poor people in that the system "fits" or "works" for you.

Another justification for progressive taxes is called the *ability to pay* principle. It simply postulates that those most able to pay should pay more. If you can do more for society, it is your duty to do so.

Our federal income tax rates are progressive—the last few

dollars you earn are subject to a higher tax rate than are "earlier" dollars, and so on, (See Table 11–2.) The impact of this tax is less progressive than the tax rate tables indicate because of *adjustments, exclusions, deductions,* and *tax credits.* Each of these reduces the amount of taxes you owe and does so in a way that reduces the progressiveness of the tax system.

1977 Tax Table A—SINGLE (Box 1)

(For single persons with tax table income of $20,000 or less who claim fewer than 4 exemptions)

To find your tax: Read down the left income column until you find your income as shown on line 34 of Form 1040. Read across to the column headed by the total number of exemptions claimed on line 7 of Form 1040. The amount shown at the point where the two lines meet is your tax. Enter on Form 1040, line 35.

The $2,200 zero bracket amount, your deduction for exemptions and the general tax credit have been taken into account in figuring the tax shown in this table. Do not take a separate deduction for them.

Caution: *If you can be claimed as a dependent on your parent's return AND you have unearned income (interest, dividends, etc.) of $750 or more AND your earned income is less than $2,200, you must first use Schedule TC (Form 1040), Part II.*

If $3,200 or less your tax is 0

If line 34, Form 1040 is— Over	But not over	1	2	3
		Your tax is—		
3,200	3,250	4	0	0
3,250	3,300	11	0	0
3,300	3,350	18	0	0
3,350	3,400	25	0	0
3,400	3,450	32	0	0
3,450	3,500	39	0	0
3,500	3,550	46	0	0
3,550	3,600	54	0	0
3,600	3,650	61	0	0
3,650	3,700	69	0	0
3,700	3,750	76	0	0
3,750	3,800	84	0	0
3,800	3,850	91	0	0
3,850	3,900	99	0	0
3,900	3,950	106	0	0
3,950	4,000	114	0	0
4,000	4,050	122	0	0
4,050	4,100	130	0	0
4,100	4,150	138	0	0
4,150	4,200	146	0	0
4,200	4,250	154	4	0
4,250	4,300	162	11	0
4,300	4,350	170	19	0
4,350	4,400	178	26	0
4,400	4,450	186	34	0
4,450	4,500	194	41	0
4,500	4,550	203	49	0
4,550	4,600	211	56	0
4,600	4,650	220	64	0
4,650	4,700	228	71	0
4,700	4,750	236	79	0
4,750	4,800	244	87	0
4,800	4,850	251	95	0
4,850	4,900	259	103	0
4,900	4,950	266	111	0
4,950	5,000	274	119	0
5,000	5,050	283	127	0
5,050	5,100	291	135	0
5,100	5,150	300	143	0
5,150	5,200	308	151	0
5,200	5,250	317	159	6
5,250	5,300	325	168	14
5,300	5,350	334	176	21
5,350	5,400	342	185	29
5,400	5,450	351	193	36
5,450	5,500	359	202	44
5,500	5,550	368	210	52
5,550	5,600	376	219	60
5,600	5,650	385	227	68
5,650	5,700	393	236	76
5,700	5,750	402	245	84
5,750	5,800	410	254	92

Continued next column

If line 34, Form 1040 is— Over	But not over	1	2	3
		Your tax is—		
5,800	5,850	419	264	100
5,850	5,900	427	273	108
5,900	5,950	436	283	116
5,950	6,000	444	292	124
6,000	6,050	453	302	133
6,050	6,100	461	311	141
6,100	6,150	470	321	150
6,150	6,200	478	330	158
6,200	6,250	487	340	167
6,250	6,300	495	349	175
6,300	6,350	504	359	184
6,350	6,400	512	368	192
6,400	6,450	521	378	201
6,450	6,500	529	387	210
6,500	6,550	538	397	219
6,550	6,600	546	406	229
6,600	6,650	555	416	238
6,650	6,700	563	425	248
6,700	6,750	572	435	257
6,750	6,800	580	444	267
6,800	6,850	589	454	276
6,850	6,900	597	463	286
6,900	6,950	606	473	295
6,950	7,000	615	482	305
7,000	7,050	624	492	314
7,050	7,100	634	501	324
7,100	7,150	643	511	333
7,150	7,200	653	520	343
7,200	7,250	662	529	352
7,250	7,300	672	538	362
7,300	7,350	681	546	371
7,350	7,400	691	555	381
7,400	7,450	700	563	390
7,450	7,500	710	572	400
7,500	7,550	719	580	409
7,550	7,600	729	589	419
7,600	7,650	738	597	428
7,650	7,700	748	606	438
7,700	7,750	757	615	447
7,750	7,800	767	624	457
7,800	7,850	776	634	466
7,850	7,900	786	643	476
7,900	7,950	795	653	485
7,950	8,000	805	662	495
8,000	8,050	814	672	504
8,050	8,100	824	681	514
8,100	8,150	833	691	523
8,150	8,200	843	700	533
8,200	8,250	852	710	542
8,250	8,300	862	719	552
8,300	8,350	871	729	561
8,350	8,400	881	738	571

Continued next column

If line 34, Form 1040 is— Over	But not over	1	2	3
		Your tax is—		
8,400	8,450	890	748	580
8,450	8,500	900	757	590
8,500	8,550	909	767	601
8,550	8,600	919	776	611
8,600	8,650	928	786	622
8,650	8,700	938	795	632
8,700	8,750	947	805	643
8,750	8,800	957	814	653
8,800	8,850	966	824	664
8,850	8,900	976	833	674
8,900	8,950	985	843	685
8,950	9,000	996	852	695
9,000	9,050	1,007	862	706
9,050	9,100	1,018	871	716
9,100	9,150	1,029	881	727
9,150	9,200	1,040	890	737
9,200	9,250	1,051	900	748
9,250	9,300	1,062	909	758
9,300	9,350	1,073	919	769
9,350	9,400	1,084	928	779
9,400	9,450	1,095	938	790
9,450	9,500	1,106	947	800
9,500	9,550	1,117	957	811
9,550	9,600	1,128	966	821
9,600	9,650	1,139	976	832
9,650	9,700	1,150	985	842
9,700	9,750	1,161	996	852
9,750	9,800	1,172	1,007	862
9,800	9,850	1,183	1,018	871
9,850	9,900	1,194	1,029	881
9,900	9,950	1,205	1,040	890
9,950	10,000	1,216	1,051	900
10,000	10,050	1,227	1,062	909
10,050	10,100	1,238	1,073	919
10,100	10,150	1,249	1,084	928
10,150	10,200	1,260	1,095	938
10,200	10,250	1,271	1,106	947
10,250	10,300	1,282	1,117	957
10,300	10,350	1,293	1,128	966
10,350	10,400	1,304	1,139	976
10,400	10,450	1,315	1,150	985
10,450	10,500	1,326	1,161	996
10,500	10,550	1,337	1,172	1,007
10,550	10,600	1,348	1,183	1,018
10,600	10,650	1,359	1,194	1,029
10,650	10,700	1,370	1,205	1,040
10,700	10,750	1,381	1,216	1,051
10,750	10,800	1,392	1,227	1,062
10,800	10,850	1,403	1,238	1,073
10,850	10,900	1,414	1,249	1,084
10,900	10,950	1,425	1,260	1,095
10,950	11,000	1,436	1,271	1,106

Continued on next page

1977 Tax Table A—SINGLE (Box 1) *(Continued)*

(If your income or exemptions are not covered, use Schedule TC (Form 1040), Part I to figure your tax)

If line 34, Form 1040 is— Over	But not over	1	2	3
		Your tax is—		
11,000	11,050	1,447	1,282	1,117
11,050	11,100	1,459	1,293	1,128
11,100	11,150	1,470	1,304	1,139
11,150	11,200	1,482	1,315	1,150
11,200	11,250	1,493	1,326	1,161
11,250	11,300	1,505	1,337	1,172
11,300	11,350	1,516	1,348	1,183
11,350	11,400	1,528	1,359	1,194
11,400	11,450	1,539	1,370	1,205
11,450	11,500	1,551	1,381	1,216
11,500	11,550	1,562	1,392	1,227
11,550	11,600	1,574	1,403	1,238
11,600	11,650	1,585	1,414	1,249
11,650	11,700	1,597	1,425	1,260
11,700	11,750	1,608	1,436	1,271
11,750	11,800	1,620	1,447	1,282
11,800	11,850	1,631	1,459	1,293
11,850	11,900	1,643	1,470	1,304
11,900	11,950	1,654	1,482	1,315
11,950	12,000	1,666	1,493	1,326
12,000	12,050	1,679	1,505	1,337
12,050	12,100	1,691	1,516	1,348
12,100	12,150	1,704	1,528	1,359
12,150	12,200	1,716	1,539	1,370
12,200	12,250	1,729	1,551	1,381
12,250	12,300	1,741	1,562	1,392
12,300	12,350	1,754	1,574	1,403
12,350	12,400	1,766	1,585	1,414
12,400	12,450	1,779	1,597	1,425
12,450	12,500	1,791	1,608	1,436
12,500	12,550	1,804	1,620	1,447
12,550	12,600	1,816	1,631	1,459
12,600	12,650	1,829	1,643	1,470
12,650	12,700	1,841	1,654	1,482
12,700	12,750	1,854	1,666	1,493
12,750	12,800	1,866	1,679	1,505
12,800	12,850	1,879	1,691	1,516
12,850	12,900	1,891	1,704	1,528
12,900	12,950	1,904	1,716	1,539
12,950	13,000	1,917	1,729	1,551
13,000	13,050	1,930	1,741	1,562
13,050	13,100	1,944	1,754	1,574
13,100	13,150	1,957	1,766	1,585
13,150	13,200	1,971	1,779	1,597
13,200	13,250	1,984	1,791	1,608
13,250	13,300	1,998	1,804	1,620
13,300	13,350	2,011	1,816	1,631
13,350	13,400	2,025	1,829	1,643
13,400	13,450	2,038	1,841	1,654
13,450	13,500	2,052	1,854	1,666
13,500	13,550	2,065	1,866	1,679
13,550	13,600	2,079	1,879	1,691
13,600	13,650	2,092	1,891	1,704
13,650	13,700	2,106	1,904	1,716
13,700	13,750	2,119	1,917	1,729
13,750	13,800	2,133	1,930	1,741
13,800	13,850	2,146	1,944	1,754
13,850	13,900	2,160	1,957	1,766
13,900	13,950	2,173	1,971	1,779
13,950	14,000	2,187	1,984	1,791

Continued next column

If line 34, Form 1040 is— Over	But not over	1	2	3
		Your tax is—		
14,000	14,050	2,200	1,998	1,804
14,050	14,100	2,214	2,011	1,816
14,100	14,150	2,227	2,025	1,829
14,150	14,200	2,241	2,038	1,841
14,200	14,250	2,254	2,052	1,854
14,250	14,300	2,268	2,065	1,866
14,300	14,350	2,281	2,079	1,879
14,350	14,400	2,295	2,092	1,891
14,400	14,450	2,308	2,106	1,904
14,450	14,500	2,322	2,119	1,917
14,500	14,550	2,335	2,133	1,930
14,550	14,600	2,349	2,146	1,944
14,600	14,650	2,362	2,160	1,957
14,650	14,700	2,376	2,173	1,971
14,700	14,750	2,389	2,187	1,984
14,750	14,800	2,403	2,200	1,998
14,800	14,850	2,416	2,214	2,011
14,850	14,900	2,430	2,227	2,025
14,900	14,950	2,443	2,241	2,038
14,950	15,000	2,457	2,254	2,052
15,000	15,050	2,472	2,268	2,065
15,050	15,100	2,486	2,281	2,079
15,100	15,150	2,501	2,295	2,092
15,150	15,200	2,515	2,308	2,106
15,200	15,250	2,530	2,322	2,119
15,250	15,300	2,544	2,335	2,133
15,300	15,350	2,559	2,349	2,146
15,350	15,400	2,573	2,362	2,160
15,400	15,450	2,588	2,376	2,173
15,450	15,500	2,602	2,389	2,187
15,500	15,550	2,617	2,403	2,200
15,550	15,600	2,631	2,416	2,214
15,600	15,650	2,646	2,430	2,227
15,650	15,700	2,660	2,443	2,241
15,700	15,750	2,675	2,457	2,254
15,750	15,800	2,689	2,472	2,268
15,800	15,850	2,704	2,486	2,281
15,850	15,900	2,718	2,501	2,295
15,900	15,950	2,733	2,515	2,308
15,950	16,000	2,747	2,530	2,322
16,000	16,050	2,762	2,544	2,335
16,050	16,100	2,776	2,559	2,349
16,100	16,150	2,791	2,573	2,362
16,150	16,200	2,805	2,588	2,376
16,200	16,250	2,820	2,602	2,389
16,250	16,300	2,834	2,617	2,403
16,300	16,350	2,849	2,631	2,416
16,350	16,400	2,863	2,646	2,430
16,400	16,450	2,878	2,660	2,443
16,450	16,500	2,892	2,675	2,457
16,500	16,550	2,907	2,689	2,472
16,550	16,600	2,921	2,704	2,486
16,600	16,650	2,936	2,718	2,501
16,650	16,700	2,950	2,733	2,515
16,700	16,750	2,965	2,747	2,530
16,750	16,800	2,979	2,762	2,544
16,800	16,850	2,994	2,776	2,559
16,850	16,900	3,008	2,791	2,573
16,900	16,950	3,023	2,805	2,588
16,950	17,000	3,038	2,820	2,602

Continued next column

If line 34, Form 1040 is— Over	But not over	1	2	3
		Your tax is—		
17,000	17,050	3,053	2,834	2,617
17,050	17,100	3,069	2,849	2,631
17,100	17,150	3,084	2,863	2,646
17,150	17,200	3,100	2,878	2,660
17,200	17,250	3,115	2,892	2,675
17,250	17,300	3,131	2,907	2,689
17,300	17,350	3,146	2,921	2,704
17,350	17,400	3,162	2,936	2,718
17,400	17,450	3,177	2,950	2,733
17,450	17,500	3,193	2,965	2,747
17,500	17,550	3,208	2,979	2,762
17,550	17,600	3,224	2,994	2,776
17,600	17,650	3,239	3,008	2,791
17,650	17,700	3,255	3,023	2,805
17,700	17,750	3,270	3,038	2,820
17,750	17,800	3,286	3,053	2,834
17,800	17,850	3,301	3,069	2,849
17,850	17,900	3,317	3,084	2,863
17,900	17,950	3,332	3,100	2,878
17,950	18,000	3,348	3,115	2,892
18,000	18,050	3,363	3,131	2,907
18,050	18,100	3,379	3,146	2,921
18,100	18,150	3,394	3,162	2,936
18,150	18,200	3,410	3,177	2,950
18,200	18,250	3,425	3,193	2,965
18,250	18,300	3,441	3,208	2,979
18,300	18,350	3,456	3,224	2,994
18,350	18,400	3,472	3,239	3,008
18,400	18,450	3,487	3,255	3,023
18,450	18,500	3,503	3,270	3,038
18,500	18,550	3,518	3,286	3,053
18,550	18,600	3,534	3,301	3,069
18,600	18,650	3,549	3,317	3,084
18,650	18,700	3,565	3,332	3,100
18,700	18,750	3,580	3,348	3,115
18,750	18,800	3,596	3,363	3,131
18,800	18,850	3,611	3,379	3,146
18,850	18,900	3,627	3,394	3,162
18,900	18,950	3,642	3,410	3,177
18,950	19,000	3,659	3,425	3,193
19,000	19,050	3,676	3,441	3,208
19,050	19,100	3,693	3,456	3,224
19,100	19,150	3,710	3,472	3,239
19,150	19,200	3,727	3,487	3,255
19,200	19,250	3,744	3,503	3,270
19,250	19,300	3,761	3,518	3,286
19,300	19,350	3,778	3,534	3,301
19,350	19,400	3,795	3,549	3,317
19,400	19,450	3,812	3,565	3,332
19,450	19,500	3,829	3,580	3,348
19,500	19,550	3,846	3,596	3,363
19,550	19,600	3,863	3,611	3,379
19,600	19,650	3,880	3,627	3,394
19,650	19,700	3,897	3,642	3,410
19,700	19,750	3,914	3,659	3,425
19,750	19,800	3,931	3,676	3,441
19,800	19,850	3,948	3,693	3,456
19,850	19,900	3,965	3,710	3,472
19,900	19,950	3,982	3,727	3,487
19,950	20,000	3,999	3,744	3,503

While a progressive tax is levied by having every additional increment to income subject to a higher tax rate than the previous increment, a *regressive* tax is levied in the exact opposite manner; thus, with a regressive tax, the lower your income, the relatively higher is your tax bill. We have no taxes specifically designed to be regressive, but we have some that are regressive in their impact. Sales taxes, for example, are proportional in that a fixed percent of the sales price of an item is charged, but in their impact on the taxpayer, they are thought to be regressive. This is because a larger part of a poor person's income is spent on things subject to sales taxes than is the case for a wealthy person. Table 11–3 shows that in some cities people are subject to a regressive tax system.

Some people desire to use the tax system to create a certain social, political, and/or economic system. An example of such a person is one who argues for progressive taxation in order to equalize incomes. When this is the purpose of progressive taxation, the tax system is being used for social engineering. Of course, whatever the reason for establishing a given tax system, it always has social, political, and economic effects. The knowledge that the system is likely to be changed in the future also has such effects, as people's current behavior is affected by expectations. (Anticipating Fidel Castro's actions, thousands of relatively wealthy people left Cuba.)

Some argue that it is the poor, not the rich, who benefit most from the expenditure of tax money by the government. Many programs, such as welfare, they point out, benefit only the poor. Others, however, contend that welfare also benefits the rich by keeping the poor placated and buying goods and services from the rich. In short, everything about taxes is seen in totally different ways by different people.

There is a widespread belief that the amount of one's income subject to tax should vary depending on what the source of that income is, and our federal income tax system does so discriminate. Many states also follow this policy. This belief has, in recent years, been challenged far more vigorously than in the past.

Income from investments is taxed at a lower rate than wages and salaries are in order to encourage investment, which creates jobs and raises the standard of living. Tax rates also vary in order to discourage or encourage the buying of given items. Both the states and the federal government, for example, tax liquor and cigarettes in order, it is said, to discourage their purchase. Raising import tariffs and lowering export duties discourages and encourages, respectively, imports and exports, as foreign goods are made more expensive to the American consumer and American goods are made less costly to foreigners, respectively.

There is no single, underlying logic to our federal tax system, so you cannot deduce what the tax code will say about a given situation. (Once you read it, you may still have trouble deciding what it says!) You must actually study it. It is quite long and complex and it cannot be completely covered in this chapter. However, most people are not affected by a large part of the tax code, so we can restrict ourselves to covering the aspects of the code that affect most people. Since the

TABLE 11–3 Family by Family: How Taxes Compare

State and Local Taxes for Typical Families of Four in 1975

	$5,000 Income		$15,000 Income		$30,000 Income		$40,000 Income	
	Taxes	Percentage of Income	Taxes	Percentage of Income	Taxes	Percentage of Income	Taxes	Percentage of Income
New York	$1,005	20.1	$2,755	18.4	$5,716	19.1	$8,037	20.1
Chicago	651	13.0	1,609	10.7	2,758	9.2	3,442	8.6
San Francisco	553	11.1	1,694	11.3	3,576	11.9	5,053	12.6
Indianapolis	537	10.7	1,326	8.8	2,312	7.7	2,894	7.2
Seattle	510	10.2	1,072	7.1	1,687	5.6	2,042	5.1
Philadelphia	473	9.5	1,487	9.9	2,674	8.9	3,421	8.6
Dallas	455	9.1	1,009	6.7	1,653	5.5	2,023	5.1
Cincinnati	441	8.8	1,144	7.6	2,248	7.5	2,978	7.4
Memphis	434	8.7	896	6.0	1,350	4.5	1,609	4.0
Milwaukee	429	8.6	2,135	14.2	4,424	14.7	5,890	14.7
Nashville	405	8.1	834	5.6	1,245	4.2	1,477	3.7
Cleveland	397	7.9	1,007	6.7	1,968	6.6	2,602	6.5
Atlanta	393	7.9	1,245	8.3	2,670	8.9	3,571	8.9
Columbus, Ohio	366	7.3	690	6.4	1,919	6.4	2,557	6.4
Jacksonville	$ 173	3.5	$ 485	3.2	$ 804	2.7	$ 966	2.4

Source: District of Columbia government.
Note: It is assumed that a family has one wage-earner, two school-age children, and lives in own home; families with $5,000 income own one car, others two.

language of the Internal Revenue Service (I.R.S.) is a strange and not-so-wonderful thing, interpretations of what the I.R.S. requires will be presented. Since tax specialists, including those with the I.R.S., don't always agree on what the tax code means, no guarantee can be made about this material. There are also many exceptions and exceptions to exceptions, and the more esoteric exceptions will not be covered.

The constant changing of the tax laws is a major reason for there being no single, underlying logic to the federal tax code. The tax code has been altered, amended, added to, and reformed numerous times, and those making these changes held a variety of opinions about what constituted fair taxation. Unfortunately, changes in the tax code have sometimes largely been a response to a powerful pressure group seeking tax benefits or the removal of some handicap, and this has often lead to another pressure group seeking the same. Some changes are for purely practical purposes, for example, increasing social security taxes because there otherwise wouldn't be enough money available in the future to pay promised benefits.

Some state tax codes are similar in their basic thrust to the federal tax code. In other cases, perhaps intentionally, their thrust is at variance with the federal government's. A state may not agree with the federal philosophy or results, and, thus, seek to mitigate the impact of federal taxation within its borders by providing for an offsetting method of taxation. For example, a state may counter, intentionally or not, a progressive federal tax with a proportional or regressive tax which will alter the nature of the overall impact of taxation on the taxpayer.

TYPES OF TAXES

Federal Taxes

There are five major types of taxes levied by the federal government: *personal income taxes, excise taxes, estate and gift taxes, social security taxes,* and *corporate income taxes.* Estate and gift and social security taxes will be discussed in Chapter 14, which is concerned with planning for your later years and taking care of your heirs. Other federal taxes, such as custom duties, gambling tax, etc., will not be considered, as they are minor sources of revenue, and most people seldom, if ever, come in contact with them.

The personal income tax is, by far, the federal government's largest source of revenue, and it probably is our most cussed and discussed tax. Few people escape paying it. It is, of course, a tax levied on the income of individuals. *Income is wealth that you receive other than that which represents a return to you of money invested.* (If you buy a house for $30,000 and later sell it for $40,000, only $10,000 of the sale price is income. If some of the rise in the price of the house is due to inflation, you don't really earn this much on the sale, but the Internal Revenue Service does not allow inflation adjustments.) Income includes any gain or profit, regardless of the source, including gains from the sale or other disposition of capital assets. A *capital asset* is any property owned and used by an individual for personal purposes, pleasure, or investment (things like your home, stocks, and bonds). If you run a business, your inventory of goods is not a capital asset.

For purposes of federal income taxation, your income is divided into two categories: ordinary and capital gains. *Ordinary income* includes compensation for services, including wages, fees, commissions, tips, and similar items; gross income from a business (revenues less expenses); gains from the sale or exchange of capital assets held less than a year; interest; rents; royalties; dividends; alimony and separate maintenance payments; annuities; income from life insurance and endowment contracts; pensions; income from discharge of indebtedness; distributive share of partnership gross income; income in respect of a decedent; and income from an interest in an estate or trust.

A *capital gain* is experienced when a capital asset is sold at a profit. *Capital assets* include such things as your home, appliances, jewelry, automobiles, and so on. If a capital asset is sold for more than was paid for it, this gain or profit is not considered ordinary income if the item was owned for a year or more. Such a gain is, instead, classed a long-term capital gain and is subject to a lower tax rate than ordinary income is. When you sell a capital asset you are likely to experience either a gain or a loss on its sale. Gains and losses on sales of capital assets are offset one against another to obtain either a net capital gain or loss, and any tax due is based on the former.

The federal government also levies *excise taxes* on purchases of tobacco, gasoline, motor vehicles, long-distance telephone calls, airline tickets, jewelry, and a number of other items it classes as "luxuries." The logic behind this tax is that if you can afford these luxuries, you can afford to pay more taxes than can those who can't. (Some cynics would say that the government, like a business might, simply charges what the market will bear, and some markets will bear more than others. Unlike a business, however, the government can force payment for its services!)

The excise tax is, like a sales tax, a tax on consumption. Excise taxes are a minor source of revenue for the federal government, but are a significant portion of the price of some items such as gasoline.

The *corporate income tax* is a tax levied on the income of corporations. (Other forms of busisess organization are not subject to an income tax; instead, their income is only taxed as income to their owners.) Out of the income left after a corporation pays taxes, it may pay out dividends to its owners. These dividends are then taxed by the federal government as personal income of the corporation's owners. This is not the only case of the double taxation of income, but it is one case about which much has been said in recent years.

An interesting and significant question is who pays the corporate income tax? Is it passed along to customers through higher prices? Do corporations' workers "pay" it via lower salaries? Do corporations' owners "pay" it via lower dividends? Do all associated with or dealing with the corporations bear, in varying amounts, the burden? Because we have no conclusive answers to these questions, the fairness of this tax cannot be determined, since we must know who pays a tax in order to determine its fairness.

STATE AND LOCAL TAXES

On the local level the property tax on real estate is by far the largest source of tax revenue. States do not depend so much on one tax. For most states a sales tax is the largest source of revenue. Many states and some local governments also levy an income tax. As can be seen in Table 11–2, the state and local tax burden varies greatly from place to place and, often, between income levels. In some places state and local taxes combined are regressive; in others they are progressive; and in others they are roughly proportional.

State and local taxes are large enough and vary enough so that they should be considered if you are offered two equally attractive jobs in different places. Taxes may be much lower in one place than the other. Sometimes a job will be located so that you can live in either of two or more states, counties, cities, or unincorporated areas. A tax variance could be the deciding factor determining exactly where you will live. Don't forget, however, to consider the level of services provided. Where taxes are low, services are often quite low, and this may be a real problem for you.

There are many other taxes and charges state and local governments are likely to levy: Both automobiles and the gasoline they use are taxed; liquor and tobacco products are taxed; hunters and fishermen must purchase licenses; businesses must obtain business licenses; various professionals and skilled tradesmen must obtain licenses; and, building permits must be obtained.

Property Taxes

Property taxes may be levied on personal property such as your automobile or boat or on real estate. The property tax on real estate is based on the assessed or appraised value of the property. The *assessed value* of the property is set at some percent of the market value of the property. (*Market value* is what it is estimated the property could be sold for.) The tax due on the property is determined by applying to the assessed value what is called the *millage rate*. (The tax rate is expressed in terms of mills per dollar. A mill is 1/1000 of a dollar.) Thus, the tax due on a piece of property can be raised or lowered by changing either the percent of market value the property is assessed at or the millage rate. Property owners often dispute their assessments. This may be because this is one of the few taxes they have much chance of successfully complaining about. There is reason to believe that the property tax is one of the, if not *the*, least popular tax to those who pay it. Two of the major complaints against it are that it hurts retired people and farmers.

Retired people's income is usually fixed, but their property tax is not, as the value of their property can, and normally does, rise over time. Thus, they may be forced to sell their property because they can't pay the taxes on it. A farmer is limited as to how much he can earn using his land for crops and livestock, but his property tax isn't limited. If the property's estimated market value is based on its most productive use (i.e., highest paying), the farmer may have to sell the property because he can't afford to pay a tax based on its use as a regional shopping center. Some also believe that high business and residential property taxes and taxation of home improvements are driving people from large cities into the suburbs. Complaints about unfair assessments due to the use of poorly qualified or easily influenced assessors are also common. Many have come to believe that people are being discouraged from improving their property because improvements will be taxed. This, of course, leads to slums.

Clearly, when you move to a new location, you should make inquiries to determine just what taxes you are liable for. You should pay any taxes you are liable for, as your property may be seized and sold to pay the tax due plus a delinquency charge.

FINANCIAL RECORD KEEPING

You can't compute how much tax you owe unless you have adequate records. You can't defend yourself against a government claim that you owe more than you paid without adequate records. Just because a year or so has gone by since you filed your tax form, and they haven't challenged you, doesn't mean they can't and won't. Thus, you must keep your financial records for several years. The federal government reserves the right to go back three years. Therefore, you need to keep your records at least this long.

The first step in setting up a record-keeping system is to study your receipts and expenditures. What kind of paperwork do they normally generate? Does each transaction you are involved in automatically generate paperwork? If a receipt or expenditure already generates paperwork, some or all this paper can be kept as your record of the transaction and proof that it took place. If this is not the case, you will have to generate this record and proof. If your financial situation is quite complex, it is best to keep a record of all significant receipts and expenditures in a ledger. One reason for using a checking account for making payments is that it provides you with a record of who you paid money to, when it was paid, and what it was paid for. The cancelled check also serves as a receipt. You also need to keep the W-2 form your employer gives you, which shows how much you earned during the calendar year, and any 1099 forms sent you annually by those who paid you dividends, interest, or other similar payments. These must be sent in with your federal tax form.

How To Keep Your Records

There are two basic methods used in keeping financial records for tax purposes. They are called the *accrual* and *cash* methods. There is also a *hybrid* method which combines these two. With the accrual method your record revenue and expenses as they occur, rather than when cash is actually received or paid out. (Sometimes you provide someone with a service or sell something before you are paid for it. Sometimes, too, you are provided with a service or sold something before you pay for it.) If you use the cash method, you recognize revenue and expenses when you receive or pay out cash rather than when you became entitled to be paid or have incurred an obligation. Individuals normally use the cash method; businesses normally use the accrual method. The accrual method requires a better record-keeping system than does the cash method. You must consistently use one method or the other, and you cannot shift back and forth between methods over the years at will.

SHOULD YOU PREPARE YOUR TAX RETURNS?

The federal income tax is based on voluntary compliance and self-assessment of tax. Thus, it is important for you to understand your rights and responsibilities as a taxpayer. Unless you have the Internal Revenue Service compute your tax for you or hire a tax preparer to do it, you will personally have to report your income and compute how much you owe the government. Having the I.R.S. compute your taxes does not guarantee that your return will not be challenged by the I.R.S. or relieve you of the responsibility for the tax form you filed. (The reason the I.R.S. will not assume responsibility for the tax forms its personnel fill out is twofold: First, and most obvious, is the fact that you may have provided false information; the second reason is that the tax code is so complex that different I.R.S. employees may disagree over what tax is owed.) Because it is swamped with work, the I.R.S. limits the number of tax forms it will actually fill out. You can, however, count on getting questions answered.

A person who, for compensation, fills out all or a substantial portion of an income tax return or a claim for a refund is called an *income tax preparer*. In recent years approximately one out of two taxpayer's returns were prepared by a tax preparer. It is hoped that this figure will decline in the future due to recent tax code reforms that are supposed to make it easier to prepare a federal tax return. Many commercial firms engage in this work. Since attorneys and Certified Public Accountants (C.P.A.'s) must have a knowledge of tax laws, many of them serve as tax preparers. Some of them specialize in this field. The I.R.S. also examines people who are not attorneys or C.P.A.'s, and those who pass this examination are called *enrolled agents*, and are eligible for enrollment to practice before the I.R.S. It is best to select a tax preparer from among attorneys, C.P.A.'s, and enrolled agents.

The preparer must sign the return and make the same declaration as the taxpayer does about the truth of the return. The only difference is that the preparer certifies the accuracy and truth of the return only to the extent of all information made available to the preparer. Some tax preparers will pay any additional tax owed as a result of a mistake they make; others will pay any interest penalties on additional tax owed.

There is no reason why a college graduate with an average set of tax circumstances cannot prepare his or her own tax return, particularly if he or she takes what used to be called the standard deduction. However, if your situation is quite complex, you may need help, and since those who work for commercial firms often are not trained to handle complex returns, it is best to consult with an attorney or a C.P.A. who specializes in tax work.

As is always the case when you have a choice between providers of goods or services, you should shop around. Make inquiries. Compare prices. Be sure you are dealing with a reputable and competent tax preparer.

COMPUTING YOUR FEDERAL INCOME TAX

In general, every U.S. citizen or resident alien whose income is greater than some specified low levels ($2950 a year for a single person under age 65) must file an income tax return. You must file by April 15, or the next weekday if April 15 falls on a weekend. You have to file even if you owe no tax. Whether single or married, if you were claimed as a dependent by someone, you must file a return if you had unearned income of $750 or more during the year. Unearned income includes trust distributions, bank interest, dividends, and capital gains. *You are required to report all income, less adjustments, received either in the form of money, property, or services that is not, by law, expressly exempt from tax.* There are two forms you may use for filing: 1040A and 1040. You may use Form 1040A (short form) if all your income consists of wages, salaries, and tips, and no more than $400 in interest or dividends. Otherwise you must use the Form 1040 (long form). You may have to file one or more additional forms called *schedules* with the 1040 form. Details about various types of income and expenses that don't appear on the 1040 form are shown on these schedules.

Normally, the following are not included in your income for income tax purposes: life insurance death proceeds; life insurance dividends paid to policyholders; benefits for military personnel for subsistence, uniform, and living quarters; dividends on veteran's government insurance; gifts and inheritances; social security benefits; unemployment compensation; workmen's compensation; interest on state and municipal bonds; and Railroad Retirement Act benefits. (Gifts and inheritances are subject to the Gift and Estate Tax.)

Adjustments

Employees, including new employees, and self-employed persons, including partners, can deduct certain moving expenses from their *gross income*. Compensation received for injuries or sickness is also generally subtracted from gross income to obtain *adjusted gross income*. Employee business expenses for such things as travel and transportation; meals and lodging; outside salesperson's expenses; and various other business expenses your employer did not reimburse you for can be subtracted from gross income. Payments to a retirement plan or arrangement can also be subtracted. Alimony can also be deducted from gross income.

Exemptions

Once you have computed your adjusted gross income, you must subtract your exemptions and deductions to obtain your taxable income. Every taxpayer is allowed to claim a $750 personal exemption. The tax tables include exemptions for you and a limited number of dependents. If you are married, you may be entitled to claim an exemption for your spouse. You cannot claim an exemption for a spouse who has income unless you file a *joint return* which includes that income. Married couples may file either jointly or separately. Exemptions for old age and blindness are also allowed for the taxpayer and/or a spouse. In addition, exemptions may be taken for each person who qualifies as a dependent.

To qualify as a *dependent,* a person must meet five tests: be a member of your household and/or related to you; be a U.S. citizenship; be supported by you; have a limited gross income; and does not file a joint return. The dependent may or may not live in the taxpayer's household if he or she is related to the taxpayer in any of several degrees (such as child, grandchild, brother, sister, mother, father, etc.). The taxpayer must provide more than one-half of the dependent's total support during the calendar year being reported unless special circumstances exist relative to multiple support agreements and divorced or separated parents. Generally, you may not claim anyone as a dependent if his or her gross income for the year was $750 or more.

How to File

In most cases married persons will pay less tax if they file a joint return rather than file separate returns. Married couples may file jointly even though they did not live together for the full year. Both parties are responsible for paying any tax due on a joint return; thus, *if one doesn't pay, the other may have to.* Married couples can file separately if both had incomes or if only one had an income. Both persons must figure their tax in the same way, that is, if one *itemizes* deductions, the other must too. Each is responsible for paying his or her own taxes; not the spouse's. If you file a separate return, you can take an exemption for your spouse only if your spouse had no income and was not the dependent of someone else. You should compute your taxes both ways— joint and separate filings—to see which produces the lowest tax bill.

If you were married and living apart from your spouse you may be able to file either as a single person or as an unmarried head of household. Tax rates vary depending on whether you file as single, married filing separately, married filing jointly, or unmarried head of a household. You can qualify as an unmarried head of household if you provided more than half the cost of a home for your mother, father, unmarried child, grandchild, foster child, or stepchild. You will pay less taxes this way than by filing as a single person. (You should count as support the fair rental value of a room, apartment, or house your dependent lives in. Unless you have records showing how much the food consumed by a dependent cost, you divide your total food bill by the members of your household to determine how much support was provided through feeding a dependent.)

Deductions

After adjusting your gross income to obtain adjusted gross income and subtracting your exemptions, you will subtract your deductions in order to obtain your *taxable income*. You have a choice between *itemizing* (listing) your deductions and claiming what used to be called the standard deduction. This is now called the *zero bracket amount*. In the past you either reduced your income by the standard deduction before computing taxes or you reduced it by deducting itemized (listed) expenses. Currently, if you do not choose to itemize your deductions, you simply use a tax table which, for example, includes no tax on $3200 of your income if you are married and filing jointly. (If you are unmarried, the amount not subject to tax is $2200. If you are married and filing separately, this amount is $1600.) In other words, the tax table does the subtracting of what used to be called the standard deduction for you. This zero bracket amount is a part of your taxable income that is not subject to tax; thus, the use of the word *zero*. You should itemize deductions if this will lower your tax bill, that is, if their size exceeds zero bracket amount. You claim only the amount by which your itemized expenses exceed the zero bracket amount, because the table incorporates this tax-free amount.

Itemized deductions are personal expenditures other than business expenditures. Excess itemized deductions are deducted from adjusted gross income in order to obtain your taxable income. Itemizable expenses include such items as medical and dental expenses, taxes, interest, contributions to charitable organizations, casualty or theft losses, and miscellaneous deductions. (You may not be able to deduct interest if it is on a debt used to finance the purchase of securities and you own state or local government securities. This is because the interest you earn on these securities escapes federal income taxation.) You should, of course, not itemize if the zero bracket amount exceeds the amount you could itemize. For most people, the zero bracket amount will be the larger.

You do not include alimony you may pay as an itemized deduction to determine the amount of excess itemized deductions. Alimony payments are deductible from gross income to arrive at adjusted gross income.

A married person filing a separate return whose spouse claims excess itemized deductions, or a child whose parents may claim (whether or not they did) a dependency exemption and the child had unearned income, must compute what is called the *unused zero bracket amount*. This is generally the zero bracket amount less itemized deductions. The unused itemized deductions are added to adjusted gross income. The following illustrates how this is done.

Adjusted gross income		$2700
Plus: Unused zero bracket amount		
Zero bracket amount	$2200	
Minus: Itemized deductions		
or earned income,		
whichever is greater	1900	
Unused zero bracket amount		300
Taxable income		$3000

The above example assumes that a dependent had $1900 in wages, $500 in dividends, and $300 in interest. Itemized deductions were $500, which is less than the earned income of $1900. If earned income had equaled or exceeded the zero bracket amount, there would have been no unused zero bracket amount.

Even if a child had gross income of $750 or more, the parents can claim him or her as a dependent if he or she was a full-time student and meets the five tests mentioned earlier. *Gross income* is all income in the form of money, property, and services that is not exempt from tax. If your child is less than 19 years old the gross income test does not apply. Your child then may have any amount of income and still be claimed as a dependent, assuming he or she meets the other four tests for dependency.

You can deduct payments for medicines, drugs, vaccines, and vitamins that your doctor tells you to take. Payments to hospitals, physicians, dentists, nurses, chiropractors, pediatrists, physiotherapists, psychiatrists, psychologists, psychoanalysts, and eye doctors may be deducted. Payments for such things as eyeglasses, false teeth, and so on, may be deducted. Payments for ambulances, X-rays, insulin treatment, may also be deducted. You can also deduct one-half (up to $150) of the amount you paid for medical care insurance even if you have no other medical expenses.

State and local income taxes and real estate taxes can be deducted. You are also allowed to deduct such things as the state tax on the gas used in your car or boat and the general sales tax. (There are optional tables you can use to derive a state purchase-based tax figure, which keeps you from having to keep records on exactly what taxes you paid your state on purchases. However, this figure might understate what you actually spent.)

You can deduct gifts to organizations operated for religious, charitable, educational, scientific, or literary purposes, or to prevent cruelty to animals or children. This means you can deduct contributions to such institutions as churches, Goodwill Industries, Red Cross, fraternal organizations, government agencies, nonprofit schools and hospitals, and so forth.

If you had property that was stolen or damaged by fire, storm, car accident, or shipwreck, you may be able to deduct your loss from these events or at least part of your losses. The interest you pay on personal debts and finance charges on installment purchases is deductible. You cannot deduct gifts to relatives, friends, or other persons. You also cannot deduct gifts to social clubs, labor unions, chambers of commerce, foreign organizations, or organizations operated for personal profit or to get people to vote for new laws or changes in old laws. *You cannot deduct educational expenses unless they are necessary to keep your present job.*

Most people who use the zero bracket amount can use the 1040A form. If you find you made an error on your 1040A or 1040 form after mailing it, you can use form 1040X to file a corrected version.

The Schedules and Tax Credits

Schedule A must be filled out by people who itemize their deductions and all others who use Form 1040. (This and the other schedules are shown at the end of this chapter.) If you received more than $400 in gross dividends and other distributions or more than $400 in in interest, you will have to fill out *Schedule B*. (The first $100 of dividends received by an individual is excluded from taxable income.) *Schedule D* is filled out by people who have sold or exchanged a capital asset at a gain or a loss. People receiving pension and annuity income must fill out *Schedule E*. Those receiving rent and/or royalty income or income from a partnership must also fill out this schedule. Persons entitled to a tax credit for the elderly must fill out *Schedule R*. A *tax credit* is a reduction in the tax that, otherwise, would be owed. Credits either make up for an advance payment of tax, prevent taxing income more than once, or provide a reward or incentive for doing something.

Capital Gains and Losses

If you sell or otherwise dispose of property, you will generally do so at either a gain or a loss, which are called, respectively, a capital gain and a capital loss. A gain or loss is the difference between the selling price and the adjusted basis. The *adjusted basis* of property is the original cost or other original basis adjusted for such things as casualty losses, improvements, and depreciation when appropriate. *Depreciation* is an annual reduction in the value of an asset to reflect the reduction in its worth as it ages. Such a reduction cannot be made in the case of land, since it does not deteriorate over time, but a depreciation-like reduction can be made to reduce the value of mineral or oil-bearing land to reflect the removal of these resources. This is called a *depletion allowance*.

In order to encourage investment in capital assets, Congress has given special tax treatment to capital gains. This special treatment is increasingly coming under attack, and in recent years capital gains treatment has been made less favorable. *When you have a gain on the sale or exchange of a capital asset held a year or longer, only one-half of this gain is included in gross income.* A capital asset held less than a year and sold at a gain produces a *short-term capital gain*. Unlike net *long-term capital gains* (held a year or longer), net short-term capital gains are taxed like ordinary income. A net short-term capital loss can be used to offset ordinary income, up to a limit of $2000. Any unused loss may be carried over to future years.

A net long-term capital gain occurs when capital gains exceed losses. There are two ways to compute the tax owed on long-term capital gains. If your tax on ordinary income is over 50 percent, you should calculate your tax as 25 percent of the net long-term gain. The other, more common, method is to include one-half the net long-term capital gain in gross income. This should be done when your tax rate on ordinary income is not more than 50 percent. (Note that if your tax rate is 50 percent, your tax will be 25 percent of the gain, in other words, 50 percent of 50 percent.) So long as your ordinary income tax rate is less than 50 percent, the tax on your net long-term capital gain will be less than 25 percent, which is the maximum capital gains rate. You may deduct 50 percent of a net long-term loss from other income, up to a limit of $2000. Any loss over $4000 may be carried forward to future years.

Special rules apply when you sell your home. You can defer the tax on a gain realized on the sale of your home if it has been your principal residence and you invest the proceeds in another principal residence within 18 months of the sale. If you pay less for the new house than you sold the old one for, you will be taxed on some of all your gain. Because of this rule, it is best to buy ever more expensive homes until after you are 65. Then if you do not buy another home or buy a cheaper one, special rules applicable to people over 65 will offset the tax due on the gain from selling your home.

Income Averaging

If your income exceeds the average income of the previous four years by more than a fifth, and the excess is over $3000, the excess may be averaged. The excess is treated as if it were earned over a five-year period and, thus, will be taxed at lower rates. The purpose of income averaging is to help people whose income fluctuates greatly from year to year. (Because income taxes are progressive, two people having, say, $40,000 in taxable income over a four-year period, would pay differing amounts of taxes over this period depending on whether they earned $10,000 each year or varying amounts annually. The most extreme variance would be between $10,000 annually and no income for three of the years and all the $40,000 in the other.)

Calculating Your Tax

The amount of tax you owe is determined either by using a tax table or computing it mathematically. You can use a tax table if one of the below describes your situation:

YOUR FILING STATUS IS:	TAXABLE INCOME IS:	EXEMPTIONS ARE:
Married—filing jointly	$40,000 or less	Nine or less
Married—filing separately	20,000 or less	Three or less
Single	20,000 or less	Three or less
Head of household	20,000 or less	Eight or less

There are four individual tax rate classifications, and there is a tax table for each. They are single (A), married filing jointly (B), married filing separately (C), and head of household (D). Tax Table A, which is for single persons who are not the head of a household, was shown in Table 11–2. You simply enter the tax table in the column headed by your proper number of exemptions and go down until you reach your taxable income. If your taxable income was $9001, this would be the row that reads "over $9000 but not over $9050." If you have one exemption, the tax is $1007. (The government considers the tax reductions due to the zero bracket amount, exemptions, and any applicable tax credits in computing the taxes listed in the table.) Unless you claim excess itemized deductions, your tax table income is adjusted gross income. If you do claim excess itemized deductions, it is adjusted gross income less excess itemized deductions.

The tax tables do not cover every set of circumstances; thus, you may have to compute your tax by using one of three tax rate schedules. *Schedule X* is for single taxpayers not qualifying for rates in Schedules *Y* or *Z*. *Schedule Y* is for married taxpayers and qualifying widows and widowers, and *Schedule Z* is for unmarried or legally separated tax-payers who qualify as heads of household. (See Table 11–4 for these schedules.)

If a good part of your income is not subject to withholding, you may have to file an estimate of how much tax you will owe over the next year and pay taxes quarterly. This estimate is filed in addition to a 1040A or 1040. The form used is called an estimated tax declaration-voucher (Form 1040-ES.) It must be filled out if you estimate that at the end of the year you will owe more than $100 in taxes.

Taxes owed on wages are collected by your employer during the year via withholding. What is withheld may be inadequate because withholding does not cover the taxes owed on other income such as dividends, interest, business income, and capital gains. Some people will have to declare and pay an estimated tax quarterly because they would owe more than $100 in taxes at the end of the year on income not subject to withholding.

WHAT TO DO IF YOU ARE AUDITED

The Audit Division of the I.R.S. examines income tax returns looking for errors, omissions, and fraud. Most audits are routine. A return isn't always selected for audit because it is thought that anything is wrong. It may have been picked as part of a random sampling of returns, or it may have been picked because the I.R.S. is checking those types of returns most likely to contain errors or omissions or be fraudulent. On the other hand, your return may be selected because it had more deductions than is considered normal for the family size and income bracket of the taxpayer. It may be selected because you added figures incorrectly.

Through long experience, the I.R.S. knows what kinds of returns are most likely to contain errors, omissions, and fraud. For the most part, however, the likelihood of your return being selected for audit is based on the size and source of your income. If your income is no more than $10,000, and you use the zero amount bracket amount, there is very little chance that you will be audited. The $10,000 to $50,000 income group is a bit more likely to be audited. If your income

1977 Tax Rate Schedules

If you cannot use one of the Tax Tables, figure your tax on the amount on Schedule TC, Part I, line 3, by using the appropriate Tax Rate Schedule on this page. Enter tax on Schedule TC, Part I, line 4.

Note: Your zero bracket amount has been built into these Tax Rate Schedules.

SCHEDULE X—Single Taxpayers Not Qualifying for Rates in Schedule Y or Z

Use this schedule if you checked Box 1 on Form 1040—

If the amount on Schedule TC, Part I, line 3, is:

Not over $2,200......—0—

Over—	But not over—	Enter on Schedule TC, Part I, line 4:	of the amount over—
$2,200	$2,700	14%	$2,200
$2,700	$3,200	$70+15%	$2,700
$3,200	$3,700	$145+16%	$3,200
$3,700	$4,200	$225+17%	$3,700
$4,200	$6,200	$310+19%	$4,200
$6,200	$8,200	$690+21%	$6,200
$8,200	$10,200	$1,110+24%	$8,200
$10,200	$12,200	$1,590+25%	$10,200
$12,200	$14,200	$2,090+27%	$12,200
$14,200	$16,200	$2,630+29%	$14,200
$16,200	$18,200	$3,210+31%	$16,200
$18,200	$20,200	$3,830+34%	$18,200
$20,200	$22,200	$4,510+36%	$20,200
$22,200	$24,200	$5,230+38%	$22,200
$24,200	$28,200	$5,990+40%	$24,200
$28,200	$34,200	$7,590+45%	$28,200
$34,200	$40,200	$10,290+50%	$34,200
$40,200	$46,200	$13,290+55%	$40,200
$46,200	$52,200	$16,590+60%	$46,200
$52,200	$62,200	$20,190+62%	$52,200
$62,200	$72,200	$26,390+64%	$62,200
$72,200	$82,200	$32,790+66%	$72,200
$82,200	$92,200	$39,390+68%	$82,200
$92,200	$102,200	$46,190+69%	$92,200
$102,200	-----	$53,090+70%	$102,200

SCHEDULE Y—Married Taxpayers and Qualifying Widows and Widowers

If you are a married person living apart from your spouse, see page 7 of the instructions to see if you can be considered to be "unmarried" for purposes of using Schedule X or Z.

Married Filing Joint Returns and Qualifying Widows and Widowers

Use this schedule if you checked Box 2 or Box 5 on Form 1040—

If the amount on Schedule TC, Part I, line 3, is:

Not over $3,200......—0—

Over—	But not over—	Enter on Schedule TC, Part I, line 4:	of the amount over—
$3,200	$4,200	14%	$3,200
$4,200	$5,200	$140+15%	$4,200
$5,200	$6,200	$290+16%	$5,200
$6,200	$7,200	$450+17%	$6,200
$7,200	$11,200	$620+19%	$7,200
$11,200	$15,200	$1,380+22%	$11,200
$15,200	$19,200	$2,260+25%	$15,200
$19,200	$23,200	$3,260+28%	$19,200
$23,200	$27,200	$4,380+32%	$23,200
$27,200	$31,200	$5,660+36%	$27,200
$31,200	$35,200	$7,100+39%	$31,200
$35,200	$39,200	$8,660+42%	$35,200
$39,200	$43,200	$10,340+45%	$39,200
$43,200	$47,200	$12,140+48%	$43,200
$47,200	$55,200	$14,060+50%	$47,200
$55,200	$67,200	$18,060+53%	$55,200
$67,200	$79,200	$24,420+55%	$67,200
$79,200	$91,200	$31,020+58%	$79,200
$91,200	$103,200	$37,980+60%	$91,200
$103,200	$123,200	$45,180+62%	$103,200
$123,200	$143,200	$57,580+64%	$123,200
$143,200	$163,200	$70,380+66%	$143,200
$163,200	$183,200	$83,580+68%	$163,200
$183,200	$203,200	$97,180+69%	$183,200
$203,200	-----	$110,980+70%	$203,200

Married Filing Separate Returns

Use this schedule if you checked Box 3 on Form 1040—

If the amount on Schedule TC, Part I, line 3, is:

Not over $1,600......—0—

Over—	But not over—	Enter on Schedule TC, Part I, line 4:	of the amount over—
$1,600	$2,100	14%	$1,600
$2,100	$2,600	$70+15%	$2,100
$2,600	$3,100	$145+16%	$2,600
$3,100	$3,600	$225+17%	$3,100
$3,600	$5,600	$310+19%	$3,600
$5,600	$7,600	$690+22%	$5,600
$7,600	$9,600	$1,130+25%	$7,600
$9,600	$11,600	$1,630+28%	$9,600
$11,600	$13,600	$2,190+32%	$11,600
$13,600	$15,600	$2,830+36%	$13,600
$15,600	$17,600	$3,550+39%	$15,600
$17,600	$19,600	$4,330+42%	$17,600
$19,600	$21,600	$5,170+45%	$19,600
$21,600	$23,600	$6,070+48%	$21,600
$23,600	$27,600	$7,030+50%	$23,600
$27,600	$33,600	$9,030+53%	$27,600
$33,600	$39,600	$12,210+55%	$33,600
$39,600	$45,600	$15,510+58%	$39,600
$45,600	$51,600	$18,990+60%	$45,600
$51,600	$61,600	$22,590+62%	$51,600
$61,600	$71,600	$28,790+64%	$61,600
$71,600	$81,600	$35,190+66%	$71,600
$81,600	$91,600	$41,790+68%	$81,600
$91,600	$101,600	$48,590+69%	$91,600
$101,600	-----	$55,490+70%	$101,600

SCHEDULE Z—Unmarried or legally separated taxpayers Who Qualify as Heads of Household

Use this schedule if you checked Box 4 on Form 1040—

If the amount on Schedule TC, Part I, line 3, is:

Not over $2,200......—0—

Over—	But not over—	Enter on Schedule TC, Part I, line 4:	of the amount over—
$2,200	$3,200	14%	$2,200
$3,200	$4,200	$140+16%	$3,200
$4,200	$6,200	$300+18%	$4,200
$6,200	$8,200	$660+19%	$6,200
$8,200	$10,200	$1,040+22%	$8,200
$10,200	$12,200	$1,480+23%	$10,200
$12,200	$14,200	$1,940+25%	$12,200
$14,200	$16,200	$2,440+27%	$14,200
$16,200	$18,200	$2,980+28%	$16,200
$18,200	$20,200	$3,540+31%	$18,200
$20,200	$22,200	$4,160+32%	$20,200
$22,200	$24,200	$4,800+35%	$22,200
$24,200	$26,200	$5,500+36%	$24,200
$26,200	$28,200	$6,220+38%	$26,200
$28,200	$30,200	$6,980+41%	$28,200
$30,200	$34,200	$7,800+42%	$30,200
$34,200	$38,200	$9,480+45%	$34,200
$38,200	$40,200	$11,280+48%	$38,200
$40,200	$42,200	$12,240+51%	$40,200
$42,200	$46,200	$13,260+52%	$42,200
$46,200	$52,200	$15,340+55%	$46,200
$52,200	$66,200	$18,640+58%	$52,200
$66,200	$72,200	$26,720+59%	$66,200
$72,200	$78,200	$30,260+61%	$72,200
$78,200	$82,200	$33,920+62%	$78,200
$82,200	$90,200	$36,400+63%	$82,200
$90,200	$102,200	$41,440+64%	$90,200
$102,200	$122,200	$49,120+66%	$102,200
$122,200	$142,200	$62,320+67%	$122,200
$142,200	$162,200	$75,720+68%	$142,200
$162,200	$182,200	$89,320+69%	$162,200
$182,200	-----	$103,120+70%	$182,200

is above $50,000, it is very likely that you will be audited. Lower-income individuals who itemize their deductions are much more likely to be audited than are those who take the zero bracket amount option. Those who live off investments are more likely to be audited than those who live off a salary. (The I.R.S. is interested in those capable of

substantially underpaying their taxes!)

If you receive a letter or phone call from the Audit Division, don't panic! There is no reason to feel or behave like a suspected criminal. Yet, do bear in mind that the I.R.S. computer is programmed to select returns with possible underpayments of taxes; not overpayments. You also need to be aware of the fact that, in contrast to when the government accuses you of anything else, if you are accused of underpaying taxes, *it is up to you to prove that you are innocent!* You can let the person who prepared your tax return for you represent you, but the responsibility for your return is yours. Be sure to take all your supporting records with you when you visit the I.R.S. for an audit.

In the tax year ending in mid-1976, I.R.S. examiners called for a change in taxes owed on 77 percent of the returns they audited. During fiscal 1975, I.R.S. service centers audited 1.6 percent and district officers 2.3 percent of the 81 million returns filed for 1974. Unallowable items (such as deducting normal living expenses) triggered 72 percent of all service center audits in fiscal 1975. Errors in computation, use of the wrong tax table, and failure of the taxpayer's data to jibe with data the I.R.S. gets from other sources may also cause an audit.

Sometimes you can avoid an audit by attaching extra documentation to your return. While the computer does not read the documentation, if it spits out your return, human classifiers can read the documentation supporting your position, and they might decide nothing is wrong. Explain anything unusual; avoid inconsistencies. The computer is programmed to spot unusual items, errors, and inconsistencies. Once you have been audited and found to have underpaid your taxes, you are more likely to be audited than are other people. You may be audited over and over again without anything being found wrong. If this persists for several years, you can protest and, perhaps, get yourself off the audit treadmill.

You have the right to appeal an I.R.S. decision. If the I.R.S. examiner proposes that you pay extra taxes, and you think he or she is wrong, you may request a meeting with a supervisor to discuss the matter. Failing to settle the issue at this point results in you being given a copy of the examination report and 30 days to respond with either a signed agreement to pay the taxes and interest on the deficiency or request a district conference. If, after this conference, an agreement is not reached, or you choose to skip the conference, you can get a hearing at the I.R.S. appellate level. At any point during this process you can go to court. You can pay and go to the U.S. Tax Court for review of your case, or, if no more than $1500 is involved, you can go to a special branch of the Tax Court and use the small-tax-case procedures. The latter route takes less in terms of both time and money. It is an informal proceeding where you represent yourself. If you take this route, neither you nor the I.R.S. can appeal the decision.

There is very little chance that you will be charged with criminal fraud, but of the 1270 cases the I.R.S. took to court charging criminal fraud in 1976, only 77 were acquitted!

In the past, many conflicts between taxpayers and the I.R.S. have been over the legitimacy of deductions, alimony, and child support. However, changes made in the tax laws since 1975 should enormously reduce such cases. But, though the causes of many disputes with the I.R.S. have been eliminated, the possibility of audit will not likely be reduced, because the I.R.S. is determined to stem the long decline in the percent of returns they examine.

HOW TO MINIMIZE YOUR TAX BILL

If all your income is from wages or salaries and your income and expenses do not vary significantly from year to year, there is little you can do to affect your tax bill. If, however, you have income from investments or can arrange to shift income from being classed as ordinary to being classed as a capital gain, you can benefit from the various tax incentives for investment. If your income fluctuates very much from year to year, you can take advantage of income averaging. In high-income years you can also make expenditures that could have been made in a later year or years when your income was lower. (In low-income years your tax rate would be lower and, thus, these expenditures would then save you less in taxes.) Since 1975, however, your ability to do this has been limited by changes in the law made in response to the fact that many taxpayers were taking advantage of the tax savings arising out of paying for things in advance of their use. Prepayments of interest for one or more years, for example, is now barred in most cases as a device for speeding deductions. Only in the case of real estate can you still deduct expenses in excess of the amount you have "at risk."

When your income doesn't fluctuate from year to year significantly, it is still to your advantage to take a deduction now rather than later. By deferring paying taxes until later, you gain the use of this money in the interval. Medical and charitable expenditures are often flexible as to timing; thus, they can be speeded up. Obviously, you must also be aware of all possible deductible expenses so that you will know if itemizing is possible and how much is possible.

You can avoid tax on part of your income by setting aside some of it in individual retirement accounts, which will be discussed in detail in Chapter 14.

A married couple can, by putting some stocks in her name and some in his, get a $200 *dividend exclusion*, rather than the $100 the couple would get if all stocks were held in one of their names. Additional exclusions can be obtained by placing stock in your children's names. Married people may also save by filing jointly.

The rule barring exemptions for dependents if they earn $750 or more doesn't apply to children who are under 19 or in school, but if a child is earning more than $750, you may not be able to claim him or her because they pay for more than half their board, clothing, education, medical, and other living expenses. Thus, you would be advised to have the child bank some of his earnings or buy a car or make some other capital investment which doesn't count as self-support.

Putting a piece of income-generating property in trust for a child will shield this income from taxation. A trust is established by transferring legal title to property to a trustee, who manages it for the benefit of the beneficiary or beneficiaries. To shield income from tax via setting up a trust, the taxpayer cannot be the beneficiary, or assign earned income to the trust.

The amount of wage and salary income you can earn after age 65 without reducing your social security payments is limited, but how much you can earn on investments isn't. Thus you should plan for supplementary retirement income to come from investments; not from working.

One way to lower your tax bill on investment income is to invest in *tax-exempt securities*. These are debt securities issued by cities, countries, and states. Interest income from these securities is exempt from federal, state, and local taxes unless they are issued by your own state or one of its subdivisions, because a state may tax its own securities held by its citizens. The higher your tax rate, the more attractive are tax-exempt securities. Since inflation, which has been substantial in recent years, throws everyone into ever-higher tax brackets, tax-exempts are becoming attractive to more people.

Most people's incomes rise as prices rise, but even if the rise in your income is less than the rise in prices, you will have to pay, absolutely and relatively, more income taxes because our tax system is progressive. For example, consider a couple with a taxable income of $18,000 in 1967. If their income had just kept pace with inflation, by 1977 it would have had to be $36,000. At the margin, their tax rate over the decade would have jumped from 28 percent to 45 percent! At a tax rate of 45 percent, a 5½ percent tax-free yield is equal to a 10 percent taxable yield, which is more than the vast majority of investments available to individuals pay. People in the top income tax bracket, which is 70 percent, would have to earn a taxable yield of 20 percent to equal a tax-exempt yield of 6 percent.. Because of this inflation-caused increase in everyone's tax bill, some suggest that tax rates be indexed, that is, tax rates would fall as prices rise, and, therefore, the value of the dollar falls.

You can compute the taxable yield you would have to earn to equal a tax-exempt yield using the following equation, where R is the tax exempt bond's return; I equals the equivalent taxable interest rate; and M is your marginal tax rate.

$$I = \frac{R}{1 - M}$$

Using the above data:

$$I = \frac{0.055}{1 - 0.45}, \ I = 10 \text{ percent}$$

There are a number of ways you can reduce your tax bill by buying and selling securities. The nature of such tactics can be illustrated by assuming that you have, to date, experienced a long-term capital loss. Only part of it can be deducted, therefore, you can save by now selling a security on which you will record a gain so that you will have a gain that the loss will cover. (If you would lose a lot by selling now rather than later, the tax-saving sale may not be advisable.)

A stock dividend is not taxed as ordinary income like a cash dividend. Instead, a capital gains tax will be paid when it is sold. Thus, you would prefer to receive a stock dividend of the same worth to one in cash.

If you exchange one house for another and make an even exchange or pay additional cash, there will be no tax on the exchange. You will pay tax only if you receive cash in addition to the other house. (This assumes that your principal residence is not involved in the exchange, as you can always defer taxes on such a transaction.) Thus, if selling a house would involve a large gain, you should consider making an exchange.

To reduce the difference between the tax you owe and the amount already withheld from your wages, you can claim for withholding purposes fewer than the number of exemptions you are entitled to. (You cannot claim more so as to reduce withholding.) If you expect to owe no tax, you can ask for an exemption from withholding via Form W-4E.

GETTING TAX HELP

In addition to going to a commercial tax advisor or the I.R.S. you can obtain a copy of "Your Federal Income Tax" from the I.R.S., which gives the official interpretation of tax laws enacted by Congress. It is published annually and goes into much greater detail than do the instructions you receive with your tax forms. There are also a number of commercial tax guides you can consult, such as J. K. Lasser's *Your Income Tax*, and Sylvia Porter's *Money Book*. Colleges and universities often offer adult education classes as well as for-credit accounting courses in federal income tax preparation. Once you learn how, you may be able to make money preparing other people's tax returns.

CASES FOR DISCUSSION

Law schools teach by the case method. Students are given the facts in an actual court case and asked to make a decision on the basis of these facts. Handle the following actual situations and court cases (with fictitious names) as would a budding lawyer. How each of the following came out in real life appears at the end of the Cases.

Case 1 Ara was a real problem child. He was hyperactive, selfish, and threw tantrums. His parents took him to a psychiatrist who said Ara's problem was his father's "perfectionistic over coercion" and his mother's "irritable over submission." Since Ara's parents were not able to change enough to help him, the psychiatrist recommended a boarding school for Ara. Ara's father took the cost of sending Ara to a boarding school as a medical expense on his federal income tax. The IRS challenged this, saying that the school didn't cater to problem children nor provide Ara with any special treatment; thus, the fact that a doctor recommended it didn't make it medical treatment. Ara's parents took the case to court.

Case 2 The Kaufman's three children all got government-guaranteed loans to help cover college costs. Their parents neither guaranteed the loans nor cosigned them, but they did make some payments on the loans. They deducted interest on these loans on their federal income tax. The IRS disallowed this deduction, saying that interest on other people's loans is not deductible. The Kaufmans went to court and argued that they had an oral contract with their children in that they had told their children that they would meet some of their loan payments.

Case 3 Mary Jo Wu is a teacher. She attended summer school at a university in order to better herself and because she likes going to school. The IRS challenged her deduction of $239.50 for summer school expenses saying that her employer did not require her to attend in order to keep her job. Mary Jo went to court with her case.

Case 4 Celia Harper's doctor told her to build a pool to swim in twice a day to prevent paralysis from a spine ailment. She built a $195,000 indoor pool. After subtracting the costs of nonessentials such as cooking facilities and the value the pool added to her home, Celia was left with $86,000, which she considered a medical expense. The IRS challenged this in its entirety, but then backed off and allowed $39,000, because she could have built a pool for only $70,000, which would have added $31,000 to the value of her house. Celia went to court over the issue.

Case 5 Both the Smiths are college professors who worked part time in a federal government-sponsored program to help deprived students. They were paid for the time they spent in the classroom, but not other time they devoted to the program. They figured that they spent 219 hours working without pay, and they deducted this time at a rate of $25 an hour from their taxes as a $5500 charitable contribution. The IRS challenged this deduction, saying that volunteers cannot deduct contributions of their time. The Smiths said that they were not, due to the professional nature of the services they provided, ordinary volunteers and took the IRS to court.

Case 6 To prevent the usual double taxation of corporate dividends, the federal government allows some small corporations' owners to be taxed like owners of an unincorporated business. This means that the corporation will not pay any income taxes. The Williams Corporation had 30 owners, 20 too many to be able to take advantage of this provision. Thus, these owners decided to split the company up into three corporations that would continue to do the business now done by Williams. Each new firm would have only ten owners, and, thus, qualify for tax treatment like that given unincorporated firms.

Case 7 Dr. Laqueur, whose income is quite high, is attempting to avoid most federal and state income taxes via income splitting. He is doing this by setting up what is called a family or equity trust. He assigns all his assets and income to the trust. He and his wife serve as the trustees and pay themselves consulting fees. The trust's income is reduced by writing off practically everything, including cars, vacations, and payments to their children as administrative expenses. The IRS says this is illegal. What do you think? Why?

Case 8 Zelda and her husband ran an auto seat cover business for many years without pay. After he died, she, her son, and another man ran the company, and she began to draw a salary. She handled the firm's receipts and disbursements and arranged loans. When the two men were away, which was frequently, she ran the business. As she was nearing 75, her pay had reached $62,800 a year, which the IRS said was $40,000 too much; thus, the business could not consider $40,000 of it as a deductible expense. The company argued that the IRS was wrong, and it took the case to court. The company pointed out that she personally guaranteed loans, coordinated colors for products, and she had suggested that the company move into auto accessories, a move that had caused sales to rise to over $4 million a year.

Case 9 The residents of Mountain City, which is located amidst some beautiful mountain scenery, were upset because much of the land in and around the city had been bought up by nonprofit organizations, such as churches and scouting groups and, therefore, this property was taken from the tax rolls. This meant that the taxes of other city and county property holders' had to be increased in order to cover the loss of these taxes and to cover the higher cost of public services caused by the arrival of the newcomers. Then Mike Arnold came to town. He had founded a new church called the Free Living Church. For a fee, he would ordain anyone as a minister in this church. These new ministers would turn their homes into churches and hold services in them. In this way they would avoid both income and property taxes. Many disgruntled taxpayers elsewhere joined Mountain City people in becoming ordained as ministers in this church. A friend has come to you suggesting that you try this. What would you say? Why?

Case 10 Laura O'Shields parents, Pat and Jim, who she does not live with, have come to her with an idea to save on taxes. Pat and Jim do not have enough expenses to itemize their deductions. If Laura will buy their house, she can deduct the maintenance and property taxes on it as business expenses by renting it to Pat and Jim. Since the house will be, for her, an income-generating property, she can also take depreciation, which her parents can't do as owner-residents of the house. Pat and Jim will transfer their mortgage loan to Laura, and she can also deduct the interest on it as a business expense. To make it a legitimate business transaction, Pat and Jim will not pay a ridiculously low rent. Pat and Jim would have left Laura the house. Laura comes to you for advice. What would you tell her?

RESULTS OF CASES FOR DISCUSSION

1. The U.S. District Court agreed with the IRS that merely because Ara has flourished in a particular environment doesn't mean that he is receiving medical treatment for tax purposes.
2. The Tax Court ruled that even if it had considered the Kaufman's agreement a valid contract that, since they

would only have been secondarily liable as guarantors for the loans, they cannot deduct this interest.

3. Mary Jo lost. You can only deduct educational expenses necessary to keep your present job.

4. The Tax Court ruled that the law didn't require "bare bone" spending. For example, private hospital rooms are deductible, though semi-private are cheaper. However, the court did reduce her swimming pool claim to $82,000.

5. The Tax Court agreed with the IRS that all volunteers should be treated alike.

6. The IRS rejected this scheme, saying that the whole thing was done for the principal purpose of beating taxes. The Supreme Court has ruled that even though the letter of the law is met, the IRS can still reject elaborate and devious schemes to avoid taxes.

7. Both the IRS and independent tax experts say schemes like this one clearly violate the law. Earned income cannot be assigned to a trust, and the taxpayer can't be the beneficiary of the trust. In addition, the trust has to have some useful purpose besides tax dodging. No court has allowed such deductions.

8. The Tax Court, after reviewing Zelda's contributions to the firm, ruled that her pay was reasonable, and, thus, it was a deductible business expense.

9. Perhaps because religious freedom is involved, this type of situation hasn't been settled, but the logic of the Case 6 judgment applies.

10. It has been reported that people doing this were told by an IRS office that if the daughter makes money off the rent she is paid, then it is legal. The daughter was taking a loss on the rent, which she said she would quit doing. This family calculated they were saving a bit more than $100 a year in taxes. Today this cannot be done, because a part of the new tax law says that any residence you own for personal purposes for any length of time during the year cannot generate deductible expenses that exceed your rental income from that residence. This law also states that renting to a parent or other close relative is, by definition, a personal purpose.

REVIEW QUESTIONS

1. What is a fair tax system?
2. What assumptions would justify a progressive tax? A proportional? A regressive?
3. What is the difference between ordinary income and capital gains and how is each taxed?
4. Compare property taxes and sales taxes in terms of efficiency and equity.
5. What is the difference between an exemption and a tax credit?
6. What is the difference between an adjustment and an exemption?
7. Why is income averaging allowed?
8. Why do you suppose the government requires employers to withhold taxes from their employees' pay rather than having employees pay what they owe when they make out their tax reports?
9. What is the difference between gross income and adjusted gross income?
10. What difference is there between adjusted gross income and taxable income?
11. What is the zero bracket amount?
12. Name several ways people reduce their federal income tax expense.

YOUR PLAN: CHAPTER 11

This section is composed of two parts. The first is a set of questions you need to answer before you start preparing your tax return. The second is a series of examples (prepared by the Internal Revenue Service) of how to fill in the various tax forms. Included in the second section are some of the tax tables.

**Answer these questions before filling
out your federal income tax return:**

1. Do you have your W-2 form?
2. Do you have all the 1099 forms for such things as interest earned this year?
3. Do you have the records you need to itemize your deductions?
4. Do you know what your earned (wages and salary) and unearned (interest, dividends) income was during the tax year?

5. Was income withheld from your pay by more than one employer?
6. Are you going to use the accrual or the cash basis for recording income and expenses?
7. Are any so-called dividends you received actually interest, as they are payments for deposits at a savings and loan association or a credit union?
8. Would it be better to file a joint return? (Only married people can do this.)
9. Should you itemize your deductions?
10. Do you pay alimony?
11. Have you sold any capital assets at a gain or a loss?
12. If you bought and sold a home, did you reinvest all the proceeds from the sale in a new home, and were both homes your primary residence?
13. How long did you hold any capital assets sold?
14. Has your income varied enough to take advantage of income averaging?
15. For how many people do you provide one-half or more of their support?
16. Have you received rent or royalty income?
17. Have you been disabled and unable to work?
18. Have you had expenses associated with your employment (moving, education, etc.) which your employer has not paid for?
19. Have you had casualty or theft losses?
20. Have you received a pension or an annuity?
21. Did you have self-employment income?
22. Have you contributed to a retirement plan? What kind?
23. Are you or your spouse blind or over 65 years old?
24. Did someone who owed you money fail to pay you back during the tax year?
25. If you are not married, can you qupalify as head of a household?
26. Did you have any tax-free income?
27. Did your children earn income? How much?
28. Are any of your dependents going to file jointly?
29. Did you receive life insurance proceeds?
30. Did you inherit or were you given any money or property? (Estate or gift taxes may be due.)

Form **1040** U.S. **Individual Income Tax Return** **1977**

Department of the Treasury—Internal Revenue Service

For the year January 1–December 31, 1977, or other taxable year beginning _____ , 1977 ending _____ , 19 ___

| Use IRS label. Otherwise, print or type. | First name and initial (if joint return, give first names and initials of both) | Last name | Your social security number |

Present home address (Number and street, including apartment number, or rural route) — For Privacy Act Notice, see page 3 of Instructions. — Spouse's social security no.

City, town or post office, State and ZIP code — Occupation: Yours ▶ Spouse's ▶

Presidential Election Campaign Fund
Do you want $1 to go to this fund? . . . . Yes ▢ No ▢
If joint return, does your spouse want $1 to go to this fund? . Yes ▢ No ▢

Note: *Checking "Yes" will not increase your tax or reduce your refund.*

Filing Status
Check Only One Box

1 ___ Single
2 ___ Married filing joint return (even if only one had income)
3 ___ Married filing separately. If spouse is also filing, give spouse's social security number in the space above and enter full name here ▶ ....
4 ___ Unmarried Head of Household. Enter qualifying name ▶ .... See page 7 of Instructions.
5 ___ Qualifying widow(er) with dependent child (Year spouse died ▶ 19 ___). See page 7 of Instructions.

Exemptions

Always check the "Yourself" box. Check other boxes if they apply.

6a ▢ Yourself ▢ 65 or over ▢ Blind — Enter number of boxes checked on 6a and b ▶ ▢

b ▢ Spouse ▢ 65 or over ▢ Blind

c First names of your dependent children who lived with you ▶ .... Enter number of children listed ▶ ▢

d Other dependents: (1) Name	(2) Relationship	(3) Number of months lived in your home.	(4) Did dependent have income of $750 or more?	(5) Did you provide more than one-half of dependent's support?

Enter number of other dependents ▶ ▢

Add numbers entered in boxes above ▶ ▢

7 Total number of exemptions claimed . . . .

Income

8	Wages, salaries, tips, and other employee compensation. (Attach Forms W–2. If unavailable, see page 5 of Instructions.)	8
9	Interest income. (If over $400, attach Schedule B.)	9
10a	Dividends (If over $400, attach Schedule B) ....:......., 10b less exclusion ....:......., Balance ▶ (See pages 9 and 17 of Instructions)	10c

(If you have no other income, skip lines 11 through 20 and go to line 21.)

11	State and local income tax refunds (does not apply if refund is for year you took standard deduction) . . .	11
12	Alimony received	12
13	Business income or (loss) (attach Schedule C)	13
14	Capital gain or (loss) (attach Schedule D)	14
15	50% of capital gain distributions not reported on Schedule D	15
16	Net gain or (loss) from Supplemental Schedule of Gains and Losses (attach Form 4797) . .	16
17	Fully taxable pensions and annuities not reported on Schedule E	17
18	Pensions, annuities, rents, royalties, partnerships, estates or trusts, etc. (attach Schedule E) .	18
19	Farm income or (loss) (attach Schedule F)	19
20	Other (state nature and source—see page 9 of Instructions) ▶	20
21	**Total income.** Add lines 8, 9, and 10c through 20 . . . . ▶	21

Adjustments to Income *(If none, skip lines 22 through 27 and enter zero on line 28.)*

22	Moving expense (attach Form 3903)	22	
23	Employee business expenses (attach Form 2106)	23	
24	Payments to an individual retirement arrangement (from attached Form 5329, Part III)	24	
25	Payments to a Keogh (H.R. 10) retirement plan	25	
26	Forfeited interest penalty for premature withdrawal	26	
27	Alimony paid (see page 11 of Instructions)	27	
28	**Total adjustments.** Add lines 22 through 27 . . . . ▶		28
29	Subtract line 28 from line 21		29
30	Disability income exclusion (sick pay) (attach Form 2440)		30
31	**Adjusted gross income.** Subtract line 30 from line 29. Enter here and on line 32. If you want IRS to figure your tax for you, see page 4 of the Instructions . . . . ▶		31

Please Attach Copy B of Forms W–2 Here

Please Attach Check or Money Order Here

325

32 Amount from line 31 . . . . | 32 | |

33 If you itemize deductions, enter excess itemized deductions from Schedule A, line 41 . . . . |

If you do NOT itemize deductions, enter zero. . . . . | 33 | |

Caution: *If you have unearned income and can be claimed as a dependent on your parent's return, check here* ▶ ☐ *and see page 11 of the Instructions. Also see page 11 of the Instructions if:*
- *You are married filing a separate return and your spouse itemizes deductions, OR*
- *You file Form 4563, OR*
- *You are a dual-status alien.*

34 Tax Table Income. Subtract line 33 from line 32 . . . . | 34 | |

Note: See Instructions for line 35 on page 11. Then find your tax on the amount on line 34 in the Tax Tables. Enter the tax on line 35. However, if line 34 is more than $20,000 ($40,000 if you checked box 2 or 5) or you have more exemptions than those covered in the Tax Tables for your filing status, use Part I of Schedule TC (Form 1040) to figure your tax. You must also use Schedule TC if you file Schedule G (Form 1040), Income Averaging.

35 Tax. Check if from ☐ Tax Tables or ☐ Schedule TC . . . . | 35 | |

36 Additional taxes. (See page 12 of Instructions.) Check if from ☐ Form 4970, ☐ Form 4972, ☐ Form 5544, ☐ Form 5405, or ☐ Section 72(m)(5) penalty tax . . . . | 36 | |

37 **Total.** Add lines 35 and 36 . . . . ▶ | 37 | |

38 Credit for contributions to candidates for public office	38		
39 Credit for the elderly (attach Schedules R&RP)	39		
40 Credit for child and dependent care expenses (attach Form 2441) .	40		
41 Investment credit (attach Form 3468)	41		
42 Foreign tax credit (attach Form 1116)	42		
43 Work Incentive (WIN) Credit (attach Form 4874)	43		
44 New jobs credit (attach Form 5884)	44		
45 See page 12 of Instructions	45		

46 **Total credits.** Add lines 38 through 45 . . . . ▶ | 46 | |

47 **Balance.** Subtract line 46 from line 37 and enter difference (but not less than zero) . . . . ▶ | 47 | |

48 Self-employment tax (attach Schedule SE) . . . . | 48 | |

49 Minimum tax. Check here ▶ ☐ and attach Form 4625 . . . . | 49 | |

50 Tax from recomputing prior-year investment credit (attach Form 4255) . . . . | 50 | |

51 Social security tax on tip income not reported to employer (attach Form 4137) . . . . . . | 51 | |

52 Uncollected employee social security tax on tips (from Form W–2) . . . . | 52 | |

53 Tax on an individual retirement arrangement (attach Form 5329) . . . . | 53 | |

54 **Total tax.** Add lines 47 through 53 . . . . ▶ | 54 | |

55 Total Federal income tax withheld (attach Forms W–2, W–2G, and W–2P to front) . . . . | 55 | |

56 1977 estimated tax payments (include amount allowed as credit from 1976 return) . . . . | 56 | |

57 Earned income credit. If line 31 is under $8,000, see page 2 of Instructions. If eligible, enter child's name ▶................................ | 57 | |

58 Amount paid with Form 4868 . . . . | 58 | |

59 Excess FICA and RRTA tax withheld (two or more employers) . . . | 59 | |

60 Credit for Federal tax on special fuels, etc. (attach Form 4136) . . | 60 | |

61 Credit from a Regulated Investment Company (attach Form 2439) . . . . . . | 61 | |

61a See page 13 of Instructions . . . . | 61a | |

62 **Total.** Add lines 55 through 61a . . . . ▶ | 62 | |

63 If line 62 is larger than line 54, enter amount **OVERPAID** . . . . ▶ | 63 | |

64 Amount of line 63 to be **REFUNDED TO YOU** . . . . ▶ | 64 | |

65 Amount of line 63 to be credited on 1978 estimated tax . . . . ▶ | 65 | |

66 If line 54 is larger than line 62, enter **BALANCE DUE.** Attach check or money order for full amount payable to "Internal Revenue Service." Write social security number on check or money order . . . ▶ (Check ▶ ☐ if Form 2210 (2210F) is attached. See page 14 of Instructions.) | 66 | |

▶ Paid preparer's signature and identifying number (see instructions)

Your signature _____   Date _____

Spouse's signature (if filing jointly, **BOTH** must sign even if only one had income)

▶ Paid preparer's address (or employer's name, address, and identifying number)

☆ U.S. GOVERNMENT PRINTING OFFICE : 1977—O-235-240   420-86476

Department of the Treasury—Internal Revenue Service

For the year January 1–December 31, 1977, or other taxable year beginning _____ 1977 ending _____ 19 _____

Use IRS label. Otherwise, print or type.

First name and initial (if joint return, give first names and initials of both) | Last name | Your social security number

FJ 516-04-1492 575-10-1776 DO 16 2
FRANK B & EVELYN H JONES
~~1150 ELM RD~~   3807 MILL WAY
~~HOMETOWN N Y 00000~~
LAKE CITY, N.Y. 00000

For Privacy Act Notice, see page 3 of Instructions.

Spouse's social security no.

Occupation Yours ► ELECTRICIAN
Spouse's ► CO-OWNER TRAVEL AGENCY

Presidential Election Campaign Fund

Do you want $1 to go to this fund? . . . . [X] Yes [ ] No
If joint return, does your spouse want $1 to go to this fund? . [X] Yes [ ] No

Note: Checking "Yes" will not increase your tax or reduce your refund.

Filing Status
Check Only One Box

1 [ ] Single
2 [X] Married filing joint return (even if only one had income)
3 [ ] Married filing separately. If spouse is also filing, give spouse's social security number in the space above and enter full name here ►
4 [ ] Unmarried Head of Household. Enter qualifying name ► . . . . See page 7 of Instructions.
5 [ ] Qualifying widow(er) with dependent child (Year spouse died ► 19 ____). See page 7 of Instructions.

Exemptions

Always check the "Yourself" box. Check other boxes if they apply.

6a [X] Yourself   [X] 65 or over   [ ] Blind   } Enter number of boxes checked on 6a and b ► **3**

b [X] Spouse   [ ] 65 or over   [ ] Blind

c First names of your dependent children who lived with you ► MARIE, JAMES

Enter number of children listed ► **2**

d Other dependents:

(1) Name	(2) Relationship	(3) Number of months lived in your home.	(4) Did dependent have income of $750 or more?	(5) Did you provide more than one-half of dependent's support?
GRACE SMITH	MOTHER	12	NO	YES
CLARA JONES	SISTER	NONE	NO	NO *

Enter number of other dependents ► **2**

7 Total number of exemptions claimed . . . .

Add numbers entered in boxes above ► **7**

Income

8	Wages, salaries, tips, and other employee compensation. (Attach Forms W–2. If unavailable, see page 5 of Instructions.)	8	10,814 65
9	Interest income. (If over $400, attach Schedule B.)	9	110 17
10a	Dividends (If over $400, attach Schedule B) 462 50, 10b less exclusion 180 00, Balance ►	10c	282 50
	(See pages 9 and 17 of Instructions)		

(If you have no other income, skip lines 11 through 20 and go to line 21.)

11	State and local income tax refunds (does not apply if refund is for year you took standard deduction) . . .	11	
12	Alimony received	12	
13	Business income or (loss) (attach Schedule C)	13	
14	Capital gain or (loss) (attach Schedule D)	14	1,290 00
15	50% of capital gain distributions not reported on Schedule D	15	
16	Net gain or (loss) from Supplemental Schedule of Gains and Losses (attach Form 4797) . .	16	300 00
17	Fully taxable pensions and annuities not reported on Schedule E	17	
18	Pensions, annuities, rents, royalties, partnerships, estates or trusts, etc. (attach Schedule E) .	18	10,727 82
19	Farm income or (loss) (attach Schedule F)	19	
20	Other (state nature and source—see page 9 of Instructions) ► 50 PRIZE $125 EXCESS REIMBURSEMENT	20	175 00
21	Total income. Add lines 8, 9, and 10c through 20	21	23,700 14

Adjustments to Income *(If none, skip lines 22 through 27 and enter zero on line 28.)*

22	Moving expense (attach Form 3903)	22	2,669 84	
23	Employee business expenses (attach Form 2106)	23		
24	Payments to an individual retirement arrangement (from attached Form 5329, Part III)	24		
25	Payments to a Keogh (H.R. 10) retirement plan	25		
26	Forfeited interest penalty for premature withdrawal	26		
27	Alimony paid (see page 11 of Instructions)	27		
28	Total adjustments. Add lines 22 through 27 . . . . ►	28	2,669 84	
29	Subtract line 28 from line 21	29	21,030 30	
30	Disability income exclusion (sick pay) (attach Form 2440)	30		
31	Adjusted gross income. Subtract line 30 from line 29. Enter here and on line 32. If you want IRS to figure your tax for you, see page 4 of the Instructions . . . . ►	31	21,030 30	

* FORMS 2120 ATTACHED

Please Attach Copy B of Forms W–2 Here

Please Attach Check or Money Order Here

327

Tax Computation

32 Amount from line 31	**32**	21,030	30
33 If you itemize deductions, enter excess itemized deductions from Schedule A, line 41 . . . . . ⎫ If you do NOT itemize deductions, enter zero . . . . ⎬	**33**	1,080	72
Caution: *If you have unearned income and can be claimed as a dependent on your parent's return, check here* ▶ ☐ *and see page 11 of the Instructions. Also see page 11 of the Instructions if:* ● You are married filing a separate return and your spouse itemizes deductions, OR ● You file Form 4563, OR ● You are a dual-status alien.			
34 Tax Table Income. Subtract line 33 from line 32	**34**	19,949	58
Note: See Instructions for line 35 on page 11. Then find your tax on the amount on line 34 in the Tax Tables. Enter the tax on line 35. However, if line 34 is more than $20,000 ($40,000 if you checked box 2 or 5) or you have more exemptions than those covered in the Tax Tables for your filing status, use Part I of Schedule TC (Form 1040) to figure your tax. You must also use Schedule TC if you file Schedule G (Form 1040), Income Averaging.			
35 Tax. Check if from ☒ Tax Tables or ☐ Schedule TC	**35**	1,900	00
36 Additional taxes. (See page 12 of Instructions.) Check if from ☐ Form 4970, ☐ Form 4972, ☐ Form 5544, ☐ Form 5405, or ☐ Section 72(m)(5) penalty tax . . . . ▶	**36**		
37 **Total.** Add lines 35 and 36 . . . . ▶	**37**	1,900	00

Credits

38 Credit for contributions to candidates for public office	**38**	7	50		
39 Credit for the elderly (attach Schedules R&RP)	**39**	300	00		
40 Credit for child and dependent care expenses (attach Form 2441) .	**40**				
41 Investment credit (attach Form 3468)	**41**				
42 Foreign tax credit (attach Form 1116)	**42**				
43 Work Incentive (WIN) Credit (attach Form 4874)	**43**				
44 New jobs credit (attach Form 5884)	**44**				
45 See page 12 of Instructions	**45**				
46 **Total credits.** Add lines 38 through 45	**46**		307	50
47 **Balance.** Subtract line 46 from line 37 and enter difference (but not less than zero) . . . . ▶	**47**		1,592	50

Other Taxes

48 Self-employment tax (attach Schedule SE)	**48**	477	36
49 Minimum tax. Check here ▶ ☐ and attach Form 4625	**49**		
50 Tax from recomputing prior-year investment credit (attach Form 4255)	**50**		
51 Social security tax on tip income not reported to employer (attach Form 4137)	**51**		
52 Uncollected employee social security tax on tips (from Form W–2)	**52**		
53 Tax on an individual retirement arrangement (attach Form 5329)	**53**		
54 **Total tax.** Add lines 47 through 53 . . . . ▶	**54**	2,069	86

Payments

55 Total Federal income tax withheld (attach Forms W–2, W–2G, and W–2P to front)	**55**	881	86		
56 1977 estimated tax payments (include amount allowed as credit from 1976 return)	**56**	1,200	00		
57 Earned income credit. If line 31 is under $8,000, see page 2 of Instructions. If eligible, enter child's name ▶...............	**57**				
58 Amount paid with Form 4868	**58**				
59 Excess FICA and RRTA tax withheld (two or more employers) . . .	**59**				
60 Credit for Federal tax on special fuels, etc. (attach Form 4136) . .	**60**	5	12		
61 Credit from a Regulated Investment Company (attach Form 2439)	**61**	27	55		
61a See page 13 of Instructions	**61a**				
62 **Total.** Add lines 55 through 61a . . . . ▶	**62**	2,114	53

Refund or Due

63 If line 62 is larger than line 54, enter amount **OVERPAID** . . . . ▶	**63**	44	67
64 Amount of line 63 to be **REFUNDED TO YOU** . . . . ▶	**64**	44	67
65 Amount of line 63 to be credited on 1978 estimated tax . . . . . ▶	**65**			
66 If line 54 is larger than line 62, enter **BALANCE DUE.** Attach check or money order for full amount payable to "Internal Revenue Service." Write social security number on check or money order . . . ▶ (Check ▶ ☐ if Form 2210 (2210F) is attached. See page 14 of Instructions.)	**66**		

Please Sign Here

Under penalties of perjury, I declare that I have examined this return, including accompanying schedules and statements, and to the best of my knowledge and belief, it is true, correct, and complete. Declaration of preparer (other than taxpayer) is based on all information of which preparer has any knowledge.

Frank B. Jones   3/31/78
Your signature   Date

Evelyn H. Jones   3/31/78
Spouse's signature (if filing jointly, BOTH must sign even if only one had income)

Paid preparer's signature and identifying number (see instructions)

Paid preparer's address (or employer's name, address, and identifying number)

☆ U.S. GOVERNMENT PRINTING OFFICE : 1977—O-235-240   420-86476

Schedules A&B—Itemized Deductions AND Interest and Dividend Income

(Form 1040)
Department of the Treasury
Internal Revenue Service
▶ Attach to Form 1040. ▶ See Instructions for Schedules A and B (Form 1040).

1977

Name(s) as shown on Form 1040

FRANK B. AND EVELYN H. JONES

Your social security number
516 04 1492

Schedule A Itemized Deductions (Schedule B is on back)

Medical and Dental Expenses (not compensated by insurance or otherwise) (See page 14 of Instructions.)

1 One-half (but not more than $150) of insurance premiums for medical care. (Be sure to include in line 10 below) . . .	138	00
2 Medicine and drugs	300	00
3 Enter 1% of line 31, Form 1040. . .	210	30
4 Subtract line 3 from line 2. Enter difference (if less than zero, enter zero) . .	89	70
5 Enter balance of insurance premiums for medical care not entered on line 1 . .	138	00
6 Enter other medical and dental expenses:		
a Doctors, dentists, nurses, etc.	589	00
b Hospitals	240	35
c Other (itemize—Include hearing aids, dentures, eyeglasses, transportation, etc.) ▶		
7 Total (add lines 4 through 6c) . . .	1,057	05
8 Enter 3% of line 31, Form 1040. . .	630	91
9 Subtract line 8 from line 7 (if less than zero, enter zero)	426	14
10 Total (add lines 1 and 9). Enter here and on line 33 . . . . ▶	564	14

Taxes (See page 14 of Instructions.)

11 State and local income	677	84
12 Real estate	424	40
13 State and local gasoline (see gas tax tables)	76	00
14 General sales (see sales tax tables) . .	244	86
15 Personal property		
16 Other (itemize) ▶		
17 Total (add lines 11 through 16). Enter here and on line 34 . . . . . . ▶	1,423	14

Interest Expense (See page 16 of Instructions.)

18 Home mortgage	537	04
19 Other (itemize) ▶		
INSTALLMENT PURCHASE	4	90
MORTGAGE PREPAYMENT		
PENALTY	60	00
20 Total (add lines 18 and 19). Enter here and on line 35 . . . . ▶	601	94

Contributions (See page 16 of Instructions for examples.)

21 a Cash contributions for which you have receipts, cancelled checks or other written evidence	529	50
b Other cash contributions. List donees and amounts. ▶		
22 Other than cash (see page 16 of Instructions for required statement)		
23 Carryover from prior years		
24 Total contributions (add lines 21a through 23). Enter here and on line 36 . . ▶	529	50

Casualty or Theft Loss(es) (See page 16 of Instructions.)

25 Loss before insurance reimbursement .	SEE	
26 Insurance reimbursement	ATTACHED	
27 Subtract line 26 from line 25. Enter difference (if less than zero, enter zero) .	FORM 4684	
28 Enter $100 or amount on line 27, whichever is smaller		
29 Casualty or theft loss (subtract line 28 from line 27). Enter here and on line 37 . ▶	929	50

Miscellaneous Deductions (See page 16 of Instructions.)

30 Union dues	150	00
31 Other (itemize) ▶		
SAFE DEPOSIT BOX RENT	7	50
SMALL TOOLS	35	00
CORRESPONDENCE COURSE	40	00
32 Total (add lines 30 and 31). Enter here and on line 38 . . . . ▶	232	50

Summary of Itemized Deductions (See page 17 of Instructions.) **A**

33 Total medical and dental—line 10 . .	564	14
34 Total taxes—line 17	1,423	14
35 Total interest—line 20	601	94
36 Total contributions—line 24	529	50
37 Casualty or theft loss(es)—line 29 . .	929	50
38 Total miscellaneous—line 32 . . .	232	50
39 Total deductions (add lines 33 through 38). ▶	4,280	72
40 If you checked Form 1040, box: 2 or 5, enter $3,200 1 or 4, enter $2,200 3, enter $1,600	3,200	00
41 Excess itemized deductions (subtract line 40 from line 39). Enter here and on Form 1040, line 33. (If line 40 is more than line 39 see "Who MUST Itemize Deductions" on page 11 of the Instructions.) . . ▶	1,080	72

329

Name(s) as shown on Form 1040 (Do not enter name and social security number if shown on other side)	Your social security number

Part I   Interest Income

1 *If you received more than $400 in interest, complete Part I.*
Interest includes earnings from savings and loan associations,
mutual savings banks, cooperative banks, and credit unions
as well as interest on bank deposits, bonds, tax refunds, etc.
Interest also includes original issue discount on bonds and
other evidences of indebtedness (see page 17 of Instructions).
(List payers and amounts.)

2 Total interest income. Enter here and
on Form 1040, line 9 . . . .

Part II   Dividend Income

3 *If you received more than $400 in* **gross dividends** *(including
capital gain distributions) and other distributions on stock,
complete Part II (see Note below and page 17 of instructions).*
**(List payers and amounts—write (H), (W), (J), for stock held
by husband, wife, or jointly.)**

(H) ACME PUBLISHING CO.	210	00
(H) SOUTH AMERICAN		
DEVELOPMENT CO.	40	00
(H) TOWN + COUNTRY INVESTORS	55	00
(H) SHARE OF JONES BROS. PTSP.	57	50
(H) ZEPCO INC.	86	00
(H) NERO POWER COMPANY	75	00
(H) TIGER FUND	6	00
(W) W+S STOCKBROKERS	60	00
(J) OPTIMIST FUND	136	00

4 Total of line 3	725	50
5 Capital gain distributions (see page 18 of Instructions. Enter here and on Schedule D, line 7). See Note below 108 00		
6 Nontaxable distributions (see page 18 of instructions) . . . 155 00		
7 Total (add lines 5 and 6)	263	00
8 Dividends before exclusion (subtract line 7 from line 4). Enter here and on Form 1040, line 10a	462	50

Note: *If you received capital gain distributions and do not need Schedule D to report any other gains or losses or to compute
the alternative tax, do not file that schedule. Instead, enter 50 percent of capital gain distributions on Form 1040,
line 15.*   **B**

Part III   Foreign Accounts and Foreign Trusts

If you are required to list interest in Part I or dividends in Part II, **OR** *if you had a foreign account or were a grantor of,
or a transferor to a foreign trust, you must answer both questions in Part III. (See page 18 of Instructions.)*

1 Did you, at any time during the taxable year, have any interest in or signature or other authority over a bank,
securities, or other financial account in a foreign country (except in a U.S. military banking facility operated by a
U.S. financial institution)? . . . . ☒ Yes   ☐ No
If "Yes," see page 3 of instructions.

2 Were you the grantor of, or transferor to, a foreign trust during any taxable year, which foreign trust was in
being during the current taxable year, whether or not you have any beneficial interest in such trust? . . . ☐ Yes ☒ No
If "Yes," you may be required to file Forms 3520, 3520–A, or 926.

☆ U.S. GOVERNMENT PRINTING OFFICE : 1977—O-235-246 58-040-1110

330

SCHEDULE D (Form 1040)

Department of the Treasury
Internal Revenue Service

Capital Gains and Losses

(Examples of property to be reported on this Schedule are gains and losses on stocks, bonds, and similar investments, and gains (but not losses) on personal assets such as a home or jewelry.)

► Attach to Form 1040.   ► See Instructions for Schedule D (Form 1040).

1977

D

Name(s) as shown on Form 1040

FRANK B. AND EVELYN H. JONES

Social security number

516 04 1492

Part I — Short-term Capital Gains and Losses—Assets Held Not More Than 9 Months

a. Kind of property and description (Example, 100 shares of "Z" Co.)	b. Date acquired (Mo., day, yr.)	c. Date sold (Mo., day, yr.)	d. Gross sales price	e. Cost or other basis, as adjusted (see Instruction F) and expense of sale	f. Gain or (loss) (d less e)
1 100 SHARES - A Co.	4-8-77	11-3-77	744.00	950.00	< 206 00
50 SHARES - B Co.	5-12-77	8-26-77	1,200.00	1,197.50	2 50
PERSONAL LOAN	7-19-77		WORTHLESS	250.00	< 250 00 >*

2	Enter your share of net short-term gain or (loss) from partnerships and fiduciaries	2	
3	Enter net gain or (loss), combine lines 1 and 2	3	< 453 50 >
4	Short-term capital loss carryover attributable to years beginning after 1969 (see Instruction I) .	4	(480 25)
5	Net short-term gain or (loss), combine lines 3 and 4	5	< 933 75 >

Part II — Long-term Capital Gains and Losses—Assets Held More Than 9 Months

6 40 SHARES- MERRY CORP.	8-2-74	1-7-77	FINAL LIQUID DIST. 60.00	110.00	< 50 00 >
150 SHARES - C Co.	6-11-76	9-18-77	1,148.00	812.50	335 50
D Co. BOND	12-1-60	12-31-77	WORTHLESS	500.00	< 500 00 >
PERSONAL RESIDENCE :					
1150 ELM ROAD					
HOMETOWN, N.Y.	11-3-66	5-5-77			3,100 00 **

7	Capital gain distributions	7	108 00
8	Enter gain, if applicable, from Form 4797, line 4(a)(1) (see Instruction A)	8	200 00
9	Enter your share of net long-term gain or (loss) from partnerships and fiduciaries	9	320 25
10	Enter your share of net long-term gain from small business corporations (Subchapter S) . . .	10	
11	Net gain or (loss), combine lines 6 through 10	11	3,513 75
12	Long-term capital loss carryover attributable to years beginning after 1969 (see Instruction I) .	12	( )
13	Net long-term gain or (loss), combine lines 11 and 12	13	3,513 75

Part III — Summary of Parts I and II (If You Have Capital Loss Carryovers From Years Beginning Before 1970, Do Not Complete This Part. See Form 4798 Instead.)

14	Combine lines 5 and 13, and enter the net gain or (loss) here	14	2,580 00
15	If line 14 shows a gain—		
	a Enter 50% of line 13 or 50% of line 14, whichever is smaller (see Part IV for computation of alternative tax). Enter zero if there is a loss or no entry on line 13	15a	1,290 00
	Note: If the amount you enter on line 15a is other than zero, you may be liable for minimum tax. See Form 4625 and instructions.		
	b Subtract line 15a from line 14. Enter here and on Form 1040, line 14	15b	1,290 00
16	If line 14 shows a loss—		
	a Enter one of the following amounts:		
	(i) If line 5 is zero or a net gain, enter 50% of line 14;		
	(ii) If line 13 is zero or a net gain, enter 50% of line 14; or,		
	(iii) If line 5 and line 13 are net losses, enter amount on line 5 added to 50% of amount on line 13	16a	
	b Enter here and enter as a (loss) on Form 1040, line 14, the smallest of:		
	(i) The amount on line 16a;		
	(ii) $2,000 ($1,000 if married and filing a separate return); or,		
	(iii) Taxable income, as adjusted (see Instruction J)	16b	( )

Note: If the amount on line 16a is larger than the loss shown on line 16b, complete Part V to determine Post-1969 Capital Loss Carryovers from 1977 to 1978.

* SEE STATEMENT ATTACHED
** FORM 2119 ATTACHED

Supplemental Income Schedule

(From pensions and annuities, rents and royalties, partnerships, estates and trusts, etc.)
► Attach to Form 1040.   ► See Instructions for Schedule E (Form 1040).

1977

Name(s) as shown on Form 1040

FRANK B. AND EVELYN H. JONES

Your social security number: 516 04 1492

Part I — Pension and Annuity Income. If fully taxable, do not complete this part. Enter amount on Form 1040, line 17. For one pension or annuity not fully taxable, complete this part. If you have more than one pension or annuity that is not fully taxable, attach a separate sheet listing each one with the appropriate data and enter combined total of taxable portions on line 5.

1 Name of payer. HOMETOWN N.Y. RETIREMENT SYSTEM

2 Did your employer contribute part of the cost? .... ☒ Yes ☐ No

If "Yes," is your contribution recoverable within 3 years of the annuity starting date? .... ☒ Yes ☐ No

If "Yes," show: Your contribution $ 4,925 , Contribution recovered in prior years ... | 2 | 4,600 |

3 Amount received this year .... | 3 | 2,400 |

4 Amount excludable this year .... | 4 | 325 |

5 Taxable portion (subtract line 4 from line 3) .... | 5 | 2,075 | 00 |

Part II — Rent and Royalty Income. If you need more space, use Form 4831.

Have you claimed expenses connected with your vacation home rented to others? ☐ Yes ☒ No

(a) Kind and location of property If residential, also write "R"	(b) Total amount of rents	(c) Total amount of royalties	(d) Depreciation (explain below) or depletion (attach computation)	(e) Other expenses (Repairs, etc.— explain below)
BRICK STORE BUILDING HOMETOWN, N.Y.	2,500.00		240.00	1,275.17
ACME PUBLISHING CO. CLEVELAND, OHIO		117.50		

6 Totals .... | 2,500.00 | 117.50 | 240.00 | 1,275.17 |

7 Net income or (loss) from rents and royalties (column (b) plus column (c) less columns (d) and (e)). | 7 | 1,102.33 |

8 Net rental income or (loss) (from Form 4831) .... | 8 | -0- |

9 Net farm rental profit or (loss) (from Form 4835) .... | 9 | -0- |

10 Total rent and royalty income (add lines 7, 8, and 9) .... | 10 | 1,102 | 33 |

Part III — Income or Losses from Partnerships, Estates or Trusts, Small Business Corporations.

Enter in column (b): P for Partnership, E for Estate or Trust, or S for Small Business Corp.

(a) Name	(b)	(c) Employer identification number	(d) Your share of gross farming or fishing income	(e) Income or (loss)	(f) Additional 1st year depreciation (applicable only to partnerships)
JONES BROS.	P	49-9148529		4,642.50	
GATEWAY TRAVEL AGENCY	P	49-6663666		1,400.00	
J. B. JONES TRUST	E	49-3169622		1,507.99	

11 Totals. | | | | 7,550.49 | |

12 Income or (loss). Total of column (e) less total of column (f) .... | 12 | 7,550 | 49 |

13 TOTAL (add lines 5, 10, and 12). Enter here and on Form 1040, line 18 .... ► | 13 | 10,727 | 82 |

Explanation of Column (e), Part II

Item	Amount	Item	Amount	Item	Amount
REAL ESTATE TAXES	465.50				
INTEREST	314.95				
INSURANCE	90.00				
PAINTING	240.00				
GENERAL REPAIRS	164.72				
TOTAL	1,275.17				

Schedule for Depreciation Claimed in Part II above. If you need more space use Form 4562.

(a) Description of property	(b) Date acquired	(c) Cost or other basis	(d) Depreciation allowed or allowable in prior years	(e) Method of computing depreciation	(f) Life or rate	(g) Depreciation for this year
1 Total additional first-year depreciation (do not include in items below) —						
BRICK STORE BUILDING	1-1-67	12,000	2,400	S.L.	50 yrs.	240.00

2 Totals .... | | 12,000 | | | | 240.00 |

E

Name(s) as shown on Form 1040	Your social security number
FRANK B. AND EVELYN H. JONES	516 04 1492

Schedule RP	Credit for the Elderly—Individual(s) Under 65 Having Gross Income from a Public Retirement System as a Result of His (Her) Services or Services of His (Her) Deceased Spouse	RP

Name of public retirement system of spouse(s) under 65

HOMETOWN, N.Y. RETIREMENT SYSTEM

Filing Status and Age (check only one)

A ☐ Single, under 65

B ☒ Married filing joint return, one spouse under 65 and having public retirement system income and other spouse 65 or over. By checking this box and completing Schedule RP, you and your spouse elect to compute your credit under this schedule. If you checked this box and live in a community property State, see Schedule RP instructions

C ☐ Married filing joint return, both spouses under 65. If you checked this box and live in a community property State, see Schedule RP instructions

D ☐ Married filing separate return, under 65, and have not lived with your spouse at any time during the taxable year

Joint return filers use column A for wife and column B for husband. All other filers use column B only.

Exception: *If you checked Filing Status and Age box B, the spouse under 65 should use column B.*

	A	B
1 Maximum amount of retirement income for credit computation: If box A checked—enter $2,500 If box B or C checked—enter $3,750 (**Note:** *The $3,750 must be divided between you and your spouse, but not more than $2,500 may be allocated to either. It will generally be more advantageous to allocate the greater amount to the spouse with the most retirement income)* If box D checked—enter $1,875	1,250 00	2,500 00
2 Deduct:		
a Amounts received as pensions or annuities under the Social Security Act, the Railroad Retirement Acts (but not supplemental annuities), and certain other exclusions from gross income (see instructions)		
b Earned income such as wages, salaries, fees, etc. received (does not apply to persons 72 or over):		
(i) If you are under 62, enter earned income in excess of $900 . . .		500 00
(ii) If you are 62 or over but under 72, enter amount determined as follows: If earned income is $1,200 or less, enter zero . . . . If earned income is over $1,200 but not over $1,700, enter one-half of amount over $1,200; or if earned income is over $1,700 enter amount over $1,450	10401 95	
3 Total of lines 2a and 2b	10401 95	500 00
4 Balance (subtract line 3 from line 1). If column A or B is more than zero, complete this schedule. If both columns are zero or less, do not file this schedule	–0–	2,000 00
5 Retirement income: **a If under 65—** Enter only income from pensions and annuities under public retirement systems (e.g. Federal, State Governments, etc.) received as a result of your services or services of your deceased spouse that is included in gross income (but not Social Security, Railroad Retirement or certain other payments excluded from gross income)		2,075 00
b If 65 or older— Enter total of pensions and annuities, interest, dividends, proceeds of retirement bonds, and amounts received from individual retirement accounts and individual retirement annuities that are included in gross income, and gross rents from Schedule E, Part II, column (b); Form 4831, line 3; or Form 4835, line 22. Also include your share of gross rents from partnerships and your proportionate share of taxable rents from estates and trusts		
6 Line 4 or line 5, whichever is smaller		2,000 00

7 Total (add amounts on line 6)	**7**	2,000 00
8 Tentative credit. Enter 15% of line 7	**8**	300 00
9 Amount of tax shown on Form 1040, line 37	**9**	1,900 00
10 **Credit for the Elderly.** Enter here and on Form 1040, line 39, the amount on line 8 or line 9, whichever is smaller . . . . ▶	**10**	300 00

☆ U.S. GOVERNMENT PRINTING OFFICE : 1977—O-235-355 23-188-5979

333

Form 2119
(Rev. Nov. 1976)
Department of the Treasury
Internal Revenue Service

Sale or Exchange of Personal Residence

▶ **Attach to Form 1040.**

Taxable year

1977

Note: *Do not include expenses which are deductible as moving expenses on Form 3903.*

Name(s) as shown on Form 1040   FRANK B. AND EVELYN H. JONES

Your social security number   516 04 1492

			Yes	No
1(a) Date former residence sold MAY 5, 1977		**(e)** Were any rooms in either residence rented or used for business purposes at any time? . . (If "Yes," explain on separate sheet and attach.)		X
(b) Have you ever deferred any gain on the sale or exchange of a personal residence? . . . . [Yes] [No X]		**(f)** If you were married, do you and your spouse have the same proportionate ownership interest in your new residence as you had in your old residence? . . . . (If "No," see the Consent on other side.)		X
(c) Have you ever claimed a credit for purchase or construction of a new principal residence? (If you answered "Yes," see Form 5405, Part II.) [X]				
2(a) Date new residence bought MAY 3, 1977		**3(a)** Were you 65 or older on date of sale? . . . . (If you answered "Yes," see Note below.)		X
(b) If new residence was constructed for or by you, date construction began —		**(b)** If you answered "Yes" to 3(a), did you use the property sold as your principal residence for a total of at least 5 years (except for short temporary absences) of the 8-year period preceding the sale?		
(c) Date you occupied new residence MAY 28, 1977				
(d) Were both the old and new properties used as your principal residence? . . . . [Yes X] [No]		**(c)** If you answered "Yes" to 3(b), do you want to elect to exclude gain on the sale from your gross income? . . .		

Computation of Gain and Adjusted Sales Price

4 Selling price of residence. (Do not include selling price of personal property items.)	**4**	28,450
5 Less: Commissions and other expenses of sale (from Schedule I on other side)	**5**	– 0 –
6 Amount realized	**6**	28,450
7 Less: Basis of residence sold (from Schedule II on other side)	**7**	19,500
8 Gain on sale (line 6 less line 7). If line 7 is more than line 6, there is no gain, so you should not make further entries on this form	**8**	8,950
9 Fixing-up expenses (from Schedule III on other side)	**9**	350
10 Adjusted sales price (line 6 less line 9)	**10**	28,100

If you answered "No" to question 3(a) or 3(c), complete only lines 11 through 14.
If you answered "Yes" to question 3(c), complete lines 15 through 17, or 15 through 20, whichever is applicable.

Computation of Gain to be Reported and Adjusted Basis of New Residence—General Rule

11 Cost of new residence	**11**	25,000
12 Gain taxable this year (line 10 less line 11, but not more than line 8). If line 11 is more than line 10, enter zero. Enter here and on Schedule D (Form 1040), in column f, line 1, or line 6, whichever is applicable	**12**	3,100
13 Gain on which tax is to be deferred (line 8 less line 12)	**13**	5,850
14 Adjusted basis of new residence (line 11 less line 13)	**14**	19,150

Computation of Exclusion, Gain to be Reported, and Adjusted Basis of New Residence—Special Rule
(For use of taxpayers 65 years of age or over who checked "Yes," in 3(c) above.)

15 If line 10 above is $20,000 or less, the entire gain shown on line 8 is excludable from gross income. If line 10 is over $20,000, determine the excludable portion of the gain as follows:		
(a) Divide amount on line 10 into $20,000 . . . . **15(a)**		
(b) Excludable portion of gain (multiply amount on line 8 by figure on line 15(a) and enter result here) .	**15(b)**	
16 Nonexcludable portion of gain (line 8 less line 15(b))	**16**	
17 Cost of new residence. If a new personal residence was not purchased, enter "None," and do not complete the following lines. Then enter the amount shown on line 16 on Schedule D (Form 1040), in column f, line 6	**17**	
18 Gain taxable this year. (Line 10 less sum of lines 15(b) and 17. But this amount may not exceed line 16.) If line 17 plus line 15(b) is more than line 10, enter zero. Enter here and on Schedule D (Form 1040), in column f, line 6	**18**	
19 Gain on which tax is to be deferred (line 16 less line 18)	**19**	
20 Adjusted basis of new residence (line 17 less line 19)	**20**	

Note: There is a special provision available if you were 65 or older on the date of the sale or exchange of your principal residence. If you met the age requirement and owned and used the residence disposed of as your principal residence for a total of 5 years out of the 8 years preceding the sale, you may elect to exclude part or all of the gain from that sale. If the property is held by you and your spouse as joint tenants, tenants by the entirety, or community property and you and your spouse file a joint return, only you or your spouse need meet the age requirement. You are only eligible for the exclusion once. This is true regardless of your marital status at the time you made the election.

Form **2119** (Rev. 11–76)

334

Form 3903

Department of the Treasury
Internal Revenue Service

Moving Expense Adjustment

▶ Attach to Form 1040.

1977

Name(s) as shown on Form 1040	Social security number
FRANK B. AND EVELYN H. JONES	516 04 1492

(a) What is the distance from your **former** residence to your new business location? ....**46**.... miles

(b) What is the distance from your **former** residence to your former business location? ....**5**...... miles

(c) If the distance in (a) is 35 or more miles farther than the distance in (b), complete the rest of this form. If the distance is less than 35 miles, you are not entitled to a moving expense deduction. (See instruction A.) This rule is not applicable to members of the armed forces.

1 Transportation expenses in moving household goods and personal effects	1	574	05
2 Travel, meals, and lodging expenses in moving from former to new residence	2	2	10
3 Pre-move travel, meals, and lodging expenses in searching for a new residence after obtaining employment . . .	3		
4 Temporary living expenses in new location or area during any 30 consecutive days after obtaining employment . .	4	42	85
5 Total (Add lines 3 and 4.)	5	42	85
6 Enter the lesser: Line 5 or $1,500 ($750 if married, filing a separate return, and you resided with your spouse who also started work during the taxable year) . .	6	42	85

7 Expenses incident to: (Check one.)
 (a) ☒ sale or exchange of your former residence; or,
 (b) ☐ if nonowner, settlement of your unexpired lease on former residence .

	7	1700	00

8 Expenses incident to: (Check one.)
 (a) ☒ purchase of a new residence; or,
 (b) ☐ if renting, acquiring a new lease . . . .

	8	350	00
9 Total (Add lines 6, 7, and 8.)	9	2,092	85

Note: Amounts on lines 7(a) and 8(a) not deducted because of the $3,000 (or $1,500) limitation may generally be used either to decrease the gain on the sale of your residence, or to increase the basis of your new residence.

10 Enter the lesser: Line 9 or $3,000 ($1,500 if married, filing a separate return, and you resided with your spouse who also started work during the taxable year). (See instruction C(2).)	10	2,092	85
11 Total moving expenses (Add lines 1, 2, and 10.)	11	2,669	00
12 Reimbursements and allowances received for this move (other than amounts included on Form W–2) (See instruction L.)	12		
13 If line 12 is less than line 11, enter the difference here and on Form 1040, line 22	13	2,669	00
14 If line 12 is larger than line 11, enter the excess here and on Form 1040, line 20, as "Excess moving reimbursement"	14		

Instructions

A. Who May Deduct Moving Expenses.— As an employed or a self-employed person, you may deduct reasonable moving expenses paid or incurred during the taxable year in connection with a move you make to a new principal work place.

The deduction is allowable to you only if (a) your change in job location has added at least 35 miles to the distance from your old residence to your work, or (b) if you had no former principal work place, your new principal work place is at least 35 miles from your former residence. (The distance between two points is considered to be the shortest of the more commonly traveled routes between those points.)

Also, the deduction is allowable only if either (a) during the 12 months immediately following your arrival in the general location of your new principal work place you are a full-time employee during at least 39 weeks, or (b) during the 24 months immediately following such arrival you are a full-time employee or self-employed on a full-time basis during at least 78 weeks, of which not less than 39 weeks are during the 12 months following your arrival.

B. The 39 Week/78 Week Test.—Disregard the 39 week/78 week test referred to in instruction A if employment is terminated because of death, disability, involuntary separation (other than for willful misconduct), or transfer for the employer's benefit.

If you have not satisfied the 39 week/78 week test before time for filing your return for the taxable year in which you paid or incurred the moving expenses, but believe you will later satisfy it, you may still deduct those expenses in the year you paid or incurred them.

(Continued on back)

Form **3903** (1977)

335

Form **4684**

Department of the Treasury
Internal Revenue Service

Casualties and Thefts

▶ See separate instructions.
▶ Attach to Form 1040.

1977

Name(s) as shown on Form 1040

FRANK B. AND EVELYN H. JONES

Social Security Number

516 04 1492

Use Part I to determine the amount of a deductible casualty or theft loss of property, other than trade, business, rental, or royalty property, provided only one casualty or theft occurred during the taxable year and any related insurance or other compensation did not exceed the property's cost or other basis, as adjusted.

Use Part II to determine the amount of a casualty or theft loss or gain if the circumstances mentioned in Part I are not applicable. For example: (1) if there is more than one casualty or theft occurrence; (2) if there are both casualty or theft losses and gains; or (3) trade, business, rental, or royalty property is involved. If Part II is used, go to Part III, on page 2, first.

Part I Casualty or Theft Loss (Use if One Loss Occurred)	Item or article	Item or article	Item or article
1 Description of property			
2 Cost or other basis, as adjusted (see instruction H) . . .			
3 Decrease in fair market value (see instruction I)			
a. Value before casualty or theft			
b. Value after casualty or theft			
c. Excess of line 3a over line 3b			
4 Lesser of line 2 or line 3c			
5 Insurance recovery or other compensation			
6 Excess of line 4 over line 5			
7 Total of amounts on line 6			
8 Amounts on line 6 attributable to income-producing property			
9 Subtract line 8 from line 7			
10 Enter $100, or amount on line 9, whichever is smaller (see instruction J)			
11 Excess of line 9 over line 10			
12 Casualty or theft loss. Add line 8 and line 11, enter here and on Schedule A (Form 1040), line 29—identify as "4684"			

Part II Summary of Gains and Losses (Use if More Than One Loss Occurred)	(B) Losses from casualties or thefts		(C) Gains from casualties or thefts includible in income
(A) Identify casualty or theft loss from Part III	(i) Property other than trade, business, rental, or royalty property	(ii) Trade, business, rental, or royalty property	

Casualty or Theft of Property Held 9 Months or Less

	(i)	(ii)	(C)
1 CASUALTY OR THEFT OCCURANCE NUMBER 2	79.50		
2 Totals, add amounts on line 1 for each column . . .	79.50		

3 Combine line 2, columns (B)(ii) and (C). Enter here and on Form 4797, Part II, line 8, column g **(Note:** if Form 4797 is not required for other transactions, enter amount on Form 1040, line 16—identify as "4684")

4 Enter amount from line 2, column (B)(i) here and on Schedule A (Form 1040), line 29—identify as "4684" .   **79.50**

Casualty or Theft of Property Held More Than 9 Months (See instruction G)

5 Any casualty or theft gains from Form 4797, Part III, line 23 . . . .

	(i)	(ii)	(C)
6 CASUALTY OR THEFT OCCURANCE NUMBER 1	850.00		
7 Total losses, add amounts on line 6, columns (B)(i) and (B)(ii) . .	850.00	/////////	

8 Total gains, add lines 5 and 6, column (C) . . . .

9 Combine line 7, columns (B)(i) and (B)(ii) **850.00**

10 If line 9 is **more than** line 8:
  a. Combine line 7, column (B)(ii) and line 8. Enter here and on Form 4797, Part II, line 8, column g **(Note:** if Form 4797 is not required for other transactions, enter amount on Form 1040, line 16—identify as "4684")

  b. Enter amount from line 7, column (B)(i) here and on Schedule A (Form 1040), line 29—identify as "4684" **850.00**

11 If line 9 is **equal to or less than** line 8, enter the difference here and on Form 4797, Part I, line 3, column g—identify as "Gain from Form 4684, Part II, line 11" . . . .

Form **4684** (1977)

Form 4684 (1977)

Part III — Applicable if Part II is used

(A) Description of property	(B) Cost or other basis, as adjusted. See Instruction H.	(C) Insurance recovery or other compensation. If col. (C) exceeds col. (B), skip to col. (I).	(D) Fair market value before casualty or theft. See Instruction I.	(E) Fair market value after casualty or theft. See Instruction I.	(F) Decrease in fair market value. Col. (D) less col. (E). If no decrease, enter zero. See Instruction I.	(G) Lesser of col. (B) or col. (F).	(H) LOSS (i) Property other than trade, business, rental or royalty property.	(H) LOSS (ii) Trade, business, rental or royalty property.	(I) GAIN Excess of col. (C) over col. (B). See Instruction K.

Property Held 9 Months or Less — Casualty or Theft Occurrence Number 1

1

2 Total of amounts on line 1, column (H)(i)

3 Amount on line 2 attributable to income-producing property

4 Subtract line 3 from line 2

5 $100 limitation, or portion of limitation used, see instruction J

6 Excess of line 4 over line 5

7 Total of amounts on lines 3 and 6, column (H)(i) and line 1, column (H)(ii) and column (I)—enter here and in Part II, line 1, and identify as "Casualty or theft occurrence number 1"

Property Held More Than 9 Months

Line	(A)	(B)	(C)	(D)	(E)	(F)	(G)	(H)(i)
8	LAKESIDE COTTAGE	13,100.00	3,050.00	14,000.00	12,000.00	4,000.00	4,000.00	950.00

9 Total of amounts on line 8, column (H)(i) ... 950.00

10 Amount on line 9 attributable to income-producing property ... -0-

11 Subtract line 10 from line 9 ... 950.00

12 Portion of $100 limitation not used on line 5 ... 100.00

13 Excess of line 11 over line 12 ... 850.00

14 Total of amounts on lines 10 and 13, column (H)(i) and line 8, column (H)(ii) and column (I)—enter here and in Part II, line 6, and identify as "Casualty or theft occurrence number 1" ... 850.00

Property Held 9 Months or Less — Casualty or Theft Occurrence Number 2

Line	(A)	(B)	(C)	(D)	(E)	(F)	(G)	(H)(i)
15	MOVIE CAMERA	300.00	-0-	179.50	-0-	179.50	179.50	179.50

16 Total of amounts on line 15, column (H)(i) ... 179.50

17 Amount on line 16 attributable to income-producing property ... -0-

18 Subtract line 17 from line 16 ... 179.50

19 $100 limitation, or portion of limitation used, see instruction J ... 100.00

20 Excess of line 18 over line 19 ... 79.50

21 Total of amounts on lines 17 and 20, column (H)(i) and line 15, column (H)(ii) and column (I)—enter here and in Part II, line 1, and identify as "Casualty or theft occurrence number 2" ... 79.50

Property Held More Than 9 Months

22

23 Total of amounts on line 22, column (H)(i)

24 Amount on line 23 attributable to income-producing property

25 Subtract line 24 from line 23

26 Portion of $100 limitation not used on line 19

27 Excess of line 25 over line 26

28 Total of amounts on lines 24 and 27, column (H)(i) and line 22, column (H)(ii) and column (I)—enter here and in Part II, line 6, and identify as "Casualty or theft occurrence number 2"

☆ U.S. GOVERNMENT PRINTING OFFICE 1977—O—245-162 58-040-1110

337

Supplemental Schedule of Gains and Losses

Sales, Exchanges and Involuntary Conversions under
Sections 1231, 1245, 1250, 1251, 1252, and 1254
To be filed with Form 1040, 1041, 1065, 1120, etc.—See Separate Instructions

1977

Name(s) as shown on return	Identifying number as shown on page 1 of your tax return
FRANK B. AND EVELYN H. JONES	516-04-1492

Part I Sales or Exchanges of Property Used in Trade or Business, and Involuntary Conversions (Section 1231)

SECTION A.—Involuntary Conversions Due to Casualty and Theft (See Instruction E)

a. Kind of property (if necessary, attach additional descriptive details not shown below)	b. Date acquired (mo., day, yr.)	c. Date sold (mo., day, yr.)	d. Gross sales price	e. Depreciation allowed (or allowable) since acquisition	f. Cost or other basis, cost of subsequent improvements (if not purchased, attach explanation) and expense of sale	g. Gain or loss (d plus e less f)
1						

2 Combine the amounts on line 1. Enter here, and on the appropriate line as follows . . . .
  (a) For all except partnership returns:
  (1) If line 2 is zero or a gain, enter that amount in column g, line 3.
  (2) If line 2 is a loss, enter the loss on line 5.
  (b) For partnership returns: Enter the amount shown on line 2 above, on Schedule K (Form 1065), line 6.

SECTION B.—Sales or Exchanges of Property Used in Trade or Business and Certain Involuntary Conversions (Not Reportable in Section A) (See Instruction E)

a. Kind of property	b. Date acquired	c. Date sold	d. Gross sales price	e. Depreciation allowed	f. Cost or other basis	g. Gain or loss
3 SHARE OF GAIN ON SALE OF BUILDING USED IN JONES BROS. PARTNERSHIP						500.00
SALE OF STORE PARKING LOT	12-31-75	1-2-77	3,500.00	400.00	4,200.00	<300.00>

4 Combine the amounts on line 3. Enter here, and on the appropriate line as follows 200.00
  (a) For all except partnership returns:
  (1) If line 4 is a gain, enter the gain as a long-term capital gain on Schedule D (Form 1040, 1120, etc.) that is being filed. See instruction E.
  (2) If line 4 is zero or a loss, enter that amount on line 6.
  (b) For partnership returns: Enter the amount shown on line 4 above, on Schedule K (Form 1065), line 7.

Part II Ordinary Gains and Losses

a. Kind of property (if necessary, attach additional descriptive details not shown below)	b. Date acquired (mo., day, yr.)	c. Date sold (mo., day, yr.)	d. Gross sales price	e. Depreciation allowed (or allowable) since acquisition	f. Cost or other basis, cost of subsequent improvements (if not purchased, attach explanation) and expense of sale	g. Gain or loss (d plus e less f)
5 Amount, if any, from line 2(a)(2)						
6 Amount, if any, from line 4(a)(2)						
7 Gain, if any, from page 2, line 22						300.00
8						

9 Combine amounts on lines 5 through 8. Enter here, and on the appropriate line as follows 300.00
  (a) For all except individual returns: Enter the gain or (loss) shown on line 9, on the line provided for on the return (Form 1120, etc.) being filed. See instruction F for specific line reference.
  (b) For individual returns:
  (1) If the gain or (loss) on line 9, includes losses which are to be treated as an itemized deduction on Schedule A (Form 1040) (see instruction F), enter the total of the loss(es) here and include on Schedule A (Form 1040), line 29—identify as "loss from Form 4797, line 9(b)(1)" . . . .
  (2) Redetermine the gain or (loss) on line 9, excluding the loss (if any) entered on line 9(b)(1). Enter here and on Form 1040, line 16 . . . .   300.00

Part III Gain From Disposition of Property Under Sections 1245, 1250, 1251, 1252, 1254—Assets Held More than Nine Months (See Separate Instructions)
Disregard lines 18 and 19 if there are no dispositions of farm property or farmland, or if this form is filed by a partnership.

10 Description of sections 1245, 1250, 1251, 1252, and 1254 property:

	Date acquired (mo., day, yr.)	Date sold (mo., day, yr.)
(A) EQUIPMENT USED IN STORE BUILDING	1-2-74	1-9-77
(B)		
(C)		
(D)		

Relate lines 10(A) through 10(D) to these columns ► ► ► ►	Property (A)	Property (B)	Property (C)	Property (D)
11 Gross sales price	900.00			
12 Cost or other basis and expense of sale	3,600.00			
13 Depreciation (or depletion) allowed (or allowable)	3,000.00			
14 Adjusted basis, subtract line 13 from line 12	600.00			
15 Total gain, subtract line 14 from line 11	300.00			
16 If section 1245 property:				
(a) Depreciation allowed (or allowable) after applicable date (see instructions)	3,000.00			
(b) Enter smaller of line 15 or 16(a)	300.00			
17 If section 1250 property:				
(a) Additional depreciation after 12/31/75				
(b) Applicable percentage times the smaller of line 15 or line 17(a) (see instruction G.4)				
(c) Excess, if any, of line 15 over line 17(a) (If line 15 does not exceed line 17(a), skip lines 17(d) through 17(h), and enter the amount from line 17(b) on line 17(i))				
(d) Additional depreciation after 12/31/69 and before 1/1/76				
(e) Applicable percentage times the smaller of line 17(c) or line 17(d) (see instruction G.4)				
(f) Excess, if any, of line 17(c) over line 17(d) (If line 17(c) does not exceed line 17(d), skip lines 17(g) and 17(h), and combine the amounts on lines 17(b) and 17(e) on line 17(i))				
(g) Additional depreciation after 12/31/63 and before 1/1/70				
(h) Applicable percentage times the smaller of line 17(f) or 17(g) (see instruction G.4)				
(i) Add lines 17(b), 17(e), and 17(h)				
18 If section 1251 property:				
(a) If farmland, enter soil, water, and land clearing expenses for current year and the. four preceding years				
(b) If farm property other than land, subtract line 16(b) from line 15; If farmland, enter smaller of line 15 or 18(a) (see instruction G.5)				
(c) Excess deductions account (see instruction G.5)				
(d) Enter smaller of line 18(b) or 18(c)				
19 If section 1252 property:				
(a) Soil, water, and land clearing expenses made after 12/31/69				
(b) Amount from line 18(d), if none enter a zero				
(c) Excess, if any, of line 19(a) over line 19(b)				
(d) Line 19(c) times applicable percentage (see instruction G.5)				
(e) Subtract line 19(b) from line 15				
(f) Enter smaller of line 19(d) or 19(e)				
20 If section 1254 property:				
(a) Intangible drilling and development costs deducted after 12/31/75 (see instruction G.6)				
(b) Enter smaller of line 15 or 20(a)				

Summary of Part III Gains (Complete Property columns (A) through (D) through line 20(b) before going to line 21)

21 Total gains for all properties (add columns (A) through (D), line 15)	300.00
22 Add columns (A) through (D), lines 16(b), 17(i), 18(d), 19(f), and 20(b). Enter here and on line 7	300.00
23 Subtract line 22 from line 21. Enter here and in appropriate Section in Part I (see instructions E and G.2)	- 0 -

☆ U.S. GOVERNMENT PRINTING OFFICE : 1977—O-235-397 58-040-1110

1977 Tax Table B—MARRIED FILING JOINTLY (Box 2) and QUALIFYING WIDOW(ER)S (Box 5)

(If your income or exemptions are not covered, use Schedule TC (Form 1040), Part I to figure your tax)

If line 34, Form 1040 is— Over	But not over	And the total number of exemptions claimed on line 7 is— 2	3	4	5	6	7	8	9
		Your tax is—							
26,000	26,050	4,624	4,384	4,151	3,941	3,701	3,456	3,211	2,966
26,050	26,100	4,640	4,400	4,165	3,955	3,715	3,470	3,225	2,980
26,100	26,150	4,656	4,416	4,179	3,969	3,729	3,484	3,239	2,994
26,150	26,200	4,672	4,432	4,193	3,983	3,743	3,498	3,253	3,008
26,200	26,250	4,688	4,448	4,208	3,997	3,757	3,512	3,267	3,022
26,250	26,300	4,704	4,464	4,224	4,011	3,771	3,526	3,281	3,036
26,300	26,350	4,720	4,480	4,240	4,025	3,785	3,540	3,295	3,050
26,350	26,400	4,736	4,496	4,256	4,039	3,799	3,554	3,309	3,064
26,400	26,450	4,752	4,512	4,272	4,053	3,813	3,568	3,323	3,078
26,450	26,500	4,768	4,528	4,288	4,067	3,827	3,582	3,337	3,092
26,500	26,550	4,784	4,544	4,304	4,081	3,841	3,596	3,351	3,106
26,550	26,600	4,800	4,560	4,320	4,095	3,855	3,610	3,365	3,120
26,600	26,650	4,816	4,576	4,336	4,109	3,869	3,624	3,379	3,134
26,650	26,700	4,832	4,592	4,352	4,123	3,883	3,638	3,393	3,148
26,700	26,750	4,848	4,608	4,368	4,137	3,897	3,652	3,407	3,162
26,750	26,800	4,864	4,624	4,384	4,151	3,911	3,666	3,421	3,176
26,800	26,850	4,880	4,640	4,400	4,165	3,925	3,680	3,435	3,190
26,850	26,900	4,896	4,656	4,416	4,179	3,939	3,694	3,449	3,204
26,900	26,950	4,912	4,672	4,432	4,193	3,953	3,708	3,463	3,218
26,950	27,000	4,928	4,688	4,448	4,208	3,967	3,722	3,477	3,232
27,000	27,050	4,944	4,704	4,464	4,224	3,981	3,736	3,491	3,246
27,050	27,100	4,960	4,720	4,480	4,240	3,995	3,750	3,505	3,260
27,100	27,150	4,976	4,736	4,496	4,256	4,009	3,764	3,519	3,274
27,150	27,200	4,992	4,752	4,512	4,272	4,023	3,778	3,533	3,288
27,200	27,250	5,008	4,768	4,528	4,288	4,037	3,792	3,547	3,302
27,250	27,300	5,024	4,784	4,544	4,304	4,051	3,806	3,561	3,316
27,300	27,350	5,040	4,800	4,560	4,320	4,065	3,820	3,575	3,330
27,350	27,400	5,056	4,816	4,576	4,336	4,079	3,834	3,589	3,344
27,400	27,450	5,072	4,832	4,592	4,352	4,093	3,848	3,603	3,358
27,450	27,500	5,088	4,848	4,608	4,368	4,107	3,862	3,617	3,372
27,500	27,550	5,104	4,864	4,624	4,384	4,121	3,876	3,631	3,386
27,550	27,600	5,120	4,880	4,640	4,400	4,135	3,890	3,645	3,400
27,600	27,650	5,136	4,896	4,656	4,416	4,149	3,904	3,659	3,414
27,650	27,700	5,152	4,912	4,672	4,432	4,163	3,918	3,673	3,428
27,700	27,750	5,168	4,928	4,688	4,448	4,178	3,932	3,687	3,442
27,750	27,800	5,184	4,944	4,704	4,464	4,194	3,946	3,701	3,456
27,800	27,850	5,200	4,960	4,720	4,480	4,210	3,960	3,715	3,470
27,850	27,900	5,216	4,976	4,736	4,496	4,226	3,974	3,729	3,484
27,900	27,950	5,232	4,992	4,752	4,512	4,242	3,988	3,743	3,498
27,950	28,000	5,248	5,008	4,768	4,528	4,258	4,002	3,757	3,512
28,000	28,050	5,264	5,024	4,784	4,544	4,274	4,016	3,771	3,526
28,050	28,100	5,280	5,040	4,800	4,560	4,290	4,030	3,785	3,540
28,100	28,150	5,296	5,056	4,816	4,576	4,306	4,044	3,799	3,554
28,150	28,200	5,312	5,072	4,832	4,592	4,322	4,058	3,813	3,568
28,200	28,250	5,328	5,088	4,848	4,608	4,338	4,072	3,827	3,582
28,250	28,300	5,344	5,104	4,864	4,624	4,354	4,086	3,841	3,596
28,300	28,350	5,360	5,120	4,880	4,640	4,370	4,100	3,855	3,610
28,350	28,400	5,376	5,136	4,896	4,656	4,386	4,114	3,869	3,624
28,400	28,450	5,392	5,152	4,912	4,672	4,402	4,128	3,883	3,638
28,450	28,500	5,408	5,168	4,928	4,688	4,418	4,143	3,897	3,652
28,500	28,550	5,424	5,184	4,944	4,704	4,434	4,159	3,911	3,666
28,550	28,600	5,440	5,200	4,960	4,720	4,450	4,175	3,925	3,680
28,600	28,650	5,456	5,216	4,976	4,736	4,466	4,191	3,939	3,694
28,650	28,700	5,472	5,232	4,992	4,752	4,482	4,207	3,953	3,708
28,700	28,750	5,489	5,248	5,008	4,768	4,498	4,223	3,967	3,722
28,750	28,800	5,507	5,264	5,024	4,784	4,514	4,239	3,981	3,736
28,800	28,850	5,525	5,280	5,040	4,800	4,530	4,255	3,995	3,750
28,850	28,900	5,543	5,296	5,056	4,816	4,546	4,271	4,009	3,764
28,900	28,950	5,561	5,312	5,072	4,832	4,562	4,287	4,023	3,778
28,950	29,000	5,579	5,328	5,088	4,848	4,578	4,303	4,037	3,792
29,000	29,050	5,597	5,344	5,104	4,864	4,594	4,319	4,051	3,806
29,050	29,100	5,615	5,360	5,120	4,880	4,610	4,335	4,065	3,820
29,100	29,150	5,633	5,376	5,136	4,896	4,626	4,351	4,079	3,834
29,150	29,200	5,651	5,392	5,152	4,912	4,642	4,367	4,093	3,848
29,200	29,250	5,669	5,408	5,168	4,928	4,658	4,383	4,108	3,862
29,250	29,300	5,687	5,424	5,184	4,944	4,674	4,399	4,124	3,876
29,300	29,350	5,705	5,440	5,200	4,960	4,690	4,415	4,140	3,890
29,350	29,400	5,723	5,456	5,216	4,976	4,706	4,431	4,156	3,904
29,400	29,450	5,741	5,472	5,232	4,992	4,722	4,447	4,172	3,918
29,450	29,500	5,759	5,489	5,248	5,008	4,738	4,463	4,188	3,932
29,500	29,550	5,777	5,507	5,264	5,024	4,754	4,479	4,204	3,946
29,550	29,600	5,795	5,525	5,280	5,040	4,770	4,495	4,220	3,960
29,600	29,650	5,813	5,543	5,296	5,056	4,786	4,511	4,236	3,974
29,650	29,700	5,831	5,561	5,312	5,072	4,802	4,527	4,252	3,988
29,700	29,750	5,849	5,579	5,328	5,088	4,818	4,543	4,268	4,002
29,750	29,800	5,867	5,597	5,344	5,104	4,834	4,559	4,284	4,016
29,800	29,850	5,885	5,615	5,360	5,120	4,850	4,575	4,300	4,030
29,850	29,900	5,903	5,633	5,376	5,136	4,866	4,591	4,316	4,044
29,900	29,950	5,921	5,651	5,392	5,152	4,882	4,607	4,332	4,058
29,950	30,000	5,939	5,669	5,408	5,168	4,898	4,623	4,348	4,073
30,000	30,050	5,957	5,687	5,424	5,184	4,914	4,639	4,364	4,089
30,050	30,100	5,975	5,705	5,440	5,200	4,930	4,655	4,380	4,105
30,100	30,150	5,993	5,723	5,456	5,216	4,946	4,671	4,396	4,121
30,150	30,200	6,011	5,741	5,472	5,232	4,962	4,687	4,412	4,137
30,200	30,250	6,029	5,759	5,489	5,248	4,978	4,703	4,428	4,153
30,250	30,300	6,047	5,777	5,507	5,264	4,994	4,719	4,444	4,169
30,300	30,350	6,065	5,795	5,525	5,280	5,010	4,735	4,460	4,185
30,350	30,400	6,083	5,813	5,543	5,296	5,026	4,751	4,476	4,201
30,400	30,450	6,101	5,831	5,561	5,312	5,042	4,767	4,492	4,217
30,450	30,500	6,119	5,849	5,579	5,328	5,058	4,783	4,508	4,233
30,500	30,550	6,137	5,867	5,597	5,344	5,074	4,799	4,524	4,249
30,550	30,600	6,155	5,885	5,615	5,360	5,090	4,815	4,540	4,265
30,600	30,650	6,173	5,903	5,633	5,376	5,106	4,831	4,556	4,281
30,650	30,700	6,191	5,921	5,651	5,392	5,122	4,847	4,572	4,297
30,700	30,750	6,209	5,939	5,669	5,408	5,138	4,863	4,588	4,313
30,750	30,800	6,227	5,957	5,687	5,424	5,154	4,879	4,604	4,329
30,800	30,850	6,245	5,975	5,705	5,440	5,170	4,895	4,620	4,345
30,850	30,900	6,263	5,993	5,723	5,456	5,186	4,911	4,636	4,361
30,900	30,950	6,281	6,011	5,741	5,472	5,202	4,927	4,652	4,377
30,950	31,000	6,299	6,029	5,759	5,489	5,218	4,943	4,668	4,393
31,000	31,050	6,317	6,047	5,777	5,507	5,234	4,959	4,684	4,409
31,050	31,100	6,335	6,065	5,795	5,525	5,250	4,975	4,700	4,425
31,100	31,150	6,353	6,083	5,813	5,543	5,266	4,991	4,716	4,441
31,150	31,200	6,371	6,101	5,831	5,561	5,282	5,007	4,732	4,457
31,200	31,250	6,389	6,119	5,849	5,579	5,298	5,023	4,748	4,473
31,250	31,300	6,407	6,137	5,867	5,597	5,314	5,039	4,764	4,489
31,300	31,350	6,425	6,155	5,885	5,615	5,330	5,055	4,780	4,505
31,350	31,400	6,443	6,173	5,903	5,633	5,346	5,071	4,796	4,521
31,400	31,450	6,461	6,191	5,921	5,651	5,362	5,087	4,812	4,537
31,450	31,500	6,479	6,209	5,939	5,669	5,378	5,103	4,828	4,553
31,500	31,550	6,497	6,227	5,957	5,687	5,394	5,119	4,844	4,569
31,550	31,600	6,515	6,245	5,975	5,705	5,410	5,135	4,860	4,585
31,600	31,650	6,533	6,263	5,993	5,723	5,426	5,151	4,876	4,601
31,650	31,700	6,551	6,281	6,011	5,741	5,442	5,167	4,892	4,617
31,700	31,750	6,569	6,299	6,029	5,759	5,459	5,183	4,908	4,633
31,750	31,800	6,587	6,317	6,047	5,777	5,477	5,199	4,924	4,649
31,800	31,850	6,605	6,335	6,065	5,795	5,495	5,215	4,940	4,665
31,850	31,900	6,623	6,353	6,083	5,813	5,513	5,231	4,956	4,681
31,900	31,950	6,641	6,371	6,101	5,831	5,531	5,247	4,972	4,697
31,950	32,000	6,659	6,389	6,119	5,849	5,549	5,263	4,988	4,713
32,000	32,050	6,677	6,407	6,137	5,867	5,567	5,279	5,004	4,729
32,050	32,100	6,695	6,425	6,155	5,885	5,585	5,295	5,020	4,745
32,100	32,150	6,713	6,443	6,173	5,903	5,603	5,311	5,036	4,761
32,150	32,200	6,731	6,461	6,191	5,921	5,621	5,327	5,052	4,777
32,200	32,250	6,749	6,479	6,209	5,939	5,639	5,343	5,068	4,793
32,250	32,300	6,767	6,497	6,227	5,957	5,657	5,359	5,084	4,809
32,300	32,350	6,785	6,515	6,245	5,975	5,675	5,375	5,100	4,825
32,350	32,400	6,803	6,533	6,263	5,993	5,693	5,391	5,116	4,841
32,400	32,450	6,821	6,551	6,281	6,011	5,711	5,407	5,132	4,857
32,450	32,500	6,839	6,569	6,299	6,029	5,729	5,424	5,148	4,873
32,500	32,550	6,857	6,587	6,317	6,047	5,747	5,442	5,164	4,889
32,550	32,600	6,875	6,605	6,335	6,065	5,765	5,460	5,180	4,905
32,600	32,650	6,893	6,623	6,353	6,083	5,783	5,478	5,196	4,921
32,650	32,700	6,911	6,641	6,371	6,101	5,801	5,496	5,212	4,937
32,700	32,750	6,930	6,659	6,389	6,119	5,819	5,514	5,228	4,953
32,750	32,800	6,949	6,677	6,407	6,137	5,837	5,532	5,244	4,969
32,800	32,850	6,969	6,695	6,425	6,155	5,855	5,550	5,260	4,985
32,850	32,900	6,988	6,713	6,443	6,173	5,873	5,568	5,276	5,001
32,900	32,950	7,008	6,731	6,461	6,191	5,891	5,586	5,292	5,017
32,950	33,000	7,027	6,749	6,479	6,209	5,909	5,604	5,308	5,033
33,000	33,050	7,047	6,767	6,497	6,227	5,927	5,622	5,324	5,049
33,050	33,100	7,066	6,785	6,515	6,245	5,945	5,640	5,340	5,065
33,100	33,150	7,086	6,803	6,533	6,263	5,963	5,658	5,356	5,081
33,150	33,200	7,105	6,821	6,551	6,281	5,981	5,676	5,372	5,097

Continued next column

Continued on next page

Protecting Yourself Against Disaster

exclusions
named peril approach
all-risk approach
subrogation
voidable
clauses
deductibles
franchises
coinsurance
   arrangements
endorsements
automobile insurance
dental insurance
time limitations
dollar limits
apportionment
terminated

stock companies
mutual companies
bodily injury
property damage
   liability
medical payments
major medical
   payments
collision coverage
homeowner's policy
basic form
broad form
special form
comprehensive
disability income
   insurance

Imagine that you are driving down a street you have gone down thousands of times. It is twilight, and everyone has just turned on their headlights. Both sides of the street are lined with stores and used car lots. Many have flashing neon signs. Others sport rows of light bulbs. Traffic going in the opposite direction is very heavy. It is only a two-lane street. A good friend is a passenger in your car. The two of you are talking. A young boy is riding a bicycle just ahead of you. He keeps weaving around, and so you are afraid to pass him until there is a big enough break in oncoming traffic for you to pull around in the opposite lane. Just as you approach an intersection, your chance comes. You pass the boy and speed up in relief. Then there is a loud crash and a tremendous jolt.

Over the weekend a traffic light was installed at the intersection. You were not aware of this. Formerly there were stop signs on the cross street; so in the past you had the right-of-way. Because of your concentration on the boy, talking to your friend, and the poor lighting conditions, you failed to see the new stop light and ran a red light, which put you in the path of a car on the cross street. One person in the other car was killed. Another is seriously injured. Your friend is critically injured, and you may have been crippled for life. Suppose you don't have any automobile insurance. What would such a situation do to you financially? Clearly, such an accident would ruin most people financially. It would hurt in many nonmonetary ways too, but there is nothing you can do to cover nonmonetary losses, but you can protect yourself from financial loss through insurance, and it may compensate you for other losses.

Perhaps you believe that you will never make a mistake that will cause an accident, and you may be right, but, even if you will never make a mistake, other drivers will. You will escape being in an accident only by pure luck. For example, if you are driving down a highway at 60 miles per hour and a car going in the opposite direction veers into your lane ten feet ahead of you, there is nothing you can do.

You don't have to be extremely lucky to avoid a major auto accident over your driving years, but you do have to be very lucky indeed to avoid having any accidents. Because this is the case, and an accident may be very expensive, a large number of people carry automobile insurance. Many states require that every driver carry some minimum amount of automobile insurance.

Now, imagine that you've been healthy all your life, but for the last several weeks you have experienced a sharp, recurring pain. You go to your physician, a general practitioner. He sends you to a specialist. Four specialists and $400 later, you find that you will need major surgery. You will be out of work for at least two months, and your surgery and hospitalization bills will total $3000, which is not costly major surgery. Suppose you have no hospitalization or medical insurance. What would this do to you financially? Everyone has medical expenses, and most people eventually have some rather high medical bills.

Now, suppose that, after several years of saving, you have enough money to take a 28-day European tour. When you return, you find that your house has burned down. A neighbor tells you that lightning struck your house, and it burst into flames in several places so quickly that even if there had been a fire engine at the corner, it couldn't have saved it. What kind of financial impact would this have on you? A home is, by far, most people's largest investment. You also would have lost nearly all of your other possessions. Your car, for example, would likely be lost if it was parked nearby; perhaps in an attached carport. You would lose all your furniture and most of your clothes. There is, of course, very little chance of a house burning down, but, if it does, your loss is staggering.

Rather than running the risk of suffering such losses as these, most people elect to spend some money to acquire insurance. Many insurance buyers, however, fail to realize that a purchase of an insurance policy should be approached like any other expenditure: What will I be getting? How much is this worth to me? These are questions they fail to answer, or, if they do, they still buy the wrong amount of insurance. The figures in Table 12–1 indicate that insurance is a pretty popular use of consumer income.

HOW INSURANCE HANDLES RISK

If a friend of yours passed you on a mountain road going 100 miles per hour, you would probably think she was taking quite a risk. What would you mean by *risk?* Most people use the word *risk* to refer to the fact she is more likely to have an accident driving at 100 mph than you are at the conservative 50 mph at which you are wisely driving. (Your mother is in the car with you, and she isn't willing to take the risk your friend takes.)

How could you measure the risk you take when you go either 50 or 100 mph? Obviously, you and your friend can't drive down a given road over and over under given conditions and see how many times each of you gets killed or injured. If, however, what you want to find out is the risk involved in playing roulette or baccarat in Las Vegas, you could set up games like these and play them over and over to see how often you would lose.

Perhaps you could find out from the highway patrol how many accidents other people have had on this road and what the investigating officer estimated their speed was on the basis of the damage done and skid marks. If they have radar set up on the road, you may be able to get more objective speed data. Maybe you would find that on a hot, dry day in January—a strange day like today—a year ago, 200 cars went over this stretch of road going 50 mph. Five percent of these

TABLE 12–1   Property and Liability Insurance, 1960 to 1974*

	1960	1965	1970	1974
Companies reporting	3,500	3,047	2,727	2,934
Premiums written[1]	14,973	20,063	32,867	45,152
Auto liability	3,883	5,424	8,958	12,010
Physical damage, auto	1,994	2,861	4,824	7,060
Liability, other than auto	963	1,137	2,140	2,990
Fire[2]	2,406	2,215	3,147	3,536
Homeowner's multiple peril	764	1,523	2,565	4,379

Source: Statistical Abstract of the United States 1976, U.S. Department of Commerce, Bureau of the Census, p. 503.

* Amounts are in millions of dollars, except companies reporting. Premiums written represent total written by these companies with *inception* dates in the years shown.

[1] Includes all property, liability, and allied lines; other data are for principal lines only.

[2] Includes extended coverage and allied lines.

had an accident. Of the 25 cars going 100 mph, 75 percent had an accident. Thus, you could say that the *probability* of having an accident at 50 mph under these conditions is 5 percent; while at 100 mph the probability of having an accident is 15 times greater, 75 percent. Obviously, it is quite unlikely that you would be able to get all this data. Even if you did, it would not really be true that you face these probabilities, because what you really have is an *average* of accident rates for various classes of drivers who may have significantly different accident rates. Insurance companies have found that both age and sex have a significant effect on one's likelihood of having an accident. Other factors, like skill and mood may have a significant effect, but can't be utilized in setting rates because of lack of data and measurement problems. Surprisingly, data shows that new drivers do not have more accidents than long-time drivers. Road and auto conditions seem to have little effect on the likelihood of an accident occurring. Men have more accidents than women. Young, single, male drivers have the highest accident rates. Sporty, high-powered automobiles are more likely to be involved in accidents than are sedans and station wagons.

The *probability* of an event is a number that expresses the likelihood of the occurrence of this event, such as the ratio of the number of experimental results that would produce the event to the total number of results considered possible. An example of this is the flipping of a fair coin. There are two possible results, assuming you arrange to prevent the coin landing on its edge. It will either land head side up or tail side up. If you flipped a coin 1000 times, it might come up heads 1000 times, but it would more likely come up heads less than 1000 times, until you get to 500 heads; then the probability of less heads starts declining. Because on each flip heads is no more likely to occur than tails, the most likely result is 500 heads.

If you flip a coin 1000 times, you are less likely to get 900 heads than you are likely to get 9 heads by flipping a coin 10 times. This is known as *the law of large numbers*. All insurance is based on this principle, that is, the larger the number of events, the more likely it is that they represent the true likelihood of the occurrence of all possible outcomes. What this means for automobile companies is twofold: First, in order to determine how likely it is that a 22-year-old, single, male driver will have an accident, they want to study as large a group of people who fall in this class as is possible before setting their rates. These persons should not differ in any way that is related to the likelihood of them having an accident, such as where they live, what use they put the car to, and what type of car they drive, so that a valid accident rate based on age can be obtained. (They don't want to, say, insure 10,000 young drivers expecting 50 accidents and have 500!) Second, they want to insure as large a number of drivers in a class as is possible, because deviations from the true probability—50 percent in the case of the coin—are less likely to be large. What they charge drivers in a class for a policy will be based on how many and what type accidents (i.e., their cost) the insurance companies expect this group to have. (You may belong to more than one class of accident-prone people. This, of course, will mean you pay a higher rate than someone in only one such group.)

Even if the rates set by an insurance company are "right" for the company (meaning their costs are covered and an adequate rate of return is earned), these rates are seldom "right" for an individual policyholder. The rate a policyholder pays will be right only if he or she is an average policyholder. Such a person may not exist. (The average of the figures 3, 7, and 8, for example, is 6; none of the three figures is, therefore, the average. Thus, if these figures represented the number of accidents experienced by the three people in an insurance class, none of these people would be average.) Invariably, many policyholders pay the insurance company either more or less than they cost the company. (The insurance company obtains additional funds by earning a return on the *premiums* paid by policyholders before they are needed to pay *claims*. This reduces the size of the premium.)

This over- and underpayment could not be corrected by setting policyholders' rates on the basis of their own past accident records because, among other things, the conditions determining the likelihood of one having an accident change over time. For the average male driver of 30, for example, other 30-year-old's experience would result in a lower premium than his own earlier driving record. An estimate based on the insured's record would also be less accurate because it would be like determining the probability of flipping a coin and getting a head by flipping one coin twice rather than 10,000 times. (Two tails are much, much more likely than 10,000!) And, of course, for new drivers, there would be no data.

Insurance classes are determined by what factors insurance companies have discovered are correlated with accidents. This doesn't mean the relationship is cause and effect. For example, as has already been noted, men are more likely to be involved in an auto accident than women, but this may not be due to something about being male, since it may be because they have more opportunities to have accidents, because, perhaps, they drive more in dangerous circumstances. Their high accident rate may be due to a combination of factors; some of which may be related to sex. For example, men may be more likely to drive when drunk.

Another technique utilized by property and casualty insurance firms is *diversification*. This can best be illustrated with fire insurance. If you were going to insure 10,000 single-family homes against fire, it would be better if all these homes were not adjacent. (In the past insurance companies have gone broke because they insured mostly in one city, and in the days of wooden shingles, fireplace heating, and small yards, a house fire was more likely than today and could more readily spread to hundreds of homes!) If every house insured was in a different city, a fire at one would not affect the others. This is diversification.

Diversification is one reason *group insurance* is cheaper than individual insurance. There is some self-selection among individual policyholders. The people who are most likely to have substantial medical expenses are more likly to purchase medical insurance or more of it than are those less likely to have such large expenses. Thus, when an insurance company sells policies to individuals, it is not getting a cross-section of society. It is dealing with high-risk individuals. However, when it sells a policy which covers, say, all the employees of a business, it is getting a cross-section of society or at least it comes closer to doing this. Group policies are also cheaper because less sales effort is required, and administrative expense per insured is less. Since group policies are usually less expensive than individual policies are, you should hesitate to buy an individual policy instead of participating in a group plan. If a group plan is available, it is likely that an individual plan is not needed or is needed only to provide supplemental benefits. Under certain circumstances, however, a group policy can be unduly expensive.

Suppose an insurance company is insuring 5,000 people against large medical expenditures. Suppose that in a year 500 of these people draw benefits of $1,500,000, or $3,000 apiece on the average. Ignoring the insurance company's costs, profits, and any interest it could earn, it would have to charge an annual premium of $300, since $300 times 5,000 is $1,500,000.

Suppose that instead this company offered a policy that covered all medical costs rather than just those over, say, $1,000. Then most everyone in the group would receive benefits, though their average size might fall from $3,000 ($1,500,000 divided by 500) to $1,000. Then the insurance company would have to pay out $5,000,000 in benefits ($1,000 times 5,000). This would require that every policyholder pay a premium of $1,000. Thus, everyone would pay $700 more in order to cover all costs rather than just those of more than $1,000.

The above figures are not drawn from a real situation, but they do illustrate what happens in real situations, that is, *as the cost of the smallest misfortune covered by an insurance policy falls, the relationship of the average benefit to the required premium falls, as the former will decline and the latter will rise.* Because allowing for self-selection will intensify this problem, insurance companies will offer groups more coverage than they will offer individuals. If the ratio of the average benefit per year to the annual premium fell to the level of the above example, more coverage is uneconomic. A $700 premium is too much to pay to cover possible costs of no more than $1,000. To spend $700 to possibly avoid spending from $700.01 to $1,000 is not a good idea, as a possible $300 loss is not worth spending this much to avoid!

The *risk class* your insurance company assigns you to can cause your premium to vary enormously. In some large metropolitan areas it costs more than three times as much to insure a given car if you live in one part of the metro area than it costs in another area; thus, moving would save some people a lot of money in automobile insurance. Moving is not the only thing you may be able to do to reduce your auto insurance premium. You can get married, take a driver's training course, drive a cheaper car, make good grades in college, drive less; in short, stop doing anything insurance companies have found increases the chance of your being in an auto accident.

Auto insurers are not free to set the premiums they will charge at any amount they wish. The states have regulatory agencies that must approve the rates they charge. These agencies consider the size of anticipated benefit claims and their likelihood, and, if a profit-making company is involved, a reasonable rate of return on owners' investment. Variances in the rate charged different classes of policyholders have to be supported by previous claims made by this class. These regulatory agencies hold public hearings on applications for rate changes.

BASIC INSURANCE CONTRACT PROVISIONS

Acquiring insurance coverage requires that you enter into a legal agreement which is specified in the contract or *policy* given to you by the insurer. In exchange for your payment of premiums, the insurance company promises to make certain payments to you under given conditions.

To obtain insurance against some particular type of misfortune you must demonstrate that you have an *insurable interest*—you antici-pate suffering a loss if a given thing happens or doesn't happen. This prevents an insurance contract from becoming simply a method of gambling. In the case of *property and liability insurance* you cannot collect more than your actual loss as a result of the occurrence or lack of occurrence of a given event. (Table 12–1 showed how much of this type of insurance is sold.) Life and many health insurance policies are not generally such contracts of *indemnity*. If a health insurance policy does include this principle, it will state that you cannot collect for any loss covered by some other insurance policy. These two principles mean that if another car runs into the car you are driving, you cannot collect for the damage to the car unless you own it, and you can't collect twice for the damage, that is, once from your insurance company and once from the other person's insurance company. *Property insurance* protects you from loss due to damage to your car. *Liability insurance* protects the driver of the other car from losses suffered as a result of being declared legally responsible for the accident by the court.

There are a number of ways to acquire an insurable interest. A secured creditor, such as one who gives you a mortgage loan on your house, has an insurable interest in the property acquired with the borrowed money. A building contractor has an insurable interest in property on which he is working. He has what is called a *mechanic's lien*. This means that if you, the owner of the property, won't or can't pay him, he can require that the property be sold to generate the necessary funds. If this doesn't enable him to be paid in full, and he has insured himself against this possibility, he can collect what he is owed from his insurance company. Your mortgage lender has a lien on your house. If you don't pay the mortgage, the house can be sold to repay him. If the lender is insured against your defaulting, he could, instead, collect from the insurance company. If someone working for you is hurt while on the job, you may be declared liable. Thus, you have an insurable interest and can insure yourself against such a loss. If your dog bites the mailman as he delivers your mail, you may be liable. Again, you have an insurable interest. If a child falls into your pool and drowns, you may be declared liable; thus, you have an insurable interest.

Another principle embodied in an insurance policy is the principle of *subrogation,* which means that if your insurance company indemnifies (reimburses) you for damages another person is liable for, it can proceed against this person to recover what it paid you, but you cannot proceed against this person. Thus, like indemnity, this provision prevents you from collecting twice for the same damages. This provision also means that a negligent uninsured person does not escape payment because the person harmed had insurance, as the injured person's insurer has a claim on the person who caused the harm.

An insurance contract is *voidable* at the option of the insurer if you misrepresent a material fact. If the insurer does not void the contract upon finding out about the misrepresentation, he may give up his right to void the contract. Usually even an innocent misrepresentation justifies voiding your policy. A *concealment* of a material fact also gives the insurer the option to void your policy. The insurer does not have to ask you if the car you are insuring is currently wrecked or if the house you are insuring just burned down. These are clearly material facts, and if you don't mention them, you are guilty of having concealed them.

Most insurance policies contain *exclusions*—certain things are not covered. For example, if you burn your own house down, your policy will not cover this. Most property contracts require you to notify the insurer as soon as possible of your loss, and you must be able to prove this loss in order to collect.

There are two common approaches used in framing the insuring agreement. One is the *named-peril approach;* the other is the *all-risk approach.* The first type of policy lists the covered perils. The second type covers all perils except those listed. Many insurance policies provide coverage for individuals who are not direct parties to the contract. These persons are known as *third parties.* For example, you may take out automobile insurance which covers anyone riding in your car; not just you.

Most insurance contracts will contain provisions excluding certain types of losses even though the policy covers the peril that causes these losses. For example, if you have automobile collision insurance, it will not cover damage you do to other people's property in a collision. Coverage of the damage done to other people's property will have to be obtained via a separate agreement.

Certain types of property may be excluded from coverage. For example, your fire insurance policy may not cover a loss experienced because money was burned up when your house burned. Sometimes a fire insurance policy on your home only covers its integral parts; not its contents. Certain locations are excluded from insurance coverage. For example, your automobile insurance usually only covers you while you are using it in the United States.

An insurer usually limits the dollar amount you may recover. This is done by including *clauses* which state the provisions of the policy. Clauses provide for *deductibles, franchises, coinsurance arrangements, time limitations, dollar limits,* and *apportionment.* A *deductible* is a specific dollar amount which will be borne by you before the insurer becomes liable for covering your losses. Accepting a deductible reduces your premium. A *franchise* is a deductible where once your loss exceeds a given amount, the insurer covers the entire claim. In the case of health insurance, *coinsurance* means that you bear a fixed percent of every loss. The purpose of this is to motivate you to try and hold down your medical bills. This also holds down the size of the premium. In the case of fire insurance, however, the meaning of coinsurance is different. If you insure your place of business for less than its replacement value, you have to bear part of the cost of a partial loss. Thus, if your place of business' replacement value is $60,000, and you insure it for only $30,000, if a fire causes $20,000 damage, you will have to cover half this amount. It is rare for residential fire insurance to involve coinsurance.

Time limits restrict the maximum period of time you can receive benefits for and/or require a waiting period before benefits can be received. The more generous these time limits are, the higher will be your premium. Health insurance policies invariably contain time limits. Most insurance policies provide for maximum dollar limits on what you can recover for a given type of loss. The higher are these limits, the higher is your premium.

An *apportionment clause* limits the insurer's liability in case other insurance contracts also cover your loss. This clause may provide that the insurer will cover the same percentage of your loss as your policy represents of your total insurance coverage for such a loss.

Your insurer will give you a certain period of time, usually 60 to 90 days, to notify him of your loss and offer proof of it. If you and the insurer cannot agree on the amount of your loss, each of you can hire a competent and disinterested person to appraise the loss. An impartial umpire will be employed to try and settle any remaining differences. If this is not successful, your only alternative will be to go to court.

All insurance policies specify the conditions under which the policy may or may not be terminated. Property and liability contracts can be cancelled by either you or the insurance company after giving a specified notice. Usually life and some health insurance policies cannot be terminated by the insurer except for a limited period of time. You are not so limited.

Most insurance companies are either stock companies or mutuals. A *stock company* is a corporation organized to earn a profit for its owners. A *mutual* is a nonprofit organization owned by its policyholders. Any excess income earned by a mutual is either returned to the policyholders as a dividend or used to reduce premiums. If you have a policy from a mutual company, you may be *assessed* (required to pay) if the company lacks the funds necessary to cover losses and meet expenses. Most mutuals, however, offer nonassessable policies. Be careful to note whether a policy offered you is assessable or not. If it is, you need to be particularly concerned with the financial strength of the company. One of the best sources of information on insurance companies and their policies is *Best's Insurance Guide with Key Ratings.*

AUTOMOBILE INSURANCE

An automobile insurance policy is a set of coverages, all or only part of which you may select to take. It is extremely foolhardy to drive a car without any type of insurance coverage. The coverages you can obtain are: *bodily injury; property damage liability; medical payments; major medical payments; collision; comprehensive; emergency road service; uninsured motor vehicle; motor vehicle rental reimbursement; auto death, dismemberment, and loss of sight;* and *total disability.*

Bodily injury insures you against any loss suffered as a result of being legally liable for bodily injury to others up to the limits of your policy. The insurance company will pay a specified amount for bodily injury or death to any one person in any one accident, and up to a specified amount for more than one person.

Property damage liability insures you up to the amount of your policy limit for whatever damage or destruction to the property of others you are legally liable for. You are also covered against any loss caused the owner of the property because he or she couldn't use it. You should never drive without liability coverage.

Medical payments covers all reasonable and necessary medical expenses incurred for services furnished by physicians, hospitals, ambulances, nurses, dentists, funeral homes, and any prosthetic devices, hearing aids, eye glasses, and so on, required by the occupants of the insured car within one year of an accident. What portion of the loss will be paid by the insurance company depends on the limit set in your policy.

Major medical payments take up where medical payments leave off. In other words, the amount of your coverage is increased. How much will be paid is limited. Losses above a certain amount are not fully covered by the insurance company.

Collision coverage provides for payment to you if your car hits another car, is hit by another car, or turns over no matter who is at fault. How much will be paid is determined by the policy's limit or the current value of your auto, depending on which is lower. *Never purchase collision insurance in excess of the current value of your car.*

Deductible collision is simply a way of obtaining collision insurance more cheaply by agreeing to pay a given amount of money in case you are involved in a collision; thus, the insurance company only covers a loss in excess of this deductible amount and up to the policy limit.

Comprehensive covers accidental loss or damage to your auto from any cause except collision, upset, or mechanical breakdown. It covers damage from fire, windstorm, theft, and other miscellaneous perils. Collision with birds or animals is also included.

Deductible comprehensive, like deductible collision, is simply a way to obtain this type of coverage at a lower cost by agreeing to pay the first few dollars of a loss.

Emergency road service covers things like having gasoline, oil, or a battery delivered to you. Changing a tire and towing to the nearest garage or service station, assuming the car can't be driven, is also covered. The cost of a mechanic necessary to make the car operable so it can be driven away is covered.

Uninsured motor vehicle coverage pays you for any injuries to persons in your car when it is hit by a motorist who carries no insurance, but is legally liable for the accident. Hit-and-run accidents are also covered.

Motor vehicle rental reimbursement pays up to some set amount the cost of a rented car to replace yours while it is being repaired. There is a time limit on these payments.

Auto death, dismemberment, and loss of sight pays specific amounts for specified major injuries or the death of the insured. Additional persons may also be covered.

Total disability provides you with a guaranteed weekly income if you are totally disabled as the result of an auto accident. You may also obtain coverage for members of your family.

Various extra benefits are available under all these coverages. You can, for example, obtain coverage for all relatives who live with you. You can cover anyone driving your car with your permission. You can obtain coverage outside the United States. If you wish to transfer insurance from your old car to a newly purchased car automatically, you can arrange this, but you will have to apply for insurance for it within a certain number of days after its purchase. You can be covered both when you drive the insured car and when, with permission, you drive someone else's car.

Under bodily injury and property damage you can arrange for coverage of a bail bond and income you lose because you have to appear in court at the insurance company's request. Under comprehensive and collision you can cover luggage and wearing apparel in the insured auto. You can also receive payments to cover the rental of a temporary replacement for your stolen auto. You may also avoid paying two deductibles when two autos insured by the same company collide.

The above does not include everything that some companies provide, and some companies do not provide all of the above. The above list is simply representative of what is available. Clearly property and bodily liability is the most necessary. Many people think you shouldn't drive out of the dealer's showroom without this coverage. Certainly if you are not well off financially this is true. Medical and comprehensive are only a bit less essential, and they are relatively inexpensive. On older cars, however, collision is not likely to be worthwhile because the car is worth too little to justify the premiums. Knowledgeable observers agree that you should opt for deductible coverage. The reason for this is twofold: The premium is lower and, because you will report fewer accidents—only those costing more than the deductible will be reported—you are less likely to have your premium raised because of your poor driving record. Other coverages are seldom worthwhile unless you face unusually large possible losses of these types. Never forget that insurance is designed to take care of large losses. It is not a maintenance or service contract; nor is it, except in the case of permanent life insurance, a prepayment of expenses.

There are, basically, two types of auto policies: the *family auto policy* and the *special auto package policy*. If your driving record is not very good, you are not eligible for the special policy. With the family auto policy you must buy liability with three limits: one for how much in medical benefits will be paid per person; one for how much in medical benefits will be paid, in total, per accident; and one for the amount paid for property damage. With the special policy there is no breakdown as to the maximum that will apply to bodily injury either in total or per person and how much to property damage. Under the family policy you can collect for medical payments even though you are also being reimbursed from another source. The special policy, in contrast, only pays medical bills in excess of other reimbursements. The special policy, however, has a substantially lower premium.

How To Lower Your Premiums

Many companies have policies which offer a relatively low premium because they can only be obtained by drivers with a good driving record—no accident record. If a policyholder has children under 21 who drive the car, the premium will be much higher because of this. This premium can be lowered by the children taking driver training or getting married. By insuring more than one car with an insurance company you can lower your premium per car. If the policyholders' children who drive are good students—upper 20 percent of the class or are B students or better—a reduction in the premium can be obtained. If a child who drives is in school more than 100 miles from home and doesn't take the car to school, the policyholder can obtain a reduction in the insurance premium. How many miles you drive a year also affects your premium. If you do not register many miles per year, your premium is lower. Premiums also vary according to the type of car you drive, particularly in the case of collision coverage. The more expensive the car, the higher the premium since repairs will be more costly. The premiums are particularly high on high-powered sports cars. Some companies will not write insurance on one of these "muscle" cars. A higher deductible will, of course, reduce your premium. Some companies also offer a special economy auto package, which differs slightly from the family policy in several areas. You may also lower your premium by shopping around. All companies do not charge the same thing!

Assigned-Risk Pools

If every insurance company you apply to turns you down, what do you do? Various states have created assigned-risk pools to cover drivers who cannot obtain standard policies because of their poor driving records. This means that they will be assigned to a particular company. Each company that writes policies in your state has to agree to take on drivers so assigned them in proportion to the number of policyholders they have in the state relative to the total number of auto insurance policies in force in the state. The premium on such a policy will be high, perhaps $3000 a year! To get this coverage you will need to contact your state insurance commissioner or the appropriate official.

No-Fault Insurance

In a number of states the court must decide who was at fault in an accident in order to determine whose insurance company must cover any resulting injuries and/or property damage. Some states have no-fault laws; so there is no need to prove who is at fault. Each person involved in the accident simply collects from his or her insurance company. Only a limited amount, often $500 or $1000, can be collected in this way, however. For amounts in excess of this "threshold" you can sue in court to make the party at fault pay. No-fault laws were expected to cut the workload of the nation's courts and lower insurance premiums by reducing legal costs and the amount insurance companies pay out in claims. So far, no-fault has not lived up to its promise. Many say it is because the threshold is too low. Few accidents cost $500 to $1000, and often when they could cost this little, they don't because people are able to pad their expenses so they can sue.

For a number of years premiums on auto insurance went up less rapidly than did prices in general. In the meanwhile three things were happening: the size of the average court settlement increased substantially, medical charges increased dramatically, and the cost of repairing autos grew rapidly. Juries began making larger awards, partly because of an increase in claims based on mental anguish, pain, suffering, and loss of income. In earlier years claims had centered on direct, immediate costs. Some think that the large increase in the number of lawyers and the fact they get a percent of the settlement also played a role. The cost of crash parts—replacement parts—increased far more than did prices in general. Medical costs increased phenomenally. There was also a substantial increase in the cost of auto repair labor. As a result, all auto insurers lost money, and the industry lost a tremendous amount of money. This forced the various state insurance regulatory agencies to allow substantial increases in premiums. This increase in premiums turned the tide for pro no-fault forces, and many states enacted such laws. There is pressure for a national no-fault law.

The following states have no-fault laws: Arkansas, Connecticut, Delaware, Florida, Georgia, Hawaii, Kansas, Kentucky, Maryland, Massachusetts, Michigan, Minnesota, Nevada, New Jersey, New York, North Dakota, Oregon, Pennsylvania, South Carolina, South Dakota, Texas, Utah, Washington, and Virginia. If you live in one of these states, the law requires that you carry a minimum amount of auto insurance. Surveys show, however, that many drivers break the law and do not carry auto insurance, and this is one reason why auto insurance premiums are higher than was expected under no-fault.

Many people advocate substantial changes be made in no-fault, and some wish to repeal no-fault laws.

HOMEOWNER'S INSURANCE

When you buy a homeowner's policy you are buying a package of basic coverages. (Table 12–1 shows the very rapid growth in this type of coverage in recent years.) These basic coverages are: *Section One,* which covers your dwelling, appurtenant structures such as a garage and tool shed, unscheduled personal property such as furniture and clothes, and additional living expense incurred while living away from home until damage is repaired; and, *Section Two,* which covers comprehensive personal liability and medical payments to others. You can add other coverages by making the appropriate *endorsement* (a provision added to the policy). This will raise your premium.

Section One coverage may fail to cover all your personal property, since its coverage is limited to 50 percent of the amount of insurance carried on your home. To handle this problem, you can add an endorsement to cover any additional amount of personal property. Your basic policy also covers only a limited amount of jewelry and furs. Via an endorsement, you can increase the amount covered. Another endorsement will cover the personal property you take with you on vacation or what your children take with them to college. You can also cover your vacation home or rental property. You can expand the basic policy coverage on money, securities, and glass breakage via endorsement, or add coverage of earthquake and theft of personal property left in your car. If you use your home as an office, it is mandatory that you take an endorsement to reflect this additional use of your home. You can also cover professional equipment stored in your home via endorsement. The basic policy's coverage of appurtenant structures can be expanded, and you may wish to do so because the amount of coverage on these is a percent of what is carried on your dwelling. This could easily be too little. A sizeable, powerful boat will not be covered by your basic policy. It can be added via an endorsement. You can take account of inflation constantly raising the replacement cost of your house via an inflation endorsement, which will automatically increase the insurance on your home and unscheduled personal property by an amount you choose. Another reason for taking this endorsement is that coverage on your furniture and household possessions normally means that the insurance company will pay you only its actual cash value less depreciation due to age and usage. Seldom can you purchase a new item for the value of the old less depreciation. Some insurance companies are offering a replacement-cost endorsement to their homeowner's policies to handle this problem. You can also obtain a debris removal endorsement. (The basic policy doesn't cover removal of any debris unless it falls on the house.)

If you live in a mobile home, a special policy can be obtained to cover it. People who live in condominiums are covered by a master policy on the building, but they may need more coverage than this provides. Many companies offer a policy that provides this additional coverage. If you rent your home, you can obtain a policy to cover your personal property from loss from fire, windstorm, theft, and other perils.

There are four forms of homeowner's policies for you to choose from. Each provides broader coverage than the previous form. The *basic form* insures you against fire or lightning; removal to protect property from damage; windstorm, tornado, or hail; explosion; riot or civil commotion; aircraft damage; nonowned vehicle damage; smoke damage; vandalism; breakage of glass; and theft. The *broad form* adds the following: falling objects; weight of ice, snow, or sleet; collapse of building; sudden and accidental tearing asunder of heating systems and appliances; accidental discharge of water or steam; freezing of plumbing, heating systems, and appliances; and sudden and accidental injury from electrical currents. The *special form* states that your dwelling is covered against all risks of physical losses with the exceptions, like war, found in all homeowner's policies. (Only the dwelling is covered against all risks; personal property is excluded.) The difference between the special and the broad form is that under the broad form only what is listed is covered. Under the special form everything not excluded is covered. This special form, in other words, insures you against unknown perils. The last form, *comprehensive*, adds to special's coverage your unscheduled personal property.

A standard policy stipulates that you must insure your home for an amount equal to 80 percent of its replacement cost in order to collect the full amount of a loss. The reason for the 80 percent figure is that your foundation is normally reusable and accounts for 20 percent of total cost. You need to beware of falling below this level via inflation. This is yet another reason for including an inflation-guard endorsement to your policy.

A homeowner's policy does not cover flooding, and insurance companies will not write flood insurance in some places because of the high probability of severe flood damage. If such a community meets federal eligibility requirements, residents of this community can participate in a program operated by the property insurance industry in cooperation with the United States government. This program is subsidized by the government, and this means you get a break in your premium cost. If you live in the flood plain of a creek or river or live where hurricanes are likely to produce flooding, you should take advantage of this program if it is available.

Like automobile insurance, homeowner's policies can be obtained with a deductible. This deductible is unique in that when the loss reaches a high enough level there will be no deductible. The larger is the deductible, the lower your premium.

The insurance value of your home is its replacement value. The insurance value is not its market value, which is what it could be sold for. This is not its actual cash value less depreciation, which is what it would cost to replace it less depreciation. It is, instead, what it would cost to replace it. This is what the insurance company will pay you; not replacement less depreciation or what a like house can be bought for. This figure does not include the land or pipes and such beneath the soil.

Your mortgage lender will insist that you carry insurance up to the value of the mortgage. If this is all you take out, and you suffer a total loss of the house, the mortgage lender will be paid, but you will lose your equity.

Keep in mind that what you can collect on a homeowner's policy exceeds the amount you insure your home for, as the policy also insures associated buildings and personal property. It is the total amount you can collect; not the amount you have insured your home for, that you should compare with your premium to decide if you are getting your money's worth. In deciding whether or not to add an endorsement or buy other than the basic form, you must compare the additional premium with the additional coverage and the likelihood that this coverage will be needed. For example, in the South there is either little or no danger of your roof caving in under snow or ice; thus, while the cost of this peril is high, you are not willing to pay much, if anything, to insure yourself against it, because it can't or isn't likely to happen.

In determining how much coverage you need, make out an inventory of your household possessions. When in doubt as to the value of an item, have it appraised. Keep in mind that if someone is injured on your property, a jury may award him $100,000 or more. It is a good idea, particularly in the case of very expensive items, to photograph your property and put these photos in your safety deposit box at your bank or savings and loan association so that you can prove the size of your loss. Table 12–1 shows how much property and liability insurance others have.

Your homeowner's policy may exclude bodily injury or property damage arising out of business pursuits. Thus, if your child cuts a neighbor's lawn, sits with their children, delivers their newspaper, and damages their property or injures them, you may find that this is not covered by your policy. You need to get in writing from your insurance company whether or not you have this coverage and how much you have. Via endorsement you can either acquire or expand this coverage.

Some liability claims can amount to millions of dollars. If you are well to do and a child drowns in your swimming pool, the child's parents may sue you for millions. To cover such possibilities, insurance companies offer insurance they may call catastrophe liability, umbrella liability, excess liability, and so on.

If you live in an area with no fire department, your premium will be much higher than that paid by people whose homes are protected by a fire department. What kind of fire department protects your home also affects your premium. Because they are usually less well equipped, and the firemen have to leave their regular jobs to come to a fire, a volunteer fire department will not reduce your premium as much as will a professional fire department. Your premium is also affected by the caliber of the professional fire department. Particularly important is how long it would take them to reach your house. Is there only one firehouse, and is it located miles from your home? Do freight trains frequently isolate your part of town? Poor police protection can also affect your premium. This is particularly likely to affect a vacation home, which, because it is often empty, attracts thieves and is likely to be located in a rural area protected by a sheriff and a few deputies.

In addition to buying a home where fire and police protection are good, you can reduce your premium by installing smoke detectors and installing a burglar alarm system if you select an insurance company that offers a reduced rate on homes so protected. Of course, places where fire and police protection are good will likely have higher taxes, and it costs money to install protective devices in your home; so, compare the premium saving with these costs.

MEDICAL INSURANCE

Tables 12–2 and 12–3 illustrates why you should consider buying some type of medical insurance: Medical expenses are large and growing rapidly. If you are very poor or elderly, you may be protected by a government program. If you are eligible and don't receive benefits, you only have to apply for coverage to get benefits. If you don't fall

TABLE 12–2   Indexes of Medical Care Prices, 1960 to 1975

	1960	1970	1975
Index, total	79.1	120.6	168.6
Drugs and prescriptions	101.5	103.6	118.8
Physicians' fees	77.0	121.4	169.4
Obstetrical care	79.4	121.8	167.2
Tonsillectomy, adenoidectomy	80.3	117.1	163.3
Dentists' fees	82.1	119.4	161.9
Optometric examination, eye glasses	85.1	113.5	149.6
Semi-private room rates	57.3	145.4	236.1

Source: Statistical Abstract of the United States 1976, U.S. Department of Commerce, Bureau of the Census, p. 72.
Note: 1967 = 100. Data prior to 1965 excludes Alaska and Hawaii.

TABLE 12–3   Per Capita Private Consumer Expenditures by Object, 1960 and 1974[1]

Type of Expenditure	1960	1974
Hospital care	$27.79	$90.44
Physicians' services	28.88	71.54
Dentists' services	10.74	31.25
Other professional services	4.49	7.27
Drugs and drug sundries	19.57	43.30
Eyeglasses and appliances[2]	4.13	10.02
Nursing home care	$ 2.24	$16.98

Source: Statistical Abstract of the United States 1976, U.S. Department of Commerce, Bureau of the Census, p. 73.

[1] Private consumer expenditures are substantially below total national expenditures. For examples, per capita national expenditures for hospital care in 1974 were $202.00.
[2] Includes fees of optometrists and expenditures for hearings aids, orthopedic appliances, artificial limbs, etc.

into either of these groups, you will have to depend on private insurance. Private insurance policies that cover your medical expenses are of two types, *individual* and *group*. Most people become eligible for group insurance through their employment. If this is the case, you probably have no choice about being covered. You may also have an opportunity to choose group coverage because you belong to some organization—a union or professional organization—that has a group policy. Even though you have group coverage, you may still wish to take out an individual policy to cover expenses not covered by the group plan. Figure 12–1 shows how people are spending their medical insurance dollars.

Individual Coverage

Since the purpose of insurance is to cover major losses, the most logical loss to cover is hospital expenses because a major illness will require

FIGURE 12–1. National Health Expenditures and Percent of Gross National Product, 1955–1975. (Health Insurance Institute, *Source Book of Health Insurance* Data 1976–1977, 1850 K Street N.W., Washington 20006)

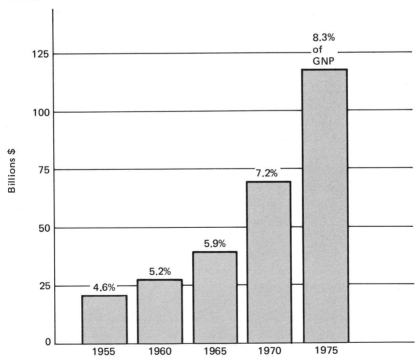

hospitalization; a minor illness will not. A *basic hospital policy* covers hospital room and board, miscellaneous expenses, and surgical expense.

Hospital room and board. This normally covers meals, special diets, and general floor nursing services. You can select from a variety of daily limits to determine how much you will be reimbursed. The higher the limit, the higher your premium.

Miscellaneous hospital expenses. This coverage reimburses you for a variety of medical services and supplies, such as: oxygen; plaster casts; blood; use of operating and recovery room; use of heart-lung machine or artificial kidney unit; services of radiologists, pathologists, and anesthetists; ambulance service; and so forth. You may either have coverage of such items based on the amount your policy covers for room and board (i.e., this is so many times that), or you may choose a limit just as you do in the case of room and board.

Surgical expense. This covers surgery both in and outside a hospital. Reimbursement is made according to a prearranged schedule of benefits, that is, a fixed amount will be paid for each type of surgery.

Supplemental coverages. Insurance companies offer a variety of additional coverages that you can obtain by paying a higher premium. You can obtain, for example, maternity benefits, in-hospital doctor calls, and accident-related medical expenses. The latter covers the cost of emergency treatment in a doctor's office as the result of an accident. Today, as shown in Figure 12–2, most medical bills are covered by insurance.

The basic policy without supplements does not usually cover sickness or injury covered by Medicare, workmen's compensation, or similar laws; confinement in a government hospital when you are not legally required to pay; treatment in a rest home, nursing home, convalescent home, or a facility for alcoholics or drug addicts; normal pregnancy and childbirth; routine baby care; war injuries; self-inflicted injury; hernia; hemorrhoids; disease of the tonsils or adenoids; disease of the reproductive organs; and dental treatment of the teeth or gums unless required by injury to natural teeth. Renewability is at the option of the insurance company.

Major Medical Insurance

A basic hospital policy fails to cover some items which can be quite expensive. Usually, for example, it covers no expenses outside a hospital or private duty nursing. In addition, its benefits are limited, and

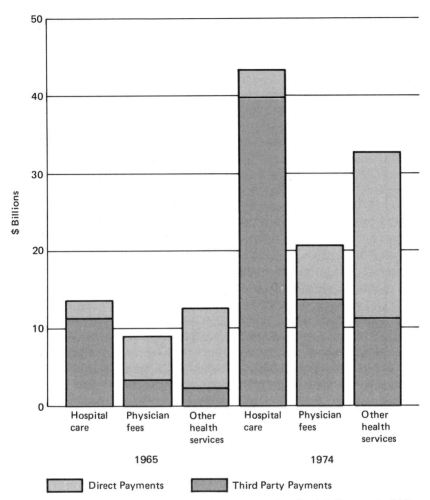

FIGURE 12–2. Insurance Benefits Cover Most Medical Bills, 1964. (U.S. Dept. of Commerce *U.S. Industrial Outlook 1977*, Washington 20006)

in case of a very serious or prolonged illness or incapacitation, you will exceed the policy's limits. *Major medical insurance takes care of the gaps in the coverage of the basic hospital policy.*

A major medical policy usually will cover all medical and surgical expenses, hospital expenses, medical supply expenses, nursing expenses, X-ray expenses, equipment rental expenses, ambulance expenses, and pregnancy complication expenses up to a high limit. (The limit may be as high as a quarter of a million dollars.)

Usually expenses arising out of a medical condition existing at the time you take out a policy are excluded, but sometimes the

insurance company will agree to cover expenses arising out of a condition they are made aware of when the policy is issued. Some policies
exclude mental illness or require that you be confined in a hospital or
mental institution. Dental treatment, plastic surgery, military injuries,
disabilities covered by workmen's compensation, and eye treatments

other than those made necessary by an accident are also usually excluded.

A major medical policy differs from other medical insurance policies in that it has a large deductible clause, a *coinsurance clause*, and a high maximum limit for benefits. The large deductible eliminates a lot of small claims that would run up your premium; in addition, since this policy supplements the basic policy, there is no need for coverage of every dollar. The purpose of coinsurance is also to hold down premiums by making you pay part of the cost. Usually you will pay 20 percent and the insurance company will pay 80 percent. Some policies have a limit on the combined amount of deductible and co-insurance you have to pay, that is, once they total a certain amount, the insurance company pays 100 percent of all additional expenses. The high limit is because covering large losses is what this type of policy is for. As figure 12–3 shows, a large number of people carry major medical protection.

FIGURE 12–3. Major Medical Expense Protection with Insurance Companies in the United States, 1960–1975. (Health Insurance Institute, *Source Book of Health Insurance Data 1976–1977*, 1850 K Street, N.W., Washington 20006)

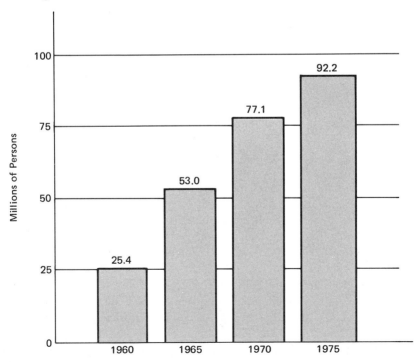

Some insurance companies offer a *comprehensive* policy which combines both the basic and major medical policies into one policy. Loss of income or disability insurance may also be included.

DISABILITY INCOME INSURANCE

The most valuable asset you possess is your earning power. Through either accident or injury this asset can be taken from you at any time either temporarily or permanently. A disability which will cause you either a temporary or permanent loss of income is much more likely if you are young than is death. Some people consider insuring themselves against loss of income to be more important than having life insurance. Certainly in the case of people with no dependents, this is true.

You are provided some income protection by the government through Medicare health insurance for the elderly and the severely disabled; disability income payments under Social Security; workmen's compensation; and a few others. Your employer or your union may provide a group plan.

Generally, a *disability income policy* provides you with a monthly income for either as long as you are unable to work or for a maximum period of time. Payment usually starts on the first day in the case of an accident, whereas in the case of illness there is a waiting period. The waiting period prevents you from collecting due to a minor illness. The policy may cover partial disability and payments will be appropriately less than for total disability. The longer the waiting period, the lower will be your premium.

Many policies provide a variety of supplemental benefits. Payments, for example, will be higher as long as you are hospitalized. Your heirs may receive a lump sum payment in the case of accidental death. Your monthly income will be higher if you are injured in an auto or common carrier accident. You are also able to obtain additional disability income without providing evidence of your insurability. Other possible supplemental benefits available are reimbursement for all medical expenses resulting from an accident; miscellaneous hospital expenses resulting from confinement for sickness or accident; and the cost of visits to doctors. Each supplemental benefit chosen, of course, will raise your premium.

In addition to how long a waiting period and what supplemental benefits, if any, you choose, your premium will be affected by your occupation, sex, and whether your policy is noncancellable, guaranteed renewable, and so forth. The noncancellable, guaranteed renewable policy is the best, but you will have to pay for this feature. It is also best to get a policy that will pay you if you can't work at your usual occupation. Some policies, however, pay only if you can't work at any job. You should think twice about accepting a policy which will pay you only if your disability shows up within a month of an accident.

DENTAL INSURANCE

You have probably noticed that the policies covered so far have not covered the cost of fillings, extractions, dentures, oral surgery, and most other dental expenses. There are insurance policies available that cover dental expenses, but they are less popular than the other forms of health insurance, and many people believe such policies are uneconomic—they cover numerous, small losses and, thus, are not appropriately covered by insurance.

Dental insurance may cover preventive treatment, emergency treatment, diagnostic services, anesthetic, drugs, extractions and oral surgery, fillings and crowns, treatment of gum diseases, root canal therapy, and dentures. Oral surgery, crowns, root canal therapy, and dentures will cost over $100 apiece and can run into the hundreds of dollars. The other items should run under $100.

Preexisting conditions and procedures not performed by a legally qualified dentist or physician will probably be excluded from coverage. Losses covered by workmen's compensation, cosmetic dental work, replacement of crowns and dentures, orthodontics (braces or straightening of teeth), and uncomplicated surgery on impacted teeth are also likely to be excluded.

Reimbursement is based on actual cost as long as it does not exceed the scheduled maximum benefit for the procedure involved. Generally there is a deductible with coinsurance involved above this amount.

CASES FOR DISCUSSION

Case 1 The Insurance Institute for Highway Safety reports that 33 percent of the damage covering claims for 1974 subcompact cars were above $600, while only 27 percent of full-size cars reached that level of loss. Full-size cars were found to have the least number of personal injury claims and subcompacts and compacts the highest. Why do you suppose this was the case? What use will insurance companies likely make of this information? What use can you make of it?

Case 2 David Busby has been shopping around for some auto insurance. He has discovered that there are two types of agents selling this insurance .One type of agent is an independent agent, she works for herself. She sells policies issued by several insurance companies. Other agents, however, work for an insurance company and only sell its policies. The independent agents tell David that they can get him the best deal, because they can select among policies and know which companies give the best service. The insurance companies' own employees tell David that they can give him a lower rate. How would you suggest David go about deciding from whom to buy?

Case 3 Ken Paulson was considering buying some hospital insurance when he got an advertisement through the mail for a special policy that insures against cancer. Ken is greatly concerned with the possibility of getting cancer since several people in his family have had it. He is considering buying cancer insurance instead of hospital insurance because he can't afford both. How would you advise him? Why?

Case 4 Lisa Muse has a tight budget, but she thinks she can afford some health insurance. Hospital insurance is cheaper than disability insurance which would pay a similar monthly benefit. Should she, therefore, buy the former? Why or why not?

Case 5 Jack Fuller lived with his parents until two months ago when he finished junior college. Wanting more freedom, he rented an apartment for $200 a month, not including utilities. Jack is 20 and earns $7500 as a computer operator. In a couple of years he expects his pay to increase substantially. He owns a 6-year-old sports car currently selling for $800. Jack is single and lives in an inner-city neighborhood of a major city. Since it is illegal for him to drive without insurance, he thinks he should get some, but he wants to spend as little money as possible. He knows you have studied personal finance, so he comes to you for advice. What would you tell him?

Case 6 Eric Kronholz is trying to decide whether to carry a $50- or a $100-deductible collision coverage. The $50 deductible would cost him $107 a year, and the $100 deductible would cost him $89 a year. Eric is a dentist, earns $20,000 a year, has a wife and two children, and is 30 years old. Cars like his are selling for about $2800, which is the amount he is insuring it for. How would you advise him? Why?

Case 7 Brian and Pam Overton are considering buying a dental insurance policy. The Overtons have three children; the oldest is ten. Their dental expenses are about average. The policy is a group policy available to the Overton's through a professional association Brian belongs to. If only Brian is covered, the premium will be $24 a quarter. If both Brian and Pam are covered, it will be $48. If all five of the Overton's are covered, the premium will be $86. The policy is like that described in the chapter, except that there is no coinsurance. There is a $50 annual deductible for each individual except that not more than $150 will be required for a family in a year. The schedule of benefits seems to the Overton's to cover no more than two-thirds of what each service will cost them at their dentist. How would you advise the Overtons? Why?

REVIEW QUESTIONS

1. What kind of losses is insurance designed to protect you against?
2. What is the law of large numbers, and how is it utilized by insurance companies?
3. How does an insurance company define a class of policy-holders?
4. Why might you find that a group policy has a lower premium than does a similar individual policy?
5. Why do you have to have an insurable interest in order to buy an insurance policy?

6. What is the difference between property and liability insurance?
7. What are exclusions?
8. What is a concealment?
9. What is a deductible?
10. What is the difference between insurance companies organized as stock companies and those organized as mutuals?
11. Name and describe the package of coverages included in an automobile policy.
12. What are the basic coverages provided by a homeowner's policy?
13. What is the insurance value of your home?
14. What is an endorsement?
15. What does a basic hospital policy cover?
16. What is the function of major medical insurance?
17. What is disability income insurance?
18. What is more important to have, life insurance or disability income insurance? Why?

YOUR PLAN: CHAPTER 12

Questions you should answer before
purchasing property, liability, health,
or disability income insurance:

1. How much can I afford to spend annually on insurance at a maximum?
2. What property do I own that is insurable and whose loss would be more than I can bear?
3. What kinds of damage to property or persons is it more than remotely possible that I or my immediate family might be declared liable for? (Clearly, if you drive a car, it is more than remotely possible you might be responsible for an accident. If you employ people, an on-the-job accident might be your responsibility. If you have children, they may damage a neighbor's property.)
4. Are my family's medical expenses likely to be below average, average, or above average? If they are likely to be above average, by how much above average are they likely to be?
5. How much money do I have in savings?
6. How much do I have invested in assets readily convertible to cash?

7. If I needed money, who could I turn to? How much could I get? Am I willing to do this? If I were in financial trouble, would I still get it? What would be the cost?
8. If I became disabled and unable to work temporarily and had no insurance, what would I do?
9. If I became disabled and unable to work for the rest of my life and had no insurance, what would I do?
10. If I or my family had a major medical expense and I had no insurance, what would I do?
11. Am I eligible for any type of group insurance? If so, what's its cost? What's its coverage?
12. Am I eligible for any government-sponsored insurance? If so, what does it cover?
13. Do I face any unusual, major risks? (Do you sky dive? Does the river near you flood every few years? Do you have a wood shingle roof on your house?) If so, to what costs do these risks expose me?
14. Do I face any risks that I could reduce, and would it cost less to reduce my risks than to insure myself against them? (You could take away your child's BB gun. You could put your bearer bonds in a safety deposit box. You can store your furs commercially, which reduces the likelihood of damage, and the storage firm is insured against theft and damage to the furs.)
15. Can I profitably take steps to reduce the risk I face and so reduce the premium I would otherwise pay to insure myself against the various perils involved? (You can install smoke alarms. You can replace your "muscle" car with a sedan.)
16. How much would it cost to replace my various assets?
17. How much money do I expect to earn in the future?
18. What size judgments are typical locally in liability suits?
19. How large a loss would it take to drive me into bankruptcy?
20. If I anticipate an expense, do I have the self-discipline to lay aside money to cover it?

How to Use Your Answers

It is never wise to buy anything without first having decided the most you can afford to pay for it. Your need for insurance is greatest for losses you cannot bear. The less risk there is of a loss, the less valuable insurance is against this loss. Thus, the losses which are the most likely are those you need insurance for the most.

CHAPTER TWELVE

The larger a possible loss is, the greater the need for insurance. Since premiums are based on the experience of the average policy-holder, insurance is relatively cheaper for those with above-average losses.

Alternatives to insurance are savings, either in the form of money or other liquid assets, and borrowing. Avoidance of the need for insurance, saving, or borrowing may be more economical than acquiring an insurance policy. Given that avoidance is too costly or is impossible, it may be cheaper to take the steps necessary to reduce your level of risk than pay an insurance premium. Even if you still need insurance, it will cost less at a lower-risk level.

To insure or not to insure is the question. If your situation would be intolerable without insurance, and you do not wish to take a chance of experiencing an intolerable situation, then insure yourself. What you need most is an income; thus, loss of it is *your* greatest loss.

Group insurance may be cheaper than individual insurance. There is no point in buying insurance that duplicates coverage you already have. Insurance policies are designed with the average person in mind. The risk you face, however, may not be average. If it is above average, you have a greater need for insurance. Obviously the size of possible losses is related to how much insurance you should buy. Presumably, you desire, at a minimum, to have enough insurance to preclude bankruptcy or lifelong poverty.

Insurance is most appropriately used to protect you against expenses larger than you could possibly pay, even if you knew you would incur them. It should also be used to protect you against expenses you cannot anticipate, and, for this reason (not their huge size), can't pay for them. If you cannot arrange to pay for expected expenses, you will also have to turn to insurance. For example, a dentist may X-ray your children's gums and tell you that in the future their wisdom teeth will have to be surgically removed. She can even tell you about when this will happen, but you may not be able to discipline yourself to set aside the money to pay for these procedures, but you are disciplined enough to pay an insurance premium for a policy that will cover these procedures.

Taking the Risk Out of Death

Long ago it was realized that everybody was subject to a variety of possible disasters that could wipe them out financially for the rest of their lives. To eliminate this problem, insurance was developed. The principle of insurance is that people subject to some risk, such as their home burning down, would, through contributions from each, create a fund from which any of their number suffering a loss could compensate themselves.

The first form of insurance was *marine insurance*; this compensated ship owners whose sailing ships sank. Next came fire insurance for businesses. Fire insurance was the first form of insurance for individuals.

Death, of course, is a certainty; not a probability like that of your home burning down. But when one will die is not certain. If you die at an early age, your family will suffer financial loss. The death of a man 28 years old who has four children under seven years of age and a wife with no job or job experience is a staggering financial disaster for his family. Life insurance was developed to insure people against dying young or "too soon." Later it was expanded to cover the risk of a living death—physical incapacity—and living too long—exhausting provisions made for old age.

TERMINOLOGY

In order to discuss life insurance, you must be familiar with its terminology. When one becomes insured, he or she is a policyholder. The policy is the contract between the life insurance company and the insured. Since nearly 70 percent of the families in the United States own some form of life insurance, it is very likely that someday you will own or be the beneficiary of a life insurance policy. Life insurance in force in the United States today amounts to $2,140 billion! This money is payable to people (beneficiaries) named by the policyholders. Often the policyholder names a *contingent beneficiary* or beneficiaries in case the primary beneficiary should die before the policyholder does. If no beneficiary is named or is deceased, the proceeds of a policy will go to the deceased's estate and be subject to creditor's claims and inheritance taxes. If there is a beneficiary to receive the proceeds, creditors of the deceased cannot get this money, and states frequently do not levy inheritance taxes on insurance policy proceeds or will not do so when the amount is not great. The federal government exempts a substantial amount from taxation.

The *face amount* of a life insurance policy is what will be paid to your beneficiary or beneficiaries when you die. To asquire the promise of the insurance company to make this payment to your beneficiary, you normally agree to pay the life insurance company a *periodic premium.* The policy will remain in force as long as you make the required premium payments. If you do not pay on time or within a *grace period,* your policy *lapses,* which means the policy comes to an end. Whether you can recover anything or can reinstate the policy depends on what type of policy it is.

Policies contain clauses, options, and riders. *Clauses* cover the various provisions of the policy. *Options* involve choices available to you, such as how dividends on a policy will be handled. Some you can't reject, such as no benefits are owed by the company if death is by suicide within one year of taking out the policy. *Riders* specify a variety of possible extra benefits your policy may provide. Each rider adds to the size of the policy's premium. Two common riders are *waiver of premium* and *double indemnity. The former waives* premiums if you become totally disabled and, thus, are in no position to continue paying the premiums. The latter provides that twice the face value of the policy will be paid the beneficiary if you die in an accident rather than of natural causes.

HOW LIFE INSURANCE WORKS

How life insurance works is most easily understood through a simple example: Suppose you and five of your friends visit a fortune teller who tells you that in one year one of you will die. The following year two of you will die. Three years from now the remaining three of you will die. She can't say who will die when. Suppose you all believe her.

Each of you realizes that if he dies within two years his assets will certainly not be large enough to even cover minimal burial expenses of $1000. One of your friends suggests that all of you should now start putting aside some money in a common fund to cover the groups' burial expenses.

This girl is pretty good at math, and after a few minutes of work with a calculator, she triumphantly announces, "If we each put $166.67 ($1000 divided by 6) into the fund now, we can pay for the burial expenses of the one of us who will die in a year. The following year the survivors will have to put up $400 ($2000 divided by 5) each to cover the expenses of these two who die that year. Three years from now the remaining three of us will have to put up $1000 each to cover their burial expenses."

"Wait a minute," you protest. "The last three will put up a total of $1566.67 ($167.67 plus $400 plus $1000) and only get a $1000 burial!"

"On the other hand," the math whiz points out, "they will be guaranteed a $1000 burial. They don't know now that they will be the last to die. If they died sooner, without the fund, they wouldn't have the $1000 available. Of course, the three that die first get a bargain. One only spends $166.67 for a $1000 burial. If we follow your logic, you get cheated if you pay for fire insurance, and your house never burns down."

"What about interest?" you ask. "We could earn something on that money, and that would reduce how much we would have to pay."

"That's a good point," smiles the math whiz. "Let me figure what that will do to the size of the payments. If we can earn 6 percent annually, we'd each have to pay $377.36 if we survive the first year to cover the $2000 needed the second year (5 times $377.36 equals $1886.80, and 1.06 times this amount equals $2000.01.) The last three survivors would each have to pay $943.40 instead of $1000 in order to have the $3000 needed the third year." ($943.40 times 1.06 equals $1000.04.)

"I don't like paying more and more money each year," you complain.

"We can avoid that," says the math whiz. "If we ignore the interest we could earn, we would have to put up $428.57 apiece each year in order to level the payments and still collect enough to cover each year's expenses. We'd collect $2571.42 the first year; $2142.85 the second year; and $1285.71 the third year for a total of $5999.98. I'll throw in the extra two cents. The extra money we collect the first two years over the $1000 and $2000 needed gives us enough to pay the $3000 needed in the third year and reduces what the last three will pay over the three years to $1285.71."

"Hey," you say, "that's a saving of $280.96 over the $1566.67 the other way! What happens if we earn interest on our money? Collecting the money early will increase the amount we can earn."

The math whiz does some more calculations and says that, "It will only cost each of us $391.60 a year if we earn 6 percent interest on our money! Then the last three survivors will each pay a total of only $1174.80! That's a saving of $391.87 over the $1566.67! Those who die the second year will pay a total of $783.20 each. The first person to die will pay $391.60, which is a lot more than would be paid under the first plan, which didn't even include any interest being earned."

You grab her calculator at that point and do some figuring yourself. "That means we will collect a total of $5482.40 and earn $517.60 in interest, giving us the $6000 we need."

Term and Whole Life Insurance

Insurance companies can't and don't depend on fortune tellers. Instead, they depend on the law of large numbers and many years of data on death rates. They can predict with a high degree of accuracy what percent of a large group of people of a given age will die each year. As in the above example, the insured is buying protection against premature death. Life insurance companies offer two basic types of insurance: term and whole life insurance. *Term* or *pure life insurance* is like the first example above, that is, each year enough money is collected from those living at that time to pay the death benefits of those who will die during the year. Because the death rate rises each year for a given age group, the premium rises each year. *Whole* or *permanent life insurance* is like the later example—the same premium is collected each year by collecting more than is needed to pay death benefits in early years and less than is needed to pay death benefits in later years. Interest is credited to the policy. *Ordinary* or *straight life* is whole's basic form.

When you are young, term insurance is cheaper than whole life. It's so much cheaper that you can buy several times as much term as whole life. Because of the high cost of term when most of an age group has died, term insurance is not sold to older people. Term policies are normally renewable only up to a certain age. If you wish to remain insured beyond that age, you must take out a whole life policy. A term policy may be convertible into some form of whole life. If a physical is required in order to get a whole life policy, you may be in trouble, as the state of your health certainly doesn't improve with age!

Some insurance salesmen may try to sell you term insurance, hoping to talk you into converting into whole life later so that they will earn two commissions. Since, through your premiums, you will pay these two commissions, conversion costs you!

Premiums

In computing premiums in the example, no consideration was given to the expenses of the insurance company. A life insurance company has to add these to the premium if it is to stay in business. Insurance companies call this the *load,* and it includes sales commissions, clerical costs, and so on. Because most life insurance companies are mutuals, the load frequently doesn't include a profit, since a mutual is a non-profit association of people for their mutual benefit. Those life insurance companies which are incorporated charge a premium high enough to provide them with a profit. (You and your friends were a mutual with no costs.) Both mutuals and incorporated life insurance companies pay out profits as dividends to their owners. A mutual's policyholders are its owners. A mutual whose costs are less than expected or whose earnings on invested premium income are more than was expected will declare dividends payable to their policyholders. (See Figure 13–1.) The policyholder can use this dividend in a variety of ways. If you don't renew your policy, you can take it in cash. It can also be applied to your premium to reduce it. You can also use it to buy paid-up insurance. *Paid-up insurance* is insurance which requires no more premium payments. It can also be used to buy one-year term insurance. (Term policies are available for various periods of time.) Another option is leaving it with the insurance company as a relatively low-earning savings account.

Premiums may be paid annually, semiannually, quarterly, or monthly. The more often you pay, the greater will be the annual total premium, for example, if there's a $200 premium if paid annually, if you pay it through the year in four payments (quarterly) you will pay more than $50 each quarter. A policy can be obtained by making only a single premium payment. This premium will be relatively quite large.

The 6 percent figure used in the example was unrealistic. Insurance companies seldom assume more than 4 percent, frequently it is much lower.

Since insurance agents are paid a much higher commission for

FIGURE 13–1. The Life Insurance Company Dollar, 1976—How Used. (American Council of Life Insurance, 1850 K Street, N.W., Washington 20006)

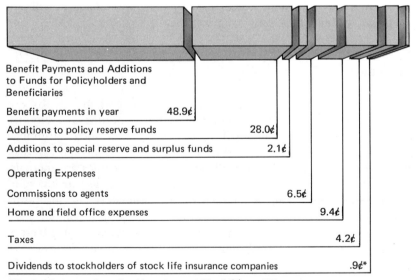

Benefit Payments and Additions to Funds for Policyholders and Beneficiaries	
Benefit payments in year	48.9¢
Additions to policy reserve funds	28.0¢
Additions to special reserve and surplus funds	2.1¢
Operating Expenses	
Commissions to agents	6.5¢
Home and field office expenses	9.4¢
Taxes	4.2¢
Dividends to stockholders of stock life insurance companies	.9¢*

*For stock companies only this ratio would be 1.8¢ per dollar.

selling a whole life policy, the load is larger for them than for term. Agents usually try harder to sell whole life than term, because of the higher commission. (Insurance companies refer to their salespeople as *agents*.) Insurance companies prefer whole life because there is less possibility they will have trouble paying claims and investment income is greater.

Cash Surrender Value

When an insurance company sells a whole life policy it is collecting money before it needs it, so these policies have what is called a cash surrender value. The *cash surrender value* is the excess money collected in premiums over what is currently needed to pay benefits. (With a whole life policy, you, in effect, have a decreasing term policy and a growing savings account—the cash surrender value. Ultimately you have no insurance at all, only a savings account. This happens when the policy's saving component reaches the face value of the policy. This is why it is said that with a whole life policy the insurance company is constantly "going off the risk," that is, what it has collected from you plus earnings on this money covers the benefit promised by the policy.)

Unlike term policies, some whole life policies become *paid-up* because at some point in time no further premiums are collected, but the policy continues in force. Ordinary insurance is paid-up when one reaches age 99 since no one is assumed to live to 100. Earlier paying up avoids burdening people in retirement with premium payments at a time when their income is usually low; thus, premium payments are raised enough so that premiums need not be collected beyond age 65 or after so many years.

A term policy lapses at the end of the term unless it is renewed. A whole life policy continues so long as premiums are paid. These premiums are level—that is, of equal size. With some whole life policies the insurance company has collected what it will pay out on the policy by the time it is paid-up; then the cash surrender value equals the policy's face value. Thus, with a whole life policy the insurance company is constantly going off the risk—the "risk" being payment of the death benefit. See Figure 13–2 which illustrates for a variety of whole life policies how the insurance company goes off the risk.

The introduction of whole life policies revolutionized the life insurance industry. Life insurance sales rose tremendously as a result of the introduction of this type of policy. After it was introduced, life insurance agents no longer had to just talk about death. They could

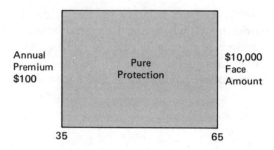

(1) Level Term to 65

Annual Premium $100 — Pure Protection — $10,000 Face Amount

35 — 65

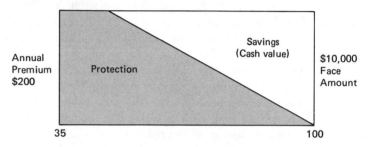

(2) Whole or Ordinary Life

Annual Premium $200 — Protection — Savings (Cash value) — $10,000 Face Amount

35 — 100

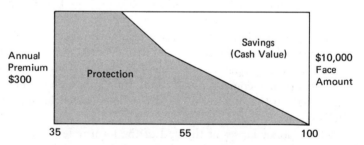

(3) 20-Pay Life

Annual Premium $300 — Protection — Savings (Cash Value) — $10,000 Face Amount

35 — 55 — 100

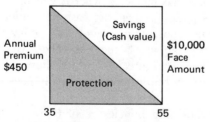

(4) 20-Year Endowment

Annual Premium $450 — Savings (Cash value) — Protection — $10,000 Face Amount

35 — 55

FIGURE 13–2. The Four Basic Types of Level Coverage. (Venita Van Caspel, Money Dynamics: *How to Build Financial Independence.* Reston, Va.: Reston Publishing Co., Inc., p. 189)

then talk about savings: the cash surrender value of a policy. If, they would point out, you give up (surrender) a term policy, you have nothing to show for it. If you surrender a whole life policy after the first few years, whose premiums go to cover the sales commission, you are entitled to its cash value. At the policy's maturity you can receive its cash value. You can also borrow, paying an interest rate stated in the policy, the cash value if you need the cash, but do not want to give up the insurance policy. Unless you repay the loan, the value of your policy is reduced by the amount of the loan. (Some people wonder why, if the cash value is yours, you have to pay interest to get it?) The cash surrender value of your policy when you die has no effect on what your beneficiary or beneficiaries get when you die. Some policies have a cash value at maturity in excess of their face value, which you will receive if you are still alive when the policy matures.

TYPES OF INSURANCE

Life insurance companies offer a bewildering variety of policies. All are either pure insurance (term) or whole life, or combinations of the two, perhaps combined with an annuity.

Ordinary or Straight Policies

A whole life policy with no additional features is called a *straight* or *ordinary* policy. Most life insurance policies are of this type. Usually these policies carry the option of converting them into a plan to pay the insured a retirement income (an annuity). Conversion means if you live to retirement age, no death benefit will be paid when you die, because when you retire, the policy's cash value is used to set up an annuity. Like a death benefit, the annuity is paid for by the accumulated premiums above that needed to pay for the pure (term) insurance portion of the policy. A policy convertible into a pension provides you with insurance against living too long.

An ordinary whole life policy is cheaper than the other forms of whole life. Thus, if an older person cannot afford the cost of term insurance, but needs insurance in this period of life, this is the best alternative in terms of cost alone.

As was observed earlier, whole life (permanent) combines, through its current collection of some of the money needed to pay benefits after the current year, term insurance with a savings account.

An insurance policy, however, may not be a very efficient method of saving, because of the relatively low interest rate credited to the policyholder's payments. If you borrow this money, the value of your policy declines by the amount of the loan. If you do not repay the loan, and you do not have to, this decrease is permanent. You should always consider the fact that if you buy a cheaper term policy rather than a whole life policy, you will have funds available to employ at interest that you would not have if you bought the whole life policy. Thus, you should compare a whole life policy with a term policy offering the same benefit plus a savings account created out of the difference between the term and whole life premiums.

Fairly frequently people take out ordinary policies and then find that they cannot afford to continue paying the premiums. Since there is initially no cash value build-up, as the insurance company first recovers its sales costs, if you give up a policy within the first two or three years, you recover none of your money. If you had purchased term instead, you would have gotten more protection for the same amount of money.

Limited Payment Policies

Since a substantial portion of an age group lives beyond age 65, when most people's income declines, life insurance companies offer limited payment policies. Usually these policies are offered for 20 or 30 years. No premiums are required after the policy matures, but the policy remains *in force*. In addition to being beneficial to those who live until this policy matures, people who currently have a high income which will decline before age 65 will find such a policy has appeal.

Clearly the greatest advantage to a limited payment life policy is the fact you only have to pay premiums for a certain number of years. A drawback is its cost, which is higher than that of ordinary life. This type of policy is often well beyond the budget of young families, who can get more insurance—as contrasted to savings—from an ordinary life policy. It is when one is young that insurance is needed most. Savings' importance grows as one ages. Therefore, older families are likely to find this type of insurance more attractive and affordable than are young families.

Endowment and Retirement Policies

These policies place heavy emphasis on savings rather than protection, and they are the most expensive type of life insurance. Endowment at age 65 and 20-year endowments are the most common types of endow-

ment policies. If the insured dies before the stated period, the beneficiary receives the full face value of the policy. If the insured lives
until the end of the stated period, he or she receives the full face value
of the policy, but is no longer insured.

The *retirement policy* will, instead of paying a lump-sum at
maturity (as does the endowment), pay you a monthly income. You
can choose to receive payments for either a given number of years or
for life, with the payments being smaller if you choose life.

Endowment policies are often sold as a way to provide the
savings necessary for your childrens' educations whether you live or
not, assuming you have a waiver of premium rider. A possible advantage of the endowment over the limited payment policy is that,
while with the limited payment policy you can collect nothing at
maturity, but are insured for life, with the endowment policy you can
collect the face value at maturity, but you lose your insurance.

Much greater savings are accumulated via these types of policies
than any other. The retirement policy will most likely be appropriate
for one with no access to a group pension plan. Such people can,
however, put money into an individual retirement plan which the
federal government will levy no income taxes on until it is disbursed,
and you are likely to earn a higher interest rate on this fund than is
credited to holders of retirement policies. (Individual retirement plans
will be discussed later.)

Many independent financial advisors believe that endowment
and retirement policies are a poor means of saving money. They
suggest that they are appropriate only for those who cannot discipline
themselves to save or are not capable of earning a reasonable rate of
return on their savings with a low degree of risk.

Other Forms of Whole Life

Straight or ordinary life policies are available which combine features
of whole life and term. These policies provide a monthly income for
the beneficiary if the insured dies before the maturity of the policy.
Common types are *family income, family, family maintenance,* and
modified life. Premiums run a little higher than those on straight life.

These policies will pay the insured's family a monthly income
until the youngest child reaches 21; then the face value of the
policy will become due and payable to the widow, either as a lump
sum or as income. These policies are popular with young families as
a way to provide more complete protection for them than does
ordinary life if the family breadwinner dies at an early age. With
ordinary life the beneficiary is left with the problem of allocating the

lump sum payment. A family can, however, easily spend too much of current income to protect itself against something so unlikely to happen. Table 13–1 shows the differences in the amount of coverage you get for a given premium with different types of policies. Table 13–2 compares premiums depending on your age and the type of policy.

Life insurance companies also provide income protection policies that insure one against a living death—disability which causes one to

TABLE 13–1 What $100 a Year Will Buy (Approximate Amounts) in Insurance for a Male, Age 22

	Amount of Insurance $100 a Year Will Buy*	Cash Value At Age 65 Per $100 Annual Premium
1. Term (5-year renewable and convertible)	$19,000	None
2. Straight life	8,000	$4,660
3. Life-paid-up-at-65	7,200	4,986
4. Family income (20 years)	7,700	4,504
5. Endowment at 65	5,700	5,700
6. 20-payment life	4,400	3,036
7. Retirement income at 65	4,000	$6,250
8. 20-year endowment	$ 2,100	Matured (age 42)

Source: Jerome B. Cohen, *Decade of Decision,* Washington, D.C.: American Council of Life Insurance, Education Services, Health Insurance Institute, 1975, p. 22.

* Most companies have minimum policy limits of $1,000, $3,000, or $5,000.

TABLE 13–2 Approximate Annual Premium Rates for $1,000 of Each of Four Types of Life Insurance Policies

Bought at Age	Straight Life	Limited Payment (20-payment)	Endowment (20-year)	Term (5-year renewable-convertible)
18	$11.95	$20.15	$43.17	$ 5.35
20	12.54	20.93	43.20	5.38
25	14.27	23.11	43.43	5.50
30	16.60	28.83	43.68	5.68
40	23.32	32.87	45.20	7.96
50	$34.51	$43.06	$48.91	$14.21

Source: Education Services, Health Insurance Institute, American Councnl of Life Insurance, Washington, D.C.

Note: Rates shown are approximate premium rates for nonparticipating life insurance policies for men. Rates for women are somewhat lower because of women's somewhat lower mortality. Rates of participating policies would be slightly higher, but the cost would be lowered by annual dividends. The premium rates shown here are per $1,000 of protection if the policies were purchased in units of $10,000.

be unable to work. This protection is provided by a rider on your life insurance policy.

Insuring children. Life insurance companies have done such a good job selling their policies that sales growth is now largely dependent on population growth unless they can come up with some new types of policies. The major new types of policies are for people who don't have any dependents, such as children and wives without outside employment. (See Figure 13-3.) While the death of a child may temporarily increase your expenses over what they would have been if the child had lived, in the long run the death of a child reduces your expenses. (Raising a child is almost certainly going to be the most expensive project you engage in; far exceeding the cost of your home, for example!) Thus, it normally doesn't make sense to take out life insurance on your children. Often policies on children are advertised as a way to provide a college education for them via the policy's cash value, but you should be able to get a better return on your money elsewhere, and if you should die, your family might not be able to afford the premium on the policy.

FIGURE 13-3. Distribution of Amount of Ordinary Life Policies Purchased by Sex of Insured in the U.S. (American Council of Life Insurance, 1850 K Street, N.W., Washington 20006)

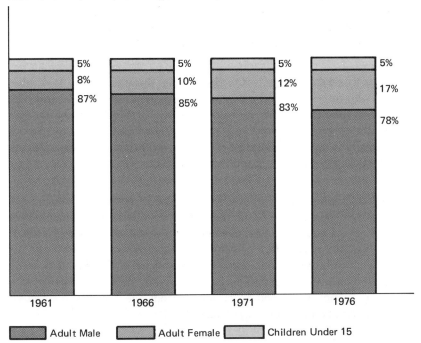

It is also said that this is a way for your children to get life insurance cheap, since premiums are low for those starting a policy as children. However, over their lifetimes they will pay out a lot more in premiums if the policy is taken out when they are children and, of course, children have no dependents to protect. (If you simply like to gamble, rather than take out a policy on a child, go somewhere like Las Vegas. You'll probably do better there!)

Insuring wives. It makes a bit more sense to insure the life of a so-called nonworking wife, that is, she works at home rather than somewhere else. If she should die and her husband has to hire some-one to do her work, he might not be able to afford to do this without insurance. He will, however, lose an expense when his wife dies, which could offset the cost of hiring a housekeeper.

As you may have concluded from what has been said, women often do not need life insurance. Their husbands often do not depend on them for support; their children may not. Does the working wife need insurance on her husband? Usually even a woman with an outside job does most of the housework and takes care of the children most of the time; thus, she, in turn, would not need to hire a replacement for her husband vis-a-vis labor around the house unless he is the handy type who does plumbing, carpentry, etc. and/or helps with the house-work and children. In short, in a family where the wife has a good job, much less insurance is needed on her husband than otherwise would be the case. In short, your loss, which may or may not equal your need, is measured by how much more than self-supporting your spouse is.

A way to strike it rich? On the surface, insurance may look like a good way to gamble. Why not take out policies on people and clean up when they die? There are two reasons why this doesn't work. First, in order to buy a policy, you have to show that you stand to lose financially from the insured's death. Second, insurance companies win most of their "bets." For gambling, stick to Las Vegas!

For your business. A relatively new type of insurance you can take out on someone else's life, or they can take out naming you as bene-ficiary, is on your business partner. As a result of a partner's death, your business may suffer greatly for lack of his or her services. You may wish to buy out your partner's heir's share of the business, but to do that you need money. The policy on your deceased partner gives you the money you need to either buy out the heirs or compensate you for the loss of his or her services.

Credit insurance.   Often someone will sell you something very expensive on a credit basis and require that you pay for a life insurance policy on yourself with them as beneficiary. This protects both them and your heirs. The policy will pay them what you owe if you die and enable your heirs to keep the item rather than, perhaps, having to let it be repossessed because they can't make the payments on it. Typically a mortgage lender will require that such a policy be taken out. Often such life insurance is the best you can buy. It is *group type* and, therefore, relatively cheap. It meets a basic need by providing your family with things like a car or a house. Nonetheless, the credit grantor may be getting a kickback from the insurance company, and you will pay for this. Be wary if your arm is twisted to take out a given company's policy.

Federal government-sponsored insurance.   Social Security provides you with some life-insurancelike benefits. However, unless you are self-employed, you have no choice about being covered. You are either working in covered employment or you are not. If you are working in a covered job, you have to pay Social Security taxes. They are automatically withheld from your pay.

While a private insurer pays benefits from a fund collected from policyholders plus earnings on their premiums, Social Security is mainly financed by passing on current Social Security tax collections to retired workers. In addition to serving as a sort of insurer, Social Security also serves as a welfare program, that is, what you receive is not totally determined by what you contribute, as is the case with private insurance.

Although Social Security taxes could rise to an unbearable level, and the system could be terribly mismanaged, one thing that can't happen is for Social Security to literally go bankrupt. No agency of the federal government, which has both the power to print money and tax, can go bankrupt! Private companies and nonfederal governments can, however. Thus, you should be very concerned with the quality of the management and the policies of nonfederal and private insurers. Use whatever powers you have as a policyholder or voter to steer them right. Of course, as a voter and payer of Social Security taxes, you should also be concerned that the Social Security program is efficiently and fairly run.

Industrial insurance. The most uneconomical type of insurance you can buy is called industrial insurance. It was originally sold to industrial workers. It is a high-cost life insurance because premiums are collected regularly, usually weekly, by collection agents. Most buyers are very poor and end up letting their policies lapse and, so, never collect a dime.

DECIDING WHAT POLICY TO BUY

The main question about life insurance is usually not whether or not to buy, but what kind to buy. Only people whose death will not place a financial burden on other people definitely do not need insurance. Thus, people with dependents or a negative net worth—what's owed exceeds the value of what's owned—need life insurance. Most agents will recommend whole life insurance, probably straight life, for people with moderate or low incomes. They will stress the value of its permanency and its unchanging annual premium. They will also exalt its living values: the policy's cash surrender value, which can be obtained by surrendering the policy or borrowing against it.

On the other hand, critics of the insurance industry, of which there are a few, note that the industry mainly sells the more profitable whole life policies, and they point out that the premiums for renewable or decreasing term contracts amount to only a fraction of those for straight life. Many people, they say, cannot afford enough whole life to give a young family the protection they need, but they can afford enough term. (With decreasing term, every time the policy is renewed, it is renewed for less. This can prevent the premium from rising.) Critics add that few people need the life-long protection whole insurance provides. So-called living values are, they say, just a cover up for a low-interest saving account. Despite their criticisms, however, whole life policies remain far more popular than term.

Straight Life Versus Term

Knowing that people do not like to talk about death, life insurance agents are likely to call themselves financial planners or life investment planners, and they sell living values more than death protection. Since a whole life policy consists of decreasing pure insurance and an increasing savings account, as a person grows older, the saving or living value of the policy clearly becomes its dominant element. Logic clearly dictates that you should buy a straight life policy only if you value its living values, because more death benefits can be obtained by a young person with a term policy for a given-sized premium, or the same death benefit can be obtained for a lower cost. (It will sometimes be uneconomical to buy term first and later switch to whole life, simply because the premium on whole life rises the older you are when you buy the policy.)

A straight life policy has certainly been uneconomical for many of its buyers. Policies sometimes stay on the average insurance company's books only seven years. The typical lapse rate in the industry is about 15 to 20 percent in the first policy year. Some companies have a dramatically higher lapse rate. After 20 years few policies terminate other than by death. Clearly many people are purchasing more insurance than they can afford. Term insurance policies are less likely to be dropped in their early years.

It is a good idea not to depend on the insurance company keeping their books properly. Keep proof that you have been paying the premiums on any policies you may have.

Whether term or straight life is better for you often hinges on what you could earn on the difference between the term and the higher-cost straight life premium that provides the same benefit. Is the rate you would earn on the difference more or less than the insurance company will credit you on your cash value? If the rate you earn is higher, is the risk also greater? You may, for example, be able to earn more in the stock market than the insurance company offers you, but the stock market is a very risky investment medium.

The problem with buying straight life is often this: A young man with a family may figure that his family will need $100,000 to replace the income lost if he dies in the near future. He can afford, however, only a $25,000 straight life policy, but a $25,000 policy will not even put his children through school, much less pay the mortgage. He could afford $100,000 of term, but the agent advising him makes a 55 percent commission on a straight policy and only 25 percent on a term policy. The young man also doesn't like the fact that neither he nor his heirs may ever collect anything from the term policy.

Many people feel gyped by term policies. If they live, they feel they've gotten nothing for the money they paid for the policy. This is, however, comparable to saying that you get nothing out of a police force unless you have to call them. Life insurance per se is merely protection against dying "too soon." If you don't die too soon, you have paid for a service just as you do when you don't utilize a policeman but could have.

Since many people don't like to think about dying, and many young people halfway believe they won't die and certainly will not soon, the introduction of whole life insurance probably did society a great service by inducing people to buy it as a way to save, which they find more attractive than protection against dying too soon.

Buying Both Policies

An increasingly common strategy is to take out a whole life policy, probably straight, when you are young and can get it at the lowest cost. The size of this policy is based on your anticipated needs when you are old. At the same time, you take out a term policy to cover your currently greater need for death protection, that is, your dependents will be more deprived if you die sooner rather than later. Because your need for death protection will probably decline with age—assuming you can initially afford to fully cover your needs—you will ultimately renew your term policy for a lesser amount. The whole life policy will be one with the option of conversion into a retirement annuity.

HOW MUCH LIFE INSURANCE IS NEEDED?

How much life insurance you need cannot be determined until you itemize and quantify the various needs that life insurance can provide. Life insurance can be used for:

Clean-up expenses—The medical bills, funeral costs, bills and loans you acquired during life, and taxes owed when you die.

Family income—How much income will your family need to get along on? Don't forget that they will need less without you and may be entitled to Social Security benefits and survivors benefits provided by your company's pension plan. (Table 13–3 shows what Social Security benefits a young family can receive.) As the children grow

TABLE 13–3   Social Security Survivor's Benefits for Young Families, 1976

| | Covered Worker's Age at Death* | | | | |
| | 30 | | | 40 | |
Final Gross Earnings	Widowed Spouse and 1 Child	Family Maximum	Widowed Spouse and 1 Child	Family Maximum
$ 7,500	$7,049	$ 8,335	$5,993	$7,390
9,000	7,949	9,271	6,768	8,110
15,000	9,991	11,658	8,114	9,467
$23,500 up	$9,991	$11,658	$8,141	$9,498

Source: "Consumer Views," Citibank, July 1976. Reprinted with permission of The Wall Street Journal, © Dow Jones & Company, Inc. (1976). All rights reserved.

Note: Annual benefits based on covered earnings from 1951, or age 22 if later, assuming earnings increased 5 percent yearly. Actual benefits have been rounded.

* Benefits decline beyond age 40. For example, the family maximum for a covered worker who dies at 50 if $9,000 is final gross earnings was $7,464.

up, less will be needed for this purpose. Also consider any income any of them may earn by taking a job. Don't forget to take account of possible future inflation!

Paying the mortgage—It is possible to take out a special policy that will provide whatever is necessary to pay off the mortgage on your home when you die.

An emergency fund—This is to take care of unforeseeable expenses or underestimates of foreseen expenses.

Income for spouse's old age—What is your spouse going to live on if he or she survives to a very old age? Is Social Security enough?

A college fund for the children—Policies are written just for this purpose.

Retirement income—If you live to be 65, will your company pension plan and Social Security provide an adequate income? If not, you will want a life insurance policy convertible into a retirement annuity.

If you cannot afford to buy enough life insurance to cover all your needs, you will have to determine which of these needs has the highest priority and cover them. (Figure 13–4 shows how much the average family in the United States has been spending on life insurance in recent years.)

The First National City Bank's (Citibank) economists and insurance specialists estimate that a family can maintain its standard of living if it receives an after-tax income which is 75 percent of its after-tax income before the breadwinner's death. If this figure falls below 60 percent, the family's living standard will be seriously lowered. Thus, Citibank advises that one aim at the 75 percent figure and at least attain the 60 percent figure. (Note that need may be less than your living standard!)

The amount of insurance needed will vary both with your level of income and your spouse's age when you die. If he or she is 25 years old and you earn $15,000 before taxes, to replace 60 percent of your after-tax income will require $45,000 (three times your income) in life insurance. If, however, he or she is 45 years old, your gross income is $30,000; and you wish to provide at the 75 percent level, a $255,000 policy is required. (Citibank's table showing how much life insurance is needed to replace the income of the deceased is shown in Table 13–4.)

The figures compiled by Citibank (Table 13–4) to show how much life insurance is needed seems to fly in the face of reason, because it shows that as your spouse ages, ever more life insurance is needed. The reason for this is that the younger a family is, the higher

FIGURE 13–4. Life Insurance and Disposable Personal Income Per Family in the U.S. (American Council of Life Insurance, 1850 K St., N.W., Washington 20006)

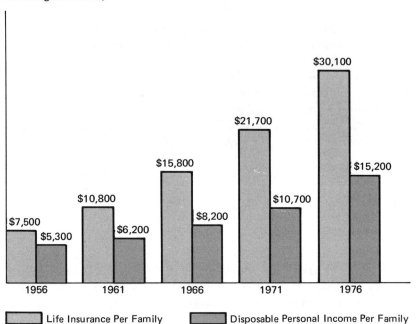

	Life Insurance per Family	Disposable Personal Income per Family		Life Insurance per Family	Disposable Personal Income per Family
Year			Year		
1930	$ 2,800	$1,900	1966	$15,800	$ 8,200
1935	2,400	1,400	1967	17,100	8,600
1940	2,700	1,700	1968	18,300	9,100
1945	3,200	3,200	1969	19,400	9,500
1950	4,600	4,000	1970	20,700	10,100
1955	6,900	5,100	1971	21,700	10,700
1960	10,200	6,100	1972	22,900	11,300
1961	10,800	6,200	1973	24,400	12,400
1962	11,400	6,500	1974	26,500	13,100
1963	12,200	6,700	1975	28,100	14,200
1964	13,200	7,300	1976	$30,100	$15,200
1965	$14,600	$7,700			

Note: Data are revised.

Sources: Spectator Year Book, *American Council of Life Insurance, and U.S. Department of Commerce. "Families" here include the units defined by the Bureau of the Census as families, subfamilies and unrelated individuals; these numbered 77,944,000 in 1976. The average amounts shown above are arithmetic means.*

TABLE 13–4   The Multiples-of-Salary Chart

Your Present Gross Earnings	25 Years*		35 Years*		45 Years*		50 Years**	
Present Age of Spouse	75%	60%	75%	60%	75%	60%	75%	60%
$ 7,500	4.0	3.0	5.5	4.0	7.5	5.5	6.5	4.5
9,000	4.0	3.0	5.5	4.0	7.5	5.5	6.5	4.5
15,000	4.5	3.0	6.5	4.5	8.0	6.0	7.0	5.5
23,500	6.5	4.5	8.0	5.5	8.5	6.0	7.5	5.5
30,000	7.5	5.0	8.0	6.0	8.5	6.5	7.0	5.5
40,000	7.5	5.0	8.0	6.0	8.0	6.0	7.0	5.5
65.000	7.5	5.5	7.5	6.0	7.5	6.0	6.5	5.0

Source: "Consumer Views," Citibank, July 1976. Reprinted with permission of The Wall Street Journal, © Dow Jones & Company, Inc. (1976). All rights reserved.

Note: The above table is concerned with how much insurance you need to replace earnings. Thus, it does not include any coverage of the expenses associated with the death of the wage earner.

* Assuming federal income taxes for a family of four (two children). There are four exemptions and the old standard deduction. State and local taxes are disregarded.

** Assuming you have only two exemptions. (Any children are now grown.)

are the Social Security benefits it receives. The more the family gets from Social Security, the less is the amount of life insurance needed. The figures do not assume any income from earning assets such as stocks and bonds or savings accounts or any other type of income other than Social Security.

SELECTING AN AGENT AND A POLICY

Insurance companies that sell life insurance often also sell other kinds of insurance such as health, fire, or auto. Thus, when you talk to an insurance agent about life insurance, he or she is likely to try to sell you several other kinds of insurance too. It may or may not be advantageous for you to buy all your insurance from one agent, for a company which is quite competitive in one line may not be in others. It is, however, convenient and may cause the agent to be more attentive to your needs.

There are two kinds of life insurance agents. One represents only one company and is an employee of the insurance company—*company agents.* The other type represents more than one company and is called an *independent life agent.* The latter are likely to be the more aggressive since they exist on commissions alone. Company agents are often more informed about the policies they sell, but the independent agent is the one who will give you help in comparison shopping. Life insur-

ance agents sell themselves as much as they sell their product. Generally they seek out their customers rather than vice versa.

A life insurance agent can be certified somewhat like a person who passes an exam to become a certified public accountant. The life insurance agent becomes a certified life underwriter. The turnover in life insurance agents is tremendous; thus, many agents know very little about their business due to their inexperience. For this reason, it is a good idea to consider dealing with a certified life underwriter (C.L.U.) or some other agent who has long been in the business and has a good reputation. When inquiring among those you know to ascertain an agent's reputation, be sure to ask how any claims made on the company or companies he represents are handled. Dealing with an agent and/or company that tries to avoid settling a claim can be very expensive in terms of both time and money. Insurance companies and their agents can differ substantially in their attitudes toward handling claims. Collecting can be a routine matter or like getting blood out of a turnip. If they are clearly unreasonable, consult a lawyer. Sometimes telling them this is your plan will change their attitude. Take your business elsewhere if you are not happy. Their tenderest nerve is the one in their pocketbook. Don't let an agent stampede you into switching companies though. The extra commission he or she is after doesn't help you.

A life insurance agent is much more likely to be a friend or relative than are the salespersons of other products and services, because life insurance companies need a personal connection more than does someone selling a more appealing and impersonal product or service. Life insurance companies encourage their agents to exploit their personal relationships with other people; thus, you can expect to find life insurance agents at church on Sunday and at the civic club luncheon on Wednesday. (What would civic clubs do without insurance agents, bankers, doctors, and lawyers?) A life insurance agent's income is extremely closely correlated with how many and what types of policies are sold. Thus, there is a strong incentive to sell you a policy whether or not you need it, and sometimes they have more incentive to sell you the policy least suitable for your needs than the policy that would be best for you. Thus, you should not accept uncritically what an agent tells you.

Most large employers and some small ones offer their employees *group insurance,* and it is normally cheaper than like policies written on an individual basis. This lower cost is in part due to the fact that there is only one agent involved and many policyholders; thus, only one sales commission is spread over many people's premiums. There are also cost savings through central administration of the policies. Before considering an individual policy you should see if you are eligible for a group policy, and then compare it with individual policies. The group policy will likely be a cheaper way to cover any needs both cover. If so, an individual policy need not be taken out unless the group policy's coverage is inadequate. A variety of organizations offer group insurance plans to their members.

Life insurance agents will often total a policy's premiums; subtract cash value at maturity and estimated dividends, and divide by the number of years in order to derive an annual cost of the protection this policy gives. Agents will show you figures for other companies' policies which are higher. Don't let them sell you on this basis alone. Insurance companies must provide you with an adjusted cost index to allow you to comparison shop for life insurance. Examine this. Since most policies have the same basic provisions, beware of letting yourself be impressed with what are only basic provisions. Evaluate the value of the "extras" a policy offers. Do you need them? If so, how much are they worth to you? Don't forget that money in the near future is worth much more to you than that in the distant future. Lower costs or dividends in the future should be discounted to reflect their lesser value than an equal amount of money today.

Always shop around for insurance. All policies and companies are not alike in terms of benefits and costs or quality of service provided. Insurance companies take great pains to make comparison shopping difficult by not offering policies that exactly duplicate other companies'. It is a good idea to discover how much each $1000 of coverage costs, and how much of each premium goes toward your coverage rather than the company's expenses. Comparison shopping can really pay off, as there are vast differences in how much the same coverage will cost between companies. It isn't enough simply to compare premiums. Policies with the same premium may pay different rates of interest on the savings portion of a whole life policy, pay different dividends, or retain less for profits and expenses. You need to consider all of these. Agents, however, will not want to provide this information. They probably will not have all this information with them when they come to your house if you don't ask for it.

Let an agent know you are shopping. Talk to your friends about the service they received from the companies and agents servicing them.

CASES FOR DISCUSSION

Case 1 Helen was divorced five years ago. She has two children, a boy 12 and a girl seven. Her mother keeps them while she works. Her ex-husband left the state, and she has been unable to get any money from him in the three years since he remarried.

Before her marriage, Helen worked as a secretary. In order to make more money, she took some courses that enabled her to get her present job as a legal secretary. She makes $10,000 a year before taxes. She is paying a mortgage on her home that costs her $200 a month. She has paid for her car, but will soon have to buy another one because it has 90,000 miles on it. She has no life insurance. She wonders if she needs some. Her ex-husband has made his out to his new wife and child. Would you recommend that Helen take out some life insurance? If so, how much and what kind?

Case 2 Steve ·was approached on campus by a fellow student who sells insurance. Steve has never thought about buying life insurance. The insurance agent told him he could get it a lot cheaper now than later. He can buy this policy on credit, paying for it after he graduates in two years. The agent suggests that he take out a $30,000 endowment policy. With inflation and all the protection he will need if he marries, that's very little insurance to have, the agent says, but it is all he can probably afford. The agent emphasized how rapidly the cash value of an endowment policy builds up compared to other types of whole life, and how it will provide Steve with a source of a loan to set up housekeeping if he should get married in five years or so. It will also provide a retirement nest egg. How would you advise Steve?

Case 3 At a recent civic club luncheon Peter was talking to a new member named Jane. Jane turned out to be an insurance broker who represents several different life insurance companies. When Peter had gotten married, he had gone to the office of an agent representing a major insurer whose ads Peter had seen for years. Peter had told the agent of his situation, and he had bought the type policy and amount the agent suggested. Since then, Peter has wondered if he did the right thing; so he asked Jane to come see him. Jane came by Peter's the next night. She showed Peter that he could get the same amount of insurance he has now from one of her companies at an annual cost of $50 less. Peter was ready to switch, but his wife, Jean, suggested they talk it over first. As soon as Jane left, Peter turned to Jean and asked her what possible reason there could be for not switching. What could Jean say?

Case 4 Harry asked an insurance agent about the possibility of his buying term insurance rather than whole life. That's O.K., the agent told him, if you just want to rent insurance. If you buy term, when the term is over, you have nothing to show for your premiums. It's like renting an apartment rather than buying a house. You can sell the house. You can borrow against the cash surrender value of your whole life insurance policy, and whole life is permanent. Term is temporary. Term is cheap for a while, but the premium will rise far above whole life's. Harry didn't know what to say. Term sure sounded bad, but why, if it's so bad, do some people say it's better? What would you tell Harry?

Case 5 Ken is really excited. He's just heard about this great way to get insurance on your life for nothing and make money too! What you do is agree to regularly buy shares in a mutual fund, and then borrow against them to pay the premium on the life insurance. The money Ken would borrow will be repaid with the earnings on his mutual fund shares. Thus, he will end up with a life insurance policy he pays nothing for and the mutual fund shares whose earnings he will then start receiving. How would you advise Ken if he came to you?

Case 6 Archie makes $20,000 a year before taxes. He has a $20,000 endowment policy and a $60,000 20-year limited payment policy on himself payable to his wife as primary beneficiary and his two children as secondary beneficiaries. He has $5,000 endowment policies on each of his two, teenaged children. He has a $30,000 straight life policy on his wife, Marjorie, with himself as the primary beneficiary and his children as secondary beneficiaries. Marjorie works part time as a photographer and makes $5,000 a year before taxes. Archie is 55, and his health is not very good. He has a demanding job as sales manager for a small manufacturing firm which keeps him under a severe strain most of the time. Marjorie is 35. They pay $325 a month on their mortgage and $200 on one of their two cars. Frequently they can't pay off their charge accounts on time. Both children want to go to expensive private colleges, one plans to do graduate work. They have insurance on their home and their cars. Marjorie is concerned about whether they have enough life insurance and the right kind. How would you advise her?

REVIEW QUESTIONS

1. Who needs life insurance?
2. What needs does life insurance meet?
3. What is the difference between whole life and term insurance?
4. What type of need would term insurance serve best?
5. What type of need would whole life insurance serve best?
6. What type of need does an annuity serve? (Consider limited payment and life annuities.)
7. Why don't term policies have cash surrender values like whole life policies?
8. Why are whole life policies sold as a way to save?
9. How do you go about deciding how much insurance to buy?
10. Compare and contrast all the different types of policies mentioned in the chapter.
11. What is the load?
12. What is an option? A rider? A clause?
13. Since they cost more, why would one want a limited-payment whole life policy?
14. Why not just compare the premiums on a term policy and a whole life policy for the same amount of insurance, and buy the one that is the cheaper?

YOUR PLAN: CHAPTER 13

**Questions you must answer
before buying life insurance:**

1. What are my total assets and liabilities, and what is the difference between the two?
2. If my liabilities (amounts due others now or later) exceed my assets, who would suffer what costs if I should die soon? What would be the case if I die many years from now?
3. If my assets exceed my liabilities, would this difference be large enough to cover the costs caused by my death?
4. If my excess of assets over liabilities is less than the amount of my cash holdings, could nonmonetary assets be liquidated quickly without significant loss so as to be used to cover death-related costs?
5. My death would cause what amount of financial hardship to whom by eliminating a source of support?
6. How would the amount of financial hardship caused by my death vary according to when I die?
7. I would not willingly allow those suffering financial hardship as a result of my death to exceed what amount?
8. By how much does my current and anticipated future income exceed necessary costs annually? (Necessary costs are those needed to cover minimal housing, food, clothing, medical services, transportation, other types of insurance, and other basic necessities.)
9. How much of the income not needed for necessities am I willing to spend to cover the amount by which my liabilities may exceed my assets, costs associated with my death, or financial loss to others resulting from my death?
10. Is the protection offered by any of the available life insurance policies equal to the amount needed to cover the costs and financial loss caused by my death for the price I'm willing and able to pay?
11. How do other savings plans available to me compare with the ones associated with whole life policies?
12. If I cannot protect others from suffering any loss as a result of my death, how can I minimize the impact of this lack? (You can give them protection when they most need it. You can give those who are the least capable of handling hardship more protection than you give others.)

13. What, if any, retirement needs do I have that might be met via life insurance?
14. What substitutes for life insurance are available to me?
15. What would be my needs if I become disabled and unable to work? Can a life insurance policy help me meet these needs?
16. Does the agents' sales talks make sense? Are they deceiving me? (Perhaps they are making a dividend-paying policy look unduly good by paying a large total dividend, but most of this money will be paid far in the future; thus, you will lose the interest you could have earned if it had been declared earlier.)
17. Have I considered several different policies and carefully compared them?
18. Am I confident that any policy I am considering is one I can afford, that is, I will not in the future be forced to let it lapse?
19. Am I aiming at keeping my family from being in need or am I aiming higher, that is, maintaining their current standard of living?

How to Use Your Answers

In answering these questions you will need to refer to the chapter material that describes the types of benefits provided by the different types of life insurance and classifies all the costs and losses caused by your death.

Clearly these questions' answers enable you to determine the amount and types of protection you need and establishes priorities so that you can logically make any necessary trade-offs. For example, if more protection than you can afford is needed, and protection is most necessary if you die soon, a term policy may be preferred to a whole life policy. If both your spouse and children need protection, but you cannot provide for both to be protected, you should protect whichever of them most needs it. If you will save the difference between the higher-priced whole life policy and a term policy for the same amount of protection, and you will earn more on this saving than the insurance company will credit you for, the term policy is probably your best bet. If you just can't save any other way, a whole life policy may be for you the best choice.

Do you, in addition to life insurance, need additional retirement income or protection against being unable to work? If so, buy a policy that includes provisions for providing such protection. If your insurance needs will vary over the years, the protection acquired today should be obtained with appropriate future alterations in mind.

As the years pass, your best estimate of your insurance needs may turn out to have been wrong, thus you should regularly re-evaluate your insurance needs.

Preparing for Retirement and Beyond

OBJECTIVES

When you have completed this chapter, you will have accomplished the following:

1. Know how to prepare for retirement.
2. Be familiar with the Social Security system.
3. Be familiar with the characteristics of the various private pension plans.
4. Be familiar with the various types of annuities.
5. Know how to draw up a will.
6. Know how to minimize the taxes due on your estate.
7. Be aware of the pitfalls in planning for retirement and beyond.

8. Be familiar with the following terms:

Employee Retirement Income Security Act	insured pension plan
vesting	trust fund plan
qualified pension plan	combination plan
profit sharing plan	intestate
employee stock option plan	executor
Keogh plan	probate
deferred annuity	joint ownership
immediate annuity	living trust
refund annuity	testamentary trust
fixed annuity	revocable trust
variable annuity	irrevocable trust

The normal reaction of people under 30 to talk about retirement planning is disinterest. Retirement is so far away that it hardly even seems a reality. Intellectually young people may recognize that, if they live long enough, they will retire, but emotionally they really don't accept the possibility of someday being old and, maybe, poverty-stricken. This only happens to other people. People are even more likely to take this attitude toward death. It isn't just happenstance that life insurance agents talk about living protection rather than life insurance and call it life rather than death insurance. Even when young people don't refuse to face this side of reality, they may believe that there's so much that can happen between now and then, that it is futile to plan for retirement and death. Yet, anyone can, at any time, be retired prematurely by an accident or illness, and each year every age group experiences deaths.

If you were walking beside a skyscraper and, upon hearing a noise, looked up and saw, several stories above you, that part of the building was collapsing, would you just stand there because there was little chance that running would save you? People who would try to avoid the building's collapse will, however, figuratively, just stand there and let retirement zap them. They explain that there is no use planning for retirement because inflation might be so great that it would enormously reduce the value of their savings for retirement. This is like saying that as the weather gets colder you are going to wear less rather than more because you can't wear enough. Inflation increases, not decreases, the need for retirement planning. Other people simply don't see retirement as a problem. Yet, it takes no great research to find out that a large portion of the current and previous generation of retirees, on the average, experienced a significant reduction in their standard of living upon retiring. Table 14–1 shows how much the average retiree had to live on in recent years. Some say that Social Security will take care of them, not realizing that its purpose is little more than keeping you free from starving to death. Table 14–2 shows how much those on Social Security have been receiving in recent years.

It is during your later years that you are most likely to encounter your largest emergency expenditures, and you will then be the least prepared, physically and emotionally, to meet these challenges. The magnitude of the problems you are likely to face, and their likelihood of occurrence, is so great that it is foolish to fail to make any plans for coping with them.

Retirement planning produces both current and future benefits. If you wait to take out health or life insurance, you may not be able to pass the necessary physical to get them later. If you can get them later, the annual premiums will be higher. Money you are now saving for retirement purposes can be used before then if a greater need arises,

TABLE 14–1   Income of Persons 65 Years Old and Older, 1960 to 1976

	1960	1965	1970	1975	1976
Male median income	$1576	$2037	$2828	$4535	$4959
Female median income	$ 797	$ 952	$1397	$2375	$2642

Source: U.S. Department of Commerce, *1976 Statistical Abstract of the United States,* table no. 473, p. 303.

TABLE 14–2   Social Security Retirement Benefits, 1960 to 1975

	1960	1970	1975
Male			
Average monthly benefit	$82	$131	$228
Full	82	139	245
Reduced: Before reduction[1]	x^2	129	228
After reduction	x	115	207
Female			
Average monthly benefit	60	101	182
Full	62	112	206
Reduced: Before reduction	64	106	NA[3]
After reduction	$56	$ 94	$169

Source: U.S. Department of Commerce, *1976 Statistical Abstract of the United States,* table no. 474, p. 303.

[1] There is a maximum and a minimum benefit (full and reduced), both of which are reduced if one starts drawing benefits before age 65.

[2] x—Not applicable for males at that time.

[3] NA—Not available.

or it can be used as collateral for a loan. You will live in the home you buy now and pay for it before your retirement. (Most people are in a much better position to make house payments before they retire than after.) You will currently enjoy the income from income-generating assets purchased today to supplement other sources of retirement income. In other words, to a substantial extent, *provision for retirement and providing for current security are accomplished together.* The same is true of providing for your heirs after your death. Thus, many of the steps you need to take to provide for retirement and death have already been discussed. For this reason, this chapter will only consider matters largely or exclusively concerned with retirement and estate planning.

PLANNING FOR RETIREMENT

No plan can be made without an objective. Therefore, the first step in retirement planning is deciding *how much money you will need.* The second step is deciding *where this money will come from.* The material on budgeting discussed in Chapter 2 explains how to go about estimating your expenses. Clearly, both the absolute and relative size of various expenses will vary between youth and old age. Medical expenses will likely be higher, but there will usually be no children to educate, and, generally, clothing needs will be less. Older people usually eat a bit less than when they were younger, and they spend less on home furnishings. Many retirees have a number of active years left, and their expenditures on recreation and travel may be relatively high, assuming they have arranged to have the money to indulge in these luxuries.

Most retired people collect Social Security. Many also collect either or both employer pensions and union pensions. Some collect veteran's benefits. Others receive interest on savings or corporate or municipal bonds. Dividends from stock and wages from part-time jobs provide some retirees with funds. Rent from property owned is yet another source for a few retirees. Some receive payments from an annuity they set up in their earlier years, a very few receive royalties. The sale of either tangible or intangible property provides a one-time source of funds for some. Health insurance and/or Medicare reduce the need for income. Destitute retirees are eligible for welfare.

A major problem in planning for retirement is that you do not know for how many years to plan. *The solution to this problem is to arrange for all or at least a substantial proportion of your retirement income to continue indefinitely after you retire.* It is dangerous to place great reliance on income from a part-time job, as you do not know if or for how long you can continue to work. The sooner you start preparing for retirement, the easier it will be. For example, if you deposit $1000 today at 5 percent, 25 years from now you will have $3386.40. If you wait 15 years to set aside this money, 25 years from now you will only have $1628.90. If you wait 15 years to set aside enough money to have $3386.40, you will have to set aside $2078.95. In other words, you will have to put up more than twice as much to accumulate the same amount! If you deposit a second $1000 one year from now, in 25 years your $2000 will have grown to $6611.54. If you deposit a third $1000 two years from now, in 25 years you will have $9683.10.

There are two reasons for setting aside money for retirement at interest. One is to reduce the amount of money you have to set aside. The other is to try to offset inflation. Only if the after-tax interest rate is higher than the rate of inflation will you reduce how much must be set aside in order to have a given future amount. If the interest rate is less than the rate of inflation, you will have to set aside additional money simply to cover the reduction in the value of your savings caused by the decline in the purchasing power of the dollar. In order to get a relatively high interest rate, you will have to take more risk. It is not a good idea to take a great deal of risk with money destined to provide you with necessities.

SOCIAL SECURITY

Social Security is a product of the Great Depression of the 1930s. It is a federal government-run pension program to aid the aged, impoverished, and disabled. It is financed by a tax both on the covered employee and the employer. If you work in a "covered" job, you have to pay this tax. Almost the only privately employed people not covered are teenage, temporary babysitters. In 1937, when Social Security taxes were first paid, the most anyone paid was $30 a year, and in 1940, when the first benefits were paid, aged recipients got a minimum of $10 a month and a maximum of $38.40. Even back then, this was not much money. With only this much money, you couldn't come close to the average standard of living then. By 1976, the combined, maximum tax paid per employee had risen to $1790. Benefits, too, had risen (see Table 14–2). For employers, both their tax payments and the employee's were expenses associated with obtaining the services of the employee. Thus, employers consider both part of their wage bills. Both wages and the Social Security tax paid are tax-deductible expenses for employers.

By 1976 self-employed persons were allowed to opt for coverage, and they paid up to $1209 plus income taxes on their Social Security

tax. In 1976 a working couple could pay up to $3580, but they might be entitled to no higher benefit payment than a couple with only one of them employed. This lack of correlation between what is paid for Social Security benefits and what is received illustrates the fact that *Social Security is not really insurance.* Social Security is responsive to need;

insurance is not. For example, if two workers die, and both paid the same amount into Social Security, but one has ten children and the other only two, the former's family will draw a larger benefit than the latter's. If, however, they had life insurance policies, they would receive the same benefit.

If Social Security was an insurance program, sufficient reserves would have to be set aside to create a fund from which the benefits promised would be paid. Insured persons would have a vested property interest in the money they paid into their account, and the amount of benefits to be paid out when the insured person retired, died, or became disabled would be directly related to the amount of premiums paid into the system. The so-called Social Security trust fund is in no way large enough to cover promised benefits. If you continue to work after 65 and earn enough money, you cannot collect any Social Security benefits. If you collect Social Security benefits, what you collect is not directly related to how much you paid into the system. Thus, some people end up paying more for less than others do, and vice versa.

Social Security is simply a system whereby the taxes paid by current workers are distributed among retired and disabled workers or the dependents of deceased workers, who worked in covered employment for enough quarters to entitle them to at least a minimum payment. (How you earn a quarter and how many you need varies with circumstances.)

More than half the families in the United States now pay more in Social Security taxes than they do in federal income taxes, and there is a good chance that the relative size of Social Security taxes will rise and/or that other tax receipts will have to be used to make Social Security benefit payments. The reason for this is that the program is underfinanced. The reason it is underfinanced is that in the past recipients as a whole have been collecting more than they paid into the system, and the ratio of active to retired workers is declining. In 1955, for example, there were seven workers paying into Social Security for each beneficiary drawing money from it. By 1976 that ratio was down to three to one, and it will go lower if the birth rate doesn't pick up.

Social Security taxes are somewhat regressive because all wages above a given level—the income base—are not subject to this tax. This income base has gone up every year since 1971. From 1972 to 1976 Social Security taxes more than doubled. Currently the income base is $17,700 and the tax rate is 6.05 percent. The average retirement benefit for single people in 1976 was $214 a month. The average benefit received by married couples was $372. In 1978 the base rose to $42,600 and the tax rate to 7.15 percent.

Social Security provides six kinds of benefits:

1. Workers receive a monthly benefit after retirement or after

age 72, even if the worker is still employed full time. If retirement occurs at age 65, a full benefit will be paid. If retirement comes before age 65, but not before age 62, a partial benefit will be paid.

2. The dependents of a retired worker also receive a monthly benefit payment. If a dependent wife has coverage through having worked in covered employment, she can take either her own benefit or her dependent benefit, *but not both.* A wife qualifies to receive a dependent's benefit at age 62, but she cannot receive a full benefit. She can receive a full benefit if she begins collecting at age 65. Her full benefit is less than the one to which her husband would have been entitled. Unmarried dependent children under 18 or full-time students up to 22 years old are entitled to benefits.

3. Benefits are also paid to the dependents of a covered worker if the worker dies. If a widow remarries before age 60, she loses her benefits.

4. A lump sum payment is made to cover burial expenses when a covered worker dies. Whoever pays this expense is entitled to this lump sum benefit.

5. Disability benefits are paid to workers under 65 if they become disabled.

6. Medicare is provided for persons 65 years or older. Medicare provides both hospital and medical insurance. You are automatically entitled to hospital care, but medical care is optional. If you elect medical insurance, you must pay a monthly premium.

The size of your benefit payment depends on (1) your age at retirement, (2) whether you retired because of disability, (3) whether you have dependents, and (4) your average annual earnings in covered employment, or the income base if your average annual earnings exceed the income base. Clearly, Social Security is arranged to encourage you to work until you are 65 and to discourage you from working if you are over 65. (If you earn wages of more than $4700 after retirement, your benefit is reduced by $1.00 for every $2.00 earned.) Interestingly, this key age was decided arbitrarily about 100 years ago by Otto von Bismark, who set up Germany's first social insurance system. Pressure from older persons who wish to work beyond age 65 and the financial problems of the Social Security system led to Congress in 1977 passing a law prohibiting employers from forcing retirement until one reaches age 70 in private industry. Government workers can't be forced to retire except via inability to perform. In private industry the inability to perform the work can be used to force retirement before age 70.

Your employer annually sends data to the Social Security Administration so that it can record both the amount of your earnings and the number of quarters worked. *You should periodically verify this information.* To do this, you can get a postcard Form OAR-7004,

"Request for Statement of Earnings," from your local Social Security office or the Postal Service. You should do this every three years because you may not be able to correct any farther back than three years.

In order to receive Social Security payments, you must apply for them and prove that you are entitled to them. You will need your Social Security number, proof of your age, and marital records. If you are claiming survivor benefits, you will need a death certificate. A wife applying for benefits must also provide proof of her age. (Widowers can also claim benefits based on their deceased wife's record.) For the benefit of any of your survivors, you should keep them informed as to what they would be entitled to and where you keep your records.

Employees of the federal government are not covered by Social Security, but they are covered by other federal government-sponsored retirement programs. Railroad workers, though employed by private firms, have their own federal retirement program, which is administered by the Railroad Retirement Board. Some state and local government employees are covered only by state-sponsored programs. Veterans are entitled to disability payments, medical care benefits, widows' and dependents' benefits, and death benefits if they served in the armed forces during certain periods of time.

TAX BREAKS FOR THE ELDERLY

To encourage people to do certain things, the federal government allows them to postpone paying taxes if they do one of these things. Postponing paying taxes can be a real boon. Suppose the government lets you put off paying $100 in taxes for 20 years. If you put this money in a 20-year government bond, which is riskless, and you earn 5 percent annually on it, when the time finally comes around for you to pay the tax collector, you would have $265.33!

To assist you in saving for retirement, the federal government, under certain conditions, will let you deduct from your taxable income contributions you make to a retirement plan. You will, however, have to pay taxes on this money later when you receive it as retirement benefits. Since your marginal tax rate will probably be lower after you retire (because your income is lower), you will end up paying a smaller tax on this money as well as putting off, to your advantage, paying income taxes on it. To encourage your employer to set up a pension plan for you, the government reduces the cost of doing so by allowing employers to deduct the contributions made to this program from their taxable incomes. If you should put after-tax money into a retirement program, the federal government will not levy income taxes on this money when you receive it as retirement benefits.

Federal tax policy is sometimes designed to help you maximize your welfare in retirement and that of your heirs. For example, for individuals dying after 1976, the value of an annuity receivable by any beneficiary (other than an executor) under an individual retirement savings program is excluded from the decedent's gross estate. Thus, this money is not subject to the estate tax. This annuity must provide for a series of substantially equal periodic payments to be made to the beneficiary for life or over a period extending for at least 36 months after the decedent's death. This exclusion is limited, however, when any payment into the plan was not allowable as a deduction for income tax purposes, and amounts payable in a lump sum will be included in the decedent's gross estate.

Another benefit to the aged is the treatment of the sale of a residence. If you are age 65 or older before the date of sale of your residence and have owned and used the property as your principal residence for at least 5 out of the 8 years preceding the sale, you may elect to exclude part or all of the gain on the sale from your gross income. Thus, this amount is not subject to income taxation. For sales in tax years beginning after 1976, you may exclude the entire gain if the adjusted sales price is $35,000 or less. Because their income is usually limited, the elderly are particularly likely to have to sell their homes because they cannot afford to pay their rising property tax bills. Some localities give elderly people a property tax break for this reason.

There is also a federal tax credit for the elderly. The credit is 15 percent of a portion of your income. The amount of income on which the credit is based depends on your age, your filing status, and, if married, the age of your spouse.

PRIVATE PENSION PLANS

A private pension plan is one where the responsibility to pay pensions lies with a private rather than a public (governmental) organization. Private pension plans may be either group or individual plans. The government is involved in private pension plans in that it regulates them and provides tax incentives to promote them. It also insures some of these plans through the Federal Pension Benefit Guaranty Corporation. If your employer goes broke and, for this reason, is unable to stand by his pension commitments, this agency may fully or partially cover your benefits. The most important pension law is the Employee Retirement Income Security Act of 1974 (ERISA).

There is no law requiring employers provide you with a pension plan. If they don't, you will be left to your own devices. Because of the relatively stringent provisions of ERISA, employers are less likely to provide pension plans now than in the past. However, there are also more individual plans available now than ever before.

Thanks to ERISA, if you are 25 or have at least one year's service with a company, you usually can't be excluded from any pension plan it offers its employees. The same pension benefits must be paid women as men. If you contribute to the plan, you are, under all circumstances, entitled to all of the benefits derived from your contributions. Usually you are vested in stages. *Vesting* refers to your right to pension benefits whether or not you stay in a company's employ. Generally, you will have to be at least 50-percent vested after ten years and fully vested in 15 years. If you are fully vested, the company must pay you a full pension. The vesting provisions of ERISA prevent a company from making you wait many years to be vested or never vesting you or firing you just before retirement in order to get out of paying you a pension. This makes it more economical for you to change jobs, since it involves little or no loss of pension benefits.

Your employer may handle his employee pension plan on either a group or an individual basis. An individual plan is one set up for an individual rather than a group of individuals. The most significant private pension plan is the *qualified pension plan* offered by corporate employers. (The first such plan was established by the American Express Company in 1875. For many years few employers had plans, but today just under 45 percent of the people employed in commerce and industry are covered under pension plans.) The qualified plan is attractive to employers because contributions made to it are deductible for federal income tax purposes, and the income earned on the investment of these funds is exempt from federal income taxation until it is distributed to the plan's beneficiaries. (Your contributions, if any, are not tax deductible.) The qualified plan is safest for the employee because it is regulated by the federal government.

Some employers provide for their employees' retirement needs through a *qualified profit sharing plan*. A profit sharing plan is advantageous to employers because they do not have to make a contribution to the plan unless a profit is earned. Profit sharing is risky for employees because they don't know what they will get—they may get more than they would with a regular pension plan, or may get less.

Employers who establish an *employee stock option plan* (ESOP) gain additional tax advantages over the standard profit sharing plan. An ESOP also allows a company's employees to acquire a significant percentage of the firm's stock without putting up any money of their own. Employees may also end up owning a business or businesses through the investment policies of a *union pension fund*. It is estimated that union pension funds already own 30 percent of America's business, and it is predicted that their share will grow substantially in the future.

Employers, of course, hope that worker ownership will cause workers to be more concerned with holding down costs and increasing profits.

Employees of duly qualified charitable organizations or public school systems may provide for their retirement needs through an annuity contract called a *tax-deferred annuity*. The amount of money paid into this plan may be deducted from your income before taxes are computed. Taxes must be paid, however, when payments are received. The tax collector always gets you in the end!

Self-employed individuals can establish a qualified pension or profit sharing plan for themselves. These plans are popularly called *Keogh plans* and were made possible by the Self-Employed Individuals Tax Retirement Act of 1962. An employer cannot set up such a plan unless the employees are also included. Up to $7500 a year can be put into such a plan and be deducted from your income before computing your income tax liability. If 15 percent of your self-employed income is less than $7500, this is all you can deduct.

If you receive a salary from some employer and also receive income from self-employment, you can have both a company pension plan and a Keogh plan. Income taxes will have to be paid on benefits as received.

If you are not eligible for any employer-sponsored pension plan, you can establish your own pension plan, which is called an *individual retirement account (IRA)*. Only earned income can be placed in this account; not investment income. You may make tax-deductible contributions (up to a limit of 15 percent of your annual pay with a ceiling of $1500) to this account, and the investment income earned on this money will generally be free from income tax. (If one spouse is unemployed, a married couple can contribute up to $1750 a year.) As is the case with a Keogh plan, withdrawals before age 59½ trigger severe tax penalties. You will pay income tax on benefits as received.

You are not eligible to set up an IRA if you are participating in a qualified pension, profit sharing, stock bonus, annuity, or bond purchase plan of an employer. This is in contrast to the Keogh plan, which may be established even though you are covered by a qualified plan. Only self-employment income, however, may be put into a Keogh plan.

A self-employed person may select either an IRA or a Keogh plan. If the IRA is selected, employees do not have to be provided a retirement plan as is the case with the Keogh plan, but the Keogh plan may produce higher deductible limits, and lump-sum distributions qualify for a more favorable tax treatment. Thus, deciding which is the better plan is not simple and will vary with circumstances. An IRA can be set up at either a bank or other thrift institution, at an insurance company, or at a brokerage house of a mutual fund. A Keogh plan can also be set up via a variety of investments, such as mutual funds, bank savings certificates, and life insurance company annuities. A special attraction of IRA's is their "roll-over" mechanism. Under certain conditions, it allows you to take money from a pension fund accumulated at a previous job and continue to shelter it until you make withdrawals.

Annuities

Instead of, or to supplement, a retirement plan provided by your employer and/or your union, you can purchase an annuity from a life insurance company. (An annuity is simply a series of payments.) An annuity may be purchased with either a single premium or periodic premium payments. You specify when you will begin receiving it. This annuity may be either *immediate* or *deferred*. An immediate annuity must be paid for with a single premium. It is an annuity that starts paying benefits within a short period of time. For a young person, an immediate annuity for life provides a much lower annual benefit than a deferred one because little of the principal can be liquidated per benefit payment. For an old person, because of a shorter life expectancy, the difference between benefits of the two types of annuities is much less, and he or she probably needs and wants to start collecting benefits in the near future. If the *annuitant* (beneficiary of the annuity) dies before payments begin, there is usually a refund, which will be paid the annuitant's beneficiary. Usually all the money paid by the annuitant is refunded. The annuity may be either *fixed* or *variable*. The latter is more risky, because you don't get a fixed return; you get a varying return, which may be either greater or less than the fixed return you could get for the same cost. (The most secure source of retirement income is a U.S. Treasury retirement bond.)

An annuity is one solution to the problem of a large, one-time, *lump-sum payout* from a company pension or profit sharing plan. This payment may come either when you are fired or quit a job, or when you retire or become disabled. Your heirs may receive such a payment when you die. There are several ways you can reduce the portion of a lump sum payment that you will have to pay Uncle Sam. You only have 60 days, however, to decide which "escape route" to take. Fortunately, most plans provide you with the option of a life annuity for you or your spouse in lieu of a lump sum payment. If you take the lump sum amount, you must consider it ordinary income, but you can subject it to a 10-year averaging device which will reduce your tax bill (as in the case of the annuity) by spreading, for tax purposes, the receipt of the money over several years. Another option is to set up an IRA. A lump sum payment will not present a severe tax problem if a large portion of the contributions to the pension plan was made by you, and, therefore, were not tax deductible as are an employer's.

An annuity can be considered a reverse life insurance policy. A life insurance policy pays off when you die; a *straight life annuity contract* pays off if you live. If you buy a deferred annuity, there is a period called the accumulation period, which is when you are paying for the annuity but receiving no benefits. If the annuity is a regular or straight annuity and you die during this period, your heirs receive nothing, even though you may have paid a lot of money to the insurance company providing the annuity. Because many people object to this possibility, life insurance companies also offer what is called a *refund annuity*. With this type of annuity, your beneficiary receives whatever you have paid for the annuity, less any benefits you have collected up until the time of your death. This can be paid to your beneficiary either as a lump sum payment or as an annuity. Another option is the *life annuity with installments certain*. This type of annuity contract guarantees that benefits will be paid a minimum length of time whether or not you live that long. Benefits will be paid as long as you live. You will have to pay more for the refund and installments certain type annuities than the straight annuity.

Many life insurance companies will allow you to convert, via its cash surrender value, an endowment or whole life insurance policy into an annuity. If this is done when you retire, clearly you will want an immediate, rather than a deferred, annuity. If you had, instead, bought a combination life insurance and retirement annuity policy originally, you would have acquired a deferred annuity. If you do not need life insurance, you should simply buy an annuity.

An annuity may be either *fixed* or *variable*. The main purpose of a variable annuity is to counter inflation. In the past people have purchased fixed annuities that seemed quite adequate, only to find that by the time they retired that prices had risen so that their annuity is inadequate to cover their expenses. Unfortunately, the average variable annuity has not, in recent years, done a very good job in equaling or beating inflation, largely due to the poor performance of the stock market. Earlier, when there were fewer variable annuities available and the rate of the inflation was low, variable annuities did rather well. But, recently some variable annuity recipients have found themselves receiving less money than they would have gotten from an equally priced fixed annuity.

Clearly in selecting a variable annuity, you must be concerned with the issuer's investment policy. Is it one that stands a good chance of success? Are it's managers competent? Do not forget that your objective is keeping up with the cost of living; not the Dow Jones Industrial average, whose fluctuations do not exactly mirror the cost of living. Since salary increases are likely to roughly match rises in the cost of living, some people simply increase the size of their fixed annuity as their salary increases. Others buy both a variable and a fixed annuity. (If prices should fall—not very likely, it seems—those with fixed annuities will be better off when they retire than they had planned for.)

Endowment and retirement income contracts purchased from life insurance companies are considered to be annuity contracts appropriate for the funding of an IRA, but any portion of your premium attributable to acquiring insurance protection is not tax deductible. Because of the tax deductibility of the retirement portion of your premium with an IRA, it is better to acquire an insurance company anuuity as part of an IRA than to buy it outside this program.

An IRA contract may be either fixed or variable in terms of both benefits and premiums. Your interest in the IRA contract must be non-forfeitable. Any dividends earned must be used to purchase additional benefits or to reduce your premium. ERISA regulations discourage premature or lump sum distributions. Only in case of your death or disability can distribution take place before age 59½. Distributions are taxed as ordinary income in the year received.

The major disadvantage of all annuities is that *they tie up your capital.* With some exceptions—for example, some few withdrawals are allowed from tax-deferred annuity plans for public school employees and employees of charitable institutions—the money you pay for an annuity cannot be used until benefits begin. Unlike the cash surrender value of life insurance or stocks and bonds, the annuity cannot be used to borrow money. Thus, the annuity has little current value—it is truly an investment for retirement.

The Company Pension Plan

A company pension plan must treat all employees alike. Employees may or may not have a choice as to whether or not they participate in the plan. If the employee contributes to the plan, he or she usually has the option to participate or not to participate. Frequently, an employee must be with a company for a certain period of time or have attained a given age before becoming eligible to join the plan. The purpose of attaining a given age before becoming eligible to join the plan is to avoid covering young employees, who are in an age group with a high rate of turnover. Persons beyond a certain age when they are employed may not be eligible because of the high cost of including them since they are so near retirement. ERISA prohibits a company from excluding any employee hired more than five years before the plan's normal retirement date. The normal retirement age in most plans has always been 65.

Most company pension plans give the employee the option to retire before 65 on a reduced pension. In some cases this is possible only in the case of total and permanent disability. ERISA requires that you, as an employee, be allowed to choose between a higher pension for the rest of your life and a lower pension for the rest of either you or your spouse's life, whichever is the longer. The amount of your benefit is usually based on the size of your salary and number of years of service with the company. Normally, only basic compensation is considered in setting the pension benefit, that is, bonuses and other extraordinary compensation is not included. Either an average of all earnings or earnings in a shorter period of time just before retirement is used in computing the benefit payment's size. Due to promotions and inflation, the use of the latter average normally results in the higher benefit payment. Some employers periodically adjust pension benefits upward with inflation, including those of people already retired. Often, however, only those not yet retired are affected.

An *insured pension* plan is the most secure. With this kind of plan, a life insurance company is the plan's funding agent. Contributions are paid to it either directly or indirectly. For given sized payment, the insurance company will provide given benefit payments. A *trust fund plan* is a plan whose funding agency is a corporate fiduciary or an individual or individuals. (Most union pension plans take this route. Controlling the pension fund are a board of trustees, who are usually union officers.) Larger companies are more likely to have a trust fund plan than small companies because for a small firm, a trust fund is not economical or safe enough. A *combination plan* involves the use of both funding agencies. Either individual contracts or a group contract may be utilized. Small employers favor the former. The individual contract plan combines whole life insurance with a retirement plan. Group pension plans are simply pension plans, but employers often take out a group term life insurance policy so that employee's dependents will receive a death benefit other than the return, if any, of the employee's contributions to the plan.

A *profit sharing plan* is a fund established for employees' benefit by an employer paying into it some percent of the business' profits. Benefits may be entirely paid currently, in the future as retirement benefits, or both currently and in the future, which, of course, is not true of pension plans. ERISA's requirements for pension funds relative to vesting, minimum funding, and employer liabilities apply to profit sharing plans. The relative size of an employee's benefit may be determined by either his or her level of compensatnon, years of service, or a combination of compensation and service. As is the case with a pension plan, employees must be *fully vested*—entitled to all contributions made in their behalf—at the time of retirement. Vesting occurs more rapidly under a profit sharing plan than under a pension plan. There is no limit as to how high your pension may be with a profit sharing plan. It all depends on how profitable the business is. Profit sharing plans are more flexible than pension plans in that you can withdraw some of the money and still remain in the plan.

An ESOP (employee stock option plan) provides benefits similar to those of a profit sharing plan, except that employer contributions are not necessarily dependent upon profits and the benefits are distributed in the form of shares of stock in the company. ESOP's have to meet the requirements of ERISA relative to participation, vesting, and prudence. (An ESOP should not be confused with a *stock option plan,* where an employee is given, in lieu of other compensation, the option to buy, at what promises to be a favorable price, company stock.) An ESOP is an employee trust that borrows money which it lends to the employer in exchange for stock. The employer provides the money to repay the loan. The employer gets a tax break by borrowing through the trust because, if the money is borrowed from a financial institution directly, only the interest on the loan would be tax deductible, but, by using the trust, both principal and interest are deductible.

WHY DRAW UP A WILL?

Don't draw up a will if you want to cause dissension in your family, make sure your wishes aren't carried out, and reduce what your heirs receive when you die. If, instead, you wish to avoid all these things, prepare a will.

Some people think there is no reason for them to prepare a will. They are young and have practically no estate. Yet, anyone can be killed in an accident and the circumstances of the accident may be such that somebody can collect a lot of money from the person or persons who caused your death. You can name who would get this money in a will. Other people say that they can't afford the legal costs. Yet, while it is best to have a lawyer draw up your will, you can draw one up for nothing. (Simple wills can be drawn up by a lawyer at only a small cost.) Another economical possibility is avoiding the need for a will by *joint ownership.* (A gift tax may be incurred except when the transfer is of your home to your spouse.) To do this, you simply put your property in your name and the name of your beneficiary. Joint ownership, however, doesn't assign your claims on others to anyone and may have a high, indirect cost in the long run, as well as a gift tax in the short run.

If you die without a will, which is called *intestate,* the state will, in effect, write a will for you. In the absence of a will or in the presence of an invalid will, state law will determine how your estate will be distributed. The *probate court* will appoint an administrator whose duties will approximate those of the executor of a will. The *executor* of a will is responsible for carrying out its provisions.

If you wait too long to draw up a will, it may be too late, as if, via illness or senility, you become incapable of carrying on your affairs, your relatives or others can get the probate court to appoint a *conservator* of your assets. (You can designate someone to handle your affairs for you by giving him or her the *power of attorney.* Be very cautious about giving someone this power!)

Unless you pass your property to others before you die, your estate will probably have to pass through the probate court of the state of your legal residence at the time of your death. (The Howard Hughes fiasco illustrates both the problems caused by a lack of a will and uncertainty about the deceased's place of legal residence.)

Some people believe that, at least in some places, the costs associated with probating a will are both excessive and frequently unnecessary. In part, this contention is part of the general argument that because of the lack of any real competition and the opportunity— through the legislature—to create work for themselves, lawyers' fees are too high and their services too often required. To sidestep the probate process, but maintain control of your property, they advocate the *inter vivos* or *living trust,* which will be discussed later.

Both the federal and state governments levy *estate taxes* on the property of deceased persons. Since tax laws are changed fairly frequently, whatever you do today to minimize taxes may have to be undone later because it no longer minimizes taxes. The Tax Reform Act of 1976, for example, radically changed the method of taxation of estates. Before this act, there were separate tax rates for gifts and estates, and prior appreciation of capital assets in an estate was not taxed. Far more estates were subject to taxation. (The IRS now estimates that by 1981, 98 percent of all estates will ecape taxation.)

The 1976 changes were so radical that any will drawn before 1977 to minimize estate taxes is probably out of date. Wills may also have to be redrawn because your circumstances change. You can adjust to changes in your circumstances either by drawing up a new will or by adding a codicil. A *codicil* is an addendum to a will that can either add to, qualify, or revoke a will. Another way to revoke a will is to simply tear up all copies of it. If you do make a change in your will, it is safest to do so formally, that is, have a lawyer handle it.

The 1976 tax reform act made it much more difficult and complicated to avoid estate taxes on large estates; thus, offsetting, at least some, the loss of tax revenues caused by exempting more estates from taxation. How you draw up a will can affect the taxes and other expenses which the estate will have to bear. The larger these expenses are the less your heirs will get.

Joint Ownership

Property can be transferred to someone automatically via joint ownership of the property. There are three forms of coownership. They are *tenancy in common, tenancy by the entirety,* and *joint tenancy.* Both personal and real property can be jointly owned. Married couples often jointly own checking and savings accounts, their home, rental property, land, and stocks and bonds. Using joint ownership to transfer property after death can produce some problems. If neither spouse has a will, and both die together in an accident, their property will be distributed according to state law; not their wishes. (If both have wills, the court will have to specify which is assumed to have died first.) In some states joint bank accounts are blocked until the will of the deceased partner is probated. The same is true of a safe deposit box both have access to. As a result, the surviving partner could be strapped for funds. (On the other hand, if the box is in the deceased's name only, the other will have to get a court order to get into it.) Two safe deposit boxes may be best!

If one spouse decides to leave the other, joint ownership enables one partner to leave the other partner holding the bag by emptying the joint bank account. If, however, a couple is not married, *joint tenancy* can prevent one partner leaving the other with nothing, that is, both paid for everything, such as a house, but one has title and gives nothing to the other when they separate. (This can be fought in court.)

If a man and a woman, each of whom has children by a previous marriage, marry, and one owns a home, joint tenancy may deny the original owner's children any share in the home. (If the original owner dies first, title will pass to his or her spouse, who may pass the house to his or her children. With a will, this could be avoided. The spouse could be given possession of the house for as long as he or she lived; then it would pass to the original owner's children or their heirs.)

Only if all property is jointly held or a trust set up is it possible to avoid probate and its cost in time and money. Only if all property is jointly held does it make any kind of sense not to have a will. Since everything of value you have or might have can't be put in joint ownership it is really never wise to have no will. Probate costs, however, will be reduced if the estate's size is reduced by joint ownership. Joint ownership, however, is not a way to avoid estate taxes. Under the 1976 tax act one-half of your estate or $250,000, whichever is greater, can be passed along to a spouse tax-free. If any property is jointly owned, this $250,000 limitation will be adjusted so that equal treatment will be accorded like couples, regardless of the way in which they hold property.

If you own property under the *tenants in common* method, each of you has an equal share in the property, that is, if there are two of you, each has one-half interest in the property. You can sell or give away your share at will. When you die, your share does not pass automatically to your coowner. Your share becomes part of your estate, and it is disposed of in accordance with your will, or, if there is no will, it is disposed of in accordance with state law. When a person dies intestate, many states will award the wife one-third and their children the other two-thirds. The court will appoint a guardian to look after minor children's interest.

The *tenancy by the entirety* method is available only to married couples. When one partner dies, the other automatically inherits his or her share. This cannot be changed by directing otherwise in a will. The property cannot be disposed of without the consent of your spouse. With *joint tenancy*, title passes to the survivor, but joint tenants need not be married to each other. Creditors can attach one owner's share.

Many states set aside what is called a *homestead exemption* or *family allowance*, which is a portion of the deceased's property which goes, without being subject to creditors' claims, to the deceased's dependents.

Drawing Up a Will

There are a variety of requirements you must meet in order to draw up a legal will. Each state sets up various requirements that must be met. All require that you be of legal age and be fully aware of what you are doing and its consequences. If you leave someone out of your will who would normally expect to be an heir, the will must indicate that you were of sound mind when you cut him or her out. Generally, it is wise to avoid bequests that hinge on the beneficiary's behavior or making vindictive statements. The will should indicate that you were aware of all the property to be distributed.

Most states will recognize a hand-written will if it is dated and signed. Under usual circumstances, such as when you have been injured in an accident, an oral will may be held valid. It is best to have a will drawn up by a lawyer, as it is then less likely to be successfully challenged. At a minimum, you should have the will notarized and witnessed. The witnesses certify that you declared to them that this instrument is your last will and testament, that you signed it, and that you appeared to do so of your own free will. They also certify that you appeared to be of sound mind and were free of undue influence from others.

You should name the person responsible for carrying out the provisions of your will. If this is a man, he is the executor; if it is a woman, she is the executrix. If you have substantial property, it is a good idea to name a bank, trust company, or a person skilled in finance as executor or coexecutor. If you name an executor and a coexecutor, the former may be a relative or family friend who will handle personal bequests, while the financial institution assumes the latter role and handles financial matters. (An executor can be a beneficiary of the will.)

It is the responsibility of the executor of a will to present the will and an inventory of the deceased's property to the probate court, which will determine if the will is legal both in form and in execution. If so, it will accept it for probate. The executor will insert a legal notice in a local newspaper to notify the deceased's creditors to present any claims they may have on this estate. The notice will also alert anyone wishing to contest the will. The court will hear these people and pass on the validity of their claims. If the will is not clear, the court will decide what the deceased meant. The executor will have the deceased's assets appraised and will file this information with the court. (Some people relieve their heirs of the cost of appraisal and provide the funds for taxes and other expenses, by liquidating part of their estate before death.) The executor will file a claim with the court for all expenses incurred in settling the estate, and he will also report all disbursements made. All expenses, including the executor's, incurred in settling an estate are paid from the estate.

Your will should be consistent with your financial plan: insurance, trusts, jointly held property, pension benefits, and so on. For example, some people might be taken care of by being named as a beneficiary of your life insurance policy. Others will get nothing unless they receive a bequest from you. Deaths, marriages, divorces, adoptions, acquisition of additional property, and other events may call for changes in your will. Beware of not even mentioning persons who would normally expect to inherit. They may challenge the will, saying they were inadvertently left out. State that these persons are not to receive anything. It is a good idea to indicate why.

Your will should include burial insructions, but this will not do any good if the will cannot be located quickly. It is a good idea to tell those closest to you what you wish as well as arrange to have the will located quickly. A safe deposit box is not a very good place to keep the only copy of a will. To keep people with access to your box from evading taxes by removing things, most states require a representative of the taxing authority to be present when the box is opened. Thus, a safety deposit box is sealed when its owner dies, and arrangements have to be made to get it open. This takes time. If only the deceased has access to the box, a court order has to be obtained to enter it. This, too, takes time. If you hid your will under a rug instead, nobody may be able to find it. Giving copies of your will to your lawyer, bank, executor and any coexecutor is a good idea. You might also keep a copy at home.

You should keep your will out of some people's hands or assure that other, more trustworthy, people also have copies. (Some individuals may profit from simply tearing up your will and letting you die intestate, as they may inherit more this way.) Be sure that a trustworthy person has or can obtain a copy of your will!

The funds in an IRA at your death will be exempt from the federal estate tax if you name a beneficiary to receive these funds in installments for life or at least three years. The proceeds of a life insurance policy, too, will not be subject to the estate tax if the policy is assigned to a beneficiary or beneficiaries other than the executor. Therefore, some property clearly shouldn't be left to be assigned in your will.

Virtually anything that is not illegal can be included in your will. You cannot, however, completely disinherit a wife. You can set down detailed instructions as to how your investments are to be handled and you can set up a trust or trusts. You can name a guardian for your children. (You can name an alternative guardian in case something happens to the first one.) Specify who will serve as executor. If there is more than one executor, you can specify the role of each. You can divide up your property in any way you wish, or specify that some property is to be liquidated before being distributed. You can bequest property to someone only as long as he or she lives, that is, they cannot in turn, will the property. (You must specify what is to become of the property upon his death.) You can specify how property is to be used. For example, you want it used by the city as a park. If the city doesn't want it or later decides it doesn't want it, the property will revert to someone you name. The will should arrange for the disposition of all assets. You should play it safe by leaving everything not mentioned in the will to somebody. (It is best that this not amount to much.)

Some people think that if a husband has a will there is no reason for his wife to have one. Yet, only if the wife has a will can her personal belongings, such as jewelry, family heirlooms, antiques, and so on, he thoughtfully distributed. If the couple should die together, and she dies last, she needs a will to direct the distribution of the assets left to her by her husband. Clearly a wife needs a will if substantial property is in her name or if she might, through gifts or an inheritance, come into a lot of property.

ESTATE TAXES

Federal gift and estate taxes were radically changed by the Tax Reform Act of 1976. This was their first major overhaul in more than 35 years. As a result, estate planning is now a whole new ball game. Old techniques of tax minimization were either eliminated or their use seriously curtailed. States also levy estate taxes, and in some cases these are coordinated with the federal tax.

The federal estate tax is levied on the fair market value of the estate at the time of death. All gifts made within three years of death are assumed to have been in contemplation of death; thus, they must be added back into the decedent's estate. The estate tax is progressive. The maximum tax rate is 70 percent. The minimum is 18 percent. Most estates will pay no estate tax because each estate gets a tax credit, which by 1981 will be large enough to cover the tax due on an estate of $175,625. (The 1981 tax credit is $47,000.) In addition, a married person is entitled to a marital deduction of one-half the estate or $250,000, whichever is greater. The gift tax also has a marital deduction. As a result of these two marital deductions, you can transfer during life and at death a combined total of over $600,000 to your spouse.

To minimize the combined estate taxes on your and your spouse's estates, you may need to take less than the maximum marital deduction. *Because the estate tax is progressive, the minimum combined tax on a couple's estate is obtained by having equal-sized estates.* If $250,000 is deducted from the first-to-die spouse's estate, the estate of the other spouse is increased by that much. Suppose the first spouse to die has the larger estate, and the deduction of $250,000 will exactly suffice to reduce the estate tax to zero. Assume the surviving spouse's estate, when he or she dies, will be subject, at the margin, to a rate well above the minimum. Clearly, under these circumstances it would have been better to leave some of that $250,000 in the first estate to be taxed at the lower rates rather than being transferred to the other estate to be taxed at a higher rate.

The person who inherits property must pay a capital gains tax on any increase in the value of the property, just as would the decedent if he or she had lived. That is, whatever gain in value occurs from the time the decedent bought the property, assuming it was after December 31, 1976, to the time the heir sells it is a taxable capital gain to the heir. For property bought before December 31, 1976, the taxable gain is computed by a complex formula. (It's important to keep receipts, brokerage statements, and other cost records for your executor's use!) Your heir pays this tax when the gain is recognized, that is, the property is sold. Unfortunately, the same basis isn't used for a capital loss. You can only consider as a capital loss any reduction in the value of an asset since you inherited it!

Charities do not have to pay a capital gains tax on property willed to them. Thus, if you have any assets on which a large capital gains tax would be due, it is best to will these to charity and will other assets to individuals. Lump sum distributions under qualified pension and profit sharing plans are subject to the estate tax, while pensions paid to beneficiaries other than the estate are not. The latter, however, are subject to the income tax. In considering how to have pension benefits paid out at death, you have to estimate income and estate taxes in order to see which method of payment has the lowest combined cost. This is a complex task, and it is best to consult a tax lawyer or a certified public accountant who specializes in tax work.

An important feature of the estate tax to couples with minor children is the provision for orphans. You can make a tax-free bequest to each child in an amount that equals $5000 multiplied by the number of years between the child's age when the parent dies and 21.

It used to be popular to leave assets in a trust whose income would go to the deceased's children, and the principal would pass on to the deceased's grandchildren, as this enabled the children to avoid taxes. Under the new law such transfers are generally subject to taxes roughly equal to those which would be paid if the property was bequeathed outright to the children. Each child can, however, pass on to a grandchild up to $250,000 tax free.

People are often surprised at how large their estates are. Their home will sell for far more than they paid for it, and they have many thousands of dollars worth of insurance and pension benefits; thus, before deciding that estate taxes are no problem, one should carefully estimate the size of his or her estate today and consider what size it is likely to be in the future.

Farms and small business property can be valued for estate purposes at current rather than best use. The purpose of this is to help families stay in farming or small businesses whose properties could be sold for far more than they are worth being used as they have been in the past. (Maybe the farm could be sold for a big shopping center.) In the past families often had to sell in order to get the money to pay estate taxes, which were based on the worth of the property in its highest paying or best use. Even the lower tax bill resulting from valuing the property at its value in its current use may be more than heirs have in ready cash. If this is likely to be the case, one should arrange for an estate to be liquid enough for heirs to pay estate taxes. (They may also need working capital for the business!) Heirs are allowed five years to pay the estate taxes. If your heirs will not wish to continue in farming or a small business, it is likely best to sell it rather than pass it on to them, assuming a reasonable price can be obtained.

THE "LIVING" TRUST

The *inter vivos* or *living trust* is one of the two principal types of trust. (*Inter vivos* means the trust is established during your lifetime). The other type is the *testamentary trust,* which is established under the provisions of your last will and testament. The testamentary trust does not become effective until your will has passed through probate. One of the more common testamentary trusts is that set up for a minor child. A trust company is named trustee and manages the trust assets, paying the beneficiary—the child—from either or both trust earnings and assets an income as specified in the will. Frequently the trust is dissolved when the child becomes an adult, and the trust assets are turned over to him or her.

A living trust does not go through probate because, as its name indicates, it is set up during your lifetime. To set it up, you put some of your assets in the care of someone or some institution that you designate as trustee. This action may be either *revocable* or *irrevocable.* In the first case, you can cancel it or alter its terms. In the second case, you can do neither. Any revocable trust made after June 22, 1936 must be included in your estate. Thus, your motive in setting up a revocable trust is not to avoid the estate tax. Your motive is to, perhaps, try out a trustee or relieve yourself of the burden of managing certain assets and to avoid probate. Through a trust, you avoid the publicity given a disposition of property made in a will, and there is less likelihood of a disgruntled person successfully upsetting this disposition of your assets than in the case of distribution via a will. Trust assets are not subject to claim by parties having a claim on the trustee. A trustee can liquidate assets much more expeditiously than can an executor; thus, in the case of business assets, disposition by trust rather than a will can save money. For obvious reasons, many people do not care to set up an irrevocable trust. Clearly, before deciding to set up a living trust, you should investigate probate costs in your state, since avoiding these is probably the major reason for considering setting up a trust. Setting up a trust does not eliminate the need for a will.

REVIEW QUESTIONS

1. Why should you plan for retirement well in advance?
2. What are the first two steps in retirement planning?
3. How do you handle the problem of not knowing how long you will live?
4. Why do some people say that Social Security isn't insurance?
5. What kind of benefits does Social Security provide?
6. What kinds of tax breaks are there for the elderly?
7. How does the tax deductibility of contributions to an annuity program help you?
8. Why do some people say that today pension plans are your best tax shelter?
9. What is the difference between a pension plan and a profit sharing plan offered by your employer?
10. What is vesting?
11. What is the difference between a Keogh plan and an IRA?
12. What is the difference between an immediate and a deferred annuity?
13. What is a refund annuity?
14. What is the difference between a trust fund plan and an insured pension plan?
15. What is the main disadvantage of using an annuity to provide for your retirement income?
16. Why does everyone need a will?
17. Why won't joint ownership substitute satisfactorily for a will?
18. What is probate?
19. What is a living trust?
20. How can you escape estate taxation?
21. Does escaping estate taxation always mean taxation has been avoided entirely? Why or why not?

CASES FOR DISCUSSION

Case 1 Amy Edison is 23 and lives at home with her parents. She has been employed as a police officer for the past three years and plans to make police work her career. She completed a junior college program in police science before taking her current position. What money she doesn't spend on food, clothes, a car, and rent to her parents, she saves at a savings and loan association. She plans to marry soon. Her mother has never worked. She stayed at home and kept house and raised Amy and her two brothers. A lawyer who works for her father's company recently talked him into drawing up a will. Her father is now after Amy and her mother to make out wills. They think this is silly. What would you tell them if they asked for your opinion?

Case 2 Dan Foures is 54, and he is determined that his children will not have to pay estate taxes on the estate he has accumulated over the years. Dan owns his own construction business, several cars, and three houses. He is divorced, and his wife has remarried. He has named his children as beneficiaries of his large life insurance policies and has put his business and homes in an irrevocable trust for his children, making himself a salaried employee who is provided a home by the firm. None of children has gone into his business. His bearded son, Pete, has rejected his hard-driving world, and rides a beat-up motorcycle to his job as groundskeeper for a golf course. His son John is a priest. His daughter Delores is a freelance artist married to a high school science teacher. They have four children. Dan's daughter Melinda does not work. She has two small children to take care of. Dan sends her a check every month, and she gets benefits from the company where her late husband worked. He was killed in an on-the-job accident. Each of Dan's children and Dan's lawyer serves as a trustee, and income from the trust is divided equally between the three children. Dan has no will. What do you think of what Dan has done? How would you advise him now?

Case 3 Tracy Ragsdale's wife left him when he was 28. He gained custody of their 5-year old daughter. At the time his prospects were bleak. Then he met Susan Herbert, the daughter of his employer. They got married, and her father helped put Tracy through college. (He had earlier completed the first two years of college.) When her father retired, Tracy stepped into his job. When they married, Susan put her home in both their names via tenancy by the entirety. The company did well after Tracy took over, and his earnings went up commensurately. They have no children and Susan doesn't work. Tracy suspects that she is running around with another man, but for appearances sake, he doesn't want to get a divorce. Then, too, the business is in Susan's name. Tracy's estate is pretty large, nonetheless, and he doesn't want Susan to get any of it after he dies. Because he is older than she is, he expects to die first. He has completely cut her off in his will, leaving everything to his daughter. What do you think of what he has done? What, if any, advice would you give him?

Case 4 Raymond and Mary Jane Whitehead have run their own restaurant for the past 35 years. They own a home worth about $50,000. All their children are through college and doing well. They have about $30,000 in stocks and savings of $60,000. They think they can sell the restaurant for $100,000. Raymond is 62 and Mary Jane is 58. They want to retire now and travel. They are covered by Social Security, but, of course, are entitled to no corporate pension plan, and they have not created their own tax-free retirement plan. How would you advise them to proceed?

Case 5 Darrell and Joan Hesmondhalgh have just returned from their honeymoon and returned to their clerical jobs with a large, electrical equipment manufacturer. Their parents have told them they should sit down right now and make plans for retirement. They have not, however, given them any advice as to what to do. Darrell is 24 and Joan is 22. How would you advise them?

YOUR PLAN: CHAPTER 14

**A simplified format for estimating the estate
tax under the 1976 Tax Reform Act:[1]**

Total assets of estate	$_____	
Gifts during last 3 years *(See Note 1)*	+_____	
Gross estate		$_____
Less: Liabilities of estate	−_____	
expenses *(Note 2)*	−_____	
Adjusted gross estate		$_____
Less: Marital deduction *(Note 3)* or	−_____	
Orphan's exclusion *(Note 4)*	−_____	
Less: Charitable deduction	−_____	
Taxable Estate		$_____
Gifts made after 1976 *(Note 5)*		+_____
Tentative taxable base		$_____
Estate tax from unified rate schedule		$_____
Less: Gift taxes previously paid		
(Note 6)	−_____	
Unified tax credit *(Note 7)*	−_____	
Other *(Note 8)*		
Net estate tax payable		$_____

Note 1: If post-1976 gifts are made within three years of death, the
full amount of the gifts, including the amount of gift taxes
paid, less the $3000 annual exclusions are includable in
the gross estate.

Note 2: Funeral and medical expenses estimate $4500–$5000. Administrative expenses estimate 3 percent of the gross
estate or 5 percent of the probate estate.

Note 3: The actual amount passing to the surviving spouse not to
exceed $250,000 or 50 percent of the adjusted gross es-
tate, whichever is greater.

[1] This format for computing the estate tax due was devised by Barry R. Schimel,
CPA, Rubin and Schimel, Rockville, Maryland, and appeared in the *Journal of
Accountancy,* July 1977, page 42. Copyright © 1977 by the American Institute of
Certified Public Accountants, Inc.

Note 4: This exclusion is available only if there is no surviving spouse nor surviving parent of the child (such as in the case of a divorce). Every year each child is under age 21 is multiplied by $5000, provided this amount of taxable estate actually passes to the child.

Note 5: Taxable gifts made after 1976, with the exception of gifts within three years of death (see Note 1 above). The taxable gift is the amount of the gift minus the marital deduction and the $3000 annual exclusion. (Your aggregate deduction since December 31, 1976 cannot exceed $100,000.)

Note 6: Gift taxes actually paid on gifts after 1976, including gifts in Notes 1 and 5.

Note 7: Varies depending on year of death:

1977 = $30,000	1980 = $42,000
1978 = $34,000	1981 = $47,000
1979 = $38,000	After 1981 = $47,000

Note 8: There is a credit for state death taxes paid. How much can be claimed is limited.

Estate Tax Schedule

**Rate Schedule for Amounts of
Not More Than $100,000**

Up to $10,000	18 percent of such amount.
Over $10,000–$20,000	$1,800, plus 20 percent of the excess of such amount over $10,000.
Over $20,000–$40,000	$3,800, plus 22 percent of the excess of such amount over $20,000.
Over $40,000–$60,000	$8,200, plus 24 percent of the excess of such amount over $40,000.
Over $60,000–$80,000	$13,000, plus 26 percent of the excess of such amount over $60,000.
Over $80,000–$100,000	$18,200, plus 28 percent of the excess of such amount over $80,000.

**How to determine how much to set aside annually
in order to have a given amount at retirement:**

Example: Suppose you will retire five years from now and want to have saved $58,000 by then. You will set aside, starting now, an equal amount annually, which will earn 5 percent compound interest. You can determine how much you need to set aside annually by using the following method. (You had better use a calculator for this.)

$$\text{Set aside annually} = \frac{\text{Amount desired (\$58,000)}}{(1.05)^5 + (1.05)^4 + (1.05)^3 + (1.05)^2 + 1.05}$$

$$\text{Set aside annually} = \frac{\$58,000}{5.8019127}$$

Set aside annually = \$9,996.70

Because: $\$9,996.70(1.05)^5 + \$9,996,70(1.05)^4 + \$9,996.70(1.05)^3 + \$9,996.70(1.05)^2 + \$9,996.70(1.05) = \$58,000$

If you had 20 years to save up \$58,000, the denominator would have begun with $(1.05)^{20}$. The next figure in it would have been $(1.05)^{19}$, and so on. If you could earn more or less than 5 percent, you would have replaced the .05 with the appropriate percent. The universal formula for solving this type of problem is, where n is the number of years you will save the money and i is the interest rate at which the money set aside will earn interest is:

$$\text{Set aside annually (\$)} = \frac{\text{Amount desired (\$)}}{(1+i)^n \ldots \ldots + (1+i)^2 + (1+i)}$$

To assist you in making such a computation, there are tables showing the value of $(1+i)^n \ldots \ldots + (1+i)^2 + (1+i)$ for a variety of values of n and i.

Questions you should answer before making plans for retirement and beyond:

1. Who would I like to receive each and all of my possessions?
2. What would be the consequences of making out a will in line with my wishes as to who gets what? (Are any of these consequences so bad that I am unwilling to cause them?)
3. What income would I have after 65 as things now stand?
4. How much less, if any, is this amount than my current income?
5. Assuming a pretty high rate of inflation (the worst that might happen), how large an annual income would I need when I retire to match my income today?

6. When I retire will I need an income equal to my current income?
7. What ways of providing a retirement income are available to me?
8. As things now stand, how much estate tax would be due when I die?
9. How could I reduce the amount of estate tax due, and what would be the consequences of doing this?
10. How could I avoid probate, and what would be the consequences of doing this?
11. What would be the consequences of my utilizing one of the forms of joint ownership?
12. How much can I afford to spend on retirement plans, and how much am I willing to spend? (The latter answer depends on what kind of sacrifices you are willing to make now to improve your standard of living after retirement.)

Avoiding Rip Offs

435

7. Be familiar with the nature of a warranty.
8. Know what to do if you find you can't pay a bill, including going bankrupt.
9. Be familiar with the following terms:

implied warranty	straight bankruptcy
late charges	wage-earner plan
title retention	National Bureau of
add-on-clause	Standards
acceleration clause	Agricultural Marketing
repossess	Service
deficiency judgment	Consumer Information
garnishment	Center
wage assignment	cross-collateral
confession of	security
judgment	writ of attachment

Generally, when you think of theft, you think of a man with a gun; yet, you are more likely to be conned than held up. The best way to avoid the con is to be savvy, that is, be familiar with the ways and means of the con man. Just as the police can identify a criminal by his modus operandi (MO), so can you identify the con man or woman. So, instead of photographs, let's look through a rogues' gallery of MOs.

THEIR MODUS OPERANDI

Bait and Switch Sam

Sam is a merchant who figures that if he offers you a big enough bargain, he can get you into his store. The only trouble is, he can't make much money, if any, selling goods so cheaply. So, after he gets you in his store, he tries to talk you into something else. He may tell you he is out of the item advertised and try to switch you to a higher-priced substitute, or he may simply say that he's sure a discriminating person like yourself won't be satisfied with the cheap item on sale. Federal law protects you against him advertising an item he doesn't have to sell you, and you should report any merchant who tries it. (A merchant who simply inadvertently runs out of an item is not engaging in fraud, but a merchant who never has the item or has an unreasonably low stock of it is.) Beware of and report also the merchant whose merchandise significantly differs from the claims and description of it in his advertisements. Contact the district attorney and/or the local Better Business Bureau or a city or state officer of consumer affairs. Often simply threatening to take one of these steps will induce a merchant to produce the proper merchandise at the proper price or provide a suitable substitute.

Greasy George

George runs a service station or a garage, and he can't find enough things really wrong with the cars that come into his place to make as much money as he wants to make. Employing his acting and creative skills, George produces some problems. He may hide an ice pick in a rag and use it to puncture your tire. Then, with a soulful look on his face, he will lean in your car window and say, "Say, Buddy, you've got a hole in your tire."

George's repertoire includes many such "cuties." He might place quarters of antacid tablets into your battery's cells. A few minutes after the caps are put on they will blow off. "Afraid you need a new battery," he tells you.

He may squirt oil from a plastic bottle concealed in his hand on your shock absorbers. Then he tells you that they are "bleeding" and need to be replaced. Or, with the same bottle, he may squirt a mixture of barbecue sauce and acid into your alternator or transmission, which will cause them to start smoking. He may simply hit your water pump —an expensive part to replace—with a wrench, causing it to leak.

He may gyp you by putting colored water into your cooling system rather than antifreeze. He may install rebuilt parts, but charge you for new parts, or he may charge for premium-grade parts or accessories, but install cheaper, lower-grade products. He may replace parts that do not need replacing, or charge you for replacements, but not make them. He may charge for services he doesn't perform. He might fail to replace bolts or not adequately tighten them. He is most likely to try to pull something on tourists.

Clearly, you need to watch those doing work on your car closely, particularly if they are strangers. Demand to see parts the mechanic claims need to be replaced and ask to have the problem pointed out and explained. Check over your car after the work is done to confirm that it has been done and done properly. When in doubt, have more than one firm's mechanics diagnose your problem. Complain. Report offenders.

Pigeon Pauline

Many people find it difficult to believe that Pauline is able to successfully ply her trade, but they underestimate how greed can blind people.
Pauline plys her trade by striking up a conversation with a stranger,

often an older woman, but not necessarily. Her accomplice then shows up, pretending not to know Pauline and to have just found a lot of money. She asks Pauline and her "pigeon" if it is theirs. Then she pretends to find evidence that some criminal lost the money. (Maybe the money is in an envelope with betting slips.) The three discuss what to do with the money. There's no telling who lost it, and the money is, they rationalize, clearly ill-gotten gains. Pauline or her accomplice suggest asking someone for their opinion, perhaps her lawyer, and goes off to get his advice. The advice is to split up the money after first determining everyone's "good faith" or ability to handle money by having them draw money from their bank account. The victim, or pigeon, ends up losing her money, often by slight of hand when the lost money plus the victim's money is handled by the con woman. One will hand the victim slips of dollar-bill sized pieces of paper masked by bills on the top and bottom.

This scam, which is called the pigeon drop, is hoary with age, but people continue to fall for it.

Banker Ben

Another scam that involves getting you to draw money out of the bank plays, not on your greed, but on your desire to be a good citizen and/or the thrill of being involved in a real, live crime drama. Ben calls on you, claiming either to represent your bank or the FBI. He asks for your help in catching a teller suspected of embezzlement. (He may show you authentic-looking credentials.) He asks that you withdraw money from your account through a certain teller. Then he or an accomplice will take it off to mark it or record the serial numbers. Then you will redeposit it. Of course, they disappear with your money.

Desperate Dan

Dan sweeps a girl off her feet. He's crazy about her. There's a fly in the ointment, however, as Dan obviously has some great problem. Reluctantly, perhaps to explain not getting married, he tells her that he is in desperate need for money. Maybe it is to go to court to fight for his children, whom his ex-wife is mistreating. Maybe it is for a desperately needed operation for one of his parents. She practically has to force the money on "honorable" Dan. Dan, of course, takes off with the money. (There are also Desperate Dianes who work this on men.)

Show Biz Art

Art spins a vista of fame and fortune for your child in show business if only you will pay for some pictures or training, or he may, instead, want you to pay to enter your child in a talent contest. His connections in the business are all a figment of his imagination. He takes your money and a powder, in that order.

Fred Fix-It

Fred drives up to your house in a pick-up truck. He says he was working on a house in your neighborhood and had enough materials left over to do your house. Since the other homeowner has paid for the materials, he can do your place cheap and still make a profit. The only problem is that the work he does will be worth far less than he charges. His work may be worth less than nothing, because you may have to spend money to correct the damage he does.

Fred comes in several varieties. He may come by and offer to inspect your house for free. He may be looking for most anything. You can rest assured that he will find what he is looking for. If he's looking for insects or rodents, he'll find them, because he will bring some with him! On top of talking you into having work done that you don't need, Fred will charge you more than would a legitimate businessman, and he will use inferior materials.

Fred's ploy might be that his company will, say, put siding on your house very cheaply because they plan to use your home to advertise to others in your neighborhood on having him work for them. The siding will turn out, at best, to be worth no more than you paid. Fred has no intention of using your home as an example of his work. He simply hopes that visions of getting something cheap will lull you into buying something you otherwise wouldn't dream of buying.

Sometimes Fred will ask for a pretty hefty price, but he points out that if you give him the names of some people you know, and he is able to sell them his product or services, you will get a commission on each sale. Usually you end up paying far more than you would have to pay elsewhere, as you get no commissions. Referral sales schemes are illegal and should be reported to the Federal Trade Commission.

Fred keeps up with the times. Right now devices to conserve fuel or insulation for your house are popular. Yet, like his grandfather and great-grandfather, Fred still sells farmers worthless lightning rods. Like any con man worth his salt, he preys on your emotions and dreams like an organist pulling out all the stops.

Dot Door-to-Door

Perhaps Dot and her sister Sue Solicitor (who telephones in the middle of dinner to tell you that if you can identify the first president of the United States, you will win some free photos of your children) are the most annoying type of the con artists. (You will get some proofs and a sales talk about some very expensive enlargements, hand-tinted photos, multiple copies, frames, etc.) Dot and Sue are the con artists you are most likely to meet, and their number is legion.

Some legitimate businesses market their products and services door-to-door, but door-to-door sales and telephone soliciting are both riddled with flimflam artists. An office costs money and makes you easy to find. Because door-to-door selling eliminates the need for a place of business, crooks prefer it.

Telephone soliciting often takes place in a so-called "boiler room." A room and some telephones are obtained for a short period of time, often under an alias, and several people spend all day for several days calling everyone in the phone book and making them an offer they can't afford to turn down. Then they move on to a new location. Shady, rather than out-and-out crooked, businessmen are also found in both these businesses. Sometimes the telephone is only used to solicit a request for a salesperosn to call at your home.

Dot may be selling almost anything. Encyclopedias, cosmetics, siding, photographs, magazines, and burial plots are among the most common. Sometimes the flimflam is total, that is, you make an advance payment and never hear from them again, or they may ask to borrow the merchandise from you to show someone else, and they conveniently lose it and/or disappear. If you do obtain satisfactory merchandise, it will usually be more expensive than if you had gone to a retail store and bought it. One way or another, you pay a high price for shopping in your home through these people.

Dot utilizes a high-pressure technique. To keep her out, you may have to slam the door in her face. Once in your home, she is almost impossible to remove without a scene. She often gains entry by appearing to be taking a poll or offering something for free. Only later do you discover she is selling something. Sometimes she poses as a poor student working her way through school or a poor widow trying to raise her children by herself.

Dot might also be casing your home for a burglar, or she may be keeping you occupied while an accomplice takes things from another part of the house. The contracts she gets you to sign usually have a lot of fine print full of "Catch 22s."

A large number of insurance policies are sold by salespeople who visit your home, but they seldom call "cold," that is, you inquired about insurance and someone is sent to talk to you. While high-pressure sales techniques are not uncommon, most insurance policies are legitimate. Insurance companies choose to sell in the home because they think this atmosphere is conducive to selling their product. Also, agents often deal with their relatives and friends.

Telling you about Dot is not designed to promote snarling at little girls selling Girl Scout cookies. It is simply to warn you to be particularly leary of those selling door-to-door and over the telephone, because these are the techniques many con artists find most suitable, and few legitimate businesses find these techniques either economical or effective.

Swamp Fox

A long distance phone call from Miami! Who could be calling you from Florida? It may be Swamp Fox. Fox is an agent for Palm Breeze, a Florida land development company. Fox offers you a free trip to Florida. He neglects to mention that the price you will have to pay for the trip is continuously listening to an intensive sales pitch and paying more for any land you may buy than it is worth.

He is more likely to simply invite you to dinner in the city where you live. There a salesperson will sit at every table, and after dinner you will look at pictures purported to be of the property.

Palm Breeze may have bought up some farm land for $50 an acre and be selling it for $5000. The property may be unimproved land, without roads, drainage, or other improvements. Much of it may be subject to flooding and/or is usually under water. The city or county government may have no intention of providing streets, drainage, or other improvements, and Palm Breeze may be under no obligation to provide any of these things. There may be no physical access to each individual tract. (Palm Breeze is, like other firms and people in this text, fictitious.)

Even though the *property report* provides this information plus the fact that the property is not suitable for building purposes, Fox will sell some of it. How? He'll do it with his sales spiel. (You had better not scoff until you've been exposed *and escaped!*)

You should never buy from Fox without reading the property report he is required to give you. Yet, the property report won't tell you the land's true value. Federal law provides that if you do not receive a property report at least three days before signing a contract, you can cancel out and receive a refund by notifying the seller within three days of signing. If you buy Florida land over the telephone, that state's law gives you 30 days to change your mind. If you personally inspect the land within six months and don't like what you see, you can get your money back. You can complain about shady practices to the U.S. Department of Housing and Urban Development's Office of Interstate Sales Registration, the Federal Trade Commission, or Florida's Office of the Division of Florida Land Sales in Tallahassee.

Florida land hustlers got started during the roaring twenties, and they have been at it ever since, despite several busts and increased regulation. When you're selling dreams, it seems that no amount of past nightmares will long seriously hinder you in making additional sales.

Millions of people have bought land in Florida and done very well for themselves. Clearly, you can get what you pay for, but it is easy to get gyped when buying real estate, particularly in Florida and similar highly desirable places.

Paul Bearer

Paul reads the death notices in the local paper. Then he sends authentic-looking bills to the families of the deceased, purportedly for things they purchased just before their deaths, perhaps as gifts for relatives. Another ploy is to deliver overpriced merchandise supposedly ordered by the deceased. (Bibles are popular.)

C. O. Dee

C. O. shows up at your door with a package he says he can't deliver to a neighbor of yours, because the neighbor is not home. If he doesn't deliver it today, he says, he will have to return it to the shipper, which will greatly inconvenience your neighbor. Would you, he asks, help out your neighbor by paying the C.O.D. charge and accepting delivery? When your puzzled neighbor opens the package, he finds a brick!

Larry Lister

Larry offers you a $20-list of all the apartments for rent in the town where you go to college. Larry got his list from the local newspaper's want ads.

When you finish college, Larry will hit you again with a list of job contacts. He gets this list out of the yellow pages in the telephone book. If you want to go into business for yourself, his cousin will sell you a bogus distributorship.

Pyramid A. Buck

Pyramid schemes may not go back to ancient Egypt, but they do go back a long way. While Buck's scam may be quite modern and sophisticated in comparison with the humble chain letter—you pay me money and, in turn, you get someone else to pay you, and so on—it works on the same principle. The optimum pyramid would be one where you are at the top with the people on the next level paying you a share of what the people on the next level pay them, who are, in turn, being paid by the people on the next level, etc. The more levels of people there are, of course, the more money you will get.

There are several things wrong with the pyramid. First, you can be sure that Buck and his pals are at the top. You don't know where on the pyramid you are. Second, getting anything depends on being able to get people to occupy the levels below you, and the number of these levels must continuously grow if pyramids are to continue. For example, B will not continue to pay A unless he or she is paid by C, and C won't pay unless he or she is paid by D, and so on. There are, however, a finite number of people in this world, and it doesn't take a very "high" pyramid to run out of people.

Suppose, for example, four people pay you. Each of them is to be paid by four people, and so forth. At the tenth level this pyramid would have 1,048,576 people. At the twelfth it would have 16,777,216! Clearly, the pyramid will quickly collapse.

Buck may also offer to sell you a distributorship. For a price, his firm will provide you with merchandise to sell or, perhaps, vending machines to sell from. If Buck sells you the right to sell distributorships, you will make money by getting a cut of your distributors' proceeds from selling distributorships and/or merchandise. Usually not too much selling of merchandise gets done, as it is far easier and, seemingly, more profitable to make money by selling distributorships. This pyramid sales technique is illegal.

Commodity Cal

Cal is commodities broker. He both represents customers and trades for his own account. Cal engages in a forbidden practice called "bucketing." He takes a customer's order to buy or sell a commodity and, instead of making the transaction in the open market, arranges a private deal rigged so he can make an illegal profit.

In both the commodities and stock markets there is a danger that a broker will unload on his customers investments he has made, but stands to lose money on if he holds them. For example, a broker, realizing that Nose Dive, Inc. is about to take one, may try to sell you on this stock because he owns some of it or one of his customers does, and he wants to unload it. Another possible ploy is, instead of buying a stock you want in the open market, he may buy it for himself there and then resell it to you at a profit. If you suspect that a broker has done any of these things, he should be reported to the regulatory agency responsible for the market involved.

Bonanza Belle

Belle cons you by placing an advertisement in a magazine for a club which, if you join, enables you to buy a variety of items at a discount. To induce people to write in for information, Belle announces that a free trip will be awarded to one of the people writing in for information about the club. Then Belle notifies everyone who writes that they have won the trip, but if they want it, they will have to pay $40 to hold it for them and cover the cost of incidentals. Belle takes the money they send her and disappears.

Nomen Peddler

Your name is a valuable piece of property and it is bought and sold by those who sell through the mail. Whether or not a seller wants your name depends on what is being sold and what type of person you are. Are you likely to be interested in his product? People who own cars are the people who would, for example, be interested in automobile accessories. Are you likely to buy something through the mail? If you have done so before, you are more likely to do so again.

Both profit-making and nonprofit organizations use the mail for soliciting. You may appear on some of their mailing lists almost as soon as you are born. (Some firms go over hospital birth records and newspaper birth announcements to make up lists to sell to companies which sell products for babies.) Government lists are sometimes the source of names being sold. City directories and telephone books are also sources. It is almost certain you are on some mailing list. You may be on 150 or more. Once you buy something through the mail, you end up on a list, because there is a company which keeps a file on everyone who has purchased a product through the mail in the past year.

You may sometime want to get off a mailing list. Usually, you can do this by writing the sender. If not, you can write to the Direct Mail Marketing Association, Inc., 6 East 43rd Street, New York, N.Y.

10017 requesting its Mail Preference Service form. When they receive this form back from you, your name will be removed from 400 cooperating mailers' list. These mailers account for 70 percent of consumer third-class mail. If you believe that some mail you are receiving is "pandering" in nature, you should fill out Form 2150 at your local post office. The law requires that you be removed from such a mailing list if this is your wish. You should also contact your postmaster if you believe a direct mail advertiser has defrauded you. It is always possible, of course, that instead of defrauding you, the direct mailer has simply made a mistake. Thus, the postmaster will want proof that you have informed the seller of the problem. One way to do this is to send the seller a registered letter. (You might also use a certified letter, as this is cheaper.)

Bob Buffon

Bob probably isn't a con man, he is simply irresponsible, but the results of his actions are the same: you are gyped. Bob may drive a moving van. He usually gets lost, arrives two days late, and drops the box containing irreplaceable antique china. Bob charges more than his competitors, and it takes months to get paid for damages he caused.

Many people believe that they have been gyped by a moving and storage company when this is not the case. A mover is not bound by his estimate. His charge depends on how far he will move your belongings and what they weigh. What they weigh cannot be determined until the truck is loaded and weighed. Thus, you should compare movers' charge per pound per mile. If you agree in writing, the mover will pay up to $.60 per pound for items lost or damaged. This seldom is enough to cover replacement cost. You can get full protection by declaring the total value of the shipment and paying extra for coverage of this amount.

As he packs your belongings, the mover will note existing damage so that you cannot collect for it. If he notes damage incorrectly, you can't collect if he does this damage. Thus, you should check what he notes. If you do your own packing, the standard damage coverage does not apply. Generally, it is better to let the mover do the packing, both for this reason and because he is experienced and will provide packages and padding at no extra charge. However, small, irreplaceable, and valuable items should, if you can possibly transport them yourself, not be entrusted to a moving company.

Unless the company has agreed to accept some other form of payment, you must pay the driver in cash or with a traveler's check, money order, or cashier's check before he will unload the truck. If the actual cost of the shipment exceeds his estimate by more than 10 percent, you get 15 days to pay the difference. You can insist on a re-weighing of the load if you question its correctness.

The mover must notify you if delivery will be a day or more late. He is required to acknowledge damage or loss claims within 30 days and pay or respond within four months. Report him if he doesn't.

The Campus Prowler

The prowler is an insurance agent who concentrates on or specializes in selling life insurance to college students. Sometimes her sales practices are deceptive, and the product she sells is suspect. The latter is the case because life insurance is seldom needed by college students because they have no dependents, and the typical student policy is too small, the wrong type, and often contains unnecessary riders. If you tell the agent you aren't interested because you have no dependents, she will come back with the fact that you probably will have in the future, and, by taking out a policy now, you can lower your premium. What she doesn't point out is that you will pay more premiums, and this often offsets the fact the premium is lower. If you do need life insurance, you probably need more than the usual $5,000 to $15,000 offered by college-student policies. These policies are usually of the whole life type, and students usually can't afford to buy enough life insurance if they buy whole life. More coverage could be obtained for the same price with a term policy. A larger whole life policy would cost less per $1,000 of coverage; thus, the whole life policy offered the college student is relatively expensive.

An insurance company may offer to give you a policy free for a short period of time, banking on the low probability of you dying during that time and gambling that you will pay the premium once the free period is over. This is simply a come-on for a relatively high-priced policy.

Student policies are also sold through the mail. This cuts the insurance company's costs and reduces the questions it will have to answer.

Dean Deceptive

Dean is the kind of guy who, before recent fur labeling rules were made, sold you Alaskan sable. He figured that sounded better than dyed skunk! His king-sized loaf of bread is 15 ounces lighter than other king sizes. Dean runs contests where the price is $50 off on the purchase of merchandise overpriced by $200!

Dean knows all the tricks. He advertises low cash prices to customers he knows will likely have to buy on credit. His credit charges are staggering. When he sells goods or services on which there is no set price, he charges what the market will bear. If you are well-to-do and/or unsophisticated, you pay more than other people do. When he sells cars, he offers you a very low price on a stripped model. Of course, he doesn't have one of these in stock, and you will have to wait at least 12 weeks for delivery if he orders one. Then he proceeds to sell you on a model he has on the floor, which is loaded with overpriced accessories. He will sell six sizes of liquid soap, and their sizes and prices will be something like 4.37 ounces for $.99. The size you are most likely to buy is the most expensive per ounce. (This is why grocery stores must display price per unit.) Dean will mix lower-octane gas with higher-octane gas, and he will mix lower-grade lumber with higher-grade lumber and sell both as the higher grade. He will charge you very little for a magazine subscription, but he will more than make up for that with his handling and postage charges. By putting less in a package, he will be able to charge the same thing for his higher-grade product that competitors charge for their lower-grade products. Clearly, Dean is a guy you'll be running into daily.

G. E. T. Rich

Rich is the guy who puts those advertisements in magazines that promise to make you rich by setting you up in business for yourself in your own home. You can't miss, he suggests, because the product is guaranteed to work, and it's something everyone can use. Send him some money and he will send you some planks, he says, to saw into blocks and sell to crush flies between. Guys like Rich also sell correspondence courses you could get for a fraction of the cost at a local school.

Jovial Jack

Jack is a helpful merchant. He's always ready to give you more credit. He gives you so much in fact, that you never get out of debt to him. Until it is too late you may not notice a clause in your contract with him called *cross-collateral security*. It requires that the payments you make to Jack be credited on a pro rata basis to all your outstanding debts to him. Thus, you don't obtain title to anything you have bought from him until you pay for it all. If you default, he takes back everything, even though you may have paid enough to cover all but one item!

Once merchandise is repossessed and sold, the proceeds of the sale are used to pay off the outstanding debt plus any costs incurred by the seller. If anything is left over, the defaulting customer gets it. If the proceeds do not cover the outstanding debt and these costs, the seller can obtain a *deficiency judgment* against the defaulting customer. By selling the repossessed merchandise cheaply and padding his expenses, the seller might obtain a deficiency judgment as large or larger than the outstanding debt.

If you refuse to pay Jack, he may obtain a *wage garnishment* against you. This will require your employer to turn over to Jack up to 25 percent of your weekly take-home pay. (The Federal Truth in Lending Law specifies that only 25 percent or that amount in excess of 30 times the minimum wage, whichever is less, can be garnished. Some states do not allow this much to be garnisheed.) You must be notified before this action can take place. If you default on an unsecured loan, your creditor can obtain a *writ of attachment,* which is carried out by the sheriff seizing some of your property or attaching your salary.

If you think a creditor is illegally harrassing you, report this to your state's attorney general or consumer protection agency. If your creditor is in another state, contact the Federal Trade Commission. Creditors cannot legally threaten you or embarrass you by telling others about your debt. (They can tell a credit bureau.) Creditors also cannot legally harrass you by telephoning you in the middle of the night.

You can get out of a contract if either it or one of its clauses is unfair or unreasonable or if the manner in which the contract was made is unfair or unreasonable. This will have to be decided by a court. If you win, all or part of the contract may be void. You may get all or part of your money back.

Professional Bill

Bill is the physician who suggests an unnecessary operation. His cousin is the lawyer who suggests to the person whose car you hit from behind that he claim a whiplash injury. "They'll never be able to prove you don't have it," he will tell his client. Another cousin is the dentist who suggests braces for a child who would be better off if nothing was done. These professionals love people who don't comparison shop, and they make it as difficult as possible for you to do so. Not bound by many of the laws that restrain other sellers, such as the antitrust laws, they are a free-wheeling bunch. Complaints should be directed to their professional associations, the courts, and lawmakers.

FEDERAL CONSUMER PROTECTION

A strong demand from consumers for protection from unscrupulous sellers began late in the 1800s. Since that time, federal, state, and local governments have, at an ever-increasing pace, been passing laws and setting regulations whose purpose is to protect the consumer. Various industry and business groups have also established self-policing groups to protect the consumer. Initially, concern centered on the purity of foods and drugs. Since then concern has spread to every corner of the marketplace.

Federal Trade Commission

The Federal Trade Commission was established in 1914. *The job of the FTC is to prevent monopoly and unfair or deceptive trade practices.* One of its major concerns is the enforcement of the antitrust provisions of the Clayton Act. In order to give it the power to prevent unfair or deceptive acts or practices in commerce, the FTC was given jurisdiction over the advertising of nonprescription items covered by the Food, Drug, and Cosmetic Act. Today it also administers the Wool Products Labeling Act, the Fur Products Labeling Act, the Textile Fiber Products Identification Act, the Fair Packaging and Labeling Act, the Truth in Lending Act, and the Fair Credit Reporting Act.

Rather than punishing offenders, the FTC generally operates through issuing *cease and desist* orders. Such an order originates with a complaint from either a consumer, competitor, or a government agency, including the FTC itself. Firms these orders are issued against may appeal to the U.S. Court of Appeals within 60 days after the FTC issues its decision. Violations of an FTC order subjects the violator to a civil penalty.

The FTC makes rules covering unfair or deceptive acts or practices. It is empowered to bring a civil suit in a U.S. District Court against anyone who knowingly violates one of its rules. The FTC has the general power to go to court to seek redress for a consumer harmed by an unfair or deceptive act or practice. This redress may take the form of a refund of money, revision or reformation of a contract, return of property, the payment of compensatory damages, and so on. Local retailers are subject to FTC regulation, as are state-licensed bodies which employ restrictive practices that harm the consumer.

The Consumer Products Safety Commission

The Consumer Product Safety Commission (CPSC) was established in 1973. It took over from the FTC the administration of the Flammable

Fabrics Act. It is responsible for setting product safety standards that are necessary to prevent or reduce an unreasonable risk of injury associated with a product. If the product cannot be made adequately safe, this Commission can remove it from the market by branding it as a "banned hazardous product." In addition to protecting the consumer from injury, this agency assists consumers in evaluating the comparative safety of consumer products and promoting research and investigation into the causes and prevention of product-related deaths, illness, and injuries. Products covered by the Food, Drug, and Cosmetic Act are beyond its purview, however.

Any interested person or organization may petition the CPSC requesting that it consider issuing, amending, or revoking a consumer product safety rule. Within 60 days of the issuance of such a rule, it may be reviewed by the U.S. Court of Appeals at the request of any person or organization adversely affected by it. Those who violate the rules of the CPSC are subject to both civil and criminal penalties.

The Departments of Agriculture and Commerce

Both of these departments have roles in consumer protection. The Department of Commerce is both directly and indirectly involved with consumer protection. Its direct involvement arises out of its role in developing industry-supported standards. The Fair Packaging and Labeling Act of 1966 charged the Department of Commerce with encouraging industry to avoid packaging proliferation. Indirectly it is involved through the product testing activity of the National Bureau of Standards. Generally the Bureau's tests involve few consumer products and are mainly concerned with developing testing methods. Most of the Department of Agriculture's involvement with consumer protection is through its Agriculture and Marketing Service (AMS). Its main role in consumer protection is the regulation of meat and poultry processing under the Meat Inspection Act of 1906, the Wholesome Meat Act of 1967, the Poultry Products Inspection Act of 1957, and the Poultry Inspection Act of 1968. The Department of Agriculture, through the AMS, also establishes grades that make it easier for the consumer to evaluate the quality of foods. The Department publishes numerous pamphlets which provide consumers with helpful information, including its annual yearbook.

A number of government departments and agencies provide consumer information. The U.S. Government Printing Office sponsors the Consumer Information Center in Pueblo, Colorado, 81009. You can obtain a free Consumer Information Catalog by writing to the Center. This catalog lists over 150 free consumer information publications and nearly 100 publications carrying a small fee.

The Food and Drug Administration

The Food and Drug Administration is a part of the Public Health Service of the Department of Health Education and Welfare. The FDA regulates a larger part of American industry than does any other regulatory agency. One-third of the products bought by consumers are regulated by the FDA. It is responsible for assuring that foods are safe, pure, and wholesome; drugs are safe and effective; cosmetics are harmless; therapeutic devices are safe and effective; products are honestly and informatively labeled and packaged; and that interstate travelers are provided with an adequate level of sanitation and are not exposed to health hazards. Its mandate arises out of the Food and Drug Act of 1906 and the Food, Drug, and Cosmetic Act of 1938 as modified by the 1962 Kefauver-Harris admendments. Of paramount concern to the FDA is the safety and effectiveness of drugs.

Warranties and Advertising

Perhaps the most interesting thing about warranties is that both the consumer and the seller feel that a warranty protects them. One reason for this is that although sellers realize that if they sell a product with no written or *explicit warranty,* they still make an *implied warranty,* often consumers don't realize this. The written warranty limits what the seller guarantees the customer. Without a written warranty, sellers are unsure what the courts might hold about their implied warranties. On the other hand, a written warranty should spare the consumer from having to go to court. Because a product carries an implied warranty when it has no explicit warranty, an explicit warranty has sometimes been used in a deceptive manner. Some sellers claim that their products are better than others' because of the warranty they provide; yet, it provides no more than one could expect from an implied warranty.

In the case of products of low value, it was seldom worth it in the past for a consumer to take the seller to court for failure to honor a warranty, either implied or explicit. The Federal Trade Commission Improvement Act of 1975 had as one of its major purposes the correction of this situation. This act gives the FTC the power to implement significant changes in warranty practices it thinks are unfair to consumers, and it provides means of redress to consumers, such as a class action suit formerly not practical.

Whenever sellers provide you with products they imply that they are *fit for the ordinary purposes for which such goods are used.* Implicitly, they also warrant that any promises or affirmations of fact made on the container or label are true. Sellers further warrant that their products are of fair or average quality relative to like items passing in trade. If a sale is made on the basis of a sample, it is implied that the items sold are like the sample.

Some critics would have us believe that through advertising sellers control the consumer, that is, the consumer is merely a puppet on a string. Those in the advertising business have a radically different view. The truth probably lies somewhere in between. What cannot be questioned, however, is that some advertising is deceptive. largely because advertising is regulated by the FTC, advertisers generally deceive by implication rather than via bald-faced lies.

It is always best to take an "I'm from Missouri; you've got to show me" attitude toward buying, that is, you must be shown, and this doesn't mean that you are shown through a product demonstration in an advertisement! (Remember the clear marbles in the bowl of soup to make the vegetables in it show?)

If You Don't Pay

If you have cut your expenses as much as possible and still can't pay all your debts, don't just not pay! Contact your creditors and explain the problem. See if they are willing to work out some sort of arrangement whereby, at least for a while, you can pay them less. If you just stop paying, you will first get a note, probably polite, from your creditors. After they give up on notes, things are liable to get rough. What they can do depends on the contract you signed.

Creditors may tack on *late charges*. This is an addition to the normal installment payment. They may obtain *title retention*—they take title to the items bought from them unil you have made full payment, including any late charges. If you signed a contract with an *add-on clause*, the creditor retains ownership of all items bought under one contract, even though you have paid enough to cover the cost of some of them; thus, default can result in you losing everything bought under a contract, no matter how much you have already paid. If the contract contains an *acceleration clause,* the seller can demand full payment as soon as you miss one payment. If the seller has the right to *repossess* the item, he can do so if a payment or payments are missed. If the seller can't sell it for enough to cover what you owe, he can have the court levy a *deficiency judgment* against you. In addition to actions specified in the contract you sign, creditors can *garnishee* your wages. The contract between you may contain a provision allowing the creditor a *wage assignment*, which is like garnishment, except that the creditor does not have to go to court or inform the debtor of the action he plans to take. Sometimes a contract contains a *confession of judgment*. This means that the buyer has agreed to let the creditor go to court to obtain a judgment against the buyer without letting the buyer know about this ahead of time.

It is highly unlikely that a seller will make a profit on a transaction if he has to repossess, so normally sellers are willing to work something out. If, however, repossession is the only answer, it is better for your reputation if you cooperate in the repossession.

Bankruptcy

If all else fails, you may have to declare bankruptcy. This should be your last resort. An estimated 255,000 Americans go bankrupt every year. Table 15–1 illustrates why going bankrupt is today much less a stigma than it used to be. Like divorce, it is much more common than it used to be. (There is some alarm, however, over the increase in bankruptcies, particularly those by students whose loans for college were underwritten by the federal and state governments. More defaults through bankruptcy were claimed in the last three years than in the previous 15. One out of every six federally guaranteed loans made since the program began in 1965 has gone into default. As a result of this huge loss, a new federal law went into effect in late 1977 that made guaranteed student loans nondischargeable in bankruptcy for five years after commencement of repayment.)

In order to go bankrupt, you or your attorney must fill out a series of forms that turn over all of your debts to the court so that they can be canceled. You also turn over all your material and real property to the court. The court appoints a referee who reviews the case and may return some possessions to you. Your assets will be divided among your creditors. After six months, during which your creditors can make further claims, you are adjudged bankrupt and released from any further obligations to pay the debts you owed at the time you filed for bankruptcy.

Some debts, such as the student loans, cannot be discharged by going bankrupt. You cannot discharge alimony and child support, mortgages, taxes, fines (traffic tickets, etc.), loans obtained through fraud, and debts arising out of injuries you caused to either people or their property. Generally, if bankrupt, you are allowed to keep your house, furniture, appliances, clothing, tools used in your employment, and, if you're a farmer, your livestock and equipment. Any item, however, which you owe money for and is subject to repossession by the creditor, can be taken from you by a creditor even after bankruptcy. Any debt you fail to list in your filing will have to be paid. Once you have gone bankrupt, you cannot file for bankruptcy again for six years.

TABLE 15–1 Growth of Bankruptcy and Population
in the United States, 1950 to 1975

	Bankruptcies	Population
1950		
Straight bankruptcies	26,632	152,271,000
Voluntary	25,263	
Involuntary	1,369	
Wage earners' plans	6,007	
1960		
Straight bankruptcies	95,710	180,671,000
Voluntary	94,414	
Involuntary	1,296	
Wage earners' plans	13,599	
1970		
Straight bankruptcies	162,451	204,878,000
Voluntary	161,366	
Involuntary	1,085	
Wage earners' plans	30,510	
1975		
Straight bankruptcies	209,330	213,540,000
Voluntary	208,064	
Involuntary	1,266	
Wage earners' plans	41,178	
Percent Growth		
1950–1960:		18.7
Straight bankruptcies	259.4	
Wage earners' plans	126.4	
1960–1970:		13.4
Straight bankruptcies	69.7	
Wage earners' plans	124.4	
1970–1975:		4.2
Straight bankruptcies	28.9	
Wage earners' plans	35.0	

Source: Statistical Abstract of the United States 1976, U.S. Department of Commerce, Bureau of the Census, table no. 1, p. 5, and table no. 867, p. 526.

There are two types of voluntary bankruptcy: *ordinary* or *straight* bankruptcy (described above) and a wage-earner plan called *Chapter 13*. The number of people selecting the latter has greatly increased in recent years. You can file for Chapter 13 as often as you wish, providing you have not filed for straight bankruptcy in six years. Under Chapter 13, the court works out a plan for you to, over a three-year period, satisfy your creditors by making full or partial payment. While the plan is in effect you are protected against collection by your creditors via attachments, garnishments, and so on. You are also not declared a bankrupt and, therefore, avoid this stigma—a stigma that can cost you in the future through denial of credit applications or higher credit charges.

You have to pay a fee in order to file for bankruptcy. Usually it is not very large. The size of this fee and the specifics of bankruptcy differ from state to state. Therefore, before filing for bankruptcy, check your state laws.

A creditor has two options available in seeking to obtain what you owe. One is to attach any unencumbered personal property in excess of that amount which is statutorily exempt. The second is to attach your salary. The former is often not available because people who cease to make payments often don't have any property not subject to claim by some creditor. Any that they once had has been either sold or offered as collateral in order to obtain funds. Thus, creditors usually either garnishee your wages or write off your account as uncollectable. *Federal statute prohibits your employer from following the once common practice of firing you because you have been garnisheed.* (Employers find garnishment both a nuisance and expensive.) This protection, however, is not quite as good as it seems since it only applies to one garnishment—after a second or third garnishment, you can be fired. Multiple garnishments are not uncommon, as the first garnishment may force a person to cease making payments to other creditors. Wage garnishment is much easier to obtain in some states than in others.

CASES FOR DISCUSSION

Case 1 A few months ago a couple of fellows opened an insurance agency a few blocks from where Jared Dykes lives. Automobile insurance in the state is very high. This new agency offered Jared a policy they said would be underwritten by a major insurer, for half the price other agencies and companies had offered him. Delighted, Jared signed up. Yesterday he read in the local newspaper that these two men had been arrested. Seems that they only forwarded a relatively small portion of what their customers paid them to an insurance company. As a result, their customers were insured for a much shorter period of time than they thought. Jared was pretty mad, but he didn't see how he could have avoided this. What do you think?

Case 2 Jared's wealthy cousin, Richard Adams, is wondering how he could have avoided what was possibly the largest Ponzi scheme of all time. (A Ponzi scheme involves the paying off of earlier investors with money, less the con man's take, obtained from later investors. Eventually some investors get less than the promised return and complain.) The scheme Richard invested in was an oil drilling firm that promised both tax write-offs and a high rate of return. Many of the nation's leading bankers, industrialists, and lawyers had invested in the firm, and Richard's lawyer and his accountant recommended it. Later, Richard discovered that they had, like other financial advisers, been paid by the oil drilling company to talk people into investing in it. This company took in about $130 million. Its investors lost about $100 million. How can one avoid falling into such traps?

Case 3 Jorge Santiago watched a life insurance company's stock go up rapidly in price for several years. While other insurance companies didn't do very well, this one was making a lot of money. He decided to put his retirement savings of $15,000 into this company's stock. Two years before his retirement it was found that this company had millions of dollars of bogus assets on its books, and Jorge's stock's value fell to a price of zero! What, if anything, could or should Jorge have done differently?

Case 4 When Scarlet Hartsfield opened her door she found a man in work clothes there who claimed to be a city plumbing inspector. She showed him how to get under her house and went back to her house-cleaning. A short while later he appeared and told her she needed $400 of work done to her plumbing. Scarlet was very surprised and disturbed. She said that she had better wait until her husband returned from an out-of-town business trip and talk with him. He then told her that the city's plumbing code required that the work be done. When she still would not agree to have him do the work right then, he told her that he had already removed a lot of pipe, and so she had no water. When she asked him to put it back, he refused unless she would sign a contract for the work he claimed was necessary. Later Scarlet discovered he was a phony. What should Scarlet have done once he refused to replace the pipe? What should she have done earlier to avoid the problem entirely?

Case 5 Margaret Sparks agreed to accept delivery on a damaged refrigerator on the condition that it would be repaired by the seller. When, after several days, no repairman showed up, she called the manager of the store where she had bought it. He said he didn't know anything about it. "Who," he asked, "told you someone would be out to repair it?" When she told him it was the man who delivered it, he said he'd check with the delivery man when he came in at five o'clock and call Margaret back the next day. He didn't call the next day, and so she called him back after waiting one more day. The manager said that the delivery man didn't remember telling her that. Margaret insisted that the store repair the refrigerator. The manager refused. "Listen, lady, he said, "you signed for it. You could have done something to it after we delivered it." What should Margaret do? What should she have done earlier?

Case 6 When Karen Shuptrine got home from work her neighbor gave her a package that had been delivered earlier in the day for Karen and her husband, Jere. Karen didn't remember ordering anything, and when Jere got home, he didn't either. A few days later they got a bill for this merchandise. What should they do?

Case 7 Gordon McClure has fallen behind on his mortgage, car payments, and credit card bill. As an airline pilot, he has a good income. A friend has suggested that he file bankruptcy. How would you advise him?

REVIEW QUESTIONS

1. What, if any, common characteristics are there among various ripoffs?

2. What kinds of people do you think are most likely to be preyed on by con artists?
3. Why is door-to-door selling so popular with con artists?
4. How does a pyramid scheme work, and why is it doomed to ultimately fail?
5. Why should you be suspicious of free offers?
6. What is cross-collateral security?
7. Is it possible to get out of a contract? If so, how?
8. What are the functions of the Food and Drug Administration, and why is it so important to the consumer?
9. What is an implicit warranty?
10. What is the difference between an ordinary bankruptcy and a wage-earner plan?

YOUR PLAN: CHAPTER 15

Consumer Tips:

1. If an offer seems too good to turn down, look twice; it may be too good to be true!
2. If something's appeal is strictly emotional, look twice; it may have no rational appeal.
3. Don't get into anything or buy anything on the basis of the involvement of well-known people. Their names may be being used without their permission, and even well-known and successful people make mistakes.
4. Know who you are dealing with.
5. If you aren't allowed to think a proposition over, say no thanks.
6. Don't let someone part you from all your savings.
7. Nothing is the only thing that is really free, and sometimes people pay for it!
8. Never sign anything without reading it, and do not depend on an interpretation made by an interested party. If in doubt, see a lawyer.
9. Always check out more than one source of a good or service before buying.
10. Do not hesitate to complain to the appropriate authorities.
11. You have no obligation to pay for unordered merchandise.
12. A creditor has no right to harass you.
13. You can get out of a contract when misrepresentation or unfairness is involved.
14. Whenever you sign a contract that could result in a credi-

tor making a claim on your home, you may cancel the contract within three business days without penalty or obligation. The seller must inform you of this.

15. Do not agree to an add-on-clause, because this means that failure to pay for part of what you buy from a seller results in you losing everything bought from him or her.
16. Even if a seller offers no explicit warranty, there is an implicit warranty.
17. Beware of extravagant claims.
18. Do not get involved in deals involving illegal actions.
19. Bankruptcy is not a step to be taken lightly. Consider trying to work out something with your creditors or the wage-earner plan.
20. The following illustrates how you might go about trying to arrange a plan for eventually repaying your creditors:[1]

Your street address
City, State, Zip Code
Date

To (All of my creditors):

At this point in time, my financial circumstances are such that I simply cannot pay all of my bills. Therefore, I am writing to you to request your cooperation in accepting a proposed schedule of reduced payments until my debt is repaid or until I can afford to increase the payments to the original figure again.

I'm sure you realize the importance of your cooperation with this request, since this adjusted payment schedule is my only alternative to filing for bankruptcy. I accept the full responsibility for my debts and would sincerely like to repay them. I simply need more time to do so under my present circumstances.

My net income from all sources (including my spouse's income and/or the children's part-time jobs) is $_____ per month. My minimum monthly expenditures for necessities are as follows:

[1] Elsie Fetterman, *Let the Buyer Be Aware,* New York: Fairchild Books, Fairchild Publications, 1976.

Housing (rent or mortgage plus taxes)	$_____
Utilities (gas, telephone, water, electricity)	_____
Food and household supplies	_____
Replacement clothing	_____
Laundry and dry cleaning	_____
Medical	_____
Transportation	_____
Insurance	_____
Other	_____
Total	$_____

This leaves me approximately $_____ for debt repayment. My total of unpaid bills is as follows:

Name of Creditor	Approximate Balance	Due Per Month
1.		
2.		
3.		
	Total: $_____	Total: $_____

Obviously, I cannot pay all of my bills on my present income. I have no savings. Therefore, my only alternative is to divide the $_____ I have available for debt repayment proportionately among all of my creditors. This would result in my paying each of you _____ percent of your regular monthly payment, until the bills are paid off or until I am able to increase the payments.

If all of my creditors will accept this plan, the proposed payment schedule will be:

Name of Creditor	Amount Per Month
1.	
2.	
3.	
	Total: $_____

If you will accept the proposed reduction in payments, please let me know immediately by signing the enclosed copy of this letter and returning it to me with an up-to-date statement of the balance I owe you. If you prefer, I will rewrite my contract according to the new terms. I hope you will also freeze the interest at its present dollar level so that I can work toward reducing the principal amount that I owe. This would serve to reduce the interest I must pay monthly by extending the total interest owed over the new longer term of the note. In effect, this means I will pay the balance on my account in full; I just need more time than I expected when I signed the original contract.

Unless all of my creditors approve this plan, it cannot work and I will be compelled to file for bankruptcy. I hope you will help me avoid this court action by accepting the proposed plan. Please reply to this request as soon as possible. I must have your answer no later than (a date ten days away).

Thank you in advance for your patience and understanding.

Sincerely yours,

We agree to the foregoing:

Name of creditor: _____

By: _____

Balance: _____

Interest will be adjusted as follows: _____

Glossary

Acceleration Clause. This gives your creditor the right to demand immediate and full payment of the unpaid balance when one or more payments are overdue.

Accrued. Cash income earned but not yet received, or an expense incurred but not yet paid out in the form of cash.

Add-on Clause. This means it is possible to purchase more than one item on an installment contract; thus, eliminating several separate contracts.

Amortization. The reduction of a debt through periodic payments.

Annuity. A contract providing you an income for a specified period of time: either for a set number of years or for life. An annuity may be purchased with a single payment and you begin receiving the annuity immediately, or it may be a deferred annuity, which means you make payments over a period of time, then you receive the annuity.

Arrears. In finance this refers to amounts that are due and not yet paid at the date set for payment, or after the period of time allowed for payment has expired.

Asset. Anything of value which is owned, whether tangible or intangible.

Assured. The assured is the person who owns a piece of property which is insured.

Automatic Premium Loan. A clause in your life insurance policy that causes a "loan" for the amount of a premium you failed to pay to be made. This amount is deducted from the cash surrender value of the policy. Once such "loans" eliminate the policy's cash value, the policy is cancelled.

Balloon Payment. This is an installment payment or payments in which the last one or ones are larger than the earlier payments.

Bankrupt. This describes a person or business which cannot pay off creditors in full and on time. Bankruptcy must be declared by a court.

Bear Market. Speculative securities traders are pessimistic because they think prices will fall. You should buy in a bear market.

Beneficiary. The person you name to receive the face value of your life insurance policy when you die.

Benefit. The amount of money an insurance company will pay under specified conditions.

Bequest. A gift of personal property or money through a will.

Bill of Sale. A formal written agreement by which one person transfers to another the rights, interest, and title to a specified piece of personal property.

Blue Cross Plan. See 'Blue Shield;" Blue Cross is a similar plan.

Blue Shield Plan. This is the name of a large, voluntary, nonprofit organization providing medical expense insurance, or prepaid medical care, to groups and individuals.

Bond. A written promissory agreement to pay a specified sum of money at a specified time in the future and to pay interest at a stated rate at specified times. It is a debt obligation.

Broker. Persons who sell real estate and those who sell securities are called brokers. They serve as agents for both buyers and sellers.

Bull Market. Speculative securities traders are optimistic because they believe prices will rise. You should sell in a bull market.

Burglary and Theft Insurance. This coverage reimburses you for property stolen from your home.

Call. In the securities trade, this is a written agreement representing an option to buy a named security on or before a certain date at a given price.

Callable Stock. Shares which may be bought back by the company at a certain price anytime during a certain time span under certain agreed-upon conditions.

Cancelled Check. A check which has been paid by a bank, charged to the drawer's account, and perforated so it can't be used again.

Capital Asset. An asset held as a long-term investment or for the production of income rather than quick resale.

Capital Gain or Loss. A profit or loss on the sale of a capital asset. To be a long-term capital gain, the asset must have been held one year.

Carat. A unit of weight for the measure of diamonds and other precious stones. It is about 3.1 grains Troy. It also measures the fineness of gold. Twenty-four-carat gold is pure gold.

Cash and Carry. In retail selling, this means you pay cash for your purchases. You must take it with you or have it delivered. Store services such as credit, free delivery, extended return privileges are not usually provided on this basis.

Cash on Delivery (C.O.D.). Payment is to be made for merchandise ordered when it is received.

Cash Surrender Value. This is the amount due you if your life insurance policy is allowed to lapse.

Casualty and Liability Insurance. These forms of insurance provide you with protection against a wide variety of miscellaneous hazards. They cover loss, damage, or injury done to others not covered by property insurance.

Certificate of Title. This is a legal document stating that your ownership of a piece of property is shown on public records.

Chattel Mortgage. This is a legal instrument that transfers title to personal property to the creditor as security for payment of a debt. If the borrower defaults, the creditor can claim this property.

Check. This is a draft drawn on a demand deposit. See also "Draft."

Closed-end Investment Company. This is a company which has a definite limit to the number of shares it can sell. It invests exclusively in securities. It is also called a mutual fund. See also "Open-end Investment Company."

Closing Costs. These are costs other than the basic purchase price of a piece of property which are imposed at the time a real estate deal is closed.

Code. A compilation or collection of existing laws into a systematic whole. The Internal Revenue Code is an example.

Codicil. A provision added to a will.

Coinsurance. You pay a certain percent of each cost covered by your policy. This reduces the size of your premium. Note the difference between this and a deductible.

Collectable Items. This refers to things you can invest in such as paintings, antique furniture, stamps, coins, antique automobiles, and so on.

Collateral. This refers to an item owned by the borrower which is pledged to the creditor as security for the loan. If the borrower defaults, the creditor takes possession of this item.

Collision Insurance (Auto). This type of coverage covers damages to a car if it is hit by another car or fixed object. It will pay only the current value of the car.

Commodity Price Index. Anyone of the various price indexes designed to measure changes in the wholesale prices of selected basic commodities prepared by the U.S. Department of Commerce. Also called the wholesale price index.

Common Disaster Clause. If the beneficiary of your life insurance policy dies in the same accident you die in, this clause causes your heirs, not your beneficiary's heirs, to be entitled to the benefit.

Compensating Balance. The proportion of a loan a bank may require a borrower to keep on deposit or the average balance required in order to obtain a loan.

Comprehensive Insurance (Auto). This type of coverage covers a variety of possible losses, such as vandalism and fire.

Comprehensive Personal Liability Insurance. This is usually included in your homeowner's policy and reimburses you for any costs you experience due to any kind of damage or injury you do other people (other than that done by an auto).

Conditional Sales Contract. This is a document used in making an installment loan to buy merchandise on credit. The buyer does not get title to the merchandise until this debt is repaid. The seller is the creditor.

Consideration. The thing of value given by one party to a contract that induces the other party to enter into it.

Consumer Price Index. This is an index of prices paid by urban wage-earning families computed by the Bureau of Labor Statistics, U.S. Department of Labor.

Contingent Beneficiary. Your second choice to receive the money from your life insurance policy. This person receives the benefit only if the first beneficiary you name dies before you do. It may be better to have the first beneficiary will the benefit to the contingent beneficiary.

Constant Dollars. This is a method of expressing prices which eliminates the effect of a change in the purchasing power of the dollar since a given year, called the base year.

Contract. A promissory agreement between two or more persons or parties that creates, modifies, or cancels some legal relationship. It is an agreement to do or not to do a specific thing in exchange for consideration.

Convertible Bond, Debenture, or Preferred Stock. This is a security that can be converted into shares of common stock at a date sometime after it is purchased.

Convertible Clause. This clause states whether or not a life insurance policy can be exchanged for another policy and what choices you have if this is allowed.

Cosigning a Loan. If the borrower does not repay a loan you have cosigned, you will have to repay it.

Cost of Living. The average cost of providing the so-called necessities of life at retail.

Coupon Bond. A bond not registered in the name of its owner. It is negotiable and payable to the bearer. Interest on it is paid on the basis of coupons attached to it, which are detached and sent to the borrower who issued it.

Credit. Broadly speaking, this is the ability to borrow money. It also is used to refer to the amount loaned or the amount due a creditor, that is, it is used like the word *debt*.

Credit Life Insurance. The benefit of this type of life policy compensates your creditor if you die before repaying money owed him.

Debenture. A promissory note backed only by the general credit of a firm.

Declining Balance. The decreasing amount owned as repayment of a loan proceeds. This balance is called the unpaid balance.

Decreasing Term Insurance. Since your need for life insurance is likely to decline as your grow older, this form of term insurance provides for you to have an ever smaller coverage until the policy expires. This reduces your premiums.

Deductible. This is a fixed amount you must pay to cover your losses before the insurance company will pay. The higher the deductible, the lower your premium. Note the difference between this and coinsurance.

Default. The failure of a borrower to make, in full, a scheduled payment or fulfill some other requirement of a loan agreement.

Default Charges. Additional charges levied when an installment payment is not paid when due.

Deposit. In selling, this is an amount of money given in partial payment for goods. In banking it is coins, currency, checks, or drafts placed by a customer in the care of a bank to be kept in an account and returned under stated circumstances.

Depreciation. This is the decline in the value of an asset as it ages. The Internal Revenue Service allows you to count as an annual expense a portion of the cost of some assets, and this is called depreciation.

Disability Income Insurance. This provides you and your family with an income if you are disabled and unable to work for a prolonged period of time.

Discounted Loan. A credit charge is computed and deducted from the total loan when credit is extended. This increases the cost of the loan.

Diversification. In insurance, this refers to the spreading of its liabilities over a large number of individual risks. In investing, this refers to investing funds in the securities of a number of companies in various industries in order to reduce risk.

Dividends. This is a payment made out of profits to the owners of a company's stock. Payments are made on a proportional basis and may be in the form of cash, additional shares of the company's own stock, or the securities of another firm it owns. Dividends do not have to be paid.

Double Indemnity. A life insurance policy that pays twice the policy's face value if you die from certain unnatural causes.

Dow Jones Average. This is an index based on selected industrial, transportation, and utility stocks. It is a composite of these that is supposed to measure the performance of the stock market.

Down Payment. This is the amount of cash required at the outset of an installment sales credit transaction and a mortgage loan.

Draft. In finance, this is an order drawn by one person upon another, calling for payment to a third person. See also "Check."

Endorsement. In insurance, this refers to a change or addition to a policy which is indicated by an attachment. It is informally known as a rider. In law, it is the only recognized way of transferring title to a negotiable instrument by writing your name on the back.

Endowment Policy. Premiums for this type of life insurance policy are paid for a specified period of time, then you are paid the policy's benefit. If you die prior to that time, your beneficiary gets this money. The premium is relatively high.

Equity. In the case of real estate, this is the value built up in a property over the years via payment of the principal of the mortgage loan. In the case of a business, this is the owner's investment in it.

Escalator Clause. A clause providing that the price as quoted in the contract may be increased at the time of delivery under certain conditions.

Escrow. An agreement under which certain documents are given to a third party to hold until specified conditions are met, then they will be delivered to the person meeting these conditions.

Estate. The interest or rights a person has in land or other real or personal property.

Estate Tax. A tax on the property of a decedent whether real or personal, tangible or intangible, located in the United States. There is a federal estate tax, and many states also have an estate tax.

Ex Dividend. This means that a share of stock, if purchased, does not include the most recent dividend that has been declared.

Executor. The person or institution responsible for settling a deceased's estate by paying debts and distributing property to beneficiaries of the will pursuant to the order of the probate court.

Extended Coverage. This protects you against loss or damage to property other than your auto caused by windstorm, hail, smoke, explosion, riots, aircraft, and so on.

Extended Term Insurance. If you can no longer pay for this policy, it will continue in force for a limited period of time.

Face Amount. The amount of money stated on the face of an instrument or contract. The term maturity value is also used, which refers to what you will receive when a security is redeemed by its issuer.

Face Value. What a life insurance company will pay your beneficiary. It also refers to the maturity value of a bond.

Family Maintenance or Family Income Insurance. This type of life insurance policy provides for both life insurance and a monthly income for the insured's family if the insured dies within a certain time period. This is a rather high-cost policy.

Fiduciary. The person or institution who manages the financial affairs of a trust.

Fixed Annuity. A contract with a life insurance company that provides for a fixed payment. You gain certainty, but run the risk of loss in purchasing power via inflation.

Float. In banking, this refers to the value of checks and drafts drawn but not yet collected.

Foreclosure. This refers to the sale by a lender of a property on which payments are seriously in default.

Fund. Any amount of cash or of assets quickly convertible into cash, which has been set aside or reserved for a particular purpose.

Grantor. This is the person who makes a conveyance or creates a trust. This person is also called a trustor or a donor.

Group Insurance. One policy insures a group of people. If you terminate your membership in the group, you lose your policy but can obtain an individual policy without having to prove insurability. Premiums are relatively low.

Hedge. This refers to taking steps to offset a possible loss due to price changes in commodities futures contracts or stocks by entering into a contract in the opposite direction.

Homestead Exemption. This refers to an amount of real property specified by statute that is set aside for the head of the family which will pass to the family when he or she dies without being liable to the claims of his or her creditors. In some states this applies to personal property.

Homeowners' Policy. This is a package of coverages including fire insurance, burglary and theft, and personal liability coverage.

Hospitalization Insurance. This type of policy covers room and board, routine nursing service, lab tests, X-rays, drugs, operating room fees, and so on.

Hypothecation. This refers to a creditor's right to order certain property sold to satisfy a claim upon default by the creditor, but, unlike a mortgage, he does not gain title to the property.

Income. An increase in wealth or resources.

Indemnity. In the case of medical insurance this refers to a policy which states that only certain dollar amounts will be paid for each type of cost covered, that is, if total cost exceeds a given amount, that difference is not covered.

Inter Vivos Trust. A trust created during the lifetime of the grantor rather than after death. See also "Trust."

Inflation. This is a sudden and sharp increase in prices or a decrease in the value of money caused by an increase in the amount of money relative to the amount of goods and services available.

Insurance Dividend. This is a payment made to the owners of mutual life insurance policies.

Insured. The person who is insured against loss. His or her life or property is insured.

Intangible. An intangible asset has value but it is not readily determinable. Securities are intangible assets. See "Tangible."

Intestate. One who dies without a will or a defective will is said to have died intestate.

Invest. This refers to the placing of money into any venture primarily for the purpose of producing an income.

Investment Company. See "Mutual Fund."

Invoice. An itemized account of goods sent or services rendered, which usually includes a request for payment.

Joint Tenancy. When two or more persons own a piece of property. Both have equal rights.

Keogh Bill. This provides for the self-employed to set up their own retirement program with tax savings.

Lapse. The termination or discontinuance of an insurance policy due to the failure to pay a premium when due or within an allowed grace period.

Lease. A contract transferring the use or occupancy of land, buildings, etc. in consideration of a payment in the form of rent.

Legacy. A gift of a particular piece of personal property. It is usually part of a will.

Legatee. A person receiving a legacy or bequest.

Leverage. This refers to investing borrowed funds hoping to increase your return without increasing your equity in the investment.

Liability Insurance (Auto). Insurance coverage for bodily injury liability and property damage liability. This, in other words, covers damages you are legally responsible for because the accident was your fault.

Lien. This is a claim against a piece of property that was pledged as security for a debt.

Limited Payment Life Insurance. This is whole life insurance on which premiums are fully paid in a limited, specified number of years.

Liquid. Those assets of a person or business which are in cash or a form readily convertible into cash.

Load. The fee which must be paid when a load-type mutual fund is purchased.

Loan Value. The amount of money that can be borrowed on a life insurance policy. This amount is subtracted from the face value of the policy until the loan is repaid. The loan doesn't have to be repaid, but interest must be paid.

Major Medical or Catastrophic Insurance. This type of policy protects you from the financial burden of a prolonged illness or serious accident that would cost more than your basic hospital and surgical insurance covers.

Margin. This is the minimum proportion of the purchase price of a share of stock you must pay when you wish to use your broker's credit to buy a security.

Marginal. That which results from the addition of one more unit, that is, additional revenue or additional expense. It also refers to something on the border between being profitable and causing a loss.

Markdown. A reduction of price below that originally charged.

Medicaid. A government program covering many medical costs for the aged, blind, disabled, and families receiving Aid to Families with Dependent Children (AFDC).

Medical Payments Insurance (Auto). This type of coverage covers the medical, hospital, and funeral expenses of those in your car when you are not at fault. See also "Major Medical or Catastrophic Insurance" and "Regular Medical Insurance."

Mortgage. This is the legal right granted by a borrower to a lender to claim the property pledged as security for the loan if the loan is defaulted.

Mortgage Bond. A bond secured by a mortgage on some piece of the issuer's property.

Municipal Bond. Strictly speaking, this is a bond issued by some subdivision of a state. Often all nonfederal government bonds are referred to by this name.

Mutual Fund. This is the popular name for an investment company. An investment company sells shares in itself and uses the proceeds to invest in other firms' securities.

Negotiable. This is an instrument that can be transferred from one person to another. It is endorsed by the payee to another individual or business.

No-Load Fund. A mutual fund which does not charge a fee to cover the cost of salesmen and advertising like a load fund does.

Nonforfeiture Option. An option available to the holder of a life insurance policy as to what is done with its cash surrender value if the holder discontinues paying for the policy.

Odd Lot. In the securities and commodities trades, this is an amount smaller than the usual and normal unit of trading, which is called a round lot. Transaction costs are greater for an odd lot than a round lot.

Open-end Investment Company. A company that has no limit as to the number of shares in itself that it may sell. It invests exclusively in securities. It is also called a mutual fund. See also "Closed-end Investment Company."

Option. This is a right to buy or sell specific securities, commodities, or other properties at a specified price within a specified time.

Par. The face value of a security.

Participating Policy. If the insurance company collects more money than it needs, this excess is paid to policy holders as a dividend.

Plat. A plan or map showing a land subdivision or housing development.

Points. In the stock market this is a $1 per share or per bond price change, that is, "The stock went up two points." Fractions of a point in ⅛'s are also used. In the case of mortgages it refers to a discounting of 1 percent or one point to increase the effective rate of interest.

Policy Loan. A loan made by an insurance company to a policyholder on the cash surrender value of the policy.

Preemptive Rights. This refers to stock that grants its holder the right to buy enough of a new issue of stock to maintain a proportionate ownership before the new stock can be offered to others.

Preferred Stock. This is stock whose possession gives one a claim on earnings and assets that precedes that of holders of common stock.

Premiums. The payments for insurance. They may be paid weekly, monthly, quarterly, semiannually or yearly. The less often you pay, the less you will pay.

Prepayment Privilege. This requires the creditor to accept payments in advance of their due date; thus, reducing the borrower's credit charges.

Probate. The presentation of a will before a court having jurisdiction over the administration of the estate of a deceased person.

Property Insurance. This insurance repays the owner of property for loss or damage due to a variety of hazards such as fire and storm. It also insures against loss of income due to loss of property.

Prospectus. The official document that describes the shares of a new security being issued. The Securities and Exchange Commission requires it be given to any prospective buyer.

Put. In the securities trade, this is a written agreement representing an option to sell a named security on or before a certain date for a given price.

Quitclaim Deed. The seller gives to the buyer any claim he may have to a piece of property.

Rebate. An amount refunded after payment.

Recourse. The right of a person to whom a note or other obligation has been endorsed to recover payment from the endorser in case of default by the original maker.

Redeem. Literally, this means to buy back. One redeems a bond by paying the principal at maturity.

Refinance. A revision of the payment schedule of an existing debt accomplished via substituting one debt instrument for another.

Reduced Paid-up Insurance. Rather than drop your insurance because you can't pay the premiums, you can, if this option is available, buy a paid-up policy with the amount of money you have already paid.

Regular Medical Insurance. This insurance policy covers visits to a doctor, extended home care, prescription drugs, diagnostic tests, and similar items.

Renewable Privilege. Some term insurance policies give you the right to renew the policy regardless of the state of your health. Usually this is not possible after you reach a certain age. Your premium will rise each time you renew.

Repossession. The reclaiming of an item sold on a credit basis from the buyer because he or she has failed to make scheduled payments.

Retirement Income Life Insurance. This type of life insurance combines life insurance with a life income after the policy's maturity date, which is usually at age 65.

Revenue Bond. A bond issued by a government or government agency that will be redeemed out of the revenue of the issuing unit of government.

Rider. A statement attached to your insurance policy adding certain benefits. You are charged for each.

Risk. In general, this refers to any element of uncertainty as to size of a return or to the possibility of loss.

Round Lot. In the securities and commodities trades, this is the standard unit, quantity, or number of shares in which a security or commodity is normally traded. Transaction costs are less for a round lot than an odd lot.

Service Benefits Insurance. A policy providing such benefits pays all hospital and physician's fees enumerated in the policy.

Simple Interest. A finance charge computed on the principal balance outstanding as long as any portion remains unpaid.

Stock Split. An increase in the number of shares of a corporation brought about by a division of existing shares and their distribution to current stockholders. This is not the same thing as a stock dividend, which refers to the payment of a dividend in shares of stock.

Straight or Ordinary Life Insurance. A benefit is paid whenever you die. The premium size is level and is paid for life. This is whole life or permanent insurance.

Street Name. A term for the recording of the ownership of a stock in the name of a brokerage house rather than in the name of the individual purchaser, who is the legal owner. This facilitates selling the stock, but opens you to some risk.

Surety. A guarantee of payment or performance. For example, a person who binds himself, or makes himself liable, for the payment of money or performance of some act by another does this by posting a surety bond to guarantee payment or performance. One who is so protected is said to be "bonded."

Surgical Insurance. A policy covering surgeons' fees and related services. It is usually sold in conjunction with hospitalization insurance.

Tangible. Literally, touchable. It has physical properties such that it can be weighed, measured, counted, and so on. It is the opposite of intangible or incorporeal. Included as tangible assets are goods, equipment, land—things a definite value can be set on.

Tenancy by the Entirety. The holding of property by a husband and wife together. The property can be sold only by joint action of the husband and wife.

Term Life Insurance. This insurance remains in force for only a limited, specified period of time. Benefits are paid only if you die within this period. See "Whole Life Insurance."

Testate. This refers to the person who made a will or a decedent who left a will.

Trust. Something is committed or entrusted to somebody to be used or cared for in behalf of the beneficiary of the trust.

Trustee. A person or institution who holds title to a piece of trust property for the purposes as stated by the terms of the trust.

Umbrella Liability Insurance. Insurance against losses above and beyond those covered by your basic liability insurance policies. It is often used by doctors and other professionals subject to malpractice claims.

Underwrite. In insurance, this means to insure. In the securities trade, it means to agree to market an issue of securities.

Uninsured Motorist Insurance (Auto). This type of coverage insures the driver and passengers against injury by an uninsured motorist or hit and run driver. Some no-fault states require this coverage.

Unsecured Note. A credit agreement involving no collateral. All the creditor has is the borrower's signature. Banks call this a signature loan.

Usury. An interest charge in excess of what the law allows.

Value. The price a thing will bring in a fair and open market.

Variable Annuity. An annuity contract with a life insurance company that provides a variable, rather than a fixed return. Funds placed in this annuity are invested in securities whose return is expected to vary with the rate of inflation; thus, protecting the recipient.

Vesting. The acquisition by an employee of a right or interest in the contributions made by an employer to a pension fund, profit sharing fund, or other employee benefit funds.

Wage Garnishment. A court order requiring that a certain amount of a borrower's wages be paid by the employer to a creditor. This action is taken only after borrower has defaulted. The law limits how much can be taken.

Waiver. Any intentional renunciation of a claim, interest, privilege or right. It may be oral, written, or implied.

Warrant. A certificate authorizing the holder to buy a specific company's stock at a specific price for a specific period of time.

Warranty Deed. The seller guarantees he or she has certain rights to a piece of property and is transferring them to the buyer.

Whole or Permanent Life Insurance. Unlike term, which insures you for a specified period, this type covers your entire life; thus, a benefit will be paid. See "Term Life Insurance."

Wholesale Price Index. See "Commodity Price Index."

Bibliography

General

Britt, Steuart Henderson. *The Spenders*. New York: McGraw-Hill, 1960.

Business Week (weekly). New York: McGraw-Hill.

Clark, Champ. "Bargain Hunting: Enough Is Enough," *Money,* March 1977.

Clendenin, John C. *Introduction to Investments*. New York: McGraw-Hill, 1969.

Cohen, Jerome B. *Decade of Decision*. Educational Division, Institute of Life Insurance, 277 Park Avenue, New York 10011. (Free).

Consumer Reports (monthly). Consumers Union of the United States.

Fortune (fortnightly). Time Inc., Chicago 60611.

Galbraith, John Kenneth. *The New Industrial State*. Boston: Houghton Mifflin, 1967.

Heilbroner, Robert. *The Making of Economic Society.* Englewood Cliffs, N.J.: Prentice-Hall, 1962.

Janeway, Elliot. *What Shall I Do With My Money?* New York: McGraw-Hill, 1970.

Lawrence, William and Stephen Leeds. *An Inventory of Federal Income Transfer Programs.* White Plains, New York: The Institute for Socioeconomic Studies, 1978.

Marlestein, David L. *How You Can Beat Inflation.* New York: McGraw-Hill, 1970.

Metz, Robert. *How To Shake the Money Tree.* New York: Putnam, 1966.

Money (monthly). Time, Inc., Chicago 60611.

Monthly Labor Review. Superintendent of Documents, Washington, D.C. 20402.

The New York Times (daily). The New York Times Company, New York 10036.

"99 New Ideas on Your Money, Job, and Living." *The Changing Times Family Success Boom.* Washington, D.C.: The Kiplinger Washington Editors, Inc. (See the latest edition.)

Nuccio, Sal. *The New York Times Guide to Personal Finance.* New York: Harper & Row, 1968.

Parke, Gibson D. *The $30 Billion Negro.* New York: Macmillan, 1969.

Poriss, Martin. *How to Live Cheap But Good.* New York: Dell, 1974.

Porter, Sylvia. *Sylvia Porter's Money Book.* Garden City, N.Y.: Doubleday, 1975.

"16 Mistakes Investors Make." *Changing Times.* August 1976.

Smith, Carlton and Richard P. Pratt. *The Time-Life Book for Family Finance.* Boston: Little, Brown, 1970.

Springer, John L. *Financial Self-Defense.* New York: McGraw-Hill, 1969.

"Strictly for Speculators." *Money.* March 1977.

Unger, Maurice A. *Personal Finance.* Rockleigh, N.J.: Ally & Bacon, 1969.

U.S. Department of Agriculture. *Shopper's Guide, The 1974 Yearbook of Agriculture.* Washington, D.C.: U.S. Government Printing Office, 1974.

U.S. Department of Commerce (monthly). *Survey of Current Business.* Washington, D.C.: U.S. Government Printing Office.

U.S. News and World Report (weekly). U.S. News and World Report, Inc.

Van Caspel, Venita. *Money Dynamics, How to Build Financial Independence.* Reston, Virginia: Reston Publishing Company, 1975.

The Wall Street Journal (daily). Dow Jones Company, New York 10007.

West, David A. and Glenn L. Wood. *Personal Financial Management.* Boston: Houghton Mifflin, 1972.

Wolf, Harold. *Personal Finance,* 4th ed. Boston: Allyn & Bacon, 1975.

Budgeting and Daily Financial Management

Blair, Lorraine L. *Answers to Your Everyday Money Questions.* Chicago: Regnery, 1968.

Buell, Victor and Carl Heyel, eds. *Handbook of Modern Marketing.* New York: McGraw-Hill, 1970.

"The Changing Times Do-It-Yourself Financial Checkup." *Changing Times.* February 1976.

A Discussion of Family Money, How Budgets Work and What They Do. Women's Division, Institute of Life Insurance, 277 Park Avenue, New York 10017, 1970.

A Guide to Budgeting for the Young Couple. Washington, D.C.: U.S. Government Superintendent of Documents (cat. no. A1. 77:98/3), n.d.

"How Does Your Spending Compare?" *Changing Times.* October 1976.

Kirk, John. *How to Manage Your Money.* New York: Simon and Schuster, 1967.

McClellan, Grant S., ed. *The Consuming Public.* New York: H. W. Wilson Company, 1968.

Padberg, Daniel I. *Economics of Food Retailing.* Ithaca, N.Y.: Cornell University Press, 1968.

Sheldon, Eleanor. *Family Economic Behavior.* Philadelphia: Lippincott, 1973.

U.S. Department of Agriculture. *A Guide to Budgeting for the Family.* Washington, D.C.: U.S. Government Superintendent of Documents (cat. no. A1. 77108/3), n.d.

"When Your Budget Signals Danger." *Changing Times.* February 1977.

Buying a Car

Donnelly, Caroline, "New Long-Term Car Loans at Short-Term Prices." *Money.* September 1976.

Moolman, Val. *Get the Most for Your Money When You Buy a Car.* New York: Simon and Schuster, 1967.

Jackson, Charles R. *How to Buy a Used Car.* Philadelphia: Chilton, 1967.

"An Owner's Manual for Financing a Car." *Money.* December 1973.

"How Much Can a Used Car Save? An Analysis By Hertz Shows Answers in Per-Mile Costs." *The Wall Street Journal,* May 1, 1978.

Collecting

"The Art of Collecting Vintage Cars." *Business Week.* August 22, 1977.
Bank Note (monthly). Camden S.C. 29020.
Bayliss, John. "Delectable Collectibles." *The Saturday Evening Post.* May–June 1977.
The Coin Wholesaler (monthly). Chattanooga, Tennessee 37401.
COINage Magazine (monthly). 16250 Ventura Blvd., Encino, Cal. 91316.
Coin World (weekly), P.O. Box 150, Sidney, Ohio 45365.
"Exotia: Rebounding from a Long Recession." *Business Week.* December 27, 1976.
"A Guide to Literary Collectibles." *Business Week.* June 27, 1977.
Hessler, Gene. *The Comprehensive Catalog of U.S. Paper Money.* Chicago: Henry Regnery Company, 1977.
Hobbies Magazine. 1006 South Michigan Avenue, Chicago 60605.
"How Investing in Gold Coins Looks Today." *Changing Times.* February, 1976.
Numismatic News (weekly). Iola, Wis. 54945.
The Numismatist (64 issues a year). American Numismatic Association, P.O. Box 2366, Colorado Springs 80901.
Pick, Franz. *Pick's Currency Yearbook.* New York: Pick Publishing Corporation. (See latest annual edition.)
Randall, Robert M. "Antiquing Down 1,000 Miles of Back Roads," *Money.* July 1973.
U.S. Postal Service, *U.S. Stamps and Stories.* Washington, D.C.: Philatelic Sales Branch, 1977.
World Coin News (weekly). Iola, Wis. 54945.
Yeoman, R. S. *A Guide Book of United States Coins.* Racine, Wis.: Western Publishing Company. (See latest annual edition.)

Consumer Protection

Andreasen, Alan R. *The Disadvantaged Consumer.* New York: The Free Press, 1975.
Berger, Robert and Joseph Teplin. *Law and the Consumer.* Boston: Houghton Mifflin, 1969.
The Consumer's Handbook. Princeton, N.J.: Dow Jones Books, 1969.

Facts You Should Know About Your Better Business Bureau. Council of Better Business Bureaus, 111 17th Street, N.W., Washington, D.C. 20036, n.d.

Feldman, Laurence. *Consumer Protection: Problems and Prospects.* St. Paul: West Publishing Co., 1974.

Fetterman, Elsie. *Let the Buyers Be Aware.* New York: Fairchild Publications, 1976.

Hancock, Ralph and Henry Chafetz. *The Complete Swindler.* New York: Macmillan, 1968.

Comarow, Avery. "Griping That Gets Action," *Money.* April 1976.

Hapgood, David. *The Screwing of the Average Man.* New York: Doubleday, 1974.

"Nine Kinds of Fraud That Come In the Mail," *Changing Times.* February 1976.

Springer, John L. *Consumer Swindles and How to Avoid Them.* Chicago: Regnery, 1970.

Credit and Saving

Consumers Quick Credit Guide. Washington, D.C.: U.S. Government Superintendent of Documents (cat. A1. 11/3: C86), n.d.

It's Your Credit: Manage It Wisely. Household Finance Corporation, Money Management Institute, Prudential Plaza, Chicago 60601, n.d.

Goldsmith, Raymond. *A Study of Saving in the United States.* New York: Greenwood Press, 1956.

Main, Jeremy. "A New Way to Score With Lenders," *Money.* February 1977.

Savings and Loan Fact Book. Chicago: United States Savings and Loan League. (See latest edition.)

Career Planning

Bolles, Richard N. *What Color Is Your Parachute? A Practical Manual for Job Hunters and Career Changers.* Berkeley, Cal.: Ten Speed Press, 1976.

The Encyclopedia of Careers and Vocational Guidance. Two vols. Chicago: J. G. Ferguson Publishing Company. (See latest edition.)

Gardiner, G. L. *How You Can Get the Job You Want.* New York: Harper & Row, 1962.

The Graduate, A Handbook for Leaving School. Approach 13-30

Corporation, 1005 Maryville Pike, SW, Knoxville 37920. (See latest edition.)

Lavoie, Rachel. "Making It in a Man's World," *Money*. May 1977.

Meyes, Caroline. "How to Think Through a Job Offer," *Money*. July 1, 1973.

U.S. Department of Labor. *Dictionary of Occupational Titles*. Washington, D.C.: U.S. Government Printing Office. (See latest edition.)

U.S. Department of Labor. *Occupational Outlook Handbook for College Graduates*. Washington, D.C.: U.S. Government Printing Office. (See latest edition.)

Taxes

"Answers to Your Tax Questions." *Changing Times*. March 1977.

Diamond, Irwin F., ed. *Working With the Revenue Code–1977*. New York: American Institute of Certified Public Accountants, 1977.

Edgerton, Jerry. "A New Way to Shelter Stock Gains." *Money*. March 1977.

"Need Help With Your Tax Return?" *Changing Times*. February 1977.

"Practical Answers to Your Tax Problems," *Changing Times*. January 1977.

Stern, Philip M. *The Rape of the Taxpayer*. New York: Random House, 1973.

The Tax Adviser (monthly). American Institute of Certified Public Accountants, 1211 Avenue of the Americas, New York 10036.

Stocks and Bonds

Comarow, Avery. "Betting on Other People's Money." *Money*. May 1973.

Engle, Louis. *How to Buy Stocks*. Boston: Little, Brown, 1967.

Homer, Sidney. *Inside the Yield Book: New Tools for Bond Market Strategy*. New York: Prentice-Hall, 1972.

Loeb, G. M. *The Battle for Investment Survival*. New York: Simon & Schuster, 1957.

Moskowitz, Milton. "Borrowing Trouble in the Stock Market," *Money*. February 1974.

"Mutuals Funds That Pay Tax-Free Income." *Changing Times*. March 1977.

Ney, Richard. *The Wall Street Jungle*. New York: Grove Press, 1970.

Quint, Barbara Gilder. "Bonds by the Bundle." *Money*. September 1976.

"Smith Adam" (Goodwin, George). *The Money Game.* New York: Random House, 1968.

"Smith, Adam" (Goodwin, George). *Supermoney.* New York: Random House, 1972.

Rolo, Charles J. "Judging What a Stock Is Worth." *Money.* May 1977.

Managing Your Own Business

Almanac of Business and Industrial Financial Ratios. Englewood Cliffs, N.J.: Prentice-Hall. (See latest annual edition.)

Annual Statement Studies. Robert Morris Associates, Credit Division, 1432 Philadelphia National Bank Building, Philadelphia, Pennsylvania 19107.

Broom, H. N. and Justin G. Longnecker. *Small Business Management.* 2nd ed. Cincinnati: South-Western Publishing Company, 1966.

Greene, Gardiner G. *How to Start and Manage Your Own Business.* New York: McGraw-Hill, 1975.

How To Read a Financial Report. Merrill Lynch, Pierce, Fenner and Smith, Inc., 70 Pine Street, New York 10005. (Free)

Kelley, P.C., Lawyer, K., and Baumbeck, C. M. *How to Organize and Operate a Small Business.* Englewood Cliffs, N.J.: Prentice-Hall, 1973.

Key Business Ratios. Dun and Bradstreet, Inc., 99 Church Street, New York 10007. (Free)

Prather, Charles L. *Financing Business Firms.* 3rd ed. Homewood, Ill.: Richard D. Irwin, 1966.

Report of the Committee on Generally Accepted Accounting Principles for Smaller and/or Closely-Held Businesses. New York: American Institute of Certified Public Accountants, 1976.

Robinson, Roland I. *Financing the Dynamic Small Firm.* Belmont, Cal.: Wadsworth 1966.

Small Business Administration. (Management, technical, and small marketers' aids are available.)

Starting and Managing a Small Business. Small Business Administration, 1441 L Street, N.W., Washington, D.C. 20416, n.d.

"Where New Small Businesses Go Wrong," *Changing Times.* December 1976.

Acquiring a Home

"Buying a Motor Home, The House You Travel In." *Changing Times.* February 1976.

Comarow, Avery. "Ins and Outs of Inspecting a House." *Money.* July 1973.

DeBenedictis, Daniel J. *The Complete Real Estate Adviser.* New York: Simon & Schuster, 1969.

Edgerton, Jerry. "Being Your Own General Contractor." *Money.* September 1976.

"Five Myths About Condominiums." *Changing Times.* December 1976.

"The Ins and Outs of Title Insurance." *Changing Times. October* 1976.

Kass, Benny. *Home Buyer's Checklist.* National Homebuyers and Homeowners Association, Suite 301, 1225 19th Street, N.W., Washington, D.C. 20036, n.d.

Maisel, Sherman J. *Financing Real Estate.* New York: McGraw-Hill, 1965.

Mobile Homes. Council of Better Business Bureaus, 1101 17th Street, N.W., Washington, D.C. 20036 (Free)

Moger, Byron and Martin Burke. *How to Buy a House.* New York: L. Stuart, 1969.

North, Nelson L. and Alfred A. Rind. *Real Estate Principles and Practices.* 5th ed. Englewood Cliffs, N.J.: Prentice-Hall, 1967.

Unger, Maurice A. *Real Estate Principles and Practices.* 4th ed. Cincinnati: South-Western, 1969.

U.S. Department of Housing and Urban Development. *Questions About Condominiums.* n.d. Consumer Information Center, Pueblo, Colorado 81009. (Free)

U.S. Department of Housing and Urban Development. *Wise Home Buying.* n.d. Consumer Information Center, Pueblo, Colorado 81009. (Free)

Watkins, A. M. "Breaking Ground as a Real Estate Investor." *Money.* December 1973.

"Yes, You Can Sell Your House Yourself." *Changing Times.* March 1977.

Buying Insurance

Best's Flitcraft Compend. Morristown, N.J.: A. M. Best Company, (See latest edition.)

"Changes in Homeowners' Insurance." *Changing Times.* March 1976.

"Does Insuring Kids Make Sense?" *Changing Times.* August 1976.

Family Health (monthly). 1271 Avenue of the Americas, New York 10020.

Green, Mark R. *Risk and Insurance.* 2d ed. Cincinnati: South-Western, 1968.

Gregg, Davis W., ed. *Life and Health Insurance Handbook.* 2d ed. Homewood, Ill.: Dow Jones/Irwin, 1966.

Goodwin, Dave. *Stop Wasting Your Insurance Dollars.* New York: Simon & Schuster, 1969.

Harris, Marlys. "Shoring Up Your Homeowners Insurance." *Money.* May 1977.

Interest-Adjusted Index. Cincinnati: The National Underwriter Company. (See latest edition.)

Keeton, Robert E. and Jeffrey O'Connell. *After Cars Crash.* Homewood, Ill.: Dow Jones/Irwin, 1967.

Leinwoll, Stanley. *So You Think You're Covered? A Consumer's Guide to Home Insurance.* New York: Scribner's, 1977.

Life Insurance Factbook (annually). New York: American Council of Life Insurance. (Free) 1850 K St. N.W., Washington, D.C. 20006.

Life Rates and Data. Cincinnati: The National Underwriter Company. (See latest edition.)

Miller, Herman P. and Richard A. Hornseth. *Present Value of Estimated Lifetime Earnings.* Washington, D.C.: U.S. Bureau of the Census. (Free)

Sokol, Saul. *Your Insurance Adviser.* New York: Barnes & Noble, 1977.

Planning for Retirement

Allen, Everett T., Joseph J. Melone, and Jerry S. Rosenbloom. *Pension Planning, Pensions, Profit Sharing, and Other Deferred Compensation Plans.* 3d ed. Homewood, Ill.: Irwin, 1976.

Burck, Charles G. "There's More to ESOP Than Meets the Eye." *Fortune.* March 1976.

Greenough, William C. and King, Francis P. *Pension Plans and Public Policy.* New York: Columbia University Press, 1976.

"How to Build a Pension Fund With an IRA." *Changing Times.* November 1976.

Margolius, Sidney. *Your Personal Guide to Successful Retirement.* New York: Random House, 1969.

Main, Jeremy. "Building a 21st Century Pension Right Now." *Money.* September 1976.

Myres, Robert J. *Social Security.* Homewood, Ill.: Irwin, 1975.

Commodity Trading

"Commodity Trading." *Business Week.* March 15, 1976.

Epstein, Eugene. *Making Money in Commodities.* New York: Praeger, 1976.

"How to Trade in Commodities." *Business Week*. September 20, 1976.
Reinach, Anthony. *The Fastest Game in Town/Trading Commodity Futures*. New York: Random House, 1973.
Teweles, Richard V., Charles V. Harlow, and Herbert L. Stone. *The Commodity Futures Game*. New York: McGraw-Hill, 1974.

Index